“What a gold mine! You have before you the keys to a world of rich, provocative, and often still startlingly relevant Jewish thinking. There was a robust Jewish theological conversation before Heschel and Soloveitchik, before Kaplan and Levinas, before Plaskow and Adler, but only now, with this wonderful volume, has this vital world opened to non-specialists and non-German readers.”

—SHAI HELD, president and dean of Hadar and author of *The Heart of Torah*

“*Modern Jewish Theology* will be an indispensable and enduring resource for scholars, students, and teachers.”

—ASHER D. BIEMANN, professor in the Department of Religious Studies, Jewish Studies Program, University of Virginia

“Exciting! This anthology has the potential to help reframe the entire field of modern Jewish thought. Its study tends to leave out the nineteenth century almost totally—and yet, as the editors show, this was an extremely important period for the development of Jewish thought and the attempt to negotiate modern sensibilities about religion and science. Additionally, because many of the nineteenth-century figures were at the intersection of Wissenschaft and philosophy, attending to them can better integrate modern Jewish thought into Jewish studies as a whole.”

—ROBERT ERLEWINE, professor and director of the Center for Jewish Studies at Eastern Michigan University and author of *Judaism and the West: From Hermann Cohen to Joseph Soloveitchik*

Modern Jewish Theology

JPS ANTHOLOGIES OF JEWISH THOUGHT

University of Nebraska Press | Lincoln

Modern Jewish Theology

The First One Hundred Years, 1835–1935

Edited by Samuel J. Kessler
and George Y. Kohler

The Jewish Publication Society | Philadelphia

Library of Congress Cataloging-in-Publication Data
Names: Kessler, Samuel Joseph, editor. | Kohler, George Y., 1966–, editor.
Title: Modern Jewish theology: the first one hundred years, 1835–1935 / edited by Samuel J. Kessler and George Y. Kohler.
Description: Lincoln: University of Nebraska Press, 2023 | Series: JPS anthologies of Jewish thought | Published by the University of Nebraska Press as a Jewish Publication Society book. | Includes bibliographical references and index.
Identifiers: LCCN 2023013590
ISBN 9780827615137 (paperback)
ISBN 9780827619128 (epub)
ISBN 9780827619135 (pdf)
Subjects: LCSH: Judaism—Doctrines. | Judaism—History—19th century—Sources. | Judaism—History—20th century—Sources. | BISAC: RELIGION / Judaism / Theology | PHILOSOPHY / Religious
Classification: LCC BM602 .M63 2023 |
DDC 296.3—dc23/eng/20230414
LC record available at https://lccn.loc.gov/2023013590

Set in Merope (Charles Ellertson) by A. Shahan.

To our colleagues,
without whom this volume
would never have existed

As it says:
Let your house be a meeting place for the sages. How so? This teaches that a person's house should always be ready for the sages, and for their students, and for their students' students, such that one can say to one's friend, "I will save a place for you there!"

—*Avot de-Rabbi Natan 6:1*

Contents

Acknowledgments

An anthology is by definition the work of many hands. We are delighted to acknowledge and thank the dozens of our friends and colleagues without whose generosity and learning this anthology would not have been possible. First and foremost, our translators, who gave of their precious time to this project, and whose lifetimes of scholarship we were pleased to call upon here. So, too, we thank the many others who read sections of the manuscript and advised on notes and bibliographical details. No two editors alone could master the range and depth of erudition reflected in this volume, and we are honored to have a community of scholars to call upon to aid us in this task. It is to all of them that we are most grateful, and to whom we have dedicated this book.

We are appreciative of the Leo Baeck Institute in New York and to Dr. James N. Dreyfus and family, the descendants of Rabbi Leo Baeck, for permitting us to reproduce selections from publications to which they retain copyright.

Finally, we thank the staffs of The Jewish Publication Society and the University of Nebraska Press. Rabbi Barry Schwartz, former director of JPS, encouraged the project from its inception, and Joy Weinberg was our indefatigable editor. While errors and infelicities remain our own, Joy's astute, careful, and wise suggestions turned a sprawling intellectual Hydra into this beautiful volume. For her efforts, we are deeply thankful.

Introduction

From the middle decades of the nineteenth century through the years following the First World War, a small but influential group of Jewish thinkers attempted to lay the foundations for a modern, systematic, academically informed discipline of Jewish theology. Building, so they believed, on the groundwork provided by the classical rabbis and medieval Jewish philosophers and exegetes, these men understood themselves to be part of a lineage of Jewish thinkers whose role was to describe and explain the specific ways in which Jews and Judaism speak about God. Written for an educated but generally lay audience, their works were intended to carry on the tradition of defining and elucidating the boundaries of Judaism's statements concerning Israel's duties toward God, God's character, and God's wants and desires for the People of Israel and for humanity as a whole.

This project of writing a modern Jewish theology could not have materialized without the social and academic background from which it grew.

German University of the Nineteenth Century

The German university of the nineteenth century was the birthplace of the modern humanities. Entirely new academic disciplines were born out of a great shift in intellectual paradigms: a new focus on the *empirical* nature of humanity and human society, and the search for knowledge based not on universal rules but from an accumulated mass of observable facts: philology (the study of the evolution of language), historiography (the study of the way history itself gets written across time), and archeology (the study of the physical development of human society itself). Likewise, older fields of thought, especially philosophy and theology, rather than being discarded (like alchemy and astrology), were completely revolutionized. With the rapid decline in influence of the German idealist philosopher Georg Wilhelm Friedrich Hegel (1770–1831) — the last great metaphysical system-builder — philosophy became a handmaiden of the empirical sciences, and with the end of the mystical belief in the holiness of texts, theology became a rational enterprise, a search for the historical and philosophical meanings of scripture and of religious traditions. Indeed, the nineteenth century was a time when a completely new intellectual ideal, that of "scientificity" (*Wissenschaftlichkeit*), came to replace that of "(moral) education" (*Bildung*), which had ruled European thought throughout the seventeenth and eighteenth centuries, during the so-called Age of Enlightenment.

If the Enlightenment — an era premised on the idea that universal truths could be realized through the use of reason and objective observation — promised a rationality that made it possible to prove or disprove dogmatic belief by the study of nature, to reveal a new rational world through science, the nineteenth century extended the critical, empirical method to the humanities. With the foundation of the University of Berlin by philosopher and linguist Wilhelm von Humboldt (1767–1835) in 1809, a new age dawned, one that replaced the aestheticist as well as the deist rationalism of the previous century with the dry technicism of the scientific state employee whom the government paid to produce useful, practical research results in increasingly specialized academic fields. Whereas the medieval universities, working on behalf of the Church, produced ever more complex formulations of theological doctrine; and the universities of the Enlightenment strove to apply the principles of rationalism and objectivity to every aspect of human knowledge and experience, in search for universal truths of physical and metaphysical reality; the universities of the nineteenth century became centers for technical expertise and practical application — the aim being to better the world in specialized ways, in everything from engineering and mathematics to new methods of teacher-training and approaches to childhood development. The nineteenth century birthed the universities of modernity, skeptical of profound, universal questions of meaning and morality, and oriented instead toward applied knowledge and measurable outcomes.

But the nineteenth century was not only the age when the trained expert replaced the aristocratic polymath; it was also the time that a new critical, empirical, and inductive method of research replaced the great metaphysical speculations and theo-philosophical concepts that had for so long shaped the development of European thought.

Wissenschaft des Judentums

From early on, Jews were part of this radical methodological shift. A generation of young Jewish intellectuals, born during the second decade of the nineteenth century, became the first Jews to study at these newly reformed German universities, thus adding the critical methods of modern academia to their traditional educations in the classical texts of Judaism. Many of them were practicing rabbis who had chosen this profession only because, after gaining their doctorates, they could not continue their academic career without accepting baptism. Nevertheless, this first generation of German *Doktor-Rabbiner* was in continual contact not only with other Jews interested in the new style of scholarship but likewise with gentile intellectuals, and regularly published their discoveries in both Jewish and non-Jewish academic journals.

These young Jewish scholars formed a new movement within Judaism, the *Wissenschaft des Judentums*, the first-ever approach to studying the history, culture, religion, and languages of Judaism with academic-critical methods. The outcome of this research, so the *Wissenschaft* scholars seriously believed, would be much more than a surplus of knowledge. These newly gained insights into Judaism's development from antiquity to the present day would also help Judaism to survive the onslaughts of modernity, because, with the talmudic lifestyle rapidly vanishing in

Western Europe, academic knowledge and methods (so it was hoped) might replace religious law and ritual observance as a means of Jewish self-identification.

Beginning as individual projects among just a handful of university-trained Jewish scholars, *Wissenschaft des Judentums* was soon institutionalized in the various modern rabbinical seminaries founded from the mid-century onward in Germany. The first journal, simply called *Zeitschrift für die Wissenschaft des Judenthums* (Journal for the study of Judaism, 1822–23), founded by Leopold Zunz, would only produce one volume in three installments. Later attempts were more successful. Abraham Geiger (see chapter 2) founded two journals, the *Wissenschaftliche Zeitschrift für jüdische Theologie* (Scientific journal for Jewish theology, 1835–47) and *Jüdische Zeitschrift für Wissenschaft und Leben* (Jewish journal for science and life, 1862–75), both of which printed essays on the model of the new university scholarship. The most important publication of them all, however, was the *Monatsschrift für die Geschichte und Wissenschaft des Judenthums* (Monthly journal for the history and study of Judaism, 1851–1939), which ran for nearly a century and published, at one point or another, all the leading thinkers in the *Wissenschaft* movement. And the *Monatsschrift* was itself closely associated with the first and most prestigious of the new rabbinical schools: the Jewish Theological Seminary of Breslau, founded in 1854 and helmed by Zecharias Frankel (see chapter 1). In the following decades, two additional seminaries emerged, both in Berlin: the liberal Hochschule für die Wissenschaft des Judentums (Higher institute for the study of Judaism, founded 1872) and the Orthodox Rabbiner-Seminar zu Berlin (founded 1873), started by Azriel Hildesheimer. Together, JTS Breslau and the two Berlin seminaries provided the model for all later institutes of modern rabbinical training, with their joint focus on the study of traditional Jewish texts paired with university-style scholarship and historical knowledge.

Through these and other likeminded journals and institutions, the impressive results of the *Wissenschaft des Judentums* were made available to larger audiences.

Discipline of Jewish Theology Debate

However, from the very beginnings of the emergence of *Wissenschaft*, and through to the present day in contemporary Jewish studies, there has remained serious debate as to whether the discipline of theology should belong alongside other academic subjects in the study of Judaism.[1] The founding fathers of *Wissenschaft*, men like Leopold Zunz and his disciple Moritz Steinschneider (1816–1907), demanded the exclusion of theology from the academic approach to Judaism. To them, theology was merely religious essentialism, full of value-laden statements and normative assumptions, and could never be a truly scholarly discipline. Instead, they believed that *Wissenschaft* must limit itself to such purely critical endeavors as historical research and technical philology.

Nevertheless, already in the first half of the nineteenth century, many young German-Jewish thinkers and academics, including Abraham Geiger and Leopold Stein (see chapter 2), were emphatically professing themselves to be Jewish theologians composing works of Jewish theology. These men roundly rejected the argument that the discipline of theology was somehow fundamentally distinct from the other branches of knowledge; in theology, too, they insisted, interpretation, reason, and evidence could lead to convincing conclusions and new ways of thinking. This anthology collects their theological texts, and thus their ideas of what the contents and propositions of a modern Jewish theology might be.

Is There Jewish Theology?

The deeper cause of this ongoing discussion has frequently been a profound misunderstanding about what is meant by the term *Jewish theology* and from where it is derived.

DEFINING THEOLOGY

Theology in itself, according to the Greek origin of the word (*theos*, "god"; *logia*, "word") in Plato and Aristotle, is the discipline of explaining the nature and being of God. It is closely connected to what would later be called metaphysics, the teaching of that which is "above" or that transcends the natural world.

In the centuries after the founding of Christianity, when theology had pride of place in Christian intellectual life, there developed two different forms of theological inquiry: historic and systematic. Historic theology describes the temporal development of a belief-system at its different stages of progress, as well as the presently valid doctrines of belief (today's dogma) as these emerged across time. Systematic theology, on the other hand, is the attempt to take the whole array of existing intrareligious doctrinal claims and organize them into a single coherent, noncontradictory account of God and God's relation to human beings.

THEOLOGY VS. PHILOSOPHY OF RELIGION

The discipline of theology, as understood by the authors included in this anthology, can best be described as *academic (critical) thought about the Divine*, that is, the act of evaluating competing internal claims, ideas, assumptions, and arguments in an effort to speak articulately about God from within a religious tradition. Theology in this sense must be distinguished from what has come to be known as "philosophy of religion," defined as the general category of metaphysical speculation about divinity, revelation, prophesy, and other such phenomena of religious belief.

The separation between theology and philosophy of religion is based on two major elements. First, theology assumes (without further proof) the possibility of rational thought about God. Second, theology focuses on the nature of God and its implications concerning the human realm within the bounds of a single specific (called in nineteenth-century terminology, "positive") religion—in the case of this volume, Judaism.

Thus, contrary to religious philosophy, every theology describes only one positive religion. Each positive religion is a combination of philosophical theory and historical content, as expressed in the biographies of its founding figures and in revelatory documents. Importantly, theology, as opposed to religious philosophy, does not cast analytical doubt on these historically derived documents, preferring instead to describe and interpret them as essential elements of the religion's belief-system. While both study under the light of reason, religious philosophy analyzes (universal) beliefs, while theology attempts to explain a specific religion's accepted notions within the context of that religion. In short, there can be no "Jewish philosophy of religion" (only a "philosophy of religion" practiced by Jews) but there can be a "Jewish theology."

History of Jewish Theology

Over the centuries, and especially in the Christian context, the term *theology* often came to be synonymous with *dogmatics,* statements outlining the content of belief—an elision which has led to the oft-repeated statement that Jews do not write theology. For Christian theologians, describing the tenets of true belief (the writing of creeds) was roughly coterminous with defining the internal workings of the proper Christian life, while in contradistinction, for most of the first millennium of Jewish-Christian coexistence, Jewish thinkers all but refrained from actively or intentionally determining any fixed set of Judaic dogmas. Classical and gaonic-era Jewish literature is awash in discussions of every kind, but outside of a few suggestive passages (in particular Mishnah *Sanhedrin* 10:1 and its commentaries, whose authority and inclusiveness remain subject to interpretation and dispute), the urge to expound and systematize doctrinal statements simply isn't present. As Solomon Schechter (see chapter 5), scholar and Jewish Theological Seminary chancellor, once summarized, "With God as a reality, Revelation as a fact, the Torah as a rule of life, and the hope of Redemption as a most vivid expectation, [the Rabbis] felt no need for formulating their dogmas into a creed."[2]

The great twelfth-century philosopher, physician, and scholar Moses Maimonides was the first to formally attempt an articulation of a Jewish creed from among the vast theological abundance of classical Judaism. Influenced by Islamic theological models, his Thirteen Attributes of Faith, building on that key Mishnaic source, expressed in rare specificity the set of doctrinal commitments he thought to be fundamental and unique to Judaism—and whose disavowal he believed could lead to excision from the community of Israel.[3] But these famous Maimonidean "dogmas" have met a strange fate. On the one hand, they garnered extensive criticism by Maimonides' own contemporaries as well as by many later authorities: their contents have been continually subject to change and their absolute authority has never been accepted.[4] But on the other hand (and owing, no doubt, to the fame of their author), their intellectual gravity (compounded by the pathbreaking courage to even proffer such a list) has persisted across the centuries, with each new generation feeling compelled to accept or combat them. (It is suggestive that nearly every author included in this anthology grapples with Maimonides' Thirteen Attributes, while also citing—and often standing with—his opponents.)

Despite the tepid acceptance of Maimonides' Thirteen Attributes, Jewish thinkers across the centuries have retained the assumption that some form of unshakable truth (call it doctrine or creed) *does* exists in Jewish theology. Importantly, however, the formative effect of such truth has always been undermined by the undefinable border between universally valid truths and those that are variable in time. In other words, because Judaism is both an intellectual tradition *and* a historical nationality, the act of establishing a universal truth could negatively affect a later generation's ability to interact with God. Take, for example, the biblical teaching that God's anger is placated through sacrifices.[5] Establishing this as a universal truth would thereby undermine Rabbinic Judaism's capacity to say that God moderates divine decrees based on one's *teshuvah* (repentance), *tefillah* (prayer), and *tzedakah* (charity). And yet canonizing these latter theological insights as immutable creed also weakens the Bible's authority as God's Word. Thus, in Judaism, basic theological dogmas have often functioned merely as boundary markers, defining the frontiers within which something is (or is not) called Judaism.

Medieval and early modern Jewish theologians never questioned certain traditional assumptions, most importantly monotheism (YHVH= "*Shema yisrael . . . YHVH echad,*" Listen, Israel . . . God is one), Revelation (*torah min-hashamayim*), and the undisrupted chain of Oral Law from

Moses onward (as expressed in Pirkei Avot 1:1). In essence, this meant that their works reflected systematic rather than historical theology (as explained above). In such writings as Saadia Gaon's *The Book of Beliefs and Opinions* (tenth century), Judah Halevi's *Kuzari* (twelfth century), and Gersonides' *The Wars of the Lord* (fourteenth century), the desire to harmonize, to find a unity of theological vision within Judaism's vast corpus and disparate periods, all but precluded a reckoning with historical development. Despite the fact that Judaism had long understood itself as *within* history rather than merely buffeted by it, premodern Jewish theology held fast to a line of theological homogeneity. And it was for this reason, perhaps more than any other, that these medieval theologians remained safely within Rabbinic tradition and eschewed the pronouncement of specific Jewish credal commitments.

Rise of Modern Jewish Theology

In 1835, Abraham Geiger, one of the leading ideologues of Jewish religious reform and an early proponent of the *Wissenschaft des Judentums*, founded a journal entitled *Wissenschaftliche Zeitschrift für jüdische Theologie* (Scientific journal for Jewish theology). Published in haphazard instalments until 1847, the WZJT printed writings by roughly a dozen European Jewish scholars on themes related to a so-called Jewish theology. In the following decades, journals like it were launched across the European world and became exemplary of a particular strain of scientifically informed Jewish theology, which critically examined, scrutinized, and questioned the languages and concepts of Rabbinic tradition and embraced contemporary advances in historical, philological, psychological, and ethnographic research. As Solomon Formstecher (see chapter 3), one of the earliest architects of the new theology, wrote in 1841, between the beginning and the end of "scientific theology" there is "wide room for historical, linguistic, hermeneutic, and archaeological research."[6] Or as German-American rabbi and Reform theologian Kaufmann Kohler (see chapter 7) described it some decades later, "A systematic theology of Judaism must . . . content itself with presenting

Jewish doctrine and belief in relation to the most advanced scientific and philosophical ideas of the age, so as to offer a comprehensive view of life and the world."[7]

In adopting the scientific methods of the nineteenth-century European academy, modern Jewish theologians diverged—often dramatically so—from their premodern forebears, for they engaged not only the medieval inclination to systematize but contemporary historicism as well, embracing genealogical developments and intellectual evolutions within Jewish theological culture. The modern Jewish theologians anthologized in this volume had at their disposal both a historical narrative of development as well as individual statements of doctrine and insight. With the rise of the modern sciences (humanistic and physical), Jewish theologians not only came to accept that Judaism was a historical religion but to view the criterion of science as the sine qua non for intellectual argumentation. In other words, for example, a new philological comparison or an archaeological finding could now outweigh any historical (literary, theological, halakhic) text whose assertions contradicted that of the new discovery. In modern Jewish theology, only those religious texts, historical facts, elements of culture and of spirit (*Geist*), and natural phenomena that could stand the trial of a critical scientific approach were regarded as tenable for making and sustaining conclusions about truths in the world—including statements about divinity.

Because modern Jewish theologians could never provide conclusive proof of the inerrancy of Jewish belief, they focused their attentions elsewhere, mainly on establishing a compilation of Jewish doctrines that would make a separate, distinct Judaic worldview comprehensible to modern people in a modern idiom. In the face of expectations from both Christian theologians and acculturating Jews eager to understand their theological inheritance, modern Jewish theologians were confronted with a unique task: that of comparing Judaism with other so-called world religions as well as justifying Judaism's continued (separate and distinct) existence. To this end, instead of defending rigid, traditional dogmas (such as Maimonides' Thirteen Attributes) in the face of radically shifting cultural dynamics, modern Jewish theologians sought to identify the driving forces of Jewish belief and expound upon their essential virtues as useful intellectual tools for the new age. As the philosopher and historian Julius Guttmann (see chapter 7) wrote in 1927 (in a seminal text on the methods of Jewish theology),

> Even if we were to assume that [one could] view the difference between the basic doctrines and the other religious truths of Judaism as having merely methodological (but not dogmatic) significance, [one] still would have to come to grips with the Talmudic statements about beliefs binding on all Jews—if they were able to find such statements. . . . [In the end,] one comes to realize that the essence of Judaism does not consist of a series of individual tenets, but of a unified fundamental religious conviction which is the very basis of these tenets and which alone gives them their religious meaning.[8]

Like Guttman, most of the authors anthologized here did not side with Maimonides, precisely because the creation of rigid dogma is not conducive to the elasticity necessary for the survival of a religion alive and responsive to history. To draw such lines, they imagined, would be as if to command the end of history. Instead, their vision for a "modern Jewish theology" was twofold. First, they sought to trace and analyze the development and evolution of Jewish theology from its biblical origins onward. In many cases, this meant the painstaking work of rediscovering, editing, and publishing as many Jewish texts from the past as were still extant in archives, libraries, and private collections. It also meant the creation of entirely new fields of inquiry, such as those focused on the debates between Maimonides and his opponents or on the rise and influence of Jewish mysticism and Kabbalah. Second, they aimed to write theological treatises for the modern era—novel works that not only employed a historical lens but also actively evaluated Jewish textual and halakhic assumptions in light of a full array of scientific findings.

About This Anthology

Modern Jewish Theology is the first comprehensive collection of Jewish theological ideas from the pathbreaking nineteenth century, featuring selections that (with few exceptions) have all been translated into English for the first time. Hence, this anthology opens to the English-language reader a true treasure house of source material from the formative years of modern Jewish thought—first-time access to the writings of the founding generations of modern Jewish theologians who defined the contours of the discipline and who made it possible to imagine that the traditional—biblical and Rabbinic—texts and *Wissenschaft* could not just complement one another but together produce a synthetic Judaic view of God, Israel, and the world.

In particular, this anthology shines novel light on what the editors consider modern Jewish theology's first hundred years, 1835–1935, an era offering a vast treasury of comprehensive theological works written by leading Jewish scholars, the majority of which have been untouched (and untranslated) by contemporary scholarship until now. In the 1830s, the first generation of modern Jewish theologians—many of them recent graduates from German universities and in their mid-twenties—published their earliest works. About a hundred years later, in the mid 1930s, the entire theological tradition (at least in Europe) would soon face a tragic end. Neither liberal nor neo-Orthodox German Jewish culture would ever recover from their expulsion and destruction by the Nazis. By 1945, German Jewry would cease to be a main driver of Jewish cultural and intellectual life, and in the post-Holocaust years, Jewish life would transform radically. The pressing question of the Holocaust or Shoah, the new military power implicit in the endurance (despite the odds) of the State of Israel, and the social and economic dominance of American Jewry, among other developments, would then become sources of Jewish theological fecundity (or, inversely, would be the events that were conspicuously avoided).

Between 1835 and 1935, however, modern Jewish theology developed almost exclusively in Central Europe, and almost all of the texts collected in this volume were originally written in German. This is more than a coincidence. German was the international scientific language of the age, and as such, it functioned as a unifying system, open to everyone who learned it. It was also a modern language, in the sense that, unlike languages traditionally used for the expression of Jewish thought, such as Hebrew or Yiddish (or even Arabic), German could articulate the finer points of new philosophical ideas in greater depth and detail. In addition, texts composed in German could interact with the broader non-Jewish world of life and culture and turn the theological ideas contained therein into common cultural property—a clearly stated intention of several of the authors anthologized here. That said, readers are to be cautioned against assuming that simply because a theologian wrote in German, he wished to assimilate his thought to gentile culture. German in the nineteenth century was what English is today. Indeed, at the very moment when Judaism was beginning to fragment in modernity, German functioned as a linguistic unifier, enabling Jews in Warsaw, Lviv, and Vilnius to interact with Jews in Berlin, Budapest, and New York.

The texts that follow span a wide variety of literary genres: sermons (which themselves sometimes include theological poetry), scientific essays published in academic journals, fictive letters of theological content, chapters from much larger works on the religious philosophy of Judaism, excerpts from university lectures on Jewish theology, introductions to Bible translations, sections from independent theological treatises, and more besides. Together, these sources attest to the vast literary range of modern Jewish theological writing and exemplify how Jewish theology can be articulated in very different modes and styles.

Organizationally, the anthology is divided into three semichronological, semithematic parts: first, the nineteenth century's discussion of the relevance and intrinsic nature of Judaism—its law and ritual; second, the twentieth-century's focus on systematic, rational theology and Judaism's relation to ethics; and third, in a great shift of paradigms that split Jewish thought after the First World War, the turn to a Jewish form of existentialism and mystical vitalism (*Lebensphilosophie*) as reflected in the writings of Martin Buber and Franz Rosenzweig.

The chapter division of the first two parts is motivated by the key subject matters to which Jewish theologians devoted their thinking during their respective centuries. Both parts begin with a chapter on "essentials," since the search for what might be identified as the theological "essence" of the Jewish religion was arguably the most pressing task modern Jewish theologians were to undertake. While modern Jewish theologians certainly aimed to provide modern Jews with a viable alternative to ritual observance as the identity marker for a continued loyalty to their religion, they also sought to find elemental markers of Jewish demarcation, theological tenets that fundamentally separated Judaism from that of, say, Protestantism. The relation of modern, acculturating Jews to the ritual traditions of Judaism (chapter 2) was another major point of theological discussion during the nineteenth century, with positions ranging from a wholesale rejection of all nonrational aspects of Jewish ceremonial law to their almost complete preservation—a debate that had repercussions regarding the concept of the law itself. Was Jewish law a dynamic, ever-changing corpus of manmade regulations, or a divinely ordained set of eternal rules? The answers to these questions, so the first modern Jewish theologians believed, had immediate consequences for the persistent relevance of Judaism (chapter 3), both for the increasingly secular Jews themselves but also for the contributions Judaism was still said to make to human civilization. Part 1 of the anthology closes with a chapter on the modern conception of God, because no feature of the Jewish religion was seen as so essential, relevant, and universally influential as what the nineteenth century termed "ethical monotheism"—that is, the theological assumption that the belief in the one and unique God, representing the idea of the Good, has direct implications for human morality.

Part 2 opens with a different, twentieth-century-based set of texts dealing with the essentials of Judaism (chapter 5), including a previously untranslated lecture by Hermann Cohen, perhaps the most important

Jewish philosopher at the turn of the century; and an extract from Leo Baeck's classic *The Essence of Judaism* (1905). Chapter 6, "Judaism and the Origin of Ethics," elaborates on the early twentieth-century notion that a modern version of Judaism, if not of religion in general, had to be exclusively about ethics. If there was still to be meaning in being religiously observant, such observance had to be for the sake of becoming a better human being and making the world a better place (*tikkun olam*). To the authors excerpted in this chapter, when considering the various world religions, Judaism was best suited for this purpose, especially the originally Jewish idea of messianism (if understood as a process, and as noneschatological). Jewish ritual and law had to be subordinated to this moral purpose; or, better, Judaism's legalistic structure was reinterpreted as being fundamentally about the spread of morality. (Note here the juxtaposition with Christianity, in which morality is based not in law but in faith and love.)[9]

Finally, part 2 concludes with a chapter (7) about the specific requirements and challenges of formulating a Jewish theology itself. The German American theologian Kaufmann Kohler made the first such attempt in 1910, in the introduction to his *Grundriss einer systematischen Theologie des Judentums auf geschichtlicher Grundlage* (Outline of a systematic theology of Judaism on a historical basis). By the 1920s, an exciting debate on Jewish dogma appeared in the pages of the *Monatsschrift*, culminating in a seminal article by Julius Guttmann concerning the emergence and authority of theological norms of Jewish belief. Eventually, under the shadow of the Nazi regime, the scholar and rabbi Alexander Altmann published an essay, "What Is Jewish Theology?," outlining a modern Orthodox position on the subject.

The more than thirty authors chosen for this volume are the widest known and most important and influential modern theologians of their time. Assembled here are a representative mixture of rabbis, preachers, historians, educators, and (increasingly toward the twentieth century) full-time academics. Only Samuel David Luzzatto and Solomon Schechter were not German citizens; all the others were born and worked (at least for significant portions of their lives) in German-speaking lands. Some of them, notably Gotthold Salomon and Ludwig Philippson, were among the most famous and sought-after Jewish intellectuals of their time, though they are almost entirely forgotten today. Others, such as the historians Heinrich Graetz and Julius Guttmann, the linguist Heyman Steinthal, and the neo-Orthodox theologian Samson Raphael Hirsch, are still known in our day, though for achievements far from the writing of theology. Still others are among the founding fathers of entire disciplines of Jewish *Wissenschaft*, such as the two Breslau medievalists David Kauffmann and Manuel Joel, and the famous Bible critic and exegete Benno Jacob. Some thinkers, such as Samuel Hirsch, Salomon Formstecher, and Hermann Cohen, were outright philosophers who authored thick volumes of Jewish philosophical thought. Most were members of the enormously broad and influential group of German *Doktor-Rabbiner*, academically trained leaders of Jewish communities who published their learned volumes combining the critical-scientific method with deep knowledge of Jewish sources and traditions. Strikingly, all of them have one commonality: an intense interest in thinking about and writing modern Jewish theology, because they were convinced that this endeavor was what guaranteed the future of Judaism in the modern age.

The new translations in this volume are all by luminaries in the field of modern Jewish thought. These scholars, above and beyond all others, understand the cultural and intellectual background of these texts and can thereby convey in English not just translations of the original words but also the resonances, influences, and subtle nuances of authorial style and intent. Their in-depth knowledge of the subjects discussed in the translated passages, as well as their familiarity with the life and work of the original authors, has hopefully helped to avoid many of the errors and misunderstandings usually found when transferring intellectual and cultural concepts from one language to another. One example is a new translation, exclusive to this volume, of the theological centerpiece of Franz Rosenzweig's *Star of Redemption* (1922) by one of the leading Rosenzweig experts of our time, Prof. Benjamin Pollock of Hebrew University in Jerusalem. (Previous English translations of what Rosenzweig famously called the "Herzbuch"—literally, the "heart" of the *Star*—have often been criticized as inadequate to the complex meaning of the original German.)

Finally, let us be clear: this is not an anthology of *exemplary Jewish theological writing* from the modern era. It is a collection of *modern Jewish theology*—that is, Jewish theology that interacts self-reflectively with the methodologies, languages, sciences, and politics of its time, not in a reactionary mode but as serious intellectual achievements from and through which a deeper understanding of Jewish theology can be derived. Because of this, we exclude, for example, the brilliant theologians of modern *Haredism*, men such as Reb Yisrael Meir Kagan (1839–1933, the Chofetz Chayim) and Reb Naftali Zvi Yehuda Berlin (1816–93, the Netziv), though they lived in the same era and in some cases shared the same teachers as those included here. These *haredi* thinkers did not write systematic theological treatises aiming to address Judaism in the context of modernity. Because of that, they are *Jewish theologians in modernity*, but not part of *modern Jewish theology*. This similarly holds true for some of the core ideologues of religious Zionism (including Abraham Isaac Kook, 1865–1935), who did not aspire to discern and describe the essential theological narratives of Judaism but rather to develop a new Jewish political and cultural future. Additionally, no female Jewish thinkers published substantive works of theology in the period covered by this anthology.[10] Jewish religious feminism would truly emerge and flower only after the Second World War.

Jewish Theology as Its Own Academic Discipline

In reawakening ourselves to the deeply normative practice of theology within Jewish culture, we can begin to recognize that theology not only thrived among Jewish scholars in the nineteenth and early twentieth centuries but remains, to this day, a discipline ripe for intellectual inquiry and continued debate. In these opening decades of the twenty-first century, university and rabbinical students, rabbis, lay leaders, and university professors are continually confronted with the challenge of both understanding and explaining Jewish theology. Not only has there been a long and deep tradition of theological investigation in modern Judaism, but it was done by mainstream, respected members of the Jewish intellectual community who understood their project as part of the broader scientific enterprise of modernity. If nature, the psyche, human social organization, even language itself are all able to be studied through scientific methods, then so can Jewish theology.

In many ways, this volume is a bridge, filling in a piece of Jewish intellectual history that has been overlooked for far too long. What happened in Jewish theology between Moses Mendelssohn and Abraham J. Heschel, between the Haskalah and Judith Plaskow? This question is not just for academic historians and graduate students in Jewish history; it is a vital inquiry for anyone interested in Jewish history and thought, especially those whose knowledge of modern Jewish philosophy rests on thinkers from the second half of the twentieth century. In illuminating the theological world out of which these—and our—philosophies arose, this volume demonstrates that a rich discourse of theology, from modern Orthodox to Reform, has been a continuous and seamless part of the Jewish tradition from the advent of modernity onward.

In that vein, the editors of this volume hope to return to discussion a wide-ranging set of ideas and methodologies for pursuing Jewish theology in the modern era, a theology alert and interested in scientific advances, and one that is equally aware of its responsibilities to the inherited history of Jewish beliefs and practices. It is the editors' contention—just as it was the contention of all the writers included in this book—that Jewish theology is a legitimate academic discipline, deserving of a place in the contemporary conversation of both Jewish studies and lived Jewish practice. Hopefully, this volume will serve as both a model and a spur to the (re)legitimation of Jewish theology as a compelling and rigorous intellectual discipline in our own day.

How to Use This Book

This book has two components, one of them present between these covers, the second available in the resources section of the volume's accompanying website (jps.org/books/modern-Jewish-theology).

First, the work. It is designed for readers of all levels, and for personal, classroom, and informal education. This introductory account of the history and development of Jewish theology will benefit students and those interested in the evolution of Jewish thought. The essays translated here tend to be but a small fraction—usually what is most exemplary or most original—of an author's full oeuvre, serving to also introduce readers of all backgrounds to new thinkers. The chapter and section introductions highlight connections between these thinkers, to help readers get a sense of the fecundity of this lost intellectual world. Explanatory and referential notes guide readers through the thicket of scriptural, Rabbinic, and historical references and point out suggestive meanings in the original language that can get lost in translation.

Second is the accompanying website, hosting materials for personal and classroom use as well as providing access to many of the essays in their original language and context. On the website (jps.org/books/modern-Jewish-theology; select the "Resources" tab), teachers and students will find a discussion guide walking them through the major ideas and innovations of each chapter; sample lesson plans and reading questions; links to the original biblical and Rabbinic texts (so readers can compare the way a text appears in its original, ancient context, and how it is then being interpreted by the modern theologian); and bibliographical references for further research and study. We encourage all readers of this volume to explore these resources if they desire an even broader and deeper experience of the texts.

Conclusion

The issues at the heart of this book lie with the defining challenges of our own age, the era of what Abraham Joshua Heschel (1907–72) called "technical civilization." We live at a time of immense practical knowledge about the physical and material world, and of a dizzying variety and richness of investigations into the past. "The making of many books is without limit" (Eccles. 12:12), we were warned long ago, and it can seem that data, information, the collection and assemblage of things to know, is the defining character of our time. We have a civilization with great material wealth and power, and immense technical proficiency. But what are we to do with it? We have information—but for meaning and responsibility we are left to ourselves. In a world of algorithms that predict want, we are expected to construct our own narratives of fulfillment. The challenge of our times is distinctly tied up with the triumph of scientific information, of historical and critical self-awareness, and of the pressures these place not just on received forms of religious and ethical knowledge, but on the way these question the claims of all prior theology itself.

The authors in this volume did not have access to the internet, of course. But they were keenly aware of the revolution in the way new forms of knowledge were mediating received philosophical and theological claims. Such awareness sits at the very heart of every word recorded in the pages of this anthology. It is this selfsame modernity—a world driven by scientific advancement and the struggle of reason, logic, and universalism against sophistry and tribalism, superstition and ignoble deception—that we still inhabit. In such an age, modern Jewish theology shows us that writing about the nature of God isn't just about providing doctrinal answers, or about solving once and for all the true essence of the Divine Being. Instead, modern Jewish theology is about grappling, straightforwardly and honestly, with the intellectual dissonances of religion and technological civilization, about trying to understand and put into words a coherent account of the nature of God and Judaism under the harsh light of historically informed self-critical thought.

Much of what is known about modern Jewish theology in the Anglophone world comes from the works of Abraham Joshua Heschel and Martin Buber. A smaller contingent of readers is likely familiar with the ideas of such twentieth-century thinkers as Joseph Soloveitchik, Abraham Isaac Kook, Mordecai Kaplan, and Judith Plaskow. Likewise, readers may have heard of the Jewish Theological Seminary and Yeshiva University, the latter of whose motto, *Torah Umadda*, "Torah and Science," is a direct application of *Wissenschaft* principles. And while the fruits of contemporary Jewish scholarship are ubiquitous — in books, magazines, journals, documentaries, museums, podcasts, videos, classrooms, the web — few people have any notion of the intellectual and methodological assumptions that make all this knowledge possible.

This is where our anthology begins. Before any of these figures were born, these institutions founded, these books written, or these classes taught, the world of Jewish theological learning and writing in the modern period was already immensely wide and deep, encompassing thinkers from across the religious and philosophical spectrum who sought a path for Jewish theology through the thicket of modernity. For those who have been influenced or intrigued by the works of Judaism's greatest theologians of the past century, we invite you into *their* libraries, to read the original works that founded modern Jewish theology. They still have many new insights to share.

Notes on Translations and Annotations

Most of the works included in this anthology originated in a language other than English. In nearly all cases, the editors have commissioned new translations by contemporary scholars, many of whom are leading experts on the author and work they've translated.

Readers should be aware that in German—the most common language translated in this volume—capitalization is used very differently than it is in English. In German, for example, it is grammatically and orthographically impossible to capitalize all the various grammatical forms of "He" when they concern God, as would be the standard practice in English when God is referred to as male. So, too, in German, nouns are generally capitalized, so it would be standard for a German author to capitalize the phrase (in English) "the Being and Essence of God," and that might not imply anything specifically theological about how that author viewed those attributes of God; by contrast, in English, saying "the being and essence of God" implies something different than "the Being and Essence of God." As a result, in this work, translators who are scholars of these authors and materials have made many individual decisions regarding the emphasis of the original and how best to render authorial intent into English.

For those selections originating in English, we have faithfully reproduced the author's original wording, including grammar and spelling. For those with an existing English translation, we have generally reprinted it here with modifications, which are noted.

All translations of the Hebrew Bible follow the New Jewish Publication Society (NJPS) translation (1999), and all New Testament translations follow the New Revised Standard Version (NRSV). When authorial interpretation has necessitated a different rendering, we have followed the author's translation in the text and commented on it in the notes. Translations of the Babylonian Talmud follow the William Davidson Talmud with occasional modifications by the editors.

As this anthology is intended primarily for an English-language readership, references to the original languages and to Hebrew have been kept to a minimum. Interested readers may consult the original-language texts on the volume's accompanying website: jps.org/books/modern-Jewish-theology.

Abbreviations

Chron.	Chronicles
Deut.	Deuteronomy
Eccles.	Ecclesiastes
Esther	Esther
Exod.	Exodus
Ezek.	Ezekiel
Ezra	Ezra
Gen.	Genesis
Hag.	Haggai
Hos.	Hosea
Isa.	Isaiah
Jer.	Jeremiah
Josh.	Joshua
Kings	Kings
Lev.	Leviticus
Mal.	Malachi
Mic.	Micah
Neh.	Nehemiah
Num.	Numbers
Prov.	Proverbs
Ps.	Psalms
Sam.	Samuel
Zech.	Zechariah
Zeph.	Zephaniah

Cor.	Corinthians
En.	Enoch
Macc.	Maccabees
Matt.	Matthew
Rom.	Romans
Tim.	Timothy

NJPS	New Jewish Publication Society Bible
NRSV	New Revised Standard Version Bible

b.	Babylonian Talmud
m.	Mishnah
t.	Tosefta
y.	Jerusalem Talmud

AdRN	Avot de-Rabbi Nathan
Deut. Rab.	Deuteronomy Rabbah
Est. Rab.	Esther Rabbah
Ex. Rab.	Exodus Rabbah
Gen. Rab.	Genesis Rabbah
MdRI	Mechilta de-Rabbi Ishmael
Mid. Tan. (B.)	Midrash Tanchuma (Buber)
Mish. Tor.	*Mishneh Torah* (Maimonides)
Mor. Nev.	*Moreh Nevukhim* (Maimonides)
PA	Pirkei Avot
PdRE	Pirkei de-Rabbi Eliezer
Pes. Rab.	*Pesikta Rabbati*
Ruth Rab.	Ruth Rabbah
Tar. Jon.	Targum Jonathan
TdER	Tanna Debei Eliyahu Rabbah
Tor. Koh.	Torat Kohanim [Sifra]
Shul. Aruk.	Shulchan Arukh

Modern Jewish Theology

1

Writing Theological Modernity

The Nineteenth Century

1

The Essentials of Judaism

Jewish theological writing in the nineteenth century often emerged in disputes with the ideas of medieval and modern philosophers, especially the two Moseses: Maimonides and Mendelssohn. Both thinkers—as well as their host of interlocutors down the generations—argued over one of the central questions of Jewish theology: Does Judaism possess dogmas or principles of belief (a dogma being understood in the nineteenth century as a rational theological principle unique to the Jewish religion)? Maimonides thought that it did, and famously defined thirteen (in his Thirteen Attributes of Jewish Faith). Mendelssohn believed that it did not, insisting instead that Judaism was a way of life bound by laws and customs but not by predefined beliefs. As a result of this mixed intellectual heritage, many nineteenth-century theologians sought to develop, or at least to glean from the classical sources, some version of a Jewish dogmatics, framed around the idea of articles of faith.

Perhaps the most prominent dogma debated among nineteenth-century theologians was a principle that eventually came to be called "ethical monotheism," the idea that the belief in one God solved the problem of competing systems of morality: if there is only one God, who is truly moral, then all humanity can likewise be united under (and then governed by) a single moral system. In a way, discussions around the concept of ethical monotheism suggested broader shifts in Jewish theology, especially when it came to negotiating the line between Jewish exclusivity and divine universality. In what ways are God's promises to Israel (e.g., Israel shall be governed morally; Israel shall be protected from enemies) distinct to Israel, and in what ways are God's promises actually indicative of God's broader care for and love of humanity?

Indeed, we see a new understanding of Jewish messianism also taking shape in the 1840s: nonpersonal (arising from the House of David but then encompassing all nations, not just Israel), this-worldly (bringing peace to the nations as we see them, rather than to an Edenic re-creation), and universal (applying not just to the return and redemption of Israel but to the peace of all humanity). While this view of messianism might feel comfortable to many contemporary Jews, it would have felt quite foreign to classical or medieval Jewish theologians.

Finally, in this new era, traditional beliefs and modes of reasoning were no longer wholly sufficient for answering the pressing religious questions of the day. To the insights of classical Rabbinic logic (reliant on the Talmud and its commentators), the findings from new methods of scientific research were increasingly added. For example, the historical era in which a given text originated, and then the various ways it was modified, adopted, or neglected, often became important data for determining the relevance, centrality or obscurity, or simply diversity of opinions regarding this or that theological concept in Judaism. Over the course of the nineteenth century, the findings of historical, archaeological, and natural historical research came to play a growing role in adjudicating and buttressing theological claims among Jewish theologians. (See the introduction for a fuller discussion of this topic.)

Nevertheless, the Torah remained the bedrock principle that united all Jewish theologians, from left to right. As one can see in this chapter, no early nineteenth-century theologians questioned the Torah's unity (i.e., the single authorship of the Pentateuch), its holiness (the words of the Torah being generative of religious faith and practice), its divinity (being the distinct work of God's instruction), or its centrality (being the heart of Judaism). Instead, the theological battlefield between liberalism and orthodoxy came to revolve around the authority of talmudic literature, and thus the continued validity of the halakhah (ritual law), and not the unique status of Torah itself.

GOTTHOLD SALOMON (1784–1862)

Gotthold Salomon (b. 1784, Sandersleben; d. 1862, Hamburg) was probably the most famous and certainly one of the most talented Jewish preachers in Europe during the first half of the nineteenth century. From 1818 until 1858 he occupied the pulpit at the Israelite Temple in Hamburg, the first Reform community established in Germany, drawing large audiences of Jews and non-Jews alike who were interested in hearing German-language sermons conveying Jewish interpretations of the Hebrew Bible.

Often compared to the leading Protestant preachers of his age, Salomon might be seen as the father of Jewish homiletics in the nineteenth century, essentially founding a whole tradition of the Reform sermon, which emphasized an ethical view of the meaning of Judaism. From 1806 to 1843, Salomon was the editor of *Sulamith*, the first German-language journal published for a Jewish public; and his German translation of the Hebrew Bible, *Deutsche Volks- und Schulbibel für Israeliten* (1837), the first Jewish Bible translation intended for use in schools, contained no Hebrew and no commentary, only the text in good, comprehensible German. Contrary to Moses Mendelssohn's sophisticated synthesis of all three elements (Hebrew, German, and commentary) in his own translation, Salomon's Bible soon became very popular among German Jewry, even beyond educational purposes.

Salomon was engaged in many controversies of his time, both intra-Jewish (especially in defending the legitimacy of Reform, whose opponents saw it as undermining the rabbinic practice of legal interpretation) and interreligious, including as a participant in the first Jewish-Christian debates on academic theology. Around 1830, for the first time, Jewish scholars began responding in substantive ways to Christian religious anti-Judaism (a tradition that sometimes even amounted to Christian denial of the Jewish religion altogether). These Jewish responses, based on a surprising wealth of knowledge of Christian theology and texts, were routinely formulated in almost academic, matter-of-fact language. Quite different from the medieval Jewish-Christian polemics (which often were not more that mutual cursing), the mid-nineteenth-century religious debates in Germany demanded seriousness from both sides and, despite the harsh argumentative tones, were by and large shaped by deep mutual respect. As part of these debates, Salomon published widely read pamphlets attacking the theological antisemitism of such prominent Christian thinkers as Anton Theodor Hartmann (in 1835) and Bruno Bauer (in 1843).

The following excerpt is a festival sermon that Salomon delivered on Simchat Torah at the Israelite Temple in Hamburg in the late 1820s.[1] Salomon structured the material in a dialogic form: a choir responds to the service leader with rhymed verses after each of Maimonides' Thirteen Attributes. In this way, Salomon emphasized the liturgical purpose and framework of the sermon's theological ideas, in a way demonstrating how integral theology is in the service of God. In addition, in giving his own theological interpretation of Maimonides' list, Salomon presents an early example of what would later become known in German Jewish thought as the doctrine of "ethical monotheism." The sermonizing tone of the text hardly hides the radical reformulations Salomon introduces into classical Jewish dogmatism—from the temporary value of some of the Torah's laws (compared to the immutability of God's teachings as such) to the reinterpretation of the Messianic Age as a worldly period of universal brotherly love. Such eternal brotherly love, Salomon argues, is the true meaning of a Jewish understanding of the term "religion."

Thirteen Basic Teachings of Religion (1829)

Translated by Dana Rubinstein

When, according to the words of Scripture (Ps. 32:11), *pious, faithfully* devoted hearts rejoice; then their joy is *pure* and *holy,* and the heavens rejoice with them, and the earth cheers, and the mountains and the hills sound songs of jubilation, and the trees of the field rustle and grow green anew (Ps. 96:2), and instead of thorns, cedars and myrtles bloom, for the high glory of the Eternal—an everlasting, unfading monument (Isa. 55:12–13).[2] And from His heights the LORD looks on and rejoices in *such* joy.

But *does* such pure, heavenly joy, in which the heavenly creatures can rejoice, also exist on earth? Is there on earth a joy that *does not end* with heartache and tears (Prov. 14:13)? How often did we rejoice in goods and treasures that we received, how often did we sound songs of jubilation, for a new possession, a new life, and—oh!—how soon, how soon did the jubilant singing turn into songs of sorrow?—I ask again: Is there on earth a joy that does not end with heartache and tears? Yes, there is on earth such joy. *It is the joy over the lasting effect of ethics and religion, how they bring happiness and bliss to humanity*! It is an elevated thought, worthy of a nation wandering before God, to dedicate certain *days* to such joy from one generation to the next.

Such a day we celebrate *today* under the Hebrew name *Simchat Torah: Joy* that the *teaching* of God never loses its power, but continues to affect us and bring happiness. This is the interpretation of the name, this is the meaning of the holiday!

When it is said about religion *let her breasts satisfy you at all times; be infatuated with love of her always* [Prov. 5:19], then we rejoice that this friend does not age or whither; that she still finds, and will always find, loving hearts among the children of man, as long as the eye sees and the heart feels. When it is said about religion *they are life to him who finds them, healing for his whole body* [Prov. 4:22], then we rejoice that this healing life-source has not yet run dry and that we still draw from it today. When it is called *a tree of life to those who grasp her* [Prov. 3:18], then we rejoice that this tree stands tall in beautiful bloom and always carries fruit. When it is called *a graceful wreath upon your head, a necklace about your throat* [Prov. 1:9], then we rejoice that this jewelry is never subject to changing fashions, that it graces and embellishes lads and young ladies, men and women. When praised that *she will adorn your head with a graceful wreath; crown you with a glorious diadem* [Prov. 4:9], then we rejoice that there are thousands and myriads that grace their appearance with this crown, always verdant, always blooming, and that, even in the coffin, it continues to adorn. Finally, when it is said about religion that it *will bestow on you length of days, years of life and well-being* [Prov. 3:2], then we rejoice that it still preserves life and increases happiness for all of humanity. Behold! This joy is pure, is divine, does not end with heartache and tears. *It is a delightful celebration for all of humanity!*

In so far as we constitute a *special* religious fellowship, and as *Israelites* celebrate today's holiday, we throw a glance at those teachings that have become *Israel's* inheritance, and we rejoice at their continued power and their unceasing light.[3] But the teachings are numerous and extensive, how can I name them all?

Thus, we will only illuminate and examine the *basic teachings* to the extent that they affect our lives and will remain eternal. The *thirteen principles* [attributes] *of the Mosaic faith,* formulated by our Maimonides shall furnish the material for our observations today. May God's word in the Scripture guide us.[4] Amen.

> Deuteronomy 31:10–13: And Moses instructed them as follows: Every seventh year, the year set for remission, at the Feast of Booths, when all Israel comes to appear before the LORD your God in the place that He will choose, you shall read this Teaching aloud in the presence of all Israel. Gather the people—men, women, children, and the strangers in your communities—that they may hear and so learn to revere the LORD your God and to observe faithfully every word of this Teaching. Their children, too, who have not had the experience, shall hear and learn to revere the LORD your God as long as they live in the land that you are about to cross the Jordan to possess.

The power of the divine teaching that was thus revealed shall serve and have its effect on men and women and children and foreigners for a *lifetime*. And it did serve, and it was effective, it still is effective and will always be effective! It must thus hold eternal power, eternal life; its spirit remains and affects eternally.

And what does it teach, that so grips and warms the heart?

There is a God!![5]

That is its *greatest, first* saying, that grips and warms human hearts with all-consuming force. As it was uttered, the universe and life gained purpose, humanity a goal, a lofty goal: to strive for an ideal with all its might!

Nature would be chaos, life senseless, the human being devoid of meaning, humanity orphaned, had you not been privy to the teaching: "*There is a God!*" All of creation would appear ghostly to you, if you had to think on it devoid of creator, devoid of God. The eye sees *effects* everywhere—but where is the *cause* of the effects? Where does it begin? Where does it end? It begins with the teaching: *There is a God!* And it ends with the teaching: *There is a God!* And if you look up at the heavens, each of its bright clouds glows: *There is a God!* Gaze at the immeasurable ocean, in each wave you hear: *There is a God!* In each tree, in each flower his name blossoms, and in your heart it calls, like in the teaching: *There is a God*:

There is a God! All lips resound,
A million worlds He created;
From pole to pole, the world around,
From east to west it is stated.

Choir: There is a God! Mountains and meadows call,
Nature attests His existence—He created it all.

The *second* basic teaching tells us: *There is only One God! One* Being called you into existence.[6] *One* Being gave the whole universe existence. *One* Being is the father of all worlds and people. *One* Being only you can embrace with all your heart and all your soul. *One* Being only whom you can love fully. *One* you can devote yourself to fully. *One* in gladness and sorrow. *One* in life and death. *One* here and there. *One* it is who stretched out the heavens. *One* who established the earth. *One* whole, one cohesive whole is nature. *One* it came forth from and therefore is still *One* with *One* purpose. And if all else would leave and expel you—*One* whose heart you will find to which you can turn! In the whole universe His fatherly heart beats in your direction. Everything exists because the *One* speaks, *Alone*. Because He and He alone created it the universe still stands today, like it did a thousand years ago, and it will withstand: *O Israel, rejoice in this second teaching! It will remain!*

> *There is only One God! His never-ending Being*
> *No earthly intellect can understand*
> *In the star-filled skies we are reading*
> *This order created by only One hand.*
>
> *Choir: This World was by One God Created,*
> *All of it! from just One Originated.*

Whatever you think of as *corporeal* is imperfect; it has flaws and infirmities. A corporeal being, be it mighty and strong, be it endowed with the highest that heavens and earth can offer—*love*: if it is corporeal, its powers must wane, its strength must pass, its love must die. Bound by *the chains of space and time* it remains weak and impotent. But one Being shall shine forth for man, in whose power he can live and in whose love he can be sustained: *God is not a body and shall not be thought of as a body,* is thus the *third* teaching of our religion.[7] As the *highest role model of our ethical perfection,* God stands before us.[8] Therefore it is strictly forbidden to think of Him as any image be it ever so refined. *Protect yourselves against this folly* if you value your life, our law giver calls to us (Deut. 4:15). What a word! What a warning! God does not wish, cannot, and may not be thought of, pictured and venerated in *form* and *image*! *Only in the spirit! Only in truth. Rejoice Israel in this third teaching! It remains!*

No image or bodily shell Him resemble,
A form for Him no one will ever descry;
Radiating holiness and wisdom so ample
He has never been seen by a mortal eye.

Choir: No image Him resembles, who ever did Him espy?
A form for Him no one will ever descry.

Do you think that the thousand times thousand worlds that you see and do not see are shells of God? Do you think that He needs them like your spirit needs a *body* on earth? If you do, then you blaspheme Him; you do not believe in the God of our religion. *He was eternally! Ere another being was ever created.*[9] He does not need His worlds, the worlds need Him, they must collapse if He so commands, they must rise once more when He calls. The father does not *need* his children, even if he *rejoices* in them; the children however need their father, they cannot breathe without him. His breath enlivens the entire universe, gives the sun its glow; gives the tree its foliage; gives the heart its life—and because He was prior to everything created, He is the Lord of all fates, He stands above nature, it is in His hand, like the cement in the hand of the builder. . . .[10]

Does this belief not uplift you, O human being? You stand under one God who acts freely and in whose hands lies all that happens. *God is* the *Lord* of destiny! *God* is the *Lord* of Nature! He uses it for his wise purposes. Therefore, He can also perform *miracles* to benefit those who love Him. Rejoice in your Lord! There is no situation in your life, be it ever so dark and convoluted, that He does not understand. He holds the strings in His hand and can guide you away from the wrong path when people cannot. *Rejoice Israel in this fourth teaching! It remains!!*

The Eternal was ere, in space open wide
The sun did its great orbit sweep,
Ere on the horizon's brink alight,
The morning sun rose and all was sleep.

Choir: The Eternal was ere the starry sky's light,
Ere the moon that brightens the gloomy night.

Could it bring you joy, O human! to live under a ruler who established his land with admirable intelligence but then relinquished the reigns to his slaves who rule it at will, without wisdom or love? What can you gain by recognizing a God as the *creator*—all wisdom and goodness—when this God's eyes do not rest on the world that He created; when it does not remain close to His heart? O there were, there still are such fools who, while believing in a *creator,* nevertheless say: *the Lord has abandoned the earth* (Ezek. 8:12); it is now subject to blind chance. *Chance*? Chance in God's world? Suppose even *one* chance event and the whole chain of events becomes chance, blind chance, devoid of meaning, devoid of purpose, devoid of love, devoid of God: because all is interdependent. Believe in a *single* chance event and you will soon stop believing in God—for a long time this delusion was spun and fools who carry God's name on their lips but do not carry it in their hearts still believe this folly—therefore rejoice O Israel in the *fifth* basic teaching! It teaches you to believe *in divine providence,* a God who implanted the ear and—hears; who formed the eye and—sees; who created the heart and—examines, hears and knows each time it beats (Ps. 94:9). If for one moment He were not watching, then everything that happened throughout *millennia* would have happened without God. Because the moment begins with what eternities, chain by chain, link by link, have brough to maturity. And you would find yourself suddenly in a world without God and life would become a corpse devoid of a warming heart. No, no, *providence* watches over you however small you think yourself; *providence* rules everything that happens in your life. Rejoice in this *fifth teaching. It remains!*

He is the Lord! The wind's and ocean's flow
obey the ruler's every word;
Lightning and thunder, just like the rainbow,
make His might and majesty heard.

Choir: He is the Lord and each creature,
exalts His glory in nature.[11]

But do you believe that humanity would have found God and providence in the *book of nature* alone?[12] Do you think it would have immediately risen up to Him? So easily raised from dust? Don't you think the dust would have pulled it to dust with all-consuming force? Aren't there entire species even today that crawl in the dust and cannot rise up to God in the face of the blooming nature that surrounds them? Thus, divinity had to minister to humans with special love and lead humanity to her heart. And she *raised* the human being up to her. *Humanity was educated, enlightened, and raised up through many men elevated by God, imparted with His spirit.*[13] Therefore our sixth teaching:

The spirit of truth and His holy will
He makes known to the men of His glory,
Lifting the veil of the future to reveal
Only to those who He finds worthy.

Choir: God only revealed His future plan;
Where He found a worthy, deserving human.

And among these forerunners of humanity, it was *Moses* who died through the mouth of God (Deut. 34:5), just like he lived by and according to God's mouth. *Moses* shone brightest among them all; *he was the most trusted in the house of the Lord* (Num. 12:7). *He was foremost among all the prophets who ever lived and taught.*[14]

Through Moses God made known His will,
Never was there a prophet like he;
The highest words he aimed to fulfill,
Only he saw God's high majesty.

Choir: Never was there in Israel a prophet like he;
Who saw God's highest majesty.

Through him came to *Earth the teaching of the Eternal*, that in its perfection refreshes the *soul.*[15] Through him came to the human race the *testimonies* of God that lend wisdom to the frivolous. Through him became known the *commands of the Lord*; their straightforward nature brings joy to one's heart. Through him we learned to practice *God's commandments*; their integrity lights up one's eyes. Through him we learned the *fear of God*, in its purity it will forever remain; and the *laws of God*; all of them fair (Ps. 19:8–10). Rejoice, Israel, in this *eighth* teaching. Rejoice because from that holy mountain shone forth the light; wherever its rays did not penetrate, it is still dark and cold. The teaching of the Lord is the healing sun, its rays reach far; where there is light and warmth, it is thanks to the light and the warmth of this sun of the teaching that God gave us through Moses.

At Sinai God gave him the Laws[16]
And spoke, encircled by sun's purest light;
This holiness protect, it has no flaws
God's word to Moses, no sinner shall spite.

Choir: Radiating the light of truth, God did us impart
on Mount Sinai His holy laws—from them do not depart!

No, no they cannot be violated, these great truths that are preserved in God's teachings; *they are eternal, like God!*[17] The worlds and souls of men are founded on them. And even if another thousand worlds and another thousand religions arise—if rational, God-believing sense inhabits these worlds and these religions, they will be illuminated by no other than the *Ur-light*; the bright sun that the Lord has shown us. And if individual laws that are limited by time and space fall prey to time and space and cease, *the teachings* that encompass humanity, and connect heaven and earth, give power to the spirit and life to the heart.[18] *These teachings* will direct you upward, helping you to suppress your inclinations and live your duty. These teachings never perish. Heaven and earth may vanish—*God stands above the ruins and with Him—God's word. Rejoice Israel! In this ninth teaching, it remains.*

Earth and firmament may someday subside
Extinguish may even the flaming sunlight;
What God commanded on that holy height,
Remains always unchanging, does not subside.

Choir: God's teachings and the truth-induced light,
Remains always unchanging, does not subside.[19]

Yes, the word of God survives eternally because He *gave it to all of humanity*. And when He gave it, all the peoples of the earth passed Him by; those of the present and those yet to come. He saw them and knew them; knew them and loved them; saw and tested them. And He well assessed that the truth He revealed in His work, in His *word,* in our *hearts,* in our *intellects,* will last forever. The master builder of the world did not design His work of law to be transient. I just named you four pillars on which the structure rests: nature, Scripture, conscience, and intellect. Those are four pillars that defy eternities. Storms may rage against them; they do not shake them! Pests may gnaw at their foundations and insolently try to soil them—these pillars stand and do not falter. Folly and foppery may jeer—this too the LORD foresaw, He already laughed off its folly. Rejoice in this *tenth* basic teaching. *It remains.*[20]

All human strivings, God sees through
He knows the deed ere it is done
The old man's life in childhood He knew
Before Him darkness turns to sun.

Choir: The Lord, He sees through future deeds,
The future in the dark He sees.[21]

And because He can see dark nights in the future, because He grasps the present, past and future in one picture, He can *mete* out reward and punishment. Because God can peer into the deepest depths of the heart, He alone can repay people's actions according to their *intentions*. This is the content of our *eleventh* basic teaching:[22] Do not be overhasty human, and do not ask: why does this sinner live in happiness while this pious person lives in misery? Leave it to the all-seeing, He who knows the creations of His hand like an artist knows the work of art he made. After all, you can only see the *here and now*, the *temporal*—how will you judge since the *hereafter* and *eternity* are hidden from you? Therefore, do not judge hastily about the condition of others. But do consider whether your own happiness is a reward or a *test; investigate* whether your own misery is a *punishment* or a *refinement*. In each case, bear it, my poor unhappy brother! Bear it, my poor unhappy sister, and look up to God with a faithful disposition.

God is just! He does the insolent sinner strike
And gives the virtuous his rightful share,
Beggar and prince are His children alike
Both will appear before His royal chair.

Choir: God is just! Before His judge's chair,
The good and bad get their rightful share.

And just like the differences do and should vanish at God's throne, because God judges regardless of a person's standing—judges the *act* and not the *actor*—so, already on earth, all the walls that *prejudice, false belief, insanity,* and *darkness* have erected between people, between brother and brother, should collapse. The prison in which human reason still lies in chains shall be blown up; the chains of a sighing mankind shall be smashed; the wounds from which humankind still sheds blood shall be healed. The fog that surrounds the human intellect should vanish, the ice that surrounds the human heart should melt. And when the fog vanishes, one brother will ask the next: How is it possible that I have so misjudged you all this time? Are you not *flesh* of my *flesh,* spirit of my spirit, a child of God like me? And when the ice has melted, the *heart* will be warmed and will glow with goodness and love. And one will look at the other, puzzled but joyful like one who has been awakened from a long winter slumber. Then, and only then, one will understand the resonant name *religion* better and will not make sport of what is holiest in the heavens and on earth. Only then will one know what it means to act according to *reason* and which enemies we have all hitherto nourished and cultivated in the greying hatred of *religion* and *superstition*. Then one *pure language that all people speak, will worship the name of the Eternal God and the Eternal will be one on this day and one will be His great name* (Zeph. 3:9; Zech. 14:9).

This is the *twelfth* basic teaching. *This is the time of the Messiah,* when the Israelite religion teaches all those who wish to penetrate its spirit and do not hold tight to the dead letter.[23] This is the *time of redemption*! O, that it may come soon! Bring it about, Israelites and Non-Israelites! Pious and world-wise, your task remains to bring about the time of celebration for humankind through wise action and pious behavior.[24]

With childlike trust we await Him,
Whatever He promised has always been fulfilled;
He sends redeemers to those who trust Him,
All tears and cries through Him are stilled.

Choir: He sends redemption; let our trust not falter;
And with hope look to Him, our father.

Yes, let us look up to Him, the Father, full of hope, and with pious Job declaim: *I know that my redeemer lives and He will wake me from the grave* (Job 19:25).[25] That is the *thirteenth* basic principle, auguring *resurrection after death. In His eternal kindness, the Lord also enlivens the deceased.*[26]

Is this belief difficult for you, my brother? Look around you and see how bit by bit the mother of the living, the blooming nature, falls ill and dies. Just a small amount and the LORD revives the deceased, sends his *odem* [ruby] and renews her to life.

Is this belief difficult for you, my brother? O how many live among us on whose *experience* I can base this belief! If he was miserable and poor and wanting—in a few moments—the LORD called forth a lovely word: he arose from his suffering and now he lives joyful, happy days: The LORD gave a corpse *its warm heart*: it lives!

Is the belief still difficult for you, my brother? O for how many, death tore away a beloved being and placed it in the lap of the cold earth. But after moons and years the LORD blessed you and you embraced a new life, a small boy, a little girl, and the child grew and blossomed and developed before your eyes and resembled in form and appearance, in expressions and behavior, in soul and heart, the one that you gave up to the earth. Didn't the LORD open the grave and call the dead back to life? Is this happy incident not the very *picture of resurrection and reunion*? So rejoice in this teaching. *It too remains!*

If however you ask me:

How will we feel, when in the depth of soul
Coming from dream's night
The image of those dear to us who call
One day awaken might?

When hot the yearning blazes fierce,
The heart demands those, dear'st, who thee,
The eye glows and seeks,
How will it be?

How will it be when they rush toward us
With love enflame
So different from last we saw them in dust
And yet somehow the same?

When they fall on our necks,
And blissful words wax
And cry blissful tears
How will it be for us?

Do you ask this, my listener? Should I answer you this question? O such secret belongs to the LORD our God. The *unspeakable* cannot be described or answered. That for which you do not have a clear concept, I do not have a word. *You will be!* That is enough! You will be because God is. Your life will be eternal because *His life* is *eternal.*

And if death should fill a grave with you
The virtuous neither shakes nor shivers
To the one who gives life anew
In joyful confidence Himself delivers.

Choir: Blessed be God! Who calls us awake,
When the graves our tired bodies take.

Hallelujah, Amen.

MICHAEL CREIZENACH (1789–1842)

Michael Creizenach (b. 1789, Mainz; d. 1842, Frankfurt) was a teacher, writer, and early moderate Reform theologian who sought to bridge traditional methods of Jewish religious education with a broad acceptance of modern European culture. Receiving a traditional Jewish education focused exclusively on Talmud and halakhah as a youth, by his late teens he began engaging with secular learning (including mathematics and the hard sciences) and literature. Creizenach spent his career as a teacher and principal, first in his hometown of Mainz, where he helped found a new, experimental Jewish school influenced by emancipatory ideas, and different even from the German Gymnasium. Not only did he teach mathematics and modern sciences alongside Jewish subjects, but he shifted the school's focus from the then dominant study of Classical languages, Latin and Greek, to modern ones. By the 1820s Creizenach was in Frankfurt, where he authored, in four volumes, a Reform version of the Shulchan Arukh (the major traditional legal compendium). Though its title suggests a focus on practical religious application, *Shulḥan 'Aruk, oder Encyklopädische Darstellung des Mosaischen Gesetzes* (Set table, or Encyclopedic presentation of the Mosaic law) was mainly a work of theology emphasizing the adaptation and evolution of Rabbinic philosophy for modern times.

In the final decades of his life, Creizenach retreated from his former belief that the Talmud held a place in Jewish modernity. The Reform camp during the first half of the nineteenth century was then deeply divided on the Talmud's importance in Jewish life. While all Reformers held the Talmud to be written by humans alone (as opposed to its identification as the divinely bestowed "Oral Law," as it traditionally was), many on the more conservative side of the movement (e.g., Samuel Hirsch; see chapter 3) believed that a new approach to the Talmud was the starting point of Reform, whereas the more radical Reformers around Abraham Geiger (see chapter 2) and David Einhorn (see chapter 3) rejected the Talmud's authority altogether, holding that it had caused nothing but extreme damage to the understanding and application of religious law in Judaism. In his earliest years, in Mainz, and his first decade in Frankfurt, Creizenach identified with the more conservative Reformers, continuing to teach and cite the Talmud. But in his later years he moved into step with the radical Reformers, many of whom suggested a return to "pure Mosaism," the notion that the Hebrew Bible was the ultimate starting point for modern Jewish theology and that Rabbinic literature after the Mishnah evinced a distinct misunderstanding of God's commands. The work translated here is from Creizenach's later intellectual period.

This selection, from an article entitled "Foundational Doctrines of Israelite Belief," lays out Creizenach's understanding of the basic structure and doctrines of Jewish theology.[27] Creizenach's use of "Israelite" throughout this essay is not necessarily intended to avoid the word "Jewish," which to some had a pejorative connotation during the nineteenth century, but rather to emphasize the historical continuity of the Jewish tradition from biblical ("Israelite") and talmudic times to Creizenach's own generation. For Creizenach, the only tenable foundation for credal statements in Jewish theological doctrine is the Bible. This, he writes, has always been the case in Judaism: the Rabbis never legislated on theological doctrine, but rather acted only within the juridical authority that they believed was extended to them in the Torah ("the religious court of ancient Judaism . . . was not legitimated to decide in questions of faith with any sort of authority"). Yet, Creizenach notes, though the Pentateuch—the firm bedrock upon which Judaism stands—is of divine origin, its words are by necessity filtered through human understanding, and therefore any and all specific theological interpretations of its text are subject to the usual human fallibilities. In the end, he says, that means that Judaism cannot enforce any single theological doctrine or tenet but must let each individual understand the biblical text in his or her own way: "One should zealously seek all the truths that the Bible teaches us without . . . presuming the right to establish one's own opinions as norms of belief for all adherents of the Jewish religion."

Foundational Doctrines of Israelite Belief (1833)

Translated by George Y. Kohler

Although it is true that the Israelite does not know duties of faith in the actual sense of the word, and that his religion does not force upon him its truths as norms of thought—but only teaches those truths using the different means to influence the human intellect without harming human freedom—still, our religion has its foundational doctrines. Those doctrines everybody who wants to belong to the community of faith has to confess as a matter of fact, and not only nominally. It would be easy, but it is not actually necessary, to prove this claim from Holy Scripture, because the concept of a religion without basic truths on which it is founded; the concept of a superior lawgiver who looks only at deeds and not at the convictions behind them; the concept of the wisest ruler of the world who would not also promote wisdom—all those concepts are very obviously self-contradicting and override themselves. "The spirit of the LORD is a spirit of wisdom and insight, a spirit of counsel and valor, a spirit of devotion and reverence of God" (Isa. 11:2)—that is why it is said "know the God of your father, and serve Him" (1 Chron. 28:9). Many Mosaic commandments have no other purpose than to draw attention to religious truths and to such historical events that proved divine intervention in the most significant ways. Moses explicitly says to the Israelites: "Take utmost care and watch yourselves scrupulously, so that you do not forget the things that you saw with your own eyes and so that they do not fade from your mind as long as you live" (Deut. 4:9).

After all, the claim made by some Jewish theologians that the Israelite meets the demands of his religion if he but keeps all commandments with unconditional obedience, and that the doctrines motivating him in so doing are unimportant, is pointless, if only because this scenario is actually impossible. Although the Mosaic commandments do not address reason directly, through actual doctrines of faith, they do so indirectly, however, by appealing to our feelings: "You shall love the LORD your God with all your heart and with all your soul and with all your might" (Deut. 6:5); "You shall love your fellow as yourself" (Lev. 19:18); "You shall love the stranger" (Deut. 10:19);[28] "You shall not covet your neighbor's house" (Exod. 20:16); "You shall not take vengeance or bear a grudge" (Lev. 19:18); "You shall not hate your kinsfolk in your heart" (Lev. 19:17); "So that you do not follow after your heart and eyes" (Num. 15:39); "Do not harden your heart" (Deut. 15:7).

The necessary condition for all these precepts, that demand that the Israelite would raise or erase feelings within his soul, is the existence of certain basic rules, the awareness of which is strong enough to generate those conditions of the soul. Or, could one reasonably expect from a person who neither believes in the eternity of his soul, nor in divine justice or providence, that the sight of material things that he is supposed to do without will not stimulate his desires? For sure, only the commandment not to covet someone else's goods is proof enough that those higher truths were known to the Israelites at the time when Moses made his laws known, and that the Mosaic legislation built on the firmness of those beliefs. The natural reason, however, for the absence of a commandment to believe in religious truths, and the presence, rather, of a recommendation to consider those truths, is that human nature cannot be forced, neither internally nor externally, to agree to given doctrines. This is because obedience to such rules does not depend on our free will and we, without inner conviction, can at best force ourselves to avoid any emphatic negative judgment concerning such rules, out of respect for the legislator, or we simply begin to mistrust our capability to think. Thus, the Israelite may make himself unhappy through skepticism, and thus may even cease to belong to his community of faith, but this would be a case not provided for by Mosaic Law. This is rather a case of mental aberration, and those who are affected by it deserve our compassion and not legal punishment.

The Israelite doctrine of faith is essentially different from the Israelite doctrine of legal duties, because no religious authority is involved here. The highest religious authority of former times [the Sanhedrin] saw itself entitled to rule in religious matters in a way that was binding on all Israelites, not because it invoked an inspiration that made the divine will known to it, but rather in reference to an authorization that was hinted at in the Pentateuch [see Deut. 17:8–11]. This passage allowed the Sanhedrin to control the continued development of Mosaic law. But its decisions were never seen as emanations of the divine spirit, and especially where difficult issues of ritual regulations had to be decided, the voice of the prophets, as prophets, was disregarded, and miracles and supernatural voices were denied probative force, because the Talmud ruled that the Law should no longer be brought down from heaven (b. *Bava Metziah* 59b). The Sanhedrin demanded obedience in matters of ritual law, but not on the precondition that the divine spirit influenced its decisions, because in that case also all minor religious courts would have to be in agreement on all biblical interpretations, which wasn't the case. Those courts issued regulations because religious discipline demanded it, and they were followed—not like one follows a messenger who brings detailed instructions on all possible points, but rather like a governor who announces in the name of the sovereign certain measures that he has conceived himself for the good of all. But he conceived them not with the intention to deceive, and thus nobody will be deceived by that. This is why the Talmud says that in case of a difference of opinion on a certain question in a religious court, both opinions are considered to be coming from God. [See b. *Eruvin* 13b.] The reason is that it is assumed to be God's will that the decision of the majority, whatever it is, is to be followed as if it were God's will.

This peculiarity of the religious court of ancient Judaism proves beyond doubt that it was not legitimated to decide on questions of faith with any sort of authority. Although the court could claim that its decisions were always sanctioned by divine will, still, nothing guaranteed that its judgments and verdicts, as products of the mere subjective convictions of its members, were consistent with truth. This limitation of the religious power of the court was never ignored, and there is not a single example of a religious court using its authority for the fixation of a dogma.[29]

Therefore, the Bible is the only source of the Israelite doctrine of faith. This is true even for the strictest followers of the Talmud who in their fervor never really go so far as to eschew all consistency of their opinion. Even tradition cannot be evoked here, because the Talmud never developed a tradition in matters of faith.[30] For analyzing Jewish dogmas, thus, we must necessarily open the Bible if we want to confirm or refute them. The development and subsequent refinement of the Jewish doctrine of faith is an object of scientific research and not of religious authority. Everybody is entitled here to decide at last instance—but only for himself. Vice versa, even the opinion of the greatest majority cannot soothe the conscience of a single dissident, if it wasn't justified by reason and by the Bible.

The countless catechisms of the Mosaic belief, published during the last twenty years, strikingly prove this point. Not two of them are like each other, neither in number nor in the limitation of the dogmas mentioned therein. This, however, has not led to serious debates, which would break out only in the case that someone denied or doubted fundamental truths that are indispensable pillars of religion, or which arise from unambiguous passages of the Bible, and which nobody can deny without thereby ceasing to be a member of the religious community.

The determination of those fundamental truths is a highly important task for the Israelite theologian. That our ancient religious teachers neglected this task had a positive result in the preservation of the freedom of belief, but in fact it is still inconceivable. Already R. Bahya [R. Bahya ibn Paquda, b. ca. 1050, Zaragoza, Spain; d. 1120, Zaragoza, rabbi, judge, and philosopher who lived in Spain during Islamic rule] expressed his astonishment about this fact in the preface to his book on the inner duties six hundred and fifty years ago, and he made it the purpose of this book to satisfy the need to give an overview of the duties that make use of the different forces of the soul.[31] Searching in this book for an instruction to a highly moral and truly religious conduct, one is not at all disappointed.[32] But the work does not contain an actual, systematically ordered and complete teaching of [Jewish] dogmas, and it seems that the author did not differentiate between the actual doctrines of belief and the duties of the heart.

The first who undertook an exhaustive enumeration of the fundamental laws of the Israelite belief was Maimonides in his commentary to Mishnah *Sanhedrin* 10:1. There he established the following Thirteen Articles [Attributes] of faith:[33]

1. There is a God without the being [*Dasein*] of whom no other being [*Dasein*] would be there, nor be possible.
2. God is a unified and unique being [*Wesen*].
3. God is no corporeal being [*Wesen*] and no corporeality can be attributed to Him.
4. The being [*Dasein*] of God is eternal and antedated the existence of all other beings [*Wesen*].
5. God is the exclusive ruler of the universe and thus the singular object of our worship.
6. Once there have been men on which the divine spirit rested and whom we call prophets.[34]
7. Moses was the greatest of all prophets and God has revealed himself to Moses in the most distinctive way.[35]
8. God has revealed to Moses the entire content of the Pentateuch.
9. The revealed teaching is unalterable.[36]
10. God takes note of human deeds and is aware of all of them.
11. God rewards good and punishes evil.[37]
12. There will be a Messiah of Davidic descent who redeems Israel.
13. The dead will rise.

Whoever is denying only one of those dogmas, Maimonides added, has left the community of the Israelites and is considered an unbeliever and freethinker.[38] This enumeration does not entirely agree with the teachings of his great book, *Mishneh Torah* (Laws of Repentance 3:6). There he established three classes of heterodox thinkers: unbelievers (*minim*), freethinkers (*apikorsim*, after some Epicureans), and deniers (*kophrim*).

In both lists, Maimonides is not supported by the Talmud and decides according to his own preferences of importance.[39] Also, Maimonides has met widespread criticism by men whose erudition and orthodoxy is beyond doubt.[40] [. . .] Most uncompromising was the resistance of [Spanish Jewish philosopher] Joseph Albo [ca. 1380–1444] against Maimonides, expressed in his book *'Ikkarim* (Principles). He rightly remarked that not every result of Biblical exegesis that manifested itself as true is at the same time a dogma of Judaism, because in this case also all miracles and promises of the Bible would be articles of faith. True, one cannot belong to the community of Israel in case one does not believe the entire content of the Mosaic books, but since most of the passages in those books can be interpreted in different ways, the Israelite theologian is merely obligated to search for the meaning of these passages with honesty and sincerity. The theologian is expected to believe what he himself has recognized as true, without being accused of a transgression, or of being less devout, in case his search has led him on the wrong pathway. When establishing basic doctrines of belief, one has to proceed with the greatest care, because there is danger lurking here to brand men of recognized devoutness as heretics. According to Maimonides, R. Hillel was an unbeliever (a *kopher*),[41] because he would not await the Messiah, but Maimonides himself assumed that the Bible does not contain any proof for the fact that before the six days of creation there was no matter in existence from which the universe was made.[42] Others, however, believe that creation *ex nihilo* is a dogma of Judaism, which would turn even the pious Talmudist R. Eliezer into a *kopher*, because he claimed to know whence heaven and earth were created.[43]

These considerations now lead to the right conclusion: Only those truths that are indispensable for the existence of religion—and of Judaism specifically—can be called fundamental doctrines of faith, so that failing to recognize them would mean an open or implicit [religious] renunciation. In addition to this, one should zealously seek all the truths that the Bible teaches us, without, however, presuming the right to establish one's own opinions as norms of belief for all adherents of the Jewish religion. Instead, everyone must be granted the same freedom of thought that one claims for himself. It is well known for the readers of Mendelssohn's *Jerusalem* that he completely agreed with this view and supported the freedom of thought of the Israelite with reasons that leave nothing to be desired.

If we now ask ourselves which truths are essential for the concept of the Israelite religion, after a moment of reflection we will arrive at the same three basic points that Joseph Albo also assumed to be fundamental doctrines: *the existence of a unique creator; God's rule of the universe; and the divine origin of the Mosaic teachings*. The prophet Isaiah hints at those points: "God is our judge, God is our lawgiver, God is our king" (Isa. 33:22). And in the middle part of the Musaf Prayer on the Day of Remembrance [Rosh Hashanah], those three fundamental teachings are developed with abundant clarity.[44] By elucidating these three fundamental doctrines and illuminating the questions consequent upon them, Israelite dogmatics is assessed in full extent and raised to a systematically ordered science.

JOSEPH DERNBURG (1811–95)

Joseph Dernburg (Derenburg/Derenbourg) (b. 1811, Mainz; d. 1895, Bad Ems) was a German-French scholar and educator who specialized in medieval Jewish philosophy from the Arabic-speaking world, especially the works of Saadia Gaon (ca. 882–942). Living much of his life in France, Dernburg was a central figure in the modernization of Jewish education in Paris, blending Jewish learning with scientific methodology. He published dozens of articles and books on Jewish Arabic literature and philosophy in both German and French, as well as translations and annotated editions. His 1867 book, *Essai sur l'histoire et la géographie de la Palestine d'après les thalmuds et les autres sources rabbiniques* (Essay on the history and geography of Palestine according to talmudic and other Rabbinic sources), was a major contribution to scholarly knowledge of Palestine during the classical Rabbinic period.

The selection here, published in the *Wissenschaftliche Zeitschrift für jüdische Theologie* (Scientific journal for Jewish theology) in 1839, when Dernburg was still in his late twenties, outlines some of Dernburg's earliest thoughts on the nature and essence of religion generally, and on the purposes and structures (*Gebäude*) of Jewish theology specifically.[45] After a general introduction acknowledging the preliminary nature of its conclusions, the essay is divided into twelve short sections, each of which reflects on one aspect of religion or theology. The work builds toward Dernburg's conclusion that although the scriptural foundations of Judaism promise little in the way of reward in the afterlife, religious life in Judaism is premised on the profound experience of the divine spirit in this world.

The Essence of Judaism According to Its Most General Principles (1839)

Translated by Michael A. Meyer

The existence of an unease in the Judaism of our time is a certain fact, the settled upon conclusion being that it is suffering and sick. However, it seems that getting to the bottom of the various indications and giving reasons for the necessary transformation have not as yet succeeded. Who can doubt that within this body much has accumulated whose elimination is necessary if stable health is to return? But who has indicated what is to be removed, what retained, what is the stuff of death and what of life?—Let us leave the metaphor behind and in clear terms express our opinion as to what it really is regarding which we desire to open a discussion. Nearly the sole gain that recent decades have brought us is that the number of those who recognize the necessity of remodeling our structure of faith has significantly increased.[46] Indeed, the necessity itself has been acknowledged without question and has been established as fact. However, what shape the true Judaism possesses—on that score only obscure talk reigns without anyone actually knowing or daring to speak out.—Here we have attempted, without developing the issues, to communicate the result of our thoughts in a few paragraphs. These paragraphs do not constitute a system, make no claim to completeness, perhaps even—despite special effort—lack consistency. They can scarcely be called building blocks for a structure of Jewish theology. Rather, we pass them on with painful awareness that we, as sons of our time, are stronger in lack of knowledge than in knowledge.

#1.

In its essence, religion is rooted in the heart, which perceives and surmises more than it distinguishes and analyzes, seeking only to satisfy the human being's most immediate and urgent needs. The limited, dissecting intellect, striving for clarity, provides it with form. Thus, the heart possesses the advantage of priority and, uncorrupted, it more adequately feels the truth. Once the intellect makes the dim suspicions of the heart into a reproach and wants to raise them to the level of clarity, firm teachings result that bear the character of temporality.

#2.

Wherever in the monuments, in the distinguishing marks of a religion, the same consciousness of faith, the same emerging feeling, manifests itself, that is where the sources of this religion can be discerned as well. Where, however, one suddenly comes upon that which cannot be united with the earlier spirit, it must naturally be separated out, the more so when it is possible to prove its origins historically.

#3.

This separation is easily done with regard to the religious writings of Judaism, and the historical event that marks the point of separation is the Exile. The pre-exilic writings are therefore principal sources of Judaism. We say principal because much that is post-exilic is equivalent in sentiment and expression to what is earlier. And even the characteristic form that the foreign [i.e., Jewish writings composed in a foreign land or under intensive foreign influence] obtains under the pervasive sunshine of Judaism nevertheless is useful for understanding actual Judaism.

#4.

The sources of Judaism consist of the history of the people, its laws, and the admonitions directed to it.—The admonitions most directly represent the feelings whereas the law represents the intellect. Both make up the theoretical side of religion. History sometimes reveals the unhindered influences of the heart, and at other times the constraining effect of the law, which is always the practical side of faith.

#5.

Revelation is a transmission of ideas that are not a product of the age in which they appear, but rather fully transcend the level of the age, that furthermore can never be contained in an intellectual formula without losing their meaning because these ideas do not concern anything temporal. Revelation, therefore, both according to the source from which it draws and the object for which it was created, essentially has to do with the heart. Every law can certainly confine revelation within a solid framework, but as a result and like the fate of the intellect, it falls victim to temporality.

#6.

Therefore, the scriptures of Judaism contain eternal revealed truth only in their admonitory and historical—or, if we may extend the term that far (Gen. 20:7; Ps. 105:15)—prophetic portions. The law, by contrast, contains formulas, which either have already submitted to the age or are able to do so.

#7.

From the viewpoint of human history, it can of necessity be assumed that within it at one time a temporal beginning for such communications from the realm of emotional life took place, and specifically from one or several men, whose unspoiled spiritual life proclaimed aloud the voice of truth to a people or an age in which the heart had taken a crooked and perverse direction.

#8.

Such a beginning, as the first attempt at expression in matters of religion, is highly significant. However, within such expression, matters of the heart immediately get mingled with matters of the law. For the language lacks the necessary abstraction for proper clarification just as the unknowing people lacks the strength to absorb whatever does not present itself in a narrowly conceived, clear form.

#9.

For Judaism, Moses is the historical beginning. How much or how little he took from other peoples, especially from the Egyptians, is of no concern for religion; it is enough that in its inspired spirit everything obtains characteristic form. The life of the patriarchs, as rich and as instructive as it is, is unable to elevate the beginning of Judaism, since for such a beginning not a single pious life, but rather instruction, dissemination, and an intended structure are essential.

#10.

Thus, the criticism that divides the Mosaic from the non-Mosaic loses its meaning for the central features of religion.[47] The question that was again discussed recently—whether the law is prototype or product of prophecy—is therefore without value here, where it is not a matter of this finer division of the temporal. Every law, even later ones, were intended to incorporate ideas alluded to by Moses—and that alone is what matters (#2)—whether they were already uttered in advance of the law or were encountered only in the heart.

#11.

As propositions that necessarily belong to the religious consciousness of Judaism we mention the following:

1. There is only one God, who as a Being that has never been perceived by mortal eyes, also can have no adequate image, and therefore may not be represented by any such image.
2. Everything that exists has received its specific form from God, is sustained and ruled by Him.
3. The human being is the crown of creation, and sovereignty is given him over all that is of the earth.
4. The human vocation is to acknowledge God, to feel and practice love and awe toward Him, and to take note of God's omnipresent, wise, and just guidance.
5. All persons stand under the guidance of God who, like a father, loves them. Yet that person who displays the most sacred earnestness in adopting these truths is the preeminent, or firstborn, son of the Father.[48]
6. Our acknowledgment of God must express itself in deeds and our conduct give evidence of our inner convictions, serving them as a point of support.
7. God is a righteous judge. Therefore, He assuredly requites good and evil persons according to their deeds.
8. The human being is free and it is within his power to fulfill or to neglect God's will.

#12.

The ambiguity in most of these propositions is due to the fact that the consciousness of faith makes no philosophical distinctions, expresses only an inner human need, and leaves any possible contradictions, which a carping intellect may discover, beyond concern. One knows nothing of God's body, for one has not seen any form. Is God a creator from nothing or a shaper of matter? We know from Judaism not to answer this question and leave it to the philosophers. For feelings [i.e., for our relationship to God], it is sufficient to know in whose hand we find ourselves; one did not notice the inconsistencies arising from the existence of a primal matter. — Historically, to be sure, Israel is that people in which alone, during antiquity, this sacred earnestness lived. But the fundamental idea is the same (Exod. 4; Jer. 31:20). The name "son of God" has indeed lost a great deal of its expansion due to the particularistic spirit following the exile, to the point where finally it was applied, instead of to the people, only to a single individual. — The Prophets sufficiently showed the value of the deed for religious conviction, so it is not necessary to present at length the retreat of Judaism in relation to Hebraism in order thereby to secure a mission for Christianity. — The nature of the reward is of no consequence to the religious consciousness as long as its existence remains beyond doubt. From this point of view all eschatological investigations are indifferent, simply wanting to satisfy the appetite for curiosity. Given the firm belief in reward that is proclaimed in Judaism and the shaky one, which naturally the other confessions also offer in this regard, one should have already spared the [Old Testament] the rebuke regarding the lack of a doctrine of immortality long ago.

The development of each of these doctrines from the spirit of Judaism would indeed be both interesting and instructive. Its result would surely depart significantly from that which until now was discerned only by Christian scholars. For our purpose it suffices that we have called attention to what is so recognizably Jewish that we have regarded the addition of Bible passages as superfluous, and that we have indicated the relations among the individual elements of Judaism more clearly.

ZECHARIAS FRANKEL (1801–75)

The rabbi and scholar Zecharias Frankel (b. 1801, Prague; d. 1875, Breslau) was one of the most important figures in the redevelopment of rabbinical education in the modern era. Born and raised in Prague, Frankel studied at the city's main yeshiva under Bezalel Ronsburg (1760–1820) before moving to Budapest, where he graduated from the university there in 1831. Taking up his first rabbinical position in Teplitz in 1832, he became the chief rabbi of Saxony in 1836. In 1854 he accepted the position of founding president of the Jewish Theological Seminary in Breslau. The first institution of its kind in German lands, JTS Breslau was designed to train rabbis along the double track of traditional texts and modern academic scholarship (and would later become the main model and inspiration for the Jewish Theological Seminary in New York, founded in 1886). Presiding over JTS Breslau for the rest of his life, Frankel educated—and employed—many of the leading modern Jewish theologians and historians of his day, including Manuel Joel and Heinrich Graetz (for both, see chapter 2).

Frankel's famous "positive-historical" outlook on Judaism shaped a whole generation of influential Jewish scholars for the next decades, and was decisive in formulating the theology of what we today call Conservative Judaism. By "positive-historical," Frankel meant that, not abstract theological ideas, but rather "the totality of Jewish history" (Graetz) was the material from which to deduce the meaning of Judaism and its basic tenets. Thus, Breslau under Frankel virtually rediscovered the great Jewish philosophers of the Middle Ages and simultaneously undertook the first efforts in the academic study of Jewish mysticism.

A respected scholar of Jewish history, especially of the Second Temple and early Rabbinic periods, in 1851 Frankel launched the *Monatsschrift für Geschichte und Wissenschaft des Judenthums* (Monthly journal for the history and study of Judaism), which quickly became the most important literary organ for modern Jewish studies in Europe. An advocate for modest alterations in religious practice and liturgy, he favored modifying some of the ceremonies associated with mourning and circumcision and eliminating the second days of certain holidays. He vehemently opposed radical Reform, especially the ideas of Abraham Geiger and Samuel Holdheim (chapter 2), going so far as to boycott teaching Geiger's book on biblical criticism. While Frankel did concede that perhaps the Oral Law was more human than divine, he rejected Reform as forced on the community from above and accepted only such changes as grew out of the Jewish people itself. Finally, his split from the Conference of Reform Rabbis (arguably, an early founding event for Conservatism) occurred in 1845 over the use of the German language in prayer as well as Reform's abandonment of the idea of an eventual return to Zion in the Messianic Age, both of which he strictly opposed.

Frankel found few friends, however, among the neo-Orthodox. In his Hebrew language book on the Mishnah, he wrote that some legal regulations of Judaism are so ancient that one could refer to them "as if they were given to Moses on Sinai." This formulation so outraged the founder of modern Orthodoxy Rabbi Samson Raphael Hirsch (see chapter 2) that after questioning Frankel on this point, he ruled that no graduate of JTS Breslau could become a rabbi of an Orthodox community.

The speech excerpted here was delivered at the January 1855 ceremony officially inaugurating the new Breslau seminary.[49] Frankel here lays out his vision for a rabbinical college that will treasure the wisdom of religious tradition (*Glaube*, faith) while embracing the knowledge gained through newfound advances in the scholarly disciplines (*Wissenschaft*, science). Faith—that is, the religious life—Frankel argues, has always been the bedrock of discovery. Humanity, living in God's world, seeks after knowledge, which is in turn the seeking after God. Yet without faith, humanity seeks only the image of itself, which is idolatry, the road to the unjust.

Speech at the Memorial Service for the Benefactor of the Jewish Theological Seminary, Breslau (1855)

Translated by Thomas Abraham Tearney

Esteemed assembly!

You have dignified today's ceremony with your presence and have enhanced a celebration dedicated to the memory of a man whose great works of charity and philanthropy bequeathed in his last will have established an everlasting memorial among his fellow citizens.[50] This day and the setting of today's commemoration tell of a new creation brought to life at his behest: a seminary for the training of rabbis and teachers. In days of old, the sprouting forth of a laurel or a rare plant from a burial mound was seen as a call for reverence of that which was buried there; and does our time not also venerate the person from whose grave such plants sprout forth, from whose ashes the spirit of faith and love ascends, upon whose death (the mark of earthly cessation and of the extinguished torch of life) a spiritual process of new life was ignited and new waves of light issued forth in all directions? On occasion, marble and precious stone should withhold certain spoils from time, which is all-destructive and which devours its own children, and these materials should wrest away a name from the rushing current of the past. According to a saying of the sages, there is no need for memorials or monuments upon the graves of the pious, for that which they left behind and established is their true monument [see y. *Shekalim* 2:5 (7a) and Gen. Rab. 82:10, quoting the same *baraita*]; and one need not visit the resting site of their earthly remains to be reminded of them: the spark gathered from the spark of life, what is spiritual and realized in the realm of the spirit, these shine far upon the horizon of time and are embedded in the lap of time with everlasting features.[51]

Grand bequeathed endowments are manifestations of the firm intuition of and inner belief in our immortality, in our continued existence in a higher light which still seeks to shine into this world. And these manifestations are most commonly given expression in works of the soul: the soul, more or less aware of its stirrings, is the seat of warmth, receptivity, and compassion; its closest outpouring, therefore, is the expression of this compassion in the relief of human suffering and pain, in the alleviation of terrestrial misery and the woeful host of troubles which are the destiny of the human being.[52] But just as the soul fails to find adequate words for its inexhaustible life, so too does its vast, world-encompassing will lack adequate deeds.[53] How far does the power of charity reach? It is usually limited to the more narrow circle of the congregation or of the city: Institutes have been established for the ill, for the abandoned and orphaned, and for the alleviation of other miseries. That which is heartfelt and sentimental prevails, but this is unable to transcend the limits imposed by human insufficiency. Only that which comes from the realm of the spiritual knows no bounds or barriers; it radiates outward, permeating and enriching the most far-reaching spaces. An institute established as a workshop of the spirit belongs to the universal, is in no way exclusionary or restrictive, and the will to establish it springs from a higher idea and from a universal conception. And if the spirit and the soul are simultaneously taken into account in their entirety, therein will be found the highest and most noble emanation of the spirit and the soul, religion and the science thereof, a position that is a testimony of one who perceives and strives toward a higher goal! Many of the institutes established for this city proclaim that which their founder felt: this institute, established for the general good and for the faith which has spread throughout the entire inhabited world, recognizes that the benefactor possessed an awareness which reached such heights that only few can achieve!

The seminary opened last year on the 10th of August among the quiet circle of the testament executor, the teachers, and the registered pupils. Aware of its difficult task which could only be achieved through faith in God, the seminary did not seek broad publicity. It recognized that it would have to be responsible for its own development: without an adequate model, without an example to be observed, emulated, and used as a guide through all of the complicated processes, it had to begin with a trust justified solely by the divine and irrefutable nature of this undertaking, supported by the hope that the solemn, spirited will would be victorious over the emerging, often unforeseen obstacles. The preparations were made and it got off to a start. The initial difficulties of organizing have now been overcome, and thus today's celebration also constitutes a first introduction to the public, and should be considered a joyous opening, elevated by the presence of this distinguished and esteemed assembly. And what could complement this opening with more dignity than the memorial ceremony of the person who brought this institute into being?

Honored guests! Allow me to touch upon the nature of this institute and the essence of its mission. When news spread of its founding, it received the most heartfelt wishes; even before coming into existence, it received tokens of the highest favor and encouragement. His Majesty the King secured in his grace and with his blessing the existence of this institute through a supreme cabinet order on August 31st, 1847.[54] And what sponsorship could be more cordial and animated for the start of a project which aims to ennoble and elevate the human than the participation of the royal cabinet! And as news spread of the actual implementation, it exhilarated the hearts of many and unleashed a joyous feeling even among the noble-minded who do not belong to this confession. For in whatever image the divine presents itself, the noble and the refined will recognize it as divine; and wherever a ladder draws a group upwards toward heaven, if the ground shall not be taken out from under it, if it shall not lose its rungs or steps, a religious structure shall not crumble or collapse. In ruins and rubble, therefore, a spirit of destruction threatens to seize all that is divine, annihilation threatens to seize all that is positive, and negate all that is holy and sanctified. This spirit threatens to stiffen hearts with its icy breath, to drive away all human warmth, and to engender apathetic indifference to everything that rises above the earthly and the material. In whatever way humanity seeks heaven, this seeking is itself an upward aspiration. Similarly, in dissolution, decline, indifference, in thoughtless gazing, there is a decrease of the divine in the human, a neglect of humanity's higher purpose, and an ignoble abandonment of one's own self. And if such a perspective can fill with sorrow even the individual who grasps the significance of the cogitative and divine nature in all humans, how harrowing then is the thought that perhaps, even if in a distant future, such a scene of destruction could emerge among a confession or a group organized around one. In recent years in Germany there are no longer academies where in the past leaders and representatives of the Mosaic faith had been trained.[55] Jewish theology could nowhere find a site particularly consecrated for itself, an institute that would cultivate and protect it according to its essence: our institute fills this deep-felt void, and its lofty and vital mission is to become an academy of the Jewish faith and the science thereof.

And this faith and this science? It is that which freed the divine within humanity from its bonds and brought this divine nature in its objectivity to humankind. It has transformed the obscure notion of striving higher, a notion which was quickly immersed in profound errors, into a clear, shining idea, into an uplifting, living awareness. Humans, created in God's image, were driven by the intuition of an archetype.[56] It was not through the observation of beneficial or harmful natural forces which conditioned the adoption of benevolent or malicious deities; rather, humanity unwittingly determined this for itself through an obscure higher drive which could not be displaced from its inner conceptions. Humanity's gods were an apotheosis of *its own* good and evil qualities. And as certain wise people maintained this error of self-idolatry in the forces of nature (which in the Hellenic world emerged aesthetically in the hypostatization of beauty), they attempted to replace the sensory concept with an idea that could be used to explain the deity. Yet the idea would not achieve the status of reality; it could not leave the realm of ideas to find an autonomous, otherworldly God. It was through the revelation at Sinai that the human was confronted with God: it was there that humankind learned to recognize the archetype which preceded all that was created, all concepts, and all thoughts, a God not conceived of by humans, but rather one who created humans and all of the beings, identified or unidentified, which surrounded them. This is the faith of Israel, a faith which gradually became the property of the educated peoples of the world, Israel's vital ether which permeated through to its innermost heartbeat, through to the deepest depths of its feeling and thinking, through to the most hidden forces of its meditation and action. Israel's consciousness begins not with the deduction: "I think, therefore I am" but rather: "I believe, therefore I am."[57] Without God, there is no sense, no thought. Faith has coalesced with Israel's innermost being such that existence without faith, without God is inconceivable. And this faith, in its simplicity and with its self-affirming truth, was converted into a firm conviction: the Hebrew language has no corresponding term for the concept "to believe."[58] The great pronouncement: "Hear, O Israel! The LORD is our God, the LORD alone" [Deut. 6:4] is followed directly by "You shall love the LORD your God with all your heart and with all your soul" [Deut. 6:5]. For wherever faith is built upon a strong conviction from within, the concept of faith is there supplanted by one of love; and even the Israelite, regardless of how the conditions and circumstances took shape and despite whatever bleak experiences he had faced, could conceive of God only in the terms of a loving father. Even the shuddering proclamation: *eheya asher eheya,* "I am that I am," a proclamation which the neo-Platonic and peripatetic Spanish school (which did not wish to assign any qualities or attributes to God) considered to be all that could be asserted about God, was translated by a faith which filled the innermost depths of the spirit and soul into the language of a sort of love only conceivable in God: "I am that I am, I am with you in this sorrow, I am with you in all other sorrows" [*Gur Aryeh* on Exod. 3:14].[59] In every proclamation of God, love is the fundamental principle, and love is the actual revelation.

And this love-emanating, invigorating, and refreshing faith would, according to its essence and its content, influence the relationship of human beings to one another. Gentleness, compassion, and kindheartedness will generally be perceived in all of its followers. Beginning with family life, the intimacy of which is supported by faith and which is elevated to an astonishing capacity for sacrifice, these more gentle feelings radiate out in all directions. The recognition of humankind's divine image and higher purpose was not lost through the many tribulations which humanity endured: in the most dismal days, the proposition which shines through the grief of all ages was formulated: "So, too, do the righteous among the nations of the world have a share in the World to Come."[60] And with such respect of human worth that was established and sustained by faith, it was further declared [b. *Sanhedrin* 59a]: "Even the non-Jew who recognizes one God and observes the ethical laws is like unto a high priest—this first promoter of faith."[61]

Let us now turn our focus to the manifestations of faith in the realm of the spiritual. Faith, which embraces and permeates the innermost core of those who profess it, establishes fidelity, the realization of all ambition in God, and the perception and investigation of doctrine as the goal of knowledge: "He said to man," it is proclaimed, "See! Fear of the LORD is wisdom; To shun evil is understanding" [Job 28:28]. Faith determined all activities of life and brought knowledge itself into this sphere. And because this examination expanded the domain of spiritual activity, faith could not be averse to it. And in fact the oldest of the most well-known Mishnaic and Talmudic writings address multiple branches of science. Astronomy was widely practiced and entire works were dedicated to this field. The old era was so familiar with geometric sums that it would often only demonstrate answers with a short arithmetic expression which in later years would require a lengthy and insightful explanation. Moreover, certain fields of agriculture, botany, and zoology were cultivated for the purpose of elucidating the Law; particular attention was paid to diet and medicine. Here again, that foundational principle of faith appeared, namely the value system of the human and the recognition of the position of humanity within creation. Therefore, the saving of a human is a rule which surpasses all else, and the preservation of human life a commandment to which even the most essential commandments yield [e.g., m. *Sanhedrin* 4:5; b. *Yoma* 85b]. And just as scientific study was pursued for its positive benefit, so too was its degeneracy into unscientific thought counteracted, although not always with the same success; chapters included warnings against miracle cures based on superstitions and narrowmindedness.[62] Metaphysical research was also not neglected, and in those brief considerations one senses an immense depth; and with what zeal the field of law was examined and the basis of the foundations of law studied! Here faith offered a wide scientific foundation upon which criminal and civil law were further built out in all directions with the most brilliant sagacity, nevertheless without ever losing a sense for justice and fairness. How splendidly did faith become apparent in the field of criminal law, given faith's principle of venerating the human! Even among the fallen, the human can be recovered: punishment does not come from a feeling of revenge but from a feeling of justice. For this reason the system of law based on this faith knew of no trials by ordeal or torture, it sought more painless methods of the death penalty, and the rare use of that punishment was the general norm.[63]—Let us note another branch in which the sense of justice and morality, elevated by faith, emerged most splendidly. The state had not come into being in accordance with its actual definition over the past centuries, and no one felt the consequences of this more than the adherents of the Mosaic faith! And nonetheless they conferred upon the state undivided authority, provided that the individual and his sacred concerns were not merged with the state. Here, the doctrine with all of its corollaries applies [b. *Nedarim* 28a and b. *Bava Kamma* 113a]: "The law of the kingdom is the law." Not only external, but also moral obedience must not be withheld from the state, and to comply with the state is a moral obligation.[64] The state did not position itself for them as the ideal of justice, and yet their constant motto was: obedience to the authorities, pray for their welfare![65]

To cultivate this faith and to train its worthy representatives is the mission of this institute. Scientific study was never foreign to faith, faith always brought it into its circle; therefore it will be sought to combine science and faith in the young pupils so that they, nurtured and steeped in faith, will be able to find that balance which allows us to perceive a divine spirit in aspiring and increasing perception. And once this path has been initiated, then some day they will enter into the world with the confidence to faithfully pursue the goal set before them. They will firmly oppose the self-idolatry and the hubris that is foreign to the true essence of scholarship, for this has no power over them; what is uplifting and enlightening in science is warmly received and supported by faith.—Faith also teaches: loyalty to the sovereign, loyalty to the fatherland; and this spirit shall be nurtured at the institute, that the [aspiring] leaders declare these teachings of faith, assured by the fidelity of which they will become fervent supporters. [. . .]

It has begun: this institute was founded with the blessing of the king; may this blessing forever remain with the institute!

It has begun with trust in God, and the project was undertaken in honor of his name: may he spread his favor and protection, such that the delicate plant ripens into a refreshing fruit which spreads blessing!

LUDWIG PHILIPPSON (1811–99)

Ludwig Philippson (b. 1811, Dessau; d. 1889, Bonn) was a rabbi, newspaper editor, Bible exegete and translator, and one of the mostly widely known Jewish intellectuals in nineteenth-century Germany. In 1837, he founded (and edited for more than fifty years) the *Allgemeine Zeitung des Judenthums* (General newspaper of Judaism), which would become the most widely read German Jewish newspaper in Central Europe. Many of its most influential editorials, especially those dealing with theological problems, were written by Philippson himself.

If Abraham Geiger (see chapter 2) was the Reform's intellectual visionary, Philippson was its organizational mastermind. In the 1840s, he played a significant role in the early growth of the German Reform movement. He convened three rabbinical conferences concerning legal reforms of the Jewish religion that succeeded in uniting all the various efforts to modernize Judaism's ceremonial laws. Likewise, Philippson acted as the publisher for many major works of Jewish scholarship. In 1855, he founded (and ran for eighteen years) the Institut zur Förderung der Israelitischen Literatur (Institute for the promotion of Jewish literature), a Jewish publication society that would print more than eighty works of Jewish history, poetry, fiction, and biography, including many volumes of Heinrich Graetz's *History of the Jews*. He also published a German translation of the Hebrew Bible (*Die Israelitische Bibel*) which featured his personal theological commentary.

The short text translated here is part of the introduction to Philippson's Bible translation, a three-volume set with Hebrew and German text, dozens of woodcut illustrations, and Philippson's extensive elaborations.[66] Throughout the volumes, his erudite commentary makes frequent references to archaeology, botany, natural history, and Egyptology, as well as biblical criticism. The introduction and commentary can be seen as exemplars of modern Jewish thought, standing between old and new. Philippson believes in the Mosaic authorship of (almost all of) the Pentateuch, but for theological, not purely dogmatic reasons. For him, the concept of God stays essentially constant throughout the whole of the Bible. He has no difficulty accepting the idea that several authors composed the book of Isaiah, but he outright rejects the *lex post prophetas* (the law comes after the prophets) thesis (that the Torah is a product of the Babylonian Diaspora and not Revelation) that would later become popular among liberal Jewish theologians. Finally, in the development of liberal Jewish theology after Philippson, the division between duties toward God and duties toward other human beings gradually disappears. In its place, "neighbor-love" comes to be seen as the full and sufficient service to a monotheistic God. In this excerpt, Philippson is still convinced of the equal importance of ritual and interpersonal ethics for the sanctification of God.

Introduction to the Five Books of Moses (1844)

Translated by Alexandra Zirkle

IDEA [OF THE FIVE BOOKS OF MOSES]

Corporeality endowed humans with sensuality. By virtue of man's free spirit, sensuality was not constrained to instinct's known and unchanging bounds. Rather, sensuality became capable of ever stronger development, waxing stronger until it attained sovereignty over the entire human, culminating in degeneracy. With corporeality, bodily appetite arose, which, once it outpaced its thoroughly natural realm, increasingly grew, desired ever more satisfaction, and demanded even more activity, until all of man was beset by bodily appetite and by the work necessitated by satisfying it.

With sociality, ownership emerged along with its various sorts of work. Ownership and inequality, however, necessarily brought about opposing ambitions, jealousy, and conflict, until these overtook all of man and his activities. Under the force of these factors, the spiritual life of man foundered and sin corrupted man's soul. Thus it came about that although the yearning for knowledge was present in the human spirit, the human spirit did not possess the aptitude for attaining true knowledge by itself. Thus the human spirit necessarily sank into the endless errors of heathendom.[67]

To redeem man's domination by sensuality; his spiritual life from the excessive pressures of work and sociality, as well as from sin; and his spirit from error; that is, to give man true understanding—namely, knowledge of law and of holiness—God had to directly share with man that which man had heretofore not known: Revelation.[68] Indeed, the divine precepts of law and holiness were unknowable by any means other than direct Revelation. But mankind as a whole should not and could not be deprived of free development, or else humanity's nature would be destroyed. Thus, to bring this divine Revelation to mankind, a particular people had to be appointed as the bearers of Revelation to humanity. This people was appointed to constantly preserve Revelation until all of mankind had succeeded, through their own path of free development, to progressively, ever more extensively and intensively, accept the divine Revelation and allow themselves to be permeated with it. This people could not be a people that was already formed, saturated with evil, and of a defined character, but rather a people who had been isolated for this purpose and who matured as a people which, from their very beginning, had nurtured their consciousness of this calling.[69]

TREND

Therefore, the Five Books of Moses intend to substantiate: 1) the necessity of Revelation, and, to this end, detail the history of Creation, in particular of mankind, humanity's primitive condition, the origin of sin through carnality, the origin of society and its troubles in its gradual development until our time; 2) the education of the People of Revelation as depicted in history; 3) the giving of Revelation, which was imparted to this people, with all of its surrounding circumstances.[70]

TEACHING

GOD is the eternal, unchanging, and single Being, who, through all His power, was able to bring forth and sustain the material world through His will, since He is Himself immaterial and pure-spirited (holy). God is Immanent to man, in that He thereby did the following:[71] He gave mankind a free, spiritual nature; created them in His own image; revealed to them truth; judges man's actions, insofar as God allows the consequences of the actions to occur; but forgives the guilt of the remorseful soul. Amongst the People of Revelation, divine guidance, as well as punishment and remuneration, are immanent to everything that relates to Revelation.

HUMAN, endowed with free will which remained his even after the revelation—destined to satisfy his corporeal needs, therefore to work and to sociality, therefore capable of sin and implicated in material life—is called to keep himself free of sin, to dissociate himself from his corporeal needs, and to live with God. Hence, he must absorb knowledge of the one God and strive toward sanctification. Sanctification occurs, in part, through spiritual elevation toward God and through the most perfect love of God; in part through neighbor-love, which should reach the same height as self-love, and which should be exercised, in particular, through absolute justice and self-sacrificing charity; and in part through bodily purity, namely abstaining from consuming blood (Gen. 9:4).

As for the bearers of Revelation specifically, Israel should be maintained through strict consistency and particular means in order to preserve the Revelation and continuously testify of it. Israel should hold fast to the knowledge of the one God by eternally remembering the happenings prior to and accompanying the giving of Revelation. The spiritual elevation toward God should be buttressed by a distinct set of rituals, enabled by observance of the sabbath and festivals to dissociate from material life at particular times, and to recall to one's consciousness the process of elevation toward God even through external symbols, such as the sublation of one's separation from God through the Day of Atonement.

Neighbor-love should arise through the exercise of the strongest laws of justice in absolute equality; through fixed but proportional, freely given [portions] for the poor; and through the reversion of inherited property and the remission of debts at appointed times. Purity should be maintained in part through marital and chastity-laws, in part through the avoidance of all dishes that accumulate too much material animal substances; in part through maintaining the most meaningful animal purifications, which have been observed for generations, such as abstention from contact with the dead and the leprous, the latter which poses an awful scourge in the Orient.[72]

The entire relationship within Revelation should be seen as a covenant into which the young child is brought shortly after birth, through circumcision.

SAMUEL DAVID LUZZATTO (1800–1865)

Theologian, poet, and biblical exegete Samuel David Luzzatto (called *Shadal*, b. 1800, Trieste; d. 1865, Padua) was an early pioneer of *Wissenschaft des Judentums* in Italy. Hailing from a relatively famous family—his great grandfather's brother was the philosopher and Kabbalist Moses Hayyim Luzzatto (the *Ramchal*, 1707–46)—Luzzatto received a traditional religious education in his native city of Trieste, studying Talmud with the chief rabbi and Classical and modern languages with a series of tutors. In 1829, he became one of the first professors at the newly opened rabbinical seminary in Padua, where he taught Bible and languages, as well as Talmud and Rabbinics.

From an early age, Luzzatto had been attracted by the new critical academic methodologies, especially by historical and philological analysis. Much of his mature scholarship on the Hebrew Bible—e.g., his willingness to emend the wording of the Masoretic (traditional) text to reflect updated philological scholarship and seek clarity of meaning, and his arguments for dating or assigning authorship of biblical texts—grew out of his exploration of those interests. Yet Luzzatto, too, was a firm adherent of Rabbinic law and theology, a lover of Talmud, and wary of ritual reform. He believed that while non-Jewish Classical and medieval philosophers had been honest in their search for knowledge and wisdom, Jewish thinkers should ultimately be wary of too great an intercourse with pagan and Christian discourse. Ultimately, God's Revelation to Israel was the only real source of truth.

This selection, from Luzzatto's book *Lezioni di teologia dogmatica Israelitica* (Lessons on Jewish dogmatic theology), originally written in Italian for a popular audience, is a near-classic example of early nineteenth-century natural theology—that is, an argument for the existence of God through reasoning and logic based on the attributes and characteristics of the physical world.[73] In the opening pages, Luzzatto writes that, following the Classical authors (the Greek and Latin writers of antiquity), the more we learn about the complexity of the structures undergirding our world, the more we are led—nay, he says, compelled—to recognize that the hand of a great intelligence must be at work in its construction and maintenance. Later, Luzzatto turns to more Judaic themes, including the centrality and reality of God's capacity to enact miracles and the importance of those miracles as proof of the historical veracity of the biblical narrative. Seeing as all of nature's laws "are not necessary by themselves, but only by the will of God," then "God can at His own pleasure suspend each of those laws and produce, then, a miracle." In this way, the biblical text relating the miracles God and Moses perform for the Israelites confirms reality, since the miracles are performed by or on behalf of God, who is capable of performing them, and not by humans, who must merely live within the natural bounds God constructs for humanity. Luzzatto ends this section by outlining what he sees as the two major dogmas of Judaism: God's justice and God's immutable covenant with Israel.

Lessons in Jewish Dogmatic Theology (1863)

Translated by Emanuel Fiano

CHAPTER 1: OF GOD'S EXISTENCE

XXXI. The most admirable magisterium, which manifests itself in all organic beings (be they plant or animal), and the more greatly so, the more progress and discoveries are made in the study of nature, this magisterium leads, nay, compels our common sense to reach the conclusion that those beings are like purposefully fashioned machines, and that such organization is the work of one Intelligence, one Mind. This Mind is what we call God.

XXXII. This argument, which some call physical and others call the argument of final causes or the teleological argument (from the Greek *telos,* aim, purpose), is the truest, the most irrefutable, and the most ancient among the arguments set forth for the existence of God.

It was used by Socrates (Xenophon, *Memorabilia* I:4). Cicero expounded it at length and with his characteristic eloquence (*De natura deorum* II). Galen regarded his seventeen books on physiology (*De usu partium corporis humani* [On the utility of the parts of the body]) as Hymns in the honor of the Deity, which would please the latter more than hecatombs and incense. [Scottish philosopher Dugald] Stewart [1753–1828] in his *Outlines of Moral Philosophy* makes use of the very same argument.[74] Among the Israelites, Maimonides (*Guide of the Perplexed* III:13) expresses himself thus: "Know too that to the mind of an equitable man, one of the strongest proofs for the production of the world in time is the fact, demonstrated with reference to natural beings, that every one of these has a certain final end, some of them existing for the sake of others; for this is a proof of purpose on the part of a being possessing purpose. And purpose can only be conceived with reference to the production in time of something so produced."[75]

xxxiii. In order to be adequately explicated, the teleological argument would demand an entire Treatise of Natural History, and particularly of Anatomy and Physiology of the human body and of the bodies of all other animals. In all these sciences, it is and it has always been a universally accepted principle, considered almost as an axiom, that Nature does nothing at random and without a purpose; and this presupposition is the same that has guided and still guides philosophers toward the investigation, and thence to the discovery, of many and many secrets in every branch of the natural sciences. . . . Now, is a purpose without a Mind, without an Intelligence, not fully inconceivable?

xxxiv. But in the infinite series of combinations to which over the infinity of centuries [Greek philosopher] Epicurus's and [Roman poet and philosopher] Lucretius's atoms must have been subjected, is it after all impossible that that felicitous combination should take place, whereby the bodies would have been formed such as to be capable of preservation and reproduction, so as to constitute the present world?[76] — No, it is true: this cannot be said to be absolutely impossible, just as it cannot be said to be absolutely impossible that our life is all a dream; that the ninety numbers of the six-number lottery would be drawn in regular progression from the first to the last in eighteen successive drawings, and thus over and over many times; or that type would be spilled out of a falling typecase composing all the verses of [Virgil's Latin epic poem] the *Aeneid* from the first to the last. These things, nonetheless, are for every man of common sense inadmissible, as his most intimate sentiment is opposed to their possibility. Therefore, we are not going to linger on examining whether [philosopher Immanuel] Kant [1724–1804] was right or wrong to refuse apodictic — that is, demonstrative — certainty to the teleological argument, which he called physico-theological; but we will be content with recognizing, as he himself did, that physical cognition reduces faith in a supreme author to an *irresistible conviction*; and that the contemplation of the marvels of nature leads us *irresistibly* to admit the existence of an infinitely wise Craftsman of the world.

xxxv. The irresistible strength of the teleological argument will become even more manifest if the following things are considered.

xxxvi. The undecomposed principles [atoms] (oxygen, hydrogen, carbon, etc.) that compose organic molecules (animal or plant) never coalesce, whether by chance or human skill, in such a way as to form one sole organic molecule; but in order to be combined in such a way as to constitute one of those molecules, they have an absolute need for vitality. When vitality ceases, the molecules surrender easily to the action of external agents and decompose, generating new products. Vitality does not exist without the organism, the organism does not exist without the organic molecules, and the organic molecules do not exist without vitality. Here we are no longer dealing with a typecase that, by spilling out its type, is to produce the *Aeneid*, but with metals of any kind, existing in any configuration, that are expected to have taken, all in the same instant, the form of typographic letters, and to have all, in that same instant, arranged themselves in the proper order to produce that poem.

xxxvii. But if all of this has been possible, and the fortuitous encounter of the elementary principles of matter has produced the first animals and vegetables, why does it no longer produce any? Epicurus responded that the earth was then young and vigorous, and that today, having aged, it has lost its fertility. But is this metaphor apt? Can fortuitous encounter, by its nature not subject to any law, ever lose its strength? Or are the very atoms capable of forming animals lost? On the other hand, we know that the earth is approximately as fertile today as it was thirty centuries ago for nurturing the plants sown or planted in it and the animals that are brought about. And what is more, as [French natural philosopher and man of letters Bernard Le Bovier de] Fontenelle [1657–1757] wisely observes, when the earth produced the animals it must have been in the same state in which it is now.[77] It must have had herbs and plants to nurture them and springs and rivers to quench their thirst, and it must have been surrounded by a breathable atmosphere: otherwise, the animals could not have preserved themselves. The earth therefore was such as it is today: thus, it should still produce organic beings or at least some parts or fibers thereof.

XXXVIII. Let us suppose that an animal was formed out of the most felicitous of coincidences, through the fortuitous encounter of the atoms; and that out of a doubly felicitous coincidence a male and a female of the same species were formed. Let us suppose again that, out of similarly most felicitous coincidences, there were formed a couple of quadrupeds and birds, fish, and insects, as well as a flower, a plant, and a tree. It will be easily understood that in this manner the earth has been able to fill itself with plants and animals of a completely different nature; but it will remain forever inconceivable that chance might have been so systematic as to produce a hundred forms of animals, all different and yet all quadrupedal, and all having an analogous organization; and similarly a hundred other forms of animals, all different and yet all winged, and all possessing an analogous organism; and likewise for a hundred varieties of fishes, insects, worms, flowers, plants, and trees. In sum, assuming that chance could produce an organic being, the latter should have produced, through its infinite combinations, many beings of very different nature, all in a different way perfect, and capable of being preserved and reproducing. But nature presents us instead with few kinds of organization, distinguished into many species that differ in few regards and are analogous and similar to one another in very many others, a sign of the fact that, as [French naturalist Julien-Joseph] Virey [1775–1846] observes (*Histoire des moeurs et de l'instinct des animaux*, Lesson 8), all vertebrate animals (that is, man, all mammals, birds, reptiles, and fishes) are composed within according to the same model.[78] Here a system, a will, and an intelligence are manifested; and chance ceases to be chance.

XXXIX. But chance becomes fully impossible if one thinks of the propagation of organic beings. Let us leave aside the systematic uniformity of almost all humans and vegetables with regard to their all being endowed with two different sexes, or of different sexual organs in the same individual, containing the germ to be fertilized and the fertilizing humor, both necessary to the reproduction of the individual; let us leave aside, I am saying, this surprising uniformity on account of the polyps, which completely lack a distinction of sex and sexual organs, and of the many plants that, though endowed of the two sexes, nevertheless reproduce without any fertilization by planting a cutting into the earth. It is certain, however, that there is no species of organic beings that needs more than two individuals to reproduce; and it is equally certain that through the infinite possible combinations it certainly should have occurred that some species would reproduce through the mating of more than two individuals.

XL. The system of the fortuitous encounter of atoms seemed too absurd even to atheists; and many among them, both among the ancient and even more among the modern, believed it appropriate to exchange the word chance for the word necessity. Everything that is, they say, is necessarily: it is by an eternal necessity, which always was and will always be. The laws of nature are eternal. These atheists are called naturalists.

XLI. The teleological argument is equally valid against the hypothesis of necessity. Where a design, a correspondence between the means and the goal, is manifested, it is impossible to suppose necessity.

XLII. Will mathematical relations, the only necessary truths, ever produce effects ordained toward a goal without an Intelligence, a Mind, industriously applying them?

XLIII. A most essential circumstance is passed over in silence, whether out of ignorance or bad faith, by those who claim that the planetary systems support themselves by mathematical and necessary laws. The movements of the planets are necessary by a hypothetical and not an absolute necessity: they are necessary as a result of the varying distances wherein they were arranged (which is what determines the degree of the centripetal force) and of the varying degree of the projective impulse they have received from God at the moment of creation (which is what determines the various degree of the centrifugal force): these distances and impulses could vary infinitely, and in fact they were varied by God in many ways. Planetary orbits depend on the proportion between the projective motion and the force of attraction, and planets and comets necessarily obey these two forces, the centrifugal and the centripetal, but the varying degree of these two forces has nothing necessary within itself except hypothetically, that is to say, according to what it pleased the supreme Craftsman to establish.

[...]

XLV. Indeed, it appears that God wanted to place within nature the print of His free will, and to prevent the suspicion of a blind eternal necessity, constituting, as He did, a marvelous variety in the different parts of nature. He divided animals and plants into multiple genera and species; and He varied the sizes, distances, and orbits of planets and comets. Nothing is as manifest and characteristic a proof of an Intelligence, of a Will, as is variety within parts coupled with systematic analogy in the whole.

CHAPTER 2: OF GOD'S UNITY

XLVI. The mutual relations and the admirable harmony which clearly make themselves manifest in the various and most remote parts of nature signal uncontestably the unity of the Intelligence, the Mind, the Will, which has constituted the universe and each of its parts such as it is. The structure of the eye, as an example, is proportioned to the laws of light and to the nature of and distance from the Sun: without this harmony, sight could not occur.

XLVII. But the unity of design does not appear only in the parts of our planetary system, but it shows itself also in the infinite number of fixed stars, which are as many suns, or centers of as many planetary systems. [. . .]

CHAPTER 3: OF GOD'S OMNIPOTENCE

XLVIII. The omnipotence of God, namely, His absolutely infinite power over anything existent, encompassing the power to create from naught and to reduce to naught, can be easily proven through metaphysical arguments. But physical arguments, supported by facts (the kind of arguments to which the reasonings in these chapters limit themselves), suffice to lead us to recognize in God a supreme power, that is to say, a power superior to all forces of nature. Therefore, although the teleological argument does not show God to be the Architect of the universe, nevertheless His action and His power need not be imagined as mechanical or chemical, but as entirely superior to any mechanical or chemical actions; and the divine Will must be acknowledged to be, rather, the only cause of all natural laws.

XLIX. In fact, Newtonian attraction or gravitation, a property supposed by some to be inherent and essential to matter and to each part thereof, cannot truly be so defined, since it is known that molecular attractions and chemical affinities do not obey the law of the inverse square of distance. If this law were inherent to the molecules of matter, they could in no circumstance follow laws different from it; and if they do so nonetheless, this proves that neither that law nor these are inherent to matter, but that they all are the effect of a supreme will.

L. The phenomenon of vitality equally demonstrates how chemical affinities, far from being inherent to matter, are nothing but the effect of the will of the supreme Intelligence, who is responsible for its organization. Vitality does not exist without the organism and, since the organism is evidently the work of an Intelligence, vitality is itself the work of the supreme Intelligence. Now, we see that the undecomposed principles composing animal molecules appear united, so long as life lasts, by forces of attraction balanced in such a way that the equilibrium, which is always at risk of being broken, does not break, and is instead always reestablished very readily; and that, once life has ceased, those principles are readily decomposed, giving rise to new products. It is therefore apparent that chemical attractions and affinities obey vitality, which is then not the work of nature, but of the supreme Intelligence.

LI. Evidence equally proves that the moral phenomena of inclination and love, which are observed among individuals in the animal kingdom and could be regarded as a third kind of attraction, are the work of the supreme Intelligence. In all animal species, individuals of one sex are naturally led to love and seek individuals of the same species of a different sex. This propensity, or as we shall say attraction, does not proceed from the analogy of forms; while the latter is greater in individuals of the same sex, the propensity among these is much less lively: it does not proceed from chemical affinities either, because these do not act but at a minimal distance, whereas propensity acts so far as sight extends; beyond being excited also by an image, by a portrait, and even by the sole imagination. This propensity does not exist outside of the organization. It is therefore apparent that the supreme Will entirely dominates even the moral part of living beings;[79] that in short, the action of God is not comparable to that of any physical, mechanical, chemical, or moral agent; and that all forces and laws—physical, mechanical, chemical, and moral—proceed only from His will: God must therefore be considered omnipotent.

LII. God's action, superior to all laws of nature, and indeed responsible for them all, is and will always be inconceivable to us, like the existence of a Being who has not received existence from others is and will always remain inconceivable to us, something that atheists themselves are forced to admit. But the theist differs from the atheist in that the latter presupposes an autonomous infinity of organized bodies wherein the design, the intelligence, and hence the Mind of a Craftsman clearly manifest themselves; whereas the theist, moved by the admirable magisterium which he observes in those bodies, admits, in order not to be at war with his intimate perception, that those bodies, and hence all of nature, have received existence from a supreme, most wise, omnipotent Intelligence. [The theist] admits then as existing by itself, and as having received [their] existence from this supreme Mind, in which, although he does not know its essence and, so to speak, its nature, he does not recognize any trace of organization or composition that might induce him to believe it, too, to be the work of another Intelligence.

CHAPTER 4: OF MIRACLES AND REVELATION

LIII. Since all the laws of nature are not necessary by themselves, but only by the will of God, who is nature's author, it is evident that God can at His own pleasure suspend each of those laws and produce, then, a miracle, that is, an event truly contrary to one or more laws of nature, without availing Himself for this purpose of any natural means; that is to say, God can produce physically impossible effects.

LIV. It is therefore manifest that [Jewish philosopher and mathematician] Gersonides [1288–1344, called Ralbag] erred in his statement (*Wars of the Lord* 6:2:12), which he falsely attributed to the Talmudists, according to which a miracle consists in the extemporaneous occurrence, without the precedence of an appropriate circumstance, of an event that would have been naturally possible only after much time and after the precedence of many circumstances. Moreover, it is naturally impossible and contrary to the laws of nature that an effect be accomplished without its necessary circumstances.

LV. A true miracle is a truly incomprehensible thing for us because we cannot comprehend God's action, which is superior to nature, and in the same way in which all natural phenomena are incomprehensible to us if we consider them seriously—that is to say that we cannot comprehend how God's will has subjected matter to those laws which matter now constantly follows. But if natural phenomena do not surprise us and everybody does not see in them the miracles of divine power, it is only because we have been seeing them since childhood;[80] and we call a miracle, or a marvelous and surprising thing, an effect produced by divine will through the suspension of one of those laws that it also produced.

LVI. Inasmuch as a miracle is produced solely by the will of God, which operates without means, it is understood that a miracle must not upset the whole machine of the world. Granted, it does occur to the human craftsman that by arresting the action of some part of a machine, the action of the entire machine becomes hindered or altered; but this occurs because the craftsman cannot but operate in a manner subordinated to the various laws of nature and to the properties of the various bodies he uses. But God, the master of nature and its every law, as well as of substances and all their properties, and the producer of everything not through means but with a pure act of His will, can easily produce any miracle without any disturbance ensuing either in the whole of nature or in any of its parts other than the one in which it pleases Him to operate the miracle.

LVII. Revelation, too, is a miracle. Nothing prevents God from sometimes wanting to manifest His will to one or more men by a more sublime, ready, and secure avenue than the natural ones. By revealing Himself to a man, God operates in such a way that the latter becomes convinced without any doubt of the divine origin of the revelation he received. Without being prophets, we cannot understand how prophecy occurs or how it does not leave any doubt (see Abarbanel on Jeremiah 23:30); we understand very clearly, however, that all of this is possible for God.

LVIII. When God wants to reveal Himself to a man in order to instruct other men, it is evident that He needs to provide that man with the means to prove to those men the divinity of His mission; and these means cannot but be miracles. A true miracle announced beforehand proves the Prophet's mission.

LIX. It is manifest that, by proving the mission of the Prophet, miracles that are announced beforehand and come to pass exactly prove the divine origin of the things he says in God's name, which assume the name of revealed things, or Revelation.

LX. Revelation tenders to us:

a) Practical precepts, which, inasmuch as they are of divine will, must be scrupulously executed;
b) Dogmas, namely theories concerning God and man, aiming to teach men those maxims which can best contribute to making them virtuous and happy; expressed in a manner proportionate not to God's infinite Wisdom, but to the limited capacity of men themselves.

DOGMAS TAUGHT BY RELIGION

LXXVIII. The dogmas taught us by religion may be traced back to two main ones, in which various others are implicitly included. These two main Dogmas are: I. God's justice, which metes out retribution through rewards and penalties all actions of all men; that is, *Sachar ve-ones* [reward and punishment]; II. that God has established a perennial and immutable alliance with the Israelite people; that is, *berit olam* [eternal covenant]. These two dogmas are clearly expressed in many passages of the Pentateuch.

LXXIX. The articles included in these two dogmas are not all expressed with equal clarity in the Pentateuch; but they are expounded at greater or lesser length according to the need of the state of the ideas and opinions of the Israelites who had left Egypt. The prophets following Moses expanded more upon some of these implicit dogmas, according to the need of the intellectual state of their contemporaries, and always in accordance with the dogmas taught by Moses.

LXXX. Thus, at the same time as Moses repeatedly taught that God rewards and punishes human actions, he did not clearly express the implicit dogma that God knows those actions. And the divine Prophet cannot have done so for any reason other than because the dogma of God's omniscience was already universally known and confessed by His contemporaries, to whom opulence and softness had not yet suggested those blasphemies typical of a more advanced civilization: "The clouds screen Him so He cannot see as He moves about the circuit of Heaven" (Job 22:14); "The Lord has abandoned the country" (Ezek. 8:12 and 9:9). Moses contents himself with saying: "Concealed acts concern the Lord our God" (Deut. 29:28).

LXXXI. Moses also did not express clearly the dogma of the immortality of the soul, since it was something known all too well to his contemporaries, to whom he had to prohibit necromancy: "[Let no one be found among you] who casts spells, or one who consults ghosts or familiar spirits, or one who inquires of the dead" (Deut. 18:11), and in whose language death was called "gathered to his kin" [Gen. 25:8], an expression that could not refer to a rejoining in the same grave, since it can be seen applied to Abraham, Aaron, and Moses, who were dead and buried in places far from the tombs of their ancestors. Furthermore, since the first pages of his sacred Book, Moses hints at this dogma through the story of Abel, whom he presents as beloved by God and hence shortly thereafter murdered by his brother; as well as through what he says about Enoch, whom he describes as a pious man, and who nevertheless died a premature death relative to the longevity of antediluvian men—"Enoch walked with God; then he was no more, for God took him" (Gen. 5:24).

LXXXII. Finally, the dogma of the resurrection of the dead was purely alluded to by Moses in the text (Deut. 32:39): "I deal death and give life,"[81] and it was clearly expressed by Daniel (12:2): "Many of those that sleep in the dust of the earth will awake, some to eternal life, others to reproaches, to everlasting abhorrence." Isaiah (26:19) also alludes to it in the text: "Oh, let Your dead revive! Let corpses arise! Awake and shout for joy, you who dwell in dust," as well as Ezekiel in Chapter 37. Religion does not offer us more precise and specific ideas about these two dogmas (of the immortality of the soul and of the resurrection of the dead); nor, were it to offer them, could they be clearly understood by us in this life. It suffices for us to know that God is just, and that our actions will all find in Him an infallible rewarder.

LXXXIII. The second main dogma, that is, God's perennial and immutable alliance with Israel, includes the following seven articles:

1. That God would give the Israelites possession of Palestine, something that was realized immediately after Moses, under Joshua;
2. That God would extraordinarily bless the Israelite nation as long as it would be faithful to His Law, something which was realized at the times of Joshua, Deborah, David, Solomon, and Hezekiah;
3. That God would harshly punish the nation if it were unfaithful to His Law, something that was realized at the time of the various kings of Judah and of Israel; and that finally it would be expelled from the homeland and scattered all over the earth, something that was realized first by the hand of Nebuchadnezzar and then of Titus;
4. That the Israelites in their dispersion would suffer all sorts of persecution and cruel treatment, something that has been realized even to an excessive degree in centuries past;
5. That despite even the most universal dispersion and persecution, the Israelite people would always subsist: "*Yet, even then, when they are in the land of their enemies, I will not reject them* or spurn them so as to destroy them, annulling My covenant with them" (Lev. 26:44), something that until now has been realized, although without an example;
6. That in case the Israelites should be scattered from the land because of their sins, God one day would reunite them again in the ancient homeland, and would accord them again His celestial favor, even more than in times of yore. "Even if your outcasts are at the ends of the world, from there the LORD your God will gather you, from there He will fetch you. And the LORD your God will bring you to the land that your fathers possessed, and you shall possess it; and He will make you more prosperous and more numerous than your fathers" (Deut. 30:4–5), a fundamental dogma, repeatedly preached by later prophets;

7. Finally, the perpetuity and immutability of the Mosaic law, a dogma which Moses, besides the frequently repeated expressions of "It is a law for all time throughout the ages" [Lev. 3:17] and similar, clearly expresses in the same chapter just cited, wherein he reasons of the future reunion of the Israelites, saying: "You, however, will again heed the LORD and obey all His commandments that I enjoin upon you this day" (Deut. 30:8).

2

Torah as Law and Ritual

Among the many themes that interested modern Jewish theologians was how best to understand—and therefore explain and adapt—Torah. What exactly *is* Torah in Judaism? Is it tantamount with "law," as many Bible translations maintained? Is it ritual—Torah as religious practice? When does Torah begin and end? Is there anything outside of Torah? Is Torah, as traditional Jewish thought had long held, more or less synonymous with the entirety of Jewish literary history—that which Jews say and write and live, from Moses on Sinai to the present? Is the circle somewhat, albeit only a little, more confined—Torah as the sum total of Bible, Talmud, midrash, halakhah, and their commentaries? Or is Torah, as radical reformers like Abraham Geiger would argue, the "natural meaning" of Holy Scripture, the exact words of the Hebrew Bible as we know them, for they, and nothing else, represent the closest echo of God's voice in the immanent world?

As this chapter lays out, the debate over the extent and content of Torah lay at the heart of modern Jewish theology from its inception. This debate is not pedantic. Torah, as everyone agreed, was the beating heart of Judaism, the font of living waters, the divine word not just out of which the religion was born but to which it could—and must—return time and again for renewal and revivification. Yet the definition of Torah—in accordance with the original meaning of the Hebrew root (*horaah*), meaning teaching, instruction—was not, and has never been, static. The Pentateuch (Five Books of Moses) is called Torah. So is the entirety of the Hebrew Bible (Tanakh—Torah, Prophets, Writings). Yet so is the tradition called Oral Torah—Mishnah, Talmud, midrash, and commentaries—that developed to interpret, elaborate, elucidate, and apply the words of written scripture, to make static words into living rituals, beliefs, laws. Indeed, for many traditional Jews, any religious learning based on any religious text from any century is understood as Torah learning.

So while Jews across the millennia have applied the word Torah to various aspects of Jewish religious expression, any individual Jewish thinker has tended to define the circle of Torah—or, to use a classic Rabbinical expression, to build a fence around Torah—at different places, motivated by different theological, cultural, or political concerns. As a consequence, theologians differ over which aspects of Judaism are reflections of Torah and which are merely the accumulation of local custom and tradition, *minhag*. *Minhag*, everyone agrees, is part of the human condition. People cannot help but create patterns of ritual practice which, as much as these hold great emotional meaning for their practitioners, are, by definition, parochial, specific to certain times, places, and communities. Therefore, one cannot expect to mandate that others who come from outside these parameters take them on, though they must respect them.[1] So while some might, as a sort of vernacular expression, refer to these *minhagim* as Torah, all would recognize that they are but instantiations of Torah values—the attempt to live by the Torah, and not Torah itself.

Torah that is not *minhag*, therefore, has a different kind of aura, a veneer of timelessness undergirded by a divine imprimatur that gives it the highest authority in matters of theological debate. As such, differentiating between custom and Torah is essential to the whole enterprise of theology. We all agree that the particular melody of a prayer is customary. But are the words of that prayer custom or Torah? We all agree that eating chicken or beef on festive occasions is customary. But are religious dietary laws (kashrut) custom or Torah? In real and meaningful ways, theologians who build their fences to encompass the oral tradition and those who do not come to very different conclusions about what is, and what is not, custom or Torah within Judaism.

The practical ramifications of these theological fences are far-reaching. Based on one's interpretation of Torah, everything can be in flux, from the mundane to the profound, from theological beliefs about sacrifices and the Messiah to liturgical wording and language to festival practices—even the day of the week on which the Sabbath falls.

Yet there must be a way, as Manuel Joel says below, in being able to distinguish when a theologian is, practically speaking, still within a recognizable Judaism, and when one's writings or beliefs have, for all intents and purposes, so disfigured the consensus as to write one out of the religion altogether. In many ways, that sentiment motivates all of the thinkers excerpted in this chapter. What *is* Torah, not just in juxtaposition to *minhagim* but as firm divine foundation on which to establish, and when necessary, from which to adapt, Judaism?

SAMSON RAPHAEL HIRSCH (1808–88)

Samson Raphael Hirsch (b. 1808, Hamburg; d. 1888, Frankfurt) was one of the most influential Orthodox rabbis of the nineteenth century. Given a traditional religious education in Hamburg, Hirsch studied with the city's chief rabbi, Isaac Bernays (1729–1849), a widely respected orator and intellectual, and then, from 1823 to 1829, in Mannheim, with Jacob Ettlinger (1798–1871). In 1830 he took up a post as rabbi in Oldenburg, and there he published the two works that would establish his name and reputation: *Iggerot Tzafun* (1836) and *Horeb* (1838). In the ensuing decade, Hirsch held two more posts, at Emden and Nikolsburg, before settling permanently in Frankfurt, where he made his greatest institutional contributions. He founded a uniquely Orthodox congregation (called the Israelitische Religions-Gesellschaft [Israelite religious society], known alternately as the German *Austritts*—that is, the "withdrawn" community—or as Neo-Orthodox) separate from the larger, more progressive Frankfurt community. Moreover, he published his five-volume commentary on the Pentateuch (*Übersetzung und Erklärung des Pentateuchs*, 1867–78), a monumental work that sought—as did so much of his writing over the course of his life—to provide a synthetic account of the Jewish approach to God and the world.

This selection is a translation of the eighteenth letter from Hirsch's *Iggerot Tzafun: Neunzehn Briefe über Judenthum* (Letters from a hidden one:[2] Nineteen letters concerning Judaism).[3] Published in German under the pseudonym Ben Usiel, perhaps an allusion to the greatest of Hillel's students (see b. *Sukkah* 28a), it purports to outline the basic tenets of traditional Jewish belief and practice through the literary device of a (fictional) correspondence between a rabbi ("Naftali") and a young intellectual ("Benjamin"). In the eighteenth letter, focused on the Jewish understanding and interpretation of Torah mainly in the Mishnah and Talmud (*Shas*), Hirsch refers to the rigorous, rational interpretation of Torah as *Jissroeïls Wissenschaft* (Israel's science), a remarkable formulation in its conflation of tradition and modernity. The Bible and its Rabbinic interpreters, Hirsch writes, were like today's scholars, studying and analyzing the truths necessary for our lives. But somewhere along the way, he says, the aura and feeling of the laws and the world they created replaced the actual adherence to the Torah's commands. Jewish ethos replaced Jewish practice: "[They] had no further need of the mitzvah [commandment]. . . . Still less did they need the science of these mitzvot, which remained, for them, spiritless." Only through a complete reengagement with Torah and mitzvot, Hirsch concludes, will one truly be able to "grasp Judaism as [an] institution for life."

Nineteen Letters Concerning Judaism: Eighteenth Letter (1836)

Translated by Paul Franks

Israel's entire essence rests on Torah; it is Israel's ground, and its goal, and the sap of life in its veins. If its Torah is healthy, Israel cannot be sick, but if its Torah is sick, then Israel can never thrive. There is therefore no deformity that is not produced—or at least sustained—through some sin in Israel's Torah-conception. Our perceptive sages already disclosed the ground of our first national downfall as the fact that "they did not bless the Torah first" [b. *Nedarim* 81a; *Bava Metzia* 85a], that is, that they were not driven to their Torah with resolve to fulfil it, thus not with respect to life and for the sake of life; life flowed from science [*Wissenschaft*]; thus science could not also penetrate life, could not truly illuminate—could not warm—life. And if you seek the origin of the contemporary sickness, you will once again find it nowhere but there.

Originally, Israel's science was maintained only in its basic norms and in writing, *Torah she-bikhtav* [Written Torah]; but its articulation, and above all its spirit, as this spirit itself is life, was supposed to maintain itself only in living word, *Torah she-be-al-peh* [Oral Torah]. The pressure of the times and the [Second] Temple's destruction led to the downfall of Israel's science—consequently, the Mishnah was transcribed, and the spirit was left to the oral word. The pressure of the times demanded more; so the spirit of the Mishnah was transcribed in the Gemara, but only in its practical expression, the spirit of the Gemara being reserved for the oral word. The pressure of the times demanded still more; so the spirit of Tanakh and the Gemara was transcribed in Aggadot; but again only in a veiled way, so that one could come to the aid of the orally inherited spirit only by penetrating the veil on one's own. Doctrine and spirit fled to two academies; but they were soon undermined—overcome—through persecution and confusion; doctrine went into exile; the letter and external practical fulfilment were saved; the spirit had escaped, except for the letters that veiled it.[4] The spirit had to be untethered from the letter and from the veiling symbol bound up with that which was saved for individuals, and then individuals could still catch a glimpse of that spirit, shining high within. But not everybody had the spirit.[5]

In non-Jewish schools, Jewish youth formed their spirit in an independent, philosophical direction. From Arabic sources, they drew Greek philosophical doctrines. They learned self-perfection in knowledge of the truth as their highest task, their view of life in contradiction to a view of life that, above all, focused on the deed, on action, and that respected knowledge only as a means to action.

The time produced a mind [*Geist*], simultaneously educated in unconceptualized Judaism and in Arabian science, that had balanced within itself the duality, as it balanced and expressed it, and thereby became the leader for all those engaged in the same struggle.[6] It is to this great man [the philosopher Maimonides], whom—and to whom alone—we are grateful for the preservation of practical Judaism up to our time, and it is he who gave birth to all good and evil due, on the other side, to the fact that he only *balanced* and to *how* he balanced, instead of creatively developing Judaism out of itself. His distinctive spiritual direction was Arabic-Greek, as was also his conception of life. He pressed into Judaism from the outside and brought with him views that had been established for him *elsewhere*—and performed his balancing act. The highest goal for him too was self-perfection through knowledge of the truth, to which the practical was subordinated. Knowledge of God was the end, not the means, and so consisted in speculations concerning God's essence, and Judaism [was] constitutively bound up with the results of these speculative inquiries as well as with propositions of science or faith. *Mitzvot* [commandments] were for him only guides, albeit necessary guides, to knowledge, and a shield against error, even in part only against partial errors arising historically within the domain of paganism. Thus *mishpatim* [rules], as well as *mitzvot*, became rules of prudence; *chukim* [laws] became rules of health, promoting feelings and warding off temporal pain; *edot* [testimony] became in part institutions for speculative and other ends. All was not grounded in the eternal essence of things; all did not flow from their eternal claim on me, from my eternal calling; all was not the eternalization of the idea through symbolism—and thus it was by means of these negations that all [Maimonides' thought] was not grounded in the totality of the *mitzvot*.[7]

And he, the great systematic organiser of the practical results of the Talmud, in the last part of his philosophical work [*Guide for the Perplexed*], laid down views concerning the spirit of the *mitzvot* that for the most part, assuming those practical results as content of the *mitzvot*, do not hold up, do not illuminate them—thus cannot accompany them in practice, in life, and in science. It is these views that have been inherited, up to the present day, by those who, in general, have desired the spirit of the *mitzvot*. Yet the relationship between precisely these [views] and that which is valid for practice remains wholly external; so that the practical results, lacking spirit, had to sink—had even to be despised. Instead of placing themselves within Judaism and asking themselves, "Since Judaism makes demands upon us, what view must it have concerning the human calling?," and instead of first grasping this demand in its totality according to Tanakh and Shas [the Talmud], and then asking themselves, "What then, indeed, can be the concept and sense of this demand?," one took one's standpoint outside Judaism and pulled it over towards oneself; from the outset, one formed views of what the *mitzvot* could be, unencumbered by the actual appearance of the *mitzvah* according to all its parts. What was the consequence? Just as now, these views produced in life the natural appearance that people who believed themselves to be the possessors of knowledge had no further need of the *mitzvah*, which to be sure was supposed to be a guide; still less did they need the science of these *mitzvot*, which remained, for them, spiritless.

People who grasped Judaism in a deeper way became enemies of this philosophical spirit, and later became enemies of the spirit in general and of the philosophical spirit in particular. Various misunderstood dicta became defensive weaponry for the deflection of all spiritually meaningful comprehension of the Talmud.[8] No distinction was made between the question, "What is stated here?" and the question, "Why is it stated?" Not even the category *Edot*, which according to its entire essence is supposed to bear nothing but spirit, was excluded from the prohibition on spirit. In the same way, later, a misunderstood passage (b. *Sanhedrin* 24a; Tos. ad. loc. "*belulah*") was even taken to order the removal of the study of Tanakh from the curriculum, an error against which warning had already (*Soferim* 15:9) prophetically been issued.[9]

Thus, since at the same time oppression and persecution stole from Israel its living views of world and life in general, and since the Talmud had been all but exhausted with respect to results for practical life, any mind [*Geist*] that wanted to be spontaneous had no option but to stray and find its occupation in sophistry. Throughout the course of this time, only a few stood purely within Judaism with their projects of intellectual research, constructing Judaism spiritually out of itself alone.[10] From these few shine forth the author of the *Kuzari* [the poet and philosopher Judah HaLevi, 1075–1141] and [philosopher, mystic, and scriptural exegete] Nachmanides [1194–1270, called Ramban]. Above all in Germany, where in any event the times of oppression and persecution suppressed any attempt of the spirit to take flight independently, did this condition of uncomprehending Judaism become dominant. To be sure, the general fundamental view that "God is the Solitary One and the Torah is God's will," and the fulfilment of the same with fear of God, love of God, and trust in God, remained *everywhere* in its vital force, and for it was life—with all its goods and joys—sacrificed joyfully and in shining devotion.

A discipline [Kabbalah] came into existence, which I—as a non-initiate—dare not judge, but which however, if I understand correctly what I believe myself to understand of it, is a priceless repository of precisely that spirit of Tanakh and Shas. But then, unfortunately, it came to be misunderstood, and what is eternal, progressive development was taken for a static mechanism, and what is inner appearance and concept was taken for external dreamworlds. This discipline came into existence, and the spirit turned either towards the external, sharp-witted development of the Talmud, or towards this discipline that appealed to the emotions. In this discipline, perhaps, practical Judaism, had it been grasped in its purity, would have been infused with spirit. But instead, since the discipline had become misunderstood, practical Judaism became a magical mechanism, an attempt to influence or to ward off theosophical worlds and non-worlds.

Gradually there came into the hands of the people a part of a work [the Shulcḥan Arukh] that was originally intended only for the review of scholars, and that presented the ultimate results of Talmudic science purely for external practice; more accurately, an extract from the systematic work of Rambam [Maimonides], differently organised, in virtue of which it appeared to us immediately as the great preserver of practical Judaism in the times of the massive *Golus* [exile] oppression.[11] But unfortunately, only one part of this work came into the hands of the people,[12] only the divisions of *Edot* and *Avodot* [rituals],[13] of divine worship and the festivals; the remaining duties were developed in the other parts, and were indeed intended for scholars, not for the people. Step by step this produced, here and there, the unfortunate view that the distinctiveness of Judaism lay in nothing other than praying and festivals. But life remained unknown.

If all these various influences are assembled, then you will be able to explain the appearance of Judaism approximately eighty years ago, as well as everything that followed. For it was then, when the external yoke began to lift and spirit felt more freely active, that a highly prominent, extremely awe-inspiring personality [the philosopher Moses Mendelssohn] stepped onto the stage once again, who by his personality has led the development up to the present day. This personality himself—who also did not acquire his independent spiritual development from Judaism, instead developing to greatness in the philosophical disciplines of metaphysics, aesthetics, and treated Tanakh only philologically and aesthetically[14]—did not build up Judaism as a science from out of itself, but rather only defended it against political incomprehension and pious Christian impositions. Personally, he was a practically religious Jew, and he showed his brethren and the world that one could be a strictly religious Jew *and yet* shine forth, highly respected, as a German Plato![15]

This "and yet!" was decisive.[16] His followers were satisfied with the avid, philological-aesthetic development of Tanakh, with the study of the *Guide, and yet* to conduct and to expand humanistic studies. But Judaism, Tanakh, and Shas as science remained neglected. Yes, not even avid study of Tanakh could lead to it, because one worked on Tanakh, not as doctrine for conceptual articulation, but rather as beautiful poetry for the imagination. Now, that [Mendelssohnian] view—suspended earlier but now set free—inevitably manifested a vitality that outstripped the neglected study of the Talmud, along with uncomprehended practical Judaism, all the way to its ultimate consequence: negating all of Judaism.

If that view of life which locates the highest calling of the human in the cognition of truth is true—and who could doubt it, since Maimonides had established it!—then, first and foremost, those views of the demands of the Torah are true—and who should doubt it, since Maimonides, the great expert on the Talmud, himself an observant Jew, had established that they are true—and so in fact the multi-volume Talmud is nothing but nit-picking sophistry. Then practical Judaism is nothing but mindless drudgery. Who could disagree!

If, for example, the meaning of the prohibition of work on the sabbath—and who could doubt it, since both Moses's [the biblical Moses and Maimonides] took it thus and since the Christian Sunday also means this—is nothing other than rest from the toil of the week, celebration of the body, but also a means by which the spirit could for once occupy itself, then who does not see what triviality-trading and hair-splitting it is to fill an entire volume with investigations of which labours to prohibit, who does not see how odd it is to stamp the writing of two letters—which may even perhaps be a spiritual occupation—as a mortal sin, while at the same time treating more leniently many a great corporeal exertion or destruction! And then to forbid even the hen herself to lay eggs! Or, for example, in another domain, if sacrifice were nothing other than, say, the offering of one's own in acknowledgment that it comes from God, and if it were, in its intricate details, nothing other than a mere antithesis to the polytheistic sacrificial practice dominant at the time, then what nonsense would it be to fill three, four volumes with investigations of how to offer this sacrifice, which parts, by whom, and when? Do you not see that all this is spirit-killing priestcraft?[17]

But one could surely, at least once, have raised the question: "Is Moses ben Maimon, or Moses ben Mendel, actually Moses ben Amram [the biblical Moses]?!" In this contradiction between the prevailing view of the *mitzvah* and its actuality, does there not lie a proof that the view is incorrect, that it is not based on the total concept of the *mitzvah*, but is instead *dreamed* into it from outside? Does the *Guide* not itself say that, for the judgment of the *mitzvot*, it takes only *Torah she-bikhtav* [Written Torah] as its standpoint, a standpoint that Maimonides himself would have declared incorrect for practice itself, and thus as a delusionary standpoint? Does Maimonides himself not say of it that, in his judgment of the *mitzvot*, he has not taken into consideration exactly those determinations of parts that, only when taken collectively, yield the total concept of the *mitzvot*, and that are precisely the principal components of *Torah she-be-al peh* [Oral Torah]? (*Guide*, pt. 3, chaps. 26 and 41). In all *mitzvot* there must be significance, and first and foremost in those that announce themselves as educational: their spirit must be capable of disclosure, for they themselves name themselves "testimony," "memorial," "symbol." How would it be if we sought this significance—if we tried, for once, to grasp it as testimony, memorial, symbol? Yet this has not been done. Many did not even want to do it. For a spirit had arrived from the west that laughed at everything sacred, and that rejoiced if it could show the sacred to be laughable; and with it came a striving for sensuality that rejoiced if it could get rid of burdensome barriers at so cheap a price. Thus one tore down the barriers, making everything flat and even.[18]

What then, today—now that one side of this spirit has already played itself out—today, now that two generations confront one another: one generation that inherits uncomprehended Judaism as *mitzvat anashim melumadah* ["a commandment of men, learned by rote"] (Isa. 29:13), holding it in their hands like a sacred mummy without spirit, fearing to awaken the spirit; the other generation, in part glowing with noble fire for the welfare of the Jews, but respecting Judaism only as spiritless appearance, as belonging to an age that went to the grave long ago—seeking spirit and finding none—and with its best effort to help the Jews in danger of severing Judaism's last nerve—out of ignorance![19] And now, when, approximating each other in a thousand nuances, these opposites testify through this very fact that they are both in error—now? Which way to salvation? Does it suffice for salvation to base our schools on this divided ground, to reform the synagogue service? The spirit, the inner, unitary life-principle is lacking—and that can never be supplied by polishing the external frame.

There is one way to salvation. Where the sin was committed, there must atonement begin. And this one way is to forget the inherited views and non-views about Judaism; to return to the sources of Judaism—Tanakh, Shas, Midrash. To read, study, comprehend them for life; from there to reconstruct Judaism's view of God, world, humanity, Israel, according to destiny and doctrine, and to know Judaism out of itself, to comprehend it out of itself, to lift its life-wisdom out of itself into a science. To begin with Tanakh! First with knowledge of language! To reconstruct, out of the spirit of the language, the spirit of its speakers. To study Tanakh, not for research into language and antiquity, or for theories of taste and amusement, but rather for the building of a science. To contemplate nature with the sensibility of David, to hear a story with the ear of Isaiah; and then, with eyes awake, with ear open, to reconstruct the teaching about God, world, humanity, Israel, and Torah from Tanakh, to bring it to comprehension. And then, to study Shas with the spirit of such an understanding, seeking in *halakhah* [legal discourse] nothing but the articulation of this comprehension, while presupposing that it is drawn from Tanakh, and seeking in *Aggadah* [exegetical discourse] nothing but the expression of this same spirit, veiled in an image.

And then, not being bothered by how the one or the other party think of your study; being untroubled by whether now in your spirit of simplicity you are no longer able to shine among the heroes of subtle disputations that do not pay homage to truth and life as their goal; being untroubled by whether you are now unable to shine in the particular disciplines that you acquire only as auxiliary sciences for your own sake; being untroubled by whether or not you become unfit for superficial presentation. You are studying for the sake of the light of truth, of the warmth and heat of life, and, having attained them, you will comprehend Israel's destiny and doctrine, along with life as expression of this doctrine, filled through and through with spirit! One spirit! In all! From the structure of the language to the structure of the actions of life. One spirit, emanating from the spirit of the Solitary One.

That would be a task for the youth of science! But it is essential to transplant the results of this science into life—through schools! Schools for Jews! The young offspring of your people should be educated as Jews—as sons and daughters of Judaism, as you have learned to know it and comprehend it and revere it and love it: as the life of your life. They should be educated in the language of Tanakh, as in the language of your land, your own, taught how to think in both, their heart educated to feeling, their spirit to thinking, to take the writings of Tanakh as their book of teaching for life, and they should be able to hear Tanakh's word throughout life.

Their eye should be opened to the contemplation of the world around them as a divine world, and to the contemplation of themselves as divine worshippers in this divine world! Their ear should be opened to history as the education of *all* humans to this synagogue service—and then their lives should be set apart for this divine worship through the results for life drawn from Torah and Shas, and they should be taught to comprehend, revere, and love, so that they may rejoice in the name "Jew" and in the life springing from this name, despite all the scorn and deprivation. And their instruction for earning a livelihood should be included in these schools for life, as once earning a livelihood was included in life, namely as a means for the fulfilment of life, not as an end. They should be taught to estimate the value of life not according to class, wealth, and brilliance, but rather according to calling, filled with the inner life, in the service of God; not to subordinate the demands of their calling to the demands of sensuality and comfort, but the other way around. And then, until Israel's houses are built out of such sons and daughters of Israel, there should be pleading, begging in the houses of their parents, that they not disturb the task of the school, that they not, with icy or dull spirit, cause the young shoots in their children's emotions to nod off or die; and that slumbering nobility also be awakened in the parents' breast—and, where comprehension is no longer possible, reverence is nevertheless achieved.

And can the situation in Israel really change? It will change in Israel! Our time leads inevitably to it. Do not look at it so gloomily, my friend. It is anxiety-provoking, like the labour hours of a woman giving birth. But better this anxiety in the house of a woman giving birth than the unanxious but also joyless and hopeless house of the infertile. May this time of flux outlast our lives, the lives of our children, and, if they want, the lives of our grandchildren. Then the great-grandchildren will rejoice in the child who has struggled into light and into life. His name is, "self-comprehending Judaism"! This time makes one guarantee only: to strive for thinking, for comprehension, for the grasping with spirit of that which ought to be revered.

Very well then! As soon as the spirit first recognises the futility of its groundless and purposeless striving, of negotiating with the exaggerated demands of the fleeting moment, once it has entered into consciousness that life can be built only on comprehension and on truth grasped internally, then spirit will awaken to the question, "What am I, then, as a Jew? What is Judaism?" And then the solution to this question will no longer be brought from non-Jewish professors and texts, from scholars who often know Judaism only through a distorting lens, some of whom believe that they have to destroy Torah and Judaism in spirit in order to build up their own; nor from the writings of reformers of the time who worked for external considerations; nor from the writings of Jewish sages who choose their standpoint outside Judaism; rather, the solution will involve going to the original sources of Judaism, to Tanakh and Shas; and it will involve this single striving: to grasp the concept of life out of Judaism, and to grasp Judaism as institution for life—this single striving, once it is included, will lead to the goal of producing the true, the vital as truth and life, in accordance with the age-old but sadly forgotten rule: "to learn in order to teach, to observe, and to do!"[20]

All of you who mean well with respect to the Judaism that you have inherited out of habit and which you intend to bequeath once again through habit—I wish that your eyes were opened and that you would recognize that you can bequeath it only through the spirit. I wish that you at least provided your sons and daughters the texts, the texts of Torah, Prophets, and Writings, so that the spirit that animates them could become their light and staff in life.

You distinguished personalities among those who now want to be active for the good of Judaism—would that you considered that helping to loosen the chains from hand and foot, and to adorn the clothing accessories, the external appearance, is not the same as producing life. I wish that you would stop the hand that is raised to tear down and would first examine whether the building does not hold something sacred and eternal, and life and truth, which, made unrecognizable by the dust of the centuries, still seems to you worthy only of trickery. I wish that you would turn your averted gaze and would first examine that from which you turn. Is it the fault of the cause? Should the cause be atoned for? Because its bearers, themselves covered in the dust of the field of battle against pressure and misery, could save it only as covered in dust? If we, to whom the mildness of the times is supposed to set the task of wiping away the dust, pay so little attention to those efforts and struggles, that we do not even consider it worth the effort to clean the jewel for ourselves and to examine what they fought for. But, rather, keeping ourselves only on the outside, throwing it away covered with dust and because it is covered with dust, throwing away as worthless the jewel for which the ancestors sacrificed life and property and freedom and all the joys of life. Yet, my Benjamin, I forget that only heaven hears this wish, only this paper sees it, and you will hear it. I forget that I am writing only to you.

Light and truth and life will be produced through this time of testing. Hold fast to that, my friend, and then you will also appreciate differently what otherwise I also regretted with you, namely the apparently helpless condition of the spiritual affairs of our people. No central agency, no authority, everything just the efforts of individuals, and in this striving for reform, the synagogue service, on which everything seems to turn, has quickly become so variegated that a Jew travelling through Germany's regions soon finds something different in each community. Do you not see how this too has its good side?

I am convinced that none of us who are now alive grasps Judaism in its purity and truth. Take for instance the divergence of views, which is also natural, since almost every rabbi must strike his own way without the guidance of any school. More generally, consider that we are still living in an age that is a time of flux. So it would be unfortunate if an authority established something. This would only make the woes eternal! For, if people are elected to leadership, even if it is unilaterally, then they will perpetuate a spectacle, and if the election is multilateral, then they will perpetuate a half-measure, and they will impede the course of development, which will bring the pure water of life only when it reaches its goal. But what time gives birth to, time will erase, always leaving room for the higher structure that awaits us.

I consider how, centuries ago, the spirit would already have attained self-awareness by means of living itself out, and how we would already now be where we will in fact be only in centuries to come, if serious concern for the preservation of Judaism's external practice had not made it necessary, in the times after Maimonides, to inhibit mutual aspirations. So I must indeed make a blessing over the fact that the scales are now hanging completely free, held only by God, to be brought into equilibrium only by spiritual endeavours, so that no force can throw its sword into them to inhibit their swinging. If they were stopped again, our great-grandchildren would still be where we are. Should we be afraid to stand the test of time for them? Let the scales swing!

The freer they hang, and the more purely they ultimately weigh truth and life, the more conspicuous must now be the height and depth of the scales' swing. And when the scales' swing is finally over, and spirit stands luminously in Israel, comprehending itself and its destiny and doctrine, and permeating all its members, and producing such life—then too the sprout that went out from Israel will have accomplished its mission. A battle of a different kind will have been fought out in the circle of our non-Jewish brothers, and there the free glance up towards the Solitary One along with the consciousness of moral force will have victoriously defeated that which threatened to darken the glance and to destroy the force. Then too, the book of history, with its conclusive doctrine, will pervade all spirits.

Let us comprehend our time, my Benjamin, each with as much force of spirit as bestowed upon him. Let us promote progress towards the goal, in our own smaller or larger circles. Even if thousands abandon the cause of life and light, if thousands break away from the destiny and name of Israel, whose way of life they already threw away long ago, the cause of truth does not count the number of its supporters. If only one still remains, one Jew with the book of doctrine in hand—with Israel's doctrine in the heart, Israel's light in the spirit—then one will be sufficient. Israel's cause will not be lost. When Israel had become unfit for its calling, the Solitary One wanted to let the solitary Moses carry Israel's destiny and doctrine. To us too, when we grow hesitant, the prophet calls:

> Look to the rock from which you were hewn,
> To the fountain-hollowing hammer that dug you out![21]
> Gaze upon Abraham, your father,
> Upon Sarah, who was destined to bear you;
> One was he, when I called him;
> Then I blessed him—and made him many![22]

Farewell, my Benjamin, teach yourself to be such a one.
Farewell.

ABRAHAM GEIGER (1810–74)

Abraham Geiger (b. 1810, Frankfurt; d. 1874, Berlin), a leading rabbi, scholar, and theologian in the middle decades of the nineteenth century, is considered one of the founding fathers and intellectual ideologues of Reform Judaism. Early on, his award-winning dissertation (granted by the University of Marburg), focusing on early Islam, asked the provocative question, "What Did Mohammed Take from Judaism?" In 1835, while working in Wiesbaden as a communal rabbi, Geiger began editing the *Wissenschaftliche Zeitschrift für jüdische Theologie* (WZJT) (Scientific journal for Jewish theology), which quickly became a leading publication for scholarship in *Wissenschaft des Judentums*, focusing on Jewish history and theology.

Beginning in 1840, Geiger held rabbinical posts in Breslau (today Wrocław, Poland), Frankfurt, and Berlin, where he worked to refine his vision of a reformed Jewish liturgy and theology. In the second half of the nineteenth century his writings were widely read and discussed, and many of his modifications—including the use of a new reformed prayer book, the *Israelitisches Gebetbuch* (Israelite prayerbook) (Breslau, 1854)—were widely adopted.

The article selected here, "The Relation of the Natural Meaning of Scripture to Its Talmudic Interpretation," published in the *WZJT* in two installments in 1844, marked the beginning of Geiger's philological-historical critique of talmudic authority.[23] In these pages, he posited a theory of Jewish legal historical development that sought a return to biblical prophetic creativity, with its ability to capture "the innermost secrets of the human being." To Geiger, the talmudic rabbis' efforts to create a scriptural basis for their own extrascriptural law had distorted the literal meaning of the Bible. In Geiger's view, the talmudic rabbis imparted to their own law both an infinite validity and a divine authority that it did not deserve, and thereby suppressed the flexibility and adaptability to time and place that the earlier strata of oral law still possessed. Such adaptability, Geiger said, could still be found in the Mishnah (the first code of Rabbinical law, dating in written form from the early third century CE) but was lost by the time of the Gemara.

Geiger's ideological power here lies in the clarity of his argument: there is a natural meaning to biblical language, and its obfuscation, even for the purpose of more deeply enumerating God's laws, must be rejected.

The Relation of the Natural Meaning of Scripture to Its Talmudic Interpretation (1844)

Translated by George Y. Kohler

At the end of the prophetic era the second period of Jewish history began. What the biblical, profoundly religious outlook had revealed was now absorbed as law. But the higher substance of the law was not yet acknowledged, and therefore one tried to observe every single commandment even more firmly. From this point forward, the commandments no longer generated the higher principle that lived in them but spawned new laws, as occurs naturally with everything that is merely external. In order to properly fulfill the commandments of the Bible (especially of the Pentateuch) at every stage of life they had to be qualified in greater detail, and subsequently those details had to be turned into law, too. For the biblical commandments not to be deprived of any of their details, new commandments were added which were binding under all circumstances—a procedure which came to prevent every possible occasion for the infringement of those rules. Nevertheless, new conditions of life emerged that now called for new regulations, and even for minor modifications, of the biblical law. The first procedure is the *interpretation* of the biblical commandments (*peirush*), the second their fencing-in (*seyag*), and the third their provisional structuring, sometimes even re-structuring (*takana*).[24] Like the latter two techniques of legal-extension—which are not part of the Bible itself and intend only to facilitate the appropriate execution of biblical commandment—biblical *interpretation* was also at first not aimed at the exegesis of words or verses in a linguistic way. Rather, it came to refer to the subject matter, to the content, and to qualify it according to the great range of situations provided by real life, according to the different circumstances of life that are connected to the law. Those interpretive qualifications are therefore also not part of the Bible. Either they arose as idiomatic consequences from the explicit sense of the text or they are necessary to additionally expand and adjust the once-comprehended purpose of the law. Thus, this [early Rabbinic] interpretation of biblical law is not yet a linguistic-exegetic activity, painstakingly contemplating every single word or verse to determine their content in a valid and right way. Instead, that was presupposed, and these short laws should rather be endowed with the right applicability for life, by formulating precise second-level provisions. These provisions, however, either transferred from theory to life, or the other way around, were seen as reflecting the *sense* of the Bible, although they are not explicitly found in the text. Increasingly now, the virtue of law-abidance and religious life were made dependent on the keeping of those sub-provisions. As a consequence, they were ever multiplied and expanded.

Despite the great significance that this expansion of the biblical law achieved, the awareness of the nonbiblical origin of this apparatus had not entirely faded at this time. Nevertheless, the legal validity that the new apparatus claimed originated from then-dominant opinions and from its own organic deductions. Explicitly, the Mishnah says:

> Chagigah 1:8: Dissolution of vows fly in the air—there is no basis for it. Laws concerning shabbat and festival peace [offerings] and misuse [of consecrated things]—these are like mountains hung from a hair: they have few verses and many laws. Judgments and [sacrificial] services and purity and impurity and improper sexual relations—they have plenty to be based on. They themselves are the body of Torah.

However, inevitably and over time, the belief was formed that everything that the [Rabbinic] schools raised to be legal regulations, and that was accepted in real life as law, must also be present in the Bible itself. The [Rabbinic] scholars themselves, who knew the Bible and were thus aware of its incompleteness (given what further extension to the laws had now achieved), must have had the wish to be able to find in the Bible at least hints of those later provisions. Especially where differing legal views existed, biblical support for every opinion was quite welcome. If the observance of the law down to the smallest detail—as it was now mandatory—is the very essence of religion (as was thus concluded), the Bible could not have been content with general outlines of the law; it could not have ignored the so-extremely-significant filling-in of the details. Once on this track, the superficial way of thought prevailing at this time also offered the possibility of finding in the Bible more than it actually contained.[25] [The new] method of interpretation was in itself superficial; it no longer referred to the context and the inner sense of the passage as decisive criteria, but instead [only] to the outer structure of it. From everything that looked like an exemption to the [linguistic] rule, single words were preferably taken into account—even if those conclusions were unwarranted under appropriate consideration.

Only the very beginnings of this method can be found in the Mishnah. In general, the Mishnah does not demand [legal] derivations from Scripture. If the Mishnah engages in discussion, it argues from the subject matter itself and its consequences rather than basing itself on a biblical verse. Sometimes, however, the Mishnah does exactly that, and in those cases the discussion sticks sharply to the letter [of the biblical law], even when the full context would not allow for it. At other times, even single words are squeezed to produce a meaning that was never in them. But the Mishnah is not yet undertaking completetly arbitrary combinations and thus deriving meaning from innocent letters that allegedly should have been positioned in a different way then they are, or that should have been missing at all. Only later, in the Gemara, can one find derivations that in true fact have not the slightest connection to supposed linguistic irregularities. [. . .]

Thus the Mishnah proceeds, firmly believing that all its interpretations are present in the Bible and that its exegesis expresses the true meaning of the relevant biblical passages. The exegetical consciousness, however, is, although not yet in a broad way, already tarnished, and finds nothing reprehensible in the literalism and the compulsivity used to interpret many passages. In this sense, there can be no talk of the teachers of the Mishnah as admitting yet another interpretation of the Bible except their own, even less had they a sense of a conflict between their own interpretations and the requirements of exegesis. If they thus use the term *drash* for the derivation of a law from a biblical passage, this does not mean for them interpreting it in an exceptional way[26]—*Drash* assumed this meaning (which Elijah rightly gave the term in Tishby) only later, when there already existed an awareness of the conflict of such interpretations with the natural meaning of Scripture.[27] The Mishnah, however, understands *drash* as the production of a law, in most cases from a biblical passage, but also sometimes completely independent of the Bible.[28]

As soon as the process of forced interpretation—which later became over-fertile—had been developed, the more its very beginnings were hidden to an ever greater extent and merged with a healthy exegesis. In some cases, where the verses contained at least a hint to the legal regulation—but no possibility to produce clear evidence from the verses themselves—the Mishnah simply admitted this with the remark: "Although there is no proof [in the verse] for this law, there is a hint to it."[29]

The Mishnah was edited and sealed. It is a subject of discussion today if this happened in writing—but I believe the course of history is irrefutable evidence for this view. In any event, the doctrines of the Mishnah were now taught in a fixed form at the [rabbinical] schools, and thus a new "book" had appeared that was to be included into [rabbinical] scholarship. Soon after the completion of the Mishnah its authority gained the strength of being binding and compelling, such that in this regard it was seen as on a par with the Bible. But since the authority of the Bible itself was built on the view that it was God's word, the same justification must needs be found for the Mishnah. The Mishnah's own view—to assume in good faith it would expand the biblical law in full compliance with the sense of the Bible itself (even if the letter of the Bible did not always agree with it) and thus to give full power to the progress of religious life and its representatives—could no longer be upheld in totality.[30] It would probably have granted the Mishnah some temporary authority, but not an eternal one, since further progress of religious life would have contradicted the Mishnah—even while the Mishnah was seen as binding for all eternity. On this account a regression to the Sadducean [view] became necessary, such that the authority of *all* legal regulations must preferably have been attributed to Scripture, while law that could not be ascribed to the Bible was then of lower authority. This had serious consequences in constraining religious life. Many regulations of the Mishnah were now to be seen under completely different considerations as compared to the Mishnah's view itself, and even the openhearted confession in *Chagigah* (quoted above)—that some laws had no biblical justification at all; others only a very general one, which could not be used to derive a wide legal interpretation—must have been completely incomprehensible for later generations. In fact, it is amusing and instructive to compare the Gemara to this Mishnah.[31] That some laws "fly in the air," that is, have no biblical explanation at all, appears to the Gemara as quite erroneous. It then tries to find those explanations in different ways, and although we have learned . . . of many laws which are "like mountains hung from a hair"—because not much regarding them can be found in the Bible—our Gemara cannot agree with that. It claims, to the contrary, that with the exception of very few, minor regulations, every law must be derived from Scripture—as all tractates dealing with those subjects attempt to show. The mountains thus turn at best into simple hummocks, hardly visible to the untrained eye. The few laws that derive from the Bible—and the numerous laws that were developed later—turn into many laws that have a biblical origin and still as many other laws that derive from the Bible and are later extended by a single modification.

Hence the frequent question asked by the Gemara when it begins to discuss the words of a Mishnah: "From which verse can those single regulations be derived?" Naturally, the need arose to create distance from the Sadducees regarding their exegetical principles, [that is,] the way to develop law from Scripture. What began only very unobtrusively in the Mishnah now grew to cover the entire ground of healthy exegesis and left no trace of [what it had once been]. Words and letters were interpreted in the most arbitrary ways; analogies were found in the most unessential and circumstantial details. This [method] was used to further justify the complete transfer of the regulations of one law onto another. One virtually now tried to *find* irregularities—unusual or redundant elements in biblical passages—and thus in fact to create uncommon details in order to tie legal interpretations to them—interpretations that, even if there really had been an "irregularity," would not have themselves to be brought in any connection to it. Therefore, it was only natural that the evidence that was earlier called a mere hint (*zekher le-davar*) was now seen—ignoring the words of the Mishnah—as valid proof.[32]

It is not necessary to further explain here the specific procedure of interpretation in the Gemara, which would necessitate illustration by example. The general fact of this "excessive" exegesis—if this expression is suitable at all—is obvious to everyone not completely unfamiliar with the Gemara—and those who are entirely remote from it could not be introduced into the meandering ways of this method of derivation without private study, even with a more complex explanation. How this method necessarily emerged and developed has by now been sufficiently described. In my opinion, it is self-evident that the Gemara took its own interpretations completely seriously and assumed that the laws it derived from Scripture—using this curious method—were indeed [actually] contained in those passages. [. . .]

It is thus clear that the Gemara considered its interpretation and derivation method as entirely truthful exegesis—even to the point of being the only truthful exegesis, without tolerance for any others. Against the Gemara's method, any contradiction of a possibly awakening exegetical conscience not yet anticipated (even where it is it stirred in the dark) was quickly silenced. Furthermore, Talmudic *aggadah*, which was not so strictly separated from halakhah, had no clear appreciation of the natural meaning of Scripture. Rather, *aggadah* and halakhah were interwoven, and only those parts of *aggadah* that had no influence on legal observance were treated more leniently; because they were [thought] inferior, there was no reason for serious discussions and legal consequences. Thus, such parts were left to subjective arbitrariness. [. . .]

[Later, however,] a certain sense emerged that the *drash* sometimes (I would even say, mostly) foisted an unnatural interpretation on the verse, and that next to this interpretation there existed a natural, "simple" explanation, now rightly called *pshat*, which sits opposed to turbid and convoluted exegesis. But the original, artificial interpretation was not rejected, and the *pshat* played only a subordinate role. This dark foreboding of a double interpretation of biblical passages gave rise sometimes, but only very seldomly, to the question of what, next to the *drash*, was actually the simple explanation of the verse (*pshita de-qra be-mai ketiv*).

This question led to a new question: What should one do with the "simple explanation"? What legal validity did it have? In theory, [the answer to] this question was soon settled: *Ein miqra yotze midei peshuto*— "no biblical passage can be understood from its literal meaning." In this way, the simple explanation was granted full rights without depriving the artificial interpretation of anything. But what was easily said as a general theorem raised great difficulties in its practical application. First of all, both Mishnah and Baraita, as well as the older Gemara, completely ignored this simple explanation, such that the regulations that *could possibly* be learned from it were thereby voided, even if they stood alongside the *drash*-interpretations. Secondly, these interpretations frequently stood in sharp contradiction to the meaning that is reasonable for any natural form of explanation. Therefore, one had to remain content with the general statement and let the matter of its practical application rest—for the awareness of [any sort of] natural exegesis was still too weak, and arose only in those cases where the healthy meaning was too-blatantly violated. This [sort of thing] happened not only through an almost silent but consistent dismissal of the natural explanation and a neglect of its consequences, but at some places simply by blatantly admitting that the general statement was not applicable at all. [. . .]

So, our above-stated results are confirmed: The Mishnah already began to feel the need to verify its expansion of the law by using the biblical substratum. But while the Mishnah admitted that it was often impossible to produce this evidence, it was also alarmed about the fate of some of its regulations, which did not have biblical explanations—until they were eventually found. This pursuit of biblical justification led to a method of interpretation that increasingly departed from natural exegesis. Eventually, natural explanations were fully replaced by this method. Natural exegesis entirely lost its rights, and at some point there was no longer even a name left for it. The Beraita went further down this dubious road in developing this method, yet still in the belief that natural exegesis would follow therewith. Hence, we find in the Beraita that some reckless interpretations are overruled because they contradict the healthy [i.e., natural] sense of the passage. Only the Babylonian Gemara developed this technique to its fullest consequence; it was determined not to leave a single law without biblical justification. Thus, the Gemara eventually arrived at such a reckless and violent treatment of the biblical word that once again the simple sense of the verse began to assert its right. But this beginning was a very quiet one, such that although a general rule acknowledged the right of a natural exegesis, this rule was almost never applied.

Who knows? Had scholarship in Babylon proceeded peacefully, would not the natural sense have asserted its right much more decisively and finally caused a radical change? But it was a time of unrest; suddenly the Talmud was closed and became an untouchable authority. Thus, the conflict between the authoritative-but-reckless interpretation—on which the entire traditional observance of the law was based—and the natural sense of Scripture was forcefully perpetuated for many centuries.

SAMUEL HOLDHEIM (1806–60)

Samuel Holdheim (b. 1806, Kempen, Posen; d. 1860, Berlin) was a leader of the German Reform movement and a proponent of extreme liturgical and theological change. Raised in a traditional household, Holdheim excelled at talmudic learning from an early age, and in his teens moved to Prague and then Berlin to study philosophy, history, and languages. Called to be rabbi in Frankfurt-on-the-Oder (1836–40), then Schwerin (1840–46), in 1847 he became rabbi of Berlin's liberal community, Congregation of the Jewish Reform Alliance (*Jüdische Reformgenossenschaft*), where he made radical changes: moving Sabbath worship to Sundays, leading most of the service in German rather than Hebrew, eliminating the second-day celebration of festivals, and officiating at Jewish-Christian marriages. Active in many rabbinic controversies then coursing through German Judaism, he was a strong, often vociferous (perhaps even cantankerous) proponent for liberal reforms. He continued to preside over his community and write extensively on Jewish theology, halakhah, and history until his sudden and untimely death at age fifty-four. Having sparred with most of the rabbinical establishment of his day, his burial in the "Rabbis' row" of the Jewish cemetery caused a major stir among Berlin Jewry. Abraham Geiger delivered the eulogy.

This chapter includes two excerpts from *Das Ceremonialgesetz im Messiareich* (The ceremonial law in the kingdom of the messiah), Holdheim's extensive essay on the possibilities and necessities of Jewish reform in a postrabbinical era.[33] He speaks about what he calls (following Moses Mendelssohn) "ceremonial law" or "separating ceremonies," by which he means the elements of Judaism that force its adherents into behaving differently from those around them, and therefore separating themselves individually and communally from other peoples, groups, nations, or religions. For Holdheim, Judaism's overweening adherence to difference has had a perfectly justifiable role in history, particularly when the surrounding nations were either pagan, partaking in practices abhorrent to the ethical values of Jewish law, or hostile toward the Jews. But in the messianic period, "where all humans will acknowledge and worship the true God . . . separate holiness of the people would be an utter absurdity—empty, meaningless, futile, aimless—unworthy of the highest wisdom of God." And, Holdheim argues, such an era is the period we are now entering: universal rights and the singular divinity of God are being acknowledged everywhere. As such, Jews must not fall behind in their recognition of this dawning emancipatory, messianic age. Just as Judaism was an ethical leader in the ancient world of the pagans, so too Judaism must be a leader in modernity, embracing the Jewish Bible's long-propounded universal morality and forgoing the overt ritual signs that for so many millennia separated the Jews from the rest of the world's peoples.

The Ceremonial Law in the Kingdom of the Messiah (1845)

Translated by George Y. Kohler

The holiness of the Jewish people—if there will ever be a Jewish people again—relies on its relation to the other, the pagan peoples and the strict separation from them, for which purpose separating ceremonial law became necessary. The ceremonial laws are the expressions, that is, the outwardly manifested appearance, of the theocratic holiness of the people. But in the messianic kingdom, where a restricted theocracy is replaced by the most liberal universalism, by the universal government of God, eliminating all national distinctions, where the place of the Jewish people is taken by humanity itself, where all humans will acknowledge and worship the true God—here such a separate holiness of the people would be an utter absurdity—empty, meaningless, futile, aimless—unworthy of the highest wisdom of God.[34] This is because theocracy is essentially nothing else but the negation of paganism, and in order to keep this negation alive in our consciousness it needs ceremonial law. But why and to what end should the Jews still separate themselves from the other peoples, after conciliation is achieved, after the process of the unification of all human beings in truthful belief—a process that demanded millennia of troublesome struggle—is happily accomplished? For a purely spiritual perception of the messianic age the continued existence of a separate people and a separate ceremonial law, that is, the continued existence of a Jewish theocracy within a monotheistic humanity, is a crying absurdity that cannot possibly be held up by an intelligent people.

But if ceremonial law is thus not eternal and is doomed to disappear without a trace in the messianic kingdom, even its validity in the present is very dubious. If the rabbis try to retain the one or the other ceremonial law (in case we will be suddenly surprised by the Messiah), then the same applies in the reverse, and one might abandon some laws for this very reason.[35]But apart from such infantilisms, a higher seriousness should challenge us to earnestly try and bring about the messianic age, to increasingly eradicate separating elements, and to magnify the spiritual unity and love of humanity. We need to ultimately abandon all our harsh references to others, born from our politically and ethnically separatist consciousness, and to unite with the peoples and the other humans in heartfelt and pure humanly relations. To speak still today of laws of separation, even in the interest of religion, would mean to postpone the messianic kingdom more and more. Theocracy has perished, and out of the last flames consuming the Temple and the Altar the Messiah was born.

Not only for our purely spiritual view of messianism, but also for the rabbinic view, must it be considered a great inconsistency to speak of the eternal validity of ceremonial law. Although the rabbis expect a personal and political Messiah from the House of David who will reestablish the old cult and with it a political rebirth of the Jewish people as the ruler over all peoples,[36] they still admit that this Messiah will force all humanity to accept the Seven Noahide Laws[37] and turn all humans into true monotheists (*b'nei noach*).[38] Only for the Jews alone the ceremonial law will be retained as the legacy for the congregation of Jacob, while all other peoples will be Noachites—if they do not convert to Judaism, although, actually, they should not be accepted, because the Jewish people is supposed to be very happy then, as in the times of David and Solomon. Thus also for the rabbis the question arises: To what end is retaining so many laws of separation if there no longer are, and cannot be, any idolaters?[39] What then is the meaning of one ceremonial law or another that only aims at separation and distancing from idolatrous customs? Nevertheless, even then the rabbis would prohibit marriages with non-Jewish peoples, only because they will still not be ready to give up the holy character of the Jewish people. We are willing to excuse this weakness of the rabbis in the specific case of intermarriage with allegedly less holy peoples, since it seems to be justified on the basis of their view that, as long as the Jews retain the ceremonial law as an exclusive privilege, they are the holy people *par excellence*.[40]

But why retain so many other laws that, according to the clear pronouncement of the Bible, were originally commanded only as a protection against idolatry? Well, the rabbis can never be embarrassed. If they would have something to say in the kingdom of the Messiah—and because they fancy the Messiah to be the most learned of all rabbis, this cannot be denied of them—they would proclaim their common rule:[41] Divine laws, even if they were given only for certain explicitly mentioned purposes and for a certain time, will not expire on their own until God revokes them, even if their purpose is achieved and their time is over. This legal ruling (b. *Beitzah* 5b) is derived from Exod. 19:15 and Deut. 5:27, but they would extend it even to rabbinical regulations that, after these became pointless and arbitrary, could only be revoked in *optima forma* by a competent authority. This demonstrates their *purely legal* approach to religion, and in the same legal way they would not fail to approach laws of separating [Jews from non-Jews] in the Messianic Age.

However, those of today's rabbis who already—and certainly even more so in the messianic condition—approach religion exclusively from a religious viewpoint, must be allowed to ask: Are we not forced to suppose, given God's wisdom, that He will repeal in the messianic fulfilment all laws of separation, because it becomes empty and meaningless—as He once, at the occasion of the revelation at Sinai, repealed the commandment *al tagshu el isha* ("do not go near a woman," Exod. 19:15) with the counterorder *shuvu lachem le'ahaleichem* ("return to your tents," Deut. 5:26)? Certainly we are. But if so, what is the *consistency* to the claim to the eternity of ceremonial law, when its abrogation from the beginning must have been part of the plan of providence for bringing about the messianic age, as it is necessarily substantiated by God's wisdom and love? And would not the same wisdom that will once completely repeal ceremonial law already now command a partial suspension, in accordance with the progress of the kingdom of the Messiah, of all those laws of separation that stand in the way of the messianic fulfilment? And will the call from the mouth of the Messiah—"go to all the peoples and become part of their national life"—be more distinct and definite than the verdict of eighteen centuries of history? Is this less [distinct and definite] than to say: "You should no longer separate yourselves from other peoples, as I commanded you in the Pentateuch, but unite with them"? Thus, however much rabbinism might try to protect itself and hide behind its claim of the eternity of ceremonial law, in the messianic kingdom it will be unable to save its consistency when it is confronted with unbridled and all-encompassing love of humanity. *Theocracy* and *idolatry* are *relative* terms, ones that can only coexist with each other or be abandoned together.[42] The eternity of a Jewish theocracy without its counterpart, idolatry, must even from the rabbinical standpoint appear to be aimless and unfounded. [. . .]

History teaches how laws of separation are making the divide between human beings only bigger and more inviolable. Exactly because the daughter religions [of Judaism] are unable to overcome those barriers of faith, we must lift them up above those barriers with our living example, since we are the ones who have made more progress towards the messianic kingdom. As long as this union with them was *impossible*, that is, as long as polytheism wielded its ruinous power over humanity and threatened to consume even us ourselves, we were forced to hold on to each other and to put up an even stronger resistance; we were *compelled* to cling to each other and close the ranks of the true monotheists, waiting for a better future. All the time that the transformation of polytheism into a particularistic and separatist Christian idea antagonistically repelled us, we had to avoid the appearance of obtrusiveness, if only in the interest of our own dignity. We were forced to stand back with our universal love of humanity, because it was repelled.

But why shouldn't we now, when on the one hand the danger has dissipated and the duty of self-preservation is no longer forcing us to do so, and when on the other hand our obligingness is less than before rejected with general hostility, when also with our Christian brothers the meanspirited particularistic view of an exclusive worthiness and authority of the Christian religious conviction makes way for the thought of universal love of humanity and the universal rights of man—why shouldn't we now meet them with the idea of universal love and brotherly union? Why wait until this idea fully takes hold and will come into practice also outside our own circle? He who has found a truth *first* should be the *first* to put it on the altar of humanity and should not hesitate while this truth is found—in difficult, roundabout ways—without him. His merit to have found it is forfeited if he—instead of spreading the truth—encloses it deep in his bosom. If this truth is a *truth of life*, a truth that should be practiced, one is even more obliged to hasten and make it real in life and to demonstrate its power by living example. Why wait with the striving for an earnest unification until others have realized its value, when in our religious feeling and thinking no impediment against it is left?

To be sure, to impose oneself [upon others] will keep everyone else from a feeling of honor [i.e., will keep them from a feeling of honor at being the first to implement a universal love of humanity in their religious community]. But to declare this a religious obligation, to declare that from a religious point of view nothing stands in the way of such striving, this cannot be withheld from anyone if we believe in the truth of it. We Jews have a higher duty to lead all the other confessions in the spirit of universalism and the ideas that will be established in the kingdom of the Messiah, because we believe that we are commanded from the very beginning to facilitate the kingdom of the Messiah through our election, and to prepare it through our history.

Now that we have moved on from legal particularism to universal messianism, we are even less allowed to hesitate and not announce this truth to all others, especially to those for whom legal particularism was just transformed into another form. And we must not leave it at the mere announcement; we are to prove it by deed. Our messianic idea is not that all human beings will become Jews, but that the Jews will become humans; after all, others have made this development, too. Christian particularism, because it views its election as not bound to a certain people but to a certain faith, is superior to legal particularism—this we admit—but messianism, because it is bound *to man himself*, is still superior. We owe our taking the lead especially to the believers in Christianity, who in fact inherited their own particularism only from Judaism. Although Christian particularism has not dealt with us in a milder way than we dealt with the inhabitants of Canaan, and although Christianity had to repulse us because it saw in Judaism only the legal aspect, that was inferior to itself, and not the messianic aspect, that was superior to Christianity—still we should repay all that by love. We should prove to Christianity through this love that the idea of universalism is still larger than all ever so refined particularism, even if it is superior to legal particularism.

Further, we should not forget that although all Christian peoples and states excluded us from the life of their people and their state, because *they* saw us as strangers, we are still not a separate people, let alone the ancient Jewish people. Hence we have to give up those specific concepts of a chosen people and all related particularistic laws, if only in the interest of the purity of our Mosaic religion, in case we want to see in the *decay* of our erstwhile peoplehood the *beginning* of the messianic kingdom, in the deconstruction of legal particularism the cornerstone for the construction of a universalism that is built on pure humanism. May, therefore, the daughter religions undergo a process of purification as they like; may they pause on the standpoint of their refined particularism and exclude us from the life of their states and peoples for as long as necessary, because we lack this specific moment of Christian particularism. We, from our own standpoint, if we understand it correctly, must no longer talk about *separating* ceremonies. We are not allowed to corrupt our own task as the herald and the harbinger of the messianic era. In us every human being must find his brother; we are free to believe in the power of truth, in its eventual victory over prejudice. We must not hamper this victory of love and truth and stand in the way of the erection of the messianic kingdom by giving a narrow-minded example of a remnant of a legal particularism that God has forever wiped out.

LEOPOLD STEIN (1810–82)

Leopold Stein (b. 1810, Burgpreppach; d. 1882, Frankfurt) was a rabbi, writer, and leader of the moderate German Reform movement, most prominently in Frankfurt, where he lived for the second half of his life. Assuming leadership over the main community in Frankfurt in 1844 after a long struggle between traditional and liberal factions within the community (the Orthodox eventually broke away altogether in 1860), he remained in his post until 1862, during which time he introduced a series of liturgical reforms, including the recitation of some prayers in German, the introduction of a triennial reading of the Torah, a weekly sermon, and the elimination of the *Musaf* service. Thus in Frankfurt Stein became the main opponent of Samson Raphael Hirsch, who founded German Neo-Orthodoxy in the city (see above). After 1862, Stein resigned as chief rabbi and receded somewhat from public view. He spent his final two decades working on dramatic writings and translations, founding and teaching at a school for Jewish girls, and preaching at the Westend Union, a Reform congregation.

This selection, "The Necessity of the Written Law," is taken from a collection of Stein's later writings *Die Schrift des Lebens: Inbegriff des gesammten Judenthums in Lehre, Gottesverehrung und Sittengesetz (Dogma, Cultus und Ethik)* (The scripture of life: the epitome of all Judaism in doctrine, worship, and moral law [dogma, cult, and ethics]).[43] In the pages translated below, Stein is concerned with understanding the relation between what he calls "inner law" (something akin to natural law) and Mosaic law (laws given—either via revelation or philosophical deduction—rather than intuited). For many pious people, Stein notes, there is no need for a written ethical code; each person observes what is right and just through his own inner orientation, her own moral compass. Yet without a written law, Stein says, that which is immoral and unjust—like the sacrifice of children, virgins, or widows; widespread lewdness and drunkenness; or legally sanctioned theft—can easily become mistaken for virtue. Therefore, in order that such "arbitrariness on a large scale . . . be controlled," the Torah was given, "so that the vacillating good, different for different people, would become an unchangeable, determined good, valid for everyone." The Torah is the epitome of this unchanging good and, notes Stein, is widely acknowledged as such, since its basic premises have become enshrined in the foundational laws of nations and states across the world. Therefore, this text becomes an interesting contribution to the ancient and still relevant question in religious thought: Why must not only ritual, but also rational, moral law be revealed? In addition, Stein strikingly emphasizes a standard doctrine of nineteenth-century German Jewish theology: the intrinsic connection between ethics and monotheism. (Compare with Joseph Lewin Saalschuetz, "Ethical Monotheism," chapter 4.)

The Necessity of the Written Law (1877)

Translated by Samuel J. Kessler

> Exod. 24:12: "The LORD said to Moses, 'Come up to Me on the mountain and wait there, and I will give you the stone tablets with the teachings and commandments which I have inscribed to instruct them.'"

The written, detailed law was initially necessary as a *civil law*. Noah and Job, who, according to the testimony of Scripture, were found to be righteous according to the inner law, and which the prophet Ezekiel (14:14) contrasts as the generally accepted pattern of piety over a whole world of perdition—they were *individual* personalities. And that general inner law—that one becomes morally free by setting limits to one's covetous nature, and, in the society in which one lives, respecting the rights of others and contributing to their well-being as much as possible—is so simple that we can well imagine how distinguished persons—whose life is the living revelation of God—can shape their moral and religious disposition out of themselves in word and deed without ever having had or having need of a written law. While the law is otherwise supposed to have a moral effect, it immediately appeared in them as a custom. And the account of Job's pious life in the closing speech of his justification (chapter 31) is such a heavenly description of righteousness as no more glorious one has flowed from Horeb.

Sinai, however, speaks to a *people*, to a numerous community of individual, often gifted and differently striving personalities, who, through the common law, should first come together to form a higher unity and be trained in holy morality. *Writing* was absolutely necessary here, engraved on stone tablets, immortalized as the "Word of the Covenant," which binds the individual within himself and at the same time binds him to the totality to which he subordinates himself. Raised out of arbitrariness and selfishness, the many thousandfold should become one will, and from the given will of God—who can only will good—

every single will should find its sure guiding line, and in this, through voluntary submission, learn to preserve its moral dignity. Because, as the freedom of many is bound and regulated by a higher law, the life of all gains in glory, in beauty and exaltation in God, just as the words of the rapturous singer gain free upswing precisely because he adheres to measure and law in arranging and structuring them. That which is excessive produces neither beauty nor freedom. The law creates the unity and harmony of the people.

There is also another aspect that is no less important. The inner law probably tells us that we should only do that which is good for us or others, but on the other hand refrain from doing anything that would ruin us or others. All peoples and religions are so necessarily united on this, as well as on the high value of virtue and the despicability of vice, when human nature is everywhere and at all times in its fundamental essence one, homogeneous.[44] And yet, with this agreement in general, peoples and religions differ widely in the most important things, in the more detailed definition of *what is individually good and moral,* with some [people and religions] considered excellent while others are called reprehensible.—All agree that achieved proficiency in good is a virtue, and yet how different is the virtue of the Spartan from that of the Athenian, of the virtue of the Greeks from that of the Romans, and even criminal acts are not infrequently celebrated as religious among otherwise educated peoples.

Here are just a few supporting instances. With the Indians, until recently the widow of a deceased was burned with him; and that was a virtue.[45] With the Phoenicians, children were placed in glowing arms of Baal-Moloch;[46] and that was virtue.[47] Among the Babylonians, virgins were sacrificed and women customarily sacrificed conjugal fidelity in the service of Mylitta; and that was virtue.[48] With Greeks and Romans—and strangely enough, even a Talmudist let himself be carried away into a similar excess for the Purim festival![49]—the celebrated wine god was glorified with extravagant sensuality; and that was virtue.[50] Likewise, what is said among the Spartans, that in certain cases the boys are allowed to steal, if only they demonstrate the laudable skill of not being caught.[51] As well as in our days, opinions emerge which say "property is theft," thus declaring the expropriation of property to be a high virtue.[52]

In particular, however, we must not fail to point out the memorable circumstance that we find reported from the *pre-Sinai* period of instances of fear of God, which, even from the standpoint of biblical piety, were later recorded as a disgrace. Abraham, who married his half-sister Sarah,[53] and Jacob, who married the sisters Rachel and Leah.[54] We see here both patriarchs commit acts which in their time did not cause moral scandal, yet both marriages are later listed at *Sinai* as great crimes.[55]

So here, too, arbitrariness on a large scale had to be controlled. It was absolutely necessary that one day the moral law should be proclaimed solemnly and with divine respect, so that the vacillating good, different for different people, would become an unchangeable, determined good, valid for everyone. *One God and one right for all humanity!*

The Ten Commandments from Sinai, with the numerous commandments of justice and love that follow it as a more detailed explanation, is the law of the world. And the Talmud celebrates this world-unifying thought in the [. . .] famous dictum[56] that every word from Sinai was immediately translated into the seventy original languages.[57] Now, the general inner law [of Job and Noah and others], that was beyond all interpretation, became the general outward law [of Sinai], for the purpose that as such it could effect back upon the inside, that it could become the unquestionable duty of conscience. The protection of *life, family, marriage, freedom, property*, justice, and humanity against *all*—these were glorious basic laws, and, for nation after nation, unshakable pillars of their constitutions, in order to one day become the bearers of the temple of all humanity.

The following, in conclusion. In addition to the natural law which is in the heart, what was written at Sinai was necessary because it was supposed to offer numerous commandments which by themselves do not flow out of the natural law. But, once given, they have also proven themselves so wise and in such accordance with human nature that one willingly submits to them.

HEINRICH GRAETZ (1817–91)

Heinrich Graetz (b. 1817, Zerkow, Posen; d. 1891, Breslau) was perhaps the most famous Jewish historian of his generation. Author of the eleven-volume *Geschichte der Juden von den ältesten Zeiten bis auf die Gegenwart* (History of the Jews from the earliest times to the present, 1853–75), he wrote knowledgeably about many areas of Jewish thought, from biblical history and exegesis to Rabbinic thought to contemporary theology. Beginning his education in Orthodox schools in Posen, he received his bachelor's degree in Breslau and his doctorate in Jena. He then spent the better part of a decade in various locales in Germany, including briefly with Samson Raphael Hirsch in Oldenberg, before finally accepting a teaching position at the new Jewish Theological Seminary in Breslau led by Zecharias Frankel (see chapter 1). He would stay at JTS Breslau for the remainder of his career, teaching history, exegesis, and Talmud.

Graetz's overall thinking is difficult to characterize. A historian by nature, he was deeply invested in Jewish communal existence and valued his service at a rabbinical college for its ability to influence the course of modern Judaism. At the same time, he was a strict adherent of Orthodoxy in his younger days, and a strong opponent of Reform for his whole life.

The selection is from a short book, *Briefwechsel einer englischen Dame über Judenthum und Semitismus* (Correspondence of an English lady about Judaism and Semitism), which was published anonymously—perhaps to allow Graetz greater freedom to historicize and reflect on Judaism beyond accepted traditions—and consists of fifteen letters exchanged between Edith, an English woman, and Graetz (who calls himself "Caspi").[58] In the fourteenth letter, excerpted here, Graetz defends the Jew's adherence to the Bible's rituals and commandments.

Moral and ethical commitments might be the "diamond core" of the biblical message, he writes, and at times the Talmud might have become "a mantle [that] disfigures the object in need of protection," but to dismiss the commandments "lock, stock, and barrel" leads to a moral free-for-all, a breakdown of community, and a loosening of the very ethical commitments the Bible cares about most deeply. As Graetz writes, with characteristic vividness, "The fence [of Jewish law around the Torah] is supposed to keep the clumsy foot from crushing the delicate plants in the garden." The text also documents Graetz's conviction that Judaism is superior to the Christian religion, whose theological language and concepts he frequently adopts here in a provocative way.

Correspondence of an English Lady about Judaism and Semitism: Fourteenth Letter (1883)

Translated by Maren Scheurer

I may [. . .] not leave your derisive remarks about the rites of Judaism and the Talmud without a response, even more so as you desire, with the anxious thoughtfulness of a mother, a standard for the religious education of your children.

First of all, please leave the Talmud out of it, as this is just a cheap trump for ignoramuses and malevolent people. Knowledgeable people, however, find rich, as yet unburied ethical treasures in it. In any case, the bright side in it by far outweighs the dark side. It is just that the form and methods of its exposition are baroque and not to everyone's taste. The Talmud was, as it were, the felt winter coat for the organism of Judaism in the most glacial times of all, the prickly protective blanket for the delicate miracle flower. Of course, such a mantle disfigures the object in need of protection and almost effaces its essence; but where it was necessary to ward off death, caring for decorative drapery would have been very inappropriate. With the onset of spring the disfiguring mantle falls by itself. How much has already crumbled away from Talmudism since a fresh breeze blew through Jewry with Moses Mendelssohn and the beginning of emancipation! Even the arch-talmudists are not capable of denying this; they sense it in their own midst. Has spring completely arrived for the Jewish tribe?[59] The opinions diverge. The gloomy experience of the last year has proven right those who have claimed that the medieval winter is nowhere near over for Israel.[60]

Incidentally, the Talmud is just the utmost consequence of the ritualism that the main document of Judaism, the Pentateuch (the Torah), peremptorily demands, though not as a fundamental dogma—this is considered to be the higher ethics and the higher idea of God—but merely as a means for the *realization* of the cardinal principles.

For Judaism—though, as it were, finished and full-grown from birth—has still formed, extended, and unfolded itself, and has thus made itself viable. The ethical ideals were supposed to be incarnated, as it were, in a national tribe, and the tribe assume the apostolate and martyrdom for them, a seemingly fantastical mandate, impossible to realize.[61] This tribe has lived in servitude for generations and was afflicted with a slavishly low mindset or had even become thoughtless. It had to fight for the occupation of its own land for a long time and became barbaric. Surely, the bulk of this people worshiped and treated their Jehovah, the God of their fathers, no different than the Moabites treated their [chief God] Chemosh. In this respect Renan is right, but we have to exclude a minority, however small, who did not hold up the Ark of the Covenant in heathen ways as a palladium promising victory in war, but venerated the two stone tablets deposed therein for their *ethical content*.[62] The neighborhood of the Canaanites, Phoenicians—who were by no means exterminated—seduced the tribes into sheer idol cult, into the worship of Adonis and Astarte as national Gods on a par with Jehovah, and this cult flattered carnality too much not to find any followers.[63] You, my friend, who are so well-read in the Bible, know that Queen *Athaliah*, the daughter of the wicked Phoenician *Jezebel*, introduced the cult of Baal and Astarte into the temple of Jerusalem and implemented it with such violent measures that those who despised these idols had to hide their sentiments.[64] Admittedly, a salutary time of reaction came to pass; the high priest Jehoiada enforced it prudently.[65] But it was easier to banish the heathen cult from the temple than the heathen conviction from the hearts of the people. Suchlike secession from pure Jehovahdom and the reaction against it has often repeated itself, as you know, in ancient Israelite history.[66]

The ritualism in Judaism can be traced back to these occurrences.[67] It was designed as a means to banish the heathen spirit from the hearts of people whose thoughts had become sluggish. Indeed, it presents itself as such a means: "so that you do not follow your heart and eyes in your lustfull urge" [Num. 15:39]—or: "thus you shall be reminded" [Num. 15:40]. A motivation that is given in the Laws of the Pentateuch tells us that the entire sacrificial system was only permitted so that the proclivity for offering sacrifices would not entice the entire people to sacrifice to the orgiastic idols of heathendom: "and that they may offer their sacrifices no more to the goat-demons after whom they stray" [Lev. 17:7]—the Talmudists designate the ritualistic provisions introduced by them as a *fence line*.[68] The fence is supposed to keep the clumsy foot from crushing the delicate plants in the garden. Admittedly, the Talmudists have not infrequently done too much of a good thing, have put up fence after fence and thus, as a result of the barricade, have spirited away the eye from the beautiful garden with the resplendent plants. The ritual laws, which take up so much space in the second and third Books of Moses, owe their origin to the same precaution and anxiety; they are fence lines as well.[69] They are, if you like, a kind of Talmudism before the Talmud. But the Talmudists themselves teach and proclaim that in Messianic times—when the ethical ideal will have triumphed everywhere—the ritualism will stop having any meaning.[70] Have we come this far already?[71]

Do not sneer at the rites lock, stock, and barrel; there are many whose expediency within the given circumstances has to be acknowledged. The dietary laws, which are also counted as a part of the ritualism of Judaism, are not agreeable to you. But ask the physiologists whether the type of aliment does not matter to the development of temperament or character. The consumption of blood or of the flesh of wild animals, if it is carried on from generation to generation, surely contributes to barbarization and the excitement of carnal desire.[72] Who knows whether the abstention from certain aliments has not contributed to mellowing the Jewish disposition and to reining in demonic passions?

One of the main accusations concerning the intolerability of the Jews consists in their self-segregation from their heterogeneous surroundings. From Haman up to [Roman historian Publius (Gaius) Cornelius] Tacitus [ca. 56–120 CE], and from him up even to sympathetic political scientists and professors, the reproach is repeated: "separati epulis, discreti cubilibus" [with separate meals and beds apart].[73] (Your son will perhaps understand enough Latin to translate this for you.) Malevolent people call this segregation: "a state within a state." But what would have become of Judaism and its ethical mandate if it had not retreated to its corner to sulk? Just keep in mind that all heathen cults were orgiastic, that all of them worshiped Aphrodite under various different names—and this has caused the downfall of the heathen nations. Ancient Israel was seduced into this cult often enough, and these relapses constitute the black pages in its history. The effort of all those who were filled with the ethical ideal of Judaism, especially of the prophets exalted by God, was needed to overcome this proclivity; otherwise the ideal would have been dissipated before it could evolve. Therefore, Judaism could only be preserved and strengthened through rigorous separatism. That is why the old law emphasizes the necessity of a partition wall: "You shall be holy to Me, for I the LORD am holy, and I have set you apart from other peoples to be Mine" [Lev. 20:26]. How many of these so-called rites may have just this separatist significance? The national-historical significance of the three joyful [annual pilgrimage] celebrations is given in the law itself.[74] Originally, they may very well have been celebrations of nature, but the energy of the religious assimilative force shows itself even more significantly in tying them to the beginnings of the development of the nation.[75] And Christianity, at least official Christianity, must always build on the recollection of this fact as well. Would you, in all seriousness, want to miss the Day of Atonement?[76] If it didn't exist, it would have to be invented. To renounce our corporeality for twenty-four hours, to reinstall harmony with God, i.e., one's conscience, and, as the ill-reputed Talmud demands imperiously, to put the reconciliation with those people whom we have hurt in word and deed over the reconciliation with God, that is by no means to be laughed at.[77] And do not even the prosaic-looking Jews, who celebrate this day with devotion, display a shimmer of ideality?

However, in the course of time the relation and the priorities have changed. The prophets, the representatives of Judaism in biblical times, stress in the strongest possible terms the ethical within Judaism, reprimand with ardent tongues the moral vices in the people and in their leaders, pass over ritualism with silence or, at most, defend the sanctification of the Sabbath. The teachers of the law who followed the prophets, in contrast, the representatives of post-biblical times, put their emphasis on ritual. Even of the sacrificial system, Jeremiah, for example, speaks with little appreciation: "Add your burnt offerings to your other sacrifices and eat the meat. I did not speak with your fathers or command them in the day that I brought them out of the land of Egypt, concerning burnt offerings or sacrifices. Do judgment and justice, administer to the needs of the poor and needy, that is to know God" [Jer. 7:21–22 and 22:15–16, following Graetz]. In contrast, the first teacher of the law in post-biblical or post-prophetic times who gets a chance to speak, Simeon the Righteous, voices an entirely different language.[78] The Jewish community rests on three things: "on the recognition of the Torah, on sacrificial service, and on charity" [PA 1:2]. The ethical takes the back row.

MANUEL JOEL (1826–90)

Manuel Joel (b. 1826, Birnbaum, Posen; d. 1890, Breslau) was a philosopher and historian of philosophy associated with the moderate

Reform movement and the early *Wissenschaft des Judentums*. Educated mainly in Berlin, where he studied Classical languages and philosophy with the leading scholars of the day, Joel can be credited with the almost single-handed rediscovery not just of much of medieval Jewish philosophy—including the writings of Maimonides, Ibn Gabirol, and Gersonides—but of the relationship between Jewish thought and Christian Scholasticism. Indeed, Joel wrote the first-ever academic work on Maimonides' *Guide*. His writings on historical philosophy and religious development, published as *Blicke in die Religionsgeschichte* (Views into religious history), would subsequently be published in four volumes, 1876–83.

In 1854, after receiving his doctorate from Halle, Joel, only 28, joined the inaugural faculty of the new Jewish Theological Seminary led by Zecharias Frankel (see chapter 1). A decade later he left the seminary to become rabbi of the New Synagogue, the main liberal community in Breslau, replacing Abraham Geiger. For the rest of his career, Joel navigated a moderate path through Reform, defending traditional prayer and talmudic learning while also participating in the modernization of Jewish historical research and advocating for German Jewry's integration into broader European culture.

The following excerpt is taken from part two of Joel's two-part 1869 essay, *Zur Orientierung in der Cultusfrage* (Toward an orientation in the question of cult).[79] In part one, Joel seeks to identify the origins of the "cult," or what we might more familiarly call "religious practice." Why does the cult arise at all? Are such irrational parts of a religion still—if they ever were—necessary? Or should only the rational, that is, ethical ideas, be preserved in the modern era? This was one of the most important questions in Jewish theology in the nineteenth century. As Joel writes, the cult was born from the same inner forces that give rise to such normal aspects of life as family and social communities—that is, from the urge to "join forces with others in expressing the . . . feelings that inspire oneself." But, he notes, the act of joining others actually changes the nature of those personal, inner feelings, transforming them into the "representation no longer of an individual but of a communal, collective sensation," and in this way imbuing them with great cohesive power. The cult, he insists, is not an arbitrary set of practices and rituals. It is instead the collective expression of the personal inner longing to relate to the Divine.

Thus established, the second part of the essay, subtitled "The Jewish Cult" and excerpted here, attempts to chart a middle ground through ritual reform, arguing on the one side for the need to recognize the historical development of religion, but defending on the other side the truth of religious experience and longing, and the importance of a given community—in this case, the Jewish community—remaining unified in its cultic expressions.[80] "Judaism still forms a unified body today," Joel concludes, "precisely because [its majority] emphasize what is common more than what divides them."

Toward an Orientation in the Question of Cult (1869)

Translated by Samuel J. Kessler

The Israelite consciousness is, through its teaching, determined and tuned differently than the Christian or the Muslim [consciousness]. In the Jewish cult, a different central fact will be the object of cultic celebration [that is unlike those] in the cults of other denominations. Our central fact is the declaration of unity, and the relation of Israel and its peoples to this one God.

But not only do *doctrines* have a determining effect on the mind. *History* does as well. All religions—the ideas of which do not live only as vague and unfixed traditions in people's heads, and which have been recorded from the outset by the *scriptures*—also have an historical plane, in which the present maintains a connection with the past. In the cult, therefore, if it is a normal one, it does not just express the *momentary* religious life that permeates a community.[81] Instead, all *historical* memories are likewise deliberately maintained, to exercise their influence on the mind and seek their cultic expressions.

Hence, the cult of every religious community that has a history cannot, intrinsically, be without a certain ancient stamp. Hence, even the best-intentioned attempts to make it merely an expression of what is *generally human* must necessarily fail, for it turns on a lack of edification. There is not today—just as at no time has there ever been—a human being in general; what is *generally* human appears at all times only in very *specific* form. There is no flower and no tree in general. In the nature of things, a flower and a tree are realized only in a rose, a tulip, etc., or in an oak, a spruce, etc. Hence, the Israelite does not simply wish to show what is generally *human* in himself but also that which satisfies his *Israelite* consciousness, just as a Christian would not declare himself satisfied if what was really Christian were not expressed in his cult.

Having indicated what is to be done with the *content* of the Jewish cult, it will now be appropriate to say something about its form as well. Which form is the best? Obviously, the one that best fits the content. There is no absolute best form, as a form that is excellent for one content could easily be unsuitable for *another*. Hence, those who believe that every possible form applies to every possible content are mistaken. The content creates for itself the form appropriate to it. And the necessity for cultural changes arises only where either the content has ceased to be a real expression of the consciousness living in the community or the form does not reflect the content in a dignified and appropriate way.

Here we come to—as one usually puts it—the burning question of the present: Can pieces of a cult become obsolete? Can the need arise in a religious community for significant changes to the existing prayers or other forms of the cult?

I know that some will smile at the question; others will reject the thought.[82] He will smile, who is in so little doubt about the right to change that he considers the raising of the question to be something completely superfluous. He who rejects the thought doesn't want—as one usually puts it—anything shaken up. But we cannot be satisfied either with the one who smiles or the one who rejects. We need to elaborate on the real meaning of the question.

Well, I do not think I am wrong in saying that there is no reasonable Jew—not even someone who counts himself among the most resolute conservatives—who will simply deny the question and reject as improper whether there could be any beneficial and necessary changes to the ritual whatsoever. He will only act on one principle, according to which he will deem the change as either permissible or as an assassination attempt [on the whole religion]. At first, he will easily see that historical circumstances must have had an influence on the addition and omission of particular prayers. For example, even if otherwise unfamiliar with the history of prayer, he will no doubt understand how [the People of] Israel—while still in Palestine—could not have prayed: "But because of our sins we have been exiled from our land" [*Musaf* prayer, Rosh Hashanah], etc. Nor will he be able to find any valid reason why historical, indeed climatic, conditions might still not retain an influence on the formulation of prayer to this day.[83] But frankly, that does not get to the point of the question. The real meaning of the question is much deeper—one that must be considered from every point of view.

The question is whether things, which, though the expression of *dogmatic* ideas, may likewise be brought into the flow of historical movement. For the following can be said: Every positive religion has certain dogmas which it regards as fixed, and which, with their denial, a member of [that religion] stops confessing [the religion altogether]. The proposition that Judaism has no dogmas is an ill-considered one, and certainly so when left as indefinite as it is usually left. Surely no positive religion can exist without a dogma. Even the most liberal Jew will have to admit that he must not only deny the existence of God but also any notions of divine essence, and only thereafter could he completely cease being able to have a relationship to religion.[84] But it has never been claimed or asserted that this [i.e., the existence of God] was the *only* dogma. At most it can be said—and certainly to Judaism's benefit—that at no time did a dogmatic fixation of all beliefs, recognized by all as final, come about. Because the Thirteen Articles of Maimonides have been scientifically challenged, they have been reduced to a smaller number. Is that why the synagogue was able to have a number of beliefs recognized by the whole of Jewry and brought to expression in the cult?[85] Does not Scripture, and later religious writings, pose a certain limit for arbitrariness, independent of the forms of belief which emerge for the one or the other from the way one conducts his research [into the Scriptural texts]? So that, for example, something decidedly and unquestionably opposed to Scripture, notoriously contradicting both its spirit and its letter, cannot be described as a real development of Jewish ideas? Here, so I believe, the liberal Jewish theologian must stop and examine his own beliefs. He does not need to accept—and cannot accept—every crass representation of common thinking about the essence of Judaism, about its conception of Scripture, or of the prophets, etc. The truly great theologians of the Middle Ages never shied away from treading new ground in these areas, ground that differed from the conception of the great mass *toto coelo* [by the whole extent of Heaven]. But does that mean he can move around [intellectually] boundless, free? Isn't there a landmark for him, which he is allowed to cross as an individual, but when crossed he must honestly explain: "Now I am no longer *inside* but *outside* of Judaism?"

I will give an example from the Christian world. [German theologian and historian] David Friedrich Strauss [1808–74], having given his conception of Christianity, feels, as an astute and clear mind, that in so doing he may have exceeded the limit that still holds him within Christianity.[86] Thus, he poses the honest question: "But can we still call ourselves Christians?" "I don't think so," he says, "but does the name matter?" Of course, Strauss is speaking about something that constitutes the foundation of Christianity.[87] But what about dogmas and beliefs that are still in flux, that have not yet been brought to a generally recognized conclusion?

To return to Judaism: it has beliefs that have never even been questioned, except by those who have broken away from it directly: [e.g.,] not just the monotheistic conception of the deity but also the fact of prophecy and revelation. [This remains a serious matter,] even if, in relation to their conception, deeper minds [e.g., Spinoza] differed from more common ones. Other [beliefs], like the messianic idea, or the idea of atonement through sacrifice, have a more eventful history (which I do not need to present to the knowledgeable and for which the ignorant may take my word). Nonetheless, the synagogue tacitly came to a certain point of view with regard to them as well, which it then also expresses in the cult. Today, theological research has seized upon these points anew—as it has every right to do—and it must bring [its research] to scientific fruition. How is it now authorized to shape this new phase of the Jewish cult?

Now, *dogmatic* disputes—and here among them we must include the dispute about the dignity of sacrifice—can have various consequences. Either they lead to a *real denominational split in Judaism* (as was the case in Christianity). [. . .] Or [. . .] within a community, which is mainly based on the same faith, differences in matters of faith emerge which, on the one hand, are not so important to justify a real denominational divorce, but on the other hand, are significant enough to create conflict (where the official expression of this conviction is concerned) in the *cult*. . . .

[Now,] questions of *cult* are always of a secondary nature. Wherever there are questions of *cult*, *dogmatic* questions must have preceded them, and not just dogmatic *questions* but, strictly speaking, dogmatic *solutions*. Has that often enough been the case? Have two denominations really formed in Judaism that sharply and precisely enough expressed their dogmatic demarcation from one another? There was once [a denominational split] in Jewish history, at the time of the rise of Karaites.[88] But since then, the Karaites have no longer had any cult questions in common with us. There has also been talk of a Jewish Reformation in recent times. Indeed, we have even received a history of it.[89] But . . . *Judaism still forms a unified body today*, within which, as a matter of course, can be found many trends and opinions in matters of faith, without the majority of them thinking of a divergence and a separation. The majority consists of those who consciously hold on to the common standard, and the spirit of understanding and the fear of God certainly rest on this majority, precisely because they emphasize what is *common* more than what *divides* them. The future of Judaism and Jewry certainly rests on this.

3

The Relevance of Judaism

Much was up for grabs, literally and philosophically, in the nineteenth century. Nations were being founded, new cities constructed, laws changed. The economy, politics, architecture, transportation, gender roles—everything seemed ripe for reinvention or renewal. Even new sports were being created. And religion was no exception.

Emancipation, the granting of civil liberties to Europe's Jews, while slower or more halting than some wished, generally proceeded apace across the decades, affecting every Jewish community from the Atlantic to the Russian border. Its repercussions proved to be momentous, not just for the material benefit of Europe's Jews but upon Jewish thought itself.

One of the fundamental questions to arise from emancipation concerned the *purpose* of Judaism in the modern world. In other words, why did Judaism *as* Judaism, need to continue to exist, if (philosophically speaking) the alternatives (especially Protestant Christianity) offered much the same monotheistic foundations and adhered to many of the same ethical principles?

For nearly all Jewish thinkers, the question was new because, by and large, it had answered itself in pre-Emancipatory times. In bygone eras, immoral undertakings had so deeply corrupted the kingdoms and empires in which Jews lived, and unjust laws had so severely restricted their lives, that Judaism represented one of the few moral buoys in a wine-dark sea. Its fences upon fences, though sometimes obscurantist or parochial, were, on the whole, the high walls necessary to protect a small and powerless people—girded only in the knowledge of God's righteousness and the practicing of divine commandments—against the ceaseless onslaught of generations upon generations of pagan immorality. Judaism had survived the nearly two millennia since Rome's destruction of Jerusalem because it was a moral necessity that it do so: a divine decree, so that God's Word should not be lost in the world.

But then came Emancipation. And as it did, the nations of Europe appeared to be embracing not only their Jewish minorities but also implementing the values that—though they attributed them to Christianity—they shared most clearly with their new Jewish citizens. In such a world enlightened by the ways of universal ethics, might Judaism, long a bastion against raw immorality, fickle tyranny, and baseless cruelty, be unnecessary?

This question—why retain Judaism at a time in which Jews and non-Jews agreed on nearly all the fundamental issues of religion, politics, and culture—had already begun to be asked in the era of Moses Mendelssohn (1729–86). In *Jerusalem,* Mendelssohn had argued that Judaism overlapped with Christianity in all ways moral, and that Judaism made no claims to special prerogatives, but that, owing to its historical lineage, traced back to the Revelation at Sinai, it was incumbent upon Jews to retain their unique rituals. Judaism, as Mendelssohn described it, mattered because the Jews were obligated in particular religious actions, but it offered no philosophical or theological vision distinctly its own.

Mendelssohn's argument was as much politically useful as it was intellectually persuasive—that is to say, it answered the question posed to him as to how he could advocate for Jewish civic equality (i.e., that Jews and Christians could agree on a moral framework for governing a shared society) but continued religious difference (i.e., that Jews and Christians could not agree on a religious framework to express that shared morality). But by the middle of the nineteenth century, it fell to a new generation of Jewish theologians to further attempt to describe why Judaism, as something separate from Christianity, or even from a nascent humanism, ought still to be retained.

As the selections in this chapter attest, the views on this matter were diverse (and touched upon by Samuel Holdheim in the prior chapter). For some, Judaism was the purest form of religion. Devoid of the Trinity and a messianic Human-God, it continued to represent the real religion of the ancient scriptures. A subset of this view held that the task of Judaism was and remained to spread the word of God as far and wide as possible. Christianity might be a handmaiden to this enterprise, but ultimately, too corrupted by Jesus and the saints, it offered an obscure vision of monotheism and biblical ethics. And still for others, Judaism represented a unique type of religion—adaptable and flexible, unfettered by centralized bureaucracy or dogmatic uniformity, and capable of looking critically at and beyond itself. These very characteristics, flexibility and self-critique, which were cultural as much as theological, were lacking in the other monotheisms and thus worth preserving in their Judaic form.

SALOMON FORMSTECHER (1808–89)

Solomon Formstecher (b. 1808, Offenbach; d. 1889, Offenbach) spent the entirety of his long career in the city of his birth, where he was community rabbi from 1842 onward. He engaged with ideas of the German reform, including altering the synagogue prayer service and tempering the focus on halakhah as a central component of Jewish life, although he ultimately demurred from seeking radical change, preferring harmonization and development in Jewish ritual and theology.

Formstecher's most famous book was *Der Religion des Geistes* (Religion of the mind, or Religion of the spirit).[1] (*Geist* can translate, depending on context, as one among the ideas that include "spirit" and "mind" and "reason," a linguistic fluidity that allows German writers to remain both more agnostic on the distinction between emotion and intellect—and more elusive.) In this work, Formstecher argued that Judaism was a logical religion whose rituals and ideas did not necessitate an unprovable preexisting belief (e.g., an immaculate conception) and whose historical development was reflective of a rational and comprehensible unfolding of humanity's increasing knowledge of God and the world.

The selection here is from the book's opening pages, where Formstecher lays out his understanding of the potentials and possibilities of a pure scientific theology, free of the prejudices he sees as endemic to the Christian study of Judaism. A staunch believer in the modern ideal of science (*Wissenschaft*) as a pure form of intellectual inquiry ("scientific research offers only naked, cold truths," he writes near the end of this selection), Formstecher argues that because Judaism does not make irrational demands of faith upon its adherents, Jews are entirely open to scientific inquiry. "Unfettered," he writes, "the Jewish researcher's scientific exploration of his religion advances, prescribing duties of knowledge—and not duties of belief."

Because of this openness to rigorous inquiry, he concludes, it is the responsibility of Jewish scholars to compose their own scientific histories of Judaism, to engage with modern research, and to seize the narrative of Judaism away from Christian scholars. Only then, he believes, will the true nature of Judaism (as opposed to the contorted view advanced by Christian polemicists) be made available for academic study.

Religion of the Spirit (1841)

Translated by Gershon Greenberg

The task to be resolved in this book is that of portraying Judaism as an absolutely necessary appearance in humanity, and to prove that it must still be considered as such. Also, that Judaism, in its essential development, rises into the universal religion of humanity. [. . .] Here, Judaism is to be grasped as a partial manifestation of the human spirit, for itself but also eyed as a totality and indivisible. [. . .]

The strictly scientific method to be followed in this inquiry allows for the presentation of a purely impartial, unconditioned standpoint, with a systematic logical consistency such as to move to a logical conclusion, while stating the sources. It seeks to prove the truth of the subjective judgment, through what is provided objectively. The method is a special property of Jewish theology. The oft-heard remark, that the acceptance of unconditionality itself involves a presupposition, is but a vapid game of a logical wit. Similarly, the assertion that anyone situated within the sphere of religion cannot judge it impartially is false. For it fails to separate between prejudice and interest in judgment.

The Jew advances to judging his religion with a totally different feeling than does the non-Jew. For the Jew, Judaism is a precious playmate from childhood, enveloped by poetical love, a friend of youth, and an ever-welcome house guest during adulthood. Judaism grants counsel, comfort, and consolation during the storms of life. For the Jew, Judaism is a bosom friend of whom one has grown fond. When the fire of this love appears to be extinguished, the Jew still suffers over any rebuke uttered against it. In judging his religion, the Jew brings along a more or less prejudiced heart—but not a prejudiced understanding. A complete philosophical system favorable to Judaism does not repose in the understanding, as the Jew does not find any philosophical system in the independent literature of Judaism.

Therefore, because the Jew finds that what comes down from a professorial chair or from a philosophical lecture directly contradicts the Judaism known to him from life, if the Jew endeavors to deal with his Judaism philosophically, or better, scientifically, he approaches the matter without any self-deception. For he already learned from his first academic study, that when it comes to a scientific treatment, he may allow no voice to his prejudiced heart and must remove the somewhat mechanically taken up philosophical or theological system right from the start—lest he be led to a result which contradicts the Judaism known to him directly. Accordingly, the Jew must begin his research *ab ovo* [from the beginning]. He must independently lay a new foundation for his system.

Otherwise, the Christian researcher will enter into judgment of Judaism.[2] Presumably, the Christian stands at least at that level of education where the Jewish judge is thought to stand, namely, where fanatical hatred against unfamiliar co-religionists, drawn and imbibed from wickedness, has been eliminated from the heart, such that the Christian researcher is liberated from all bias, both for and against Judaism.[3] Not only is such an unprejudiced heart required, but an unprejudiced understanding as well. The Christian judge of Judaism often lacks that understanding. Also, the Christian researcher leaves no room in the heart, beating with love for the Christianity which has become so precious to him, for the influence of scientific research. Instead, all historically observed philosophical and theological systems harmonize so well with the voice of the heart, that with all the striving for unconditionality there is always a residue of prejudice at the ground of thought which cannot be removed. Who does not know of the grotesque and bizarre garments with which Judaism has often been dressed in order to direct Judaism to that place in the salon of nations where it should most appropriately sit according to a previously prepared order? Who does not know how the Jew is stereotyped? Or attributed with negative or polarized roles? Or, how Judaism is explained as a ghostly corpse formation or as representative of the cursed eternal Jew Ahasuerus?[4] Or as remnant of a Semitic race which, on account of its Oriental type, is declared to be totally unacceptable to the civilization of a Japhetic, Indo-Germanic tribe?[5] Because, with this ugly mask already in place, Judaism could be better accommodated in some corner of the systematic structure? Judaism cannot easily hope for such a bias-free judge in the area of Christianity as it finds on its own ground.

Thus: Regarding the relationship of the Jewish researcher to the Christian offered by education and training, it would be justified to assert that the strictly scientific method involving unconditionality would be the exclusive property of Jewish theology. Nevertheless, the reason for asserting this is more internal than external. Even if contemporary Protestant Christian theology no longer wanted to respect the scholastic axiom *fides praecedit intellectum* [faith preceded knowledge] or *credo ut intelligam, no quaero intelligere, ut credum* [I believe so I may understand, I do not understand so I may believe]; if it wished to be true to its Christian character, it must always assume a concept of revelation, inspiration, and illumination. It must be directed by a concept of Trinity where religion, as enveloping a mystery, always remained the object of belief but never became the object of knowledge. The illumination, which is sent from God, is considered the subject of grace. The ability to believe is received in the subject. Grace and faith are one and the same. Without grace there is no faith, and without faith there is no grace. Christianity is knowable only through Christianity. Only someone infused with Christianity can grasp it in its truth. So reads the axiom of contemporary churchly-Christian speculative theology. The requirement of being a Christian, so as to be able to perceive the mystery of Christianity, hardly follows that scholastic axiom. The requirement assumes belief in order to be worthy of the grace of illumination.

By contrast, Judaism recognizes the task to believe that which once happened, what history has transmitted as a fact, and to believe to be true that offered as the claimed necessary result of unrestrained reflection about an experience. This is the case with teaching about God and His relationship to the world and the world's relationship to God. Judaism does not recognize the duty to believe in a mystery of God's immanence, to become worthy of His grace. For Judaism, God is not searchable in terms of inner essence. The human being can already rejoice in blessedness as soon as he recognizes the existence of the single God and His loving relationship to the world—and without believing in a mystery which contradicts reason. Christian theology requires belief. That which is believed is what is presupposed, and what scientific thinking must find in its research. This is also why Christian theology, given its Orthodox-Christian standpoint, can only ridicule the joyful outcry of *heyrikamen* [we have found] of philosophical research. Jewish theology does not require such a belief, and rather always turns to intellectual power and to free power of judgment. It requires that intellectual power goes to work to examine the prophet who knew to validate himself through signs and wonders which were announced in advance and later fulfilled (Deut. 13:2–6). A religious duty to believe, mandating acceptance of any kind of teaching as religious truth, even when it contradicts reason and only because it has been communicated by a higher, divine authority, is alien to Judaism. The term "to believe," meaning to hold as true without having comprehended something as true, is missing in the language of its religious sources. *Amen* indicates entrusting another, physically or spiritually; *emunah* [indicates] trust, dependability.[6] This is why even God is not believed. Rather, God is to be known through His works by means of the *Weltanschauung* (Deut. 4:35; 1 Kings 8:6; Hos. 2:22, 6:3; Ps. 46:11, 83:19).

The Jew should believe as true that God once concluded a covenant with Israel, just as he believes any fact—solely because he extends trust to the narrator thereof because of his rigorously certain communication. Not because of his gift to perform miracles (Maimonides, *Yesodei haTorah* 8, 9, 10; Joseph Albo, *Ikkarim* 1:18). Nor is the Jew obliged to accept a person's declarations as religious truths because that person declared that he was inspired by a divine spirit or is recognized to have been so inspired. This is because in Judaism every religious truth must at the same time be a rational truth. And a rational truth lets itself be discovered and proven through a *Weltanschauung* of continual vigilance, even without an inspiration from the outside. Judaism thereby recognizes only a belief in an historical fact, and in a knowledge-result achieved through proper thinking. Not in any authoritative belief.[7] Unfettered, the Jewish researcher's scientific exploration of his religion advances, prescribing duties of knowledge—and not duties of belief. Scientific exploration does not commit to ratified dogma, whose theses *must* be proven philosophically by the researcher. It commits rather to comprehend only the words of God, with the warrant to ever-more clearly and explicitly comprehend eminent doctrines of knowledge through free research. This way of exploration is special to Judaism. It does not point the researcher to a goal which he must reach, where freedom is only allowed to search out an agreeable path which leads him most easily and quickly to this goal. Rather, this way of exploration invites him to free advances in thought, without concern about the result to which this leads. It recommends only strict consequentiality and precise knowledge of the object.

The task to be resolved here, that Judaism be considered as an absolutely necessary appearance in humanity, requires achieving a double aim. First, an illumination of Judaism in and of itself. Then, its relationship to humanity. As the expression "Judaism" has such a variety of meanings and often exhibits contradictory definitions, it is necessary to call special attention to the difference between Judaism as appearance and Judaism in the idea—indicating relative and absolute truths, home-bred and imported elements, with the former; and acquaintance with Judaism in its purity, with the latter. In the presentation of Judaism according to its idea, a norm-giving measure is provided. According to it, Judaism as appearance must be judged at each and every stage of its path of development. Through this exploration, the confessor of Judaism comes to be convinced of the truth that his religion, inherited from the patriarchs, does not require a path of development in terms of the essence. In terms of the appearance, Judaism of the present no longer wears the same garment as in antiquity, and the contemporary garment is changed for the future. Having been convinced of that truth, the confessor may be led to the distinction between essence and appearance, between shell and core, and cause him to separate the edible from the bran in a pious, but never in a careless way. Being so convinced could also teach him that his religion has not yet died from the weakness of old age and is in need of burial. Rather, that it still finds itself full of vital strength. And, that sometimes Judaism must clothe itself in a frightening shroud for the sake of self-preservation and to protect the inner seed securely against the hefty winter storm of world history with a torpid external. The truth teaches that this seed of life develops again with full power as soon as the spring sunlight of tolerance, of civilization and humanity, permits—advancing the spirit and its pursuit of knowledge, ennobling the heart with higher feelings; and glorifying and sweetening the blessed life with its graceful and cheerful form.

The distinction between Judaism according to its idea and Judaism according to its appearance should also persuade anyone situated outside the domain of Judaism that Judaism wants to be considered at each and every stage of its development as a member of humanity. And that on account of its uninterrupted participation in the vital life of the humanistic organism it had to exhibit those movements which it displayed in the course of world history. Judaism has stepped forwards and backwards with humanity. Despite its isolation, it has nevertheless participated most intimately both in humanity's errors and weaknesses, and in its discoveries and expressions of power. Jews fought for hearth and fatherland in the ancient world, reveled in images of fantasy just as much as [the Neoplatonic philosophers] Plotinus [204–70 CE], Iamblichus [ca. 242–325 CE], or Porphyry [ca. 234–305 CE]. It competed with the Moors for victory in Aristotelian philosophy and in rhymed poetry. With their contemporaries, Jews set astrology and alchemy into motion. They fabricated their contemporaries' amulets and talismans. And they opposed horrible persecutions and torture-agonies inflamed with hatred and thirst for revenge which were allowed to happen.

The contemporary judge of Judaism according to its appearance should, above all, consider Judaism's confessors in the context of their respective time and place. He should place them at the same stage of scientific and moral education as their close associates, and only then allow himself to judge. He would then convey a totally different judgment of Judaism than what is still, regrettably too often, being made. Likewise, he would do so if he could only conceive of the path of humanity's development in its dramatic totality and find the law of association of ideas also among a nation's individuals, and consider the human as human—and not require a human to be either angelic and have no bitter bile, or be like a servile dog licking the hand of the one who barbarically whips it soundly.

The path of development in Judaism cannot be grasped in some juvenile and childish manner—as it is by judging the poetry of the *midrash* according to the measure of today's scientific study. Namely, in terms of *Hermeneutic* and *Weltanschauung*. Or, as morality sometimes expressed inwardly, and outwardly as barbarism which has been smuggled in; or as the most popular rags from all times and places in corners of the earth to make a jacket fit for some burlesque character. Then, *à la* [the German scholar Johann Andreas] Eisenmenger [1654–1704], Judaism is disposed of into the obscene rabble.[8] Is there any doubt that a Jewish Eisenmenger, using the same satanic logic and devilish love, could deliver up the literature of Christianity—beginning somehow with the revelation of John, then rushing through the apocryphal books of the New Testament, the Church fathers, the annals of the Crusades, the chronicles of the Inquisition, the writings of the theosophists and mystics down to [the Swedish Lutheran theologian and scientist] Emanuel von Swedenborg [1688–1772] and his school—and successfully suspend a counterpart alongside *Entdecktes Judentum* [Judaism unmasked] entitled *Entdecktes Christentum* [Christianity unmasked] in literature's picture gallery? And nevertheless it is this Eisenmenger-Hartmann–like picture that is copied and embellished with new anachronistic flourishes as soon as one needs a portrayal of Judaism, perchance to deliver a vote about the emancipation of Jews in the assembly of states; or show in lectures about the state economy how Jews would be the bloodsuckers of humanity, and be able to establish also a representative of negativity, of polarity, etc. in the philosophy of history. [. . .][9]

The exploration [in this book] should be considered an apology. It does not try to explain away the errors and deficiencies cast against Judaism, by saying that it detects them as well in the developmental path and life of other religions. Rather, it seeks to excuse the errors and deficiencies as having been conditioned by time and space, as necessary crises in the course of sickness of the human spirit. Anyway, what is the point of crude quarrels and shoving one another on the sanctified ground of scientific literature? Where spirit, in its pure sublimity, above lowly egoistic drives of vain earthly children, decisively advocates the results of spirit, thinking, and research alone? Where spirit should rejoice, having become aware of its errors through the affable exchange of ideas and required to follow a better path? How low does even truth itself appear if it is made available only amid offence and poisonous animosity?

Above all, scientific research offers only naked, cold truths. Truth should be sought out for its own sake, without concern that success in practical life emanates from it. Nevertheless, research is permitted to indicate the impact expected from discovered results, independent of other aims. "Truth is the inscription on the seal of God."[10] Because truth, like God Himself, is singular. If truth is generally recognized in its absolute form, unity will reign in dispositions, feelings, and strivings. Humanity will rejoice in one spirit and heart, and world peace will create blessed heaven out of earth. The one who risks directing even one ray of this prismatically dispersed truth into spiritual focus will complete a work of love, helping to build this peace, sought for by all, in the time to come.

SIGISMUND STERN (1812–67)

Sigismund Stern (b. 1812, Kargowa; d. 1867, Frankfurt) was a leading member of the German Reform community and a respected Jewish educator. After studying philology at the University of Berlin, Stern became headmaster of the Berlin Jewish Boys' School in 1835, remaining there until accepting the principalship in 1855 of the Philanthropin, the Jewish gymnasium (high school) in Frankfurt, where he remained until his death.

In his position as schoolmaster, Stern initiated numerous pedagogical reforms to help bring liberal Jewish education into line with the latest methods developed in Europe for children's scholastic instruction, a task for which he was widely lauded. In 1845, he founded one of the most radical Reform congregations in Germany, the Berlin Reformgenossenschaft, which had emerged from a group of Jewish intellectuals who had met regularly for some time to listen to Stern's lectures on Judaism. (Two years later, the community would engage Samuel Holdheim—see chapter 2—as their rabbi.)

The Berlin Reformgenossenschaft was a "Jewish Church" in the sense of the text translated below. To Stern, a "church" was a body that wielded power on behalf of its followers in the pursuance of their political goals. Since he and his followers aimed to assert ethical influence on the politics of the state, he believed that Judaism must reconstitute itself as a "church" in order to have the standing to act within the power structure of states and nations.

Stern's writings on Jewish history and religious life were broadly influential among Germany's liberal Jews and contributed to the intellectual substrate on which German Reform took fertile root. The selection translated here is from *Die Aufgabe des Judenthums und des Juden in der Gegenwart (The task of Judaism and the Jews in the present age)*,[11] a collection of his lectures delivered in Berlin in 1845, which caused considerable controversy for its radically reform-minded agenda.

In this lecture, Stern describes the social and political history of Israel (from monarchy to Diaspora) as intimately tied up with Judaism's moral responsibility to spread monotheism and its incumbent ethical norms. As Stern writes, the arc of Israel's wanderings is too clear "to doubt the intention history aimed to reach by the dissolution of the political-national bonds in Judaism." The divine purpose for the resulting diasporic religion, Stern relates, was to "make the knowledge of God the common property of humanity as a whole," thereby ensuring a universal morality based on biblical ethics. While Stern's argument sounds anti-Zionist, it is too early in nineteenth-century Jewish history to be participating in that discourse. Instead, Stern's words were aimed squarely at the Orthodox, who insisted on a traditional liturgy that yearned for the return to Zion and the rebuilding of Jerusalem. Instead of clinging to such "wishful dreams whose fulfillment it cannot hope to achieve," Stern imagines a future Judaism that embraces its diasporic existence and, in so doing, creates a new sociopolitical institution, a "Jewish Church," that works to disseminate an ethical vision of God and the world.

The Task of Jews and Judaism in the Present Age (1845)

Translated by Michael Zank

Few of the great phenomena of world history show themselves so clearly as to the core and content of their essence and its meaning for humanity as Judaism; few show in their development such a steady and broadening progress in the same direction as Judaism since its first entry into history down to its seeming disappearance from history. Nowhere does the shape of external forms correspond so visibly to the contemporaneous stage of the development as in Judaism.[12]

The content and essence of Judaism is knowledge of God, the awareness of the existence of a single one and incorporeal God as the creator and loving preserver of the world. [Judaism's] task for humanity cannot be other than making this, its possession, the common property of all.[13] The development of Judaism is thereby discerned simply in its progressive dissemination across humanity, and even more so in the ever higher moral arrangements that rest on it.[14] In Abraham, the knowledge of God is the possession of a single individual whose personal morality is sustained by it.[15] Within his family, it became the common property of a narrowly defined whole, giving it the moral form of patriarchy.[16] But when eventually the entire people reached this knowledge of God, it provided the moral bond that united these people as the enclosed whole of a nation,[17] and theocracy was the form in which that developmental stage of Judaism appeared.[18]

But here the thread of history seems suddenly torn and the river of development dried up.[19] The bond of the nation is dissolved, theocracy destroyed, and no new shape wants to arise from the chaos of destruction; no new whole exists around which the unifying bond of religion is woven, no new and higher moral phenomenon appears, called into existence by the continuous development of Judaism.

But the path that the history of Judaism followed to this point pursues a particular direction. The eventual goal to which it is to lead can be anticipated too certainly to doubt the intention history aimed to reach by the dissolution of the political-national bonds in Judaism. Freed of the bonds of a particular nationality and a particular organism of state, the new task of Judaism could be none other than to make the knowledge of God the common property of humanity as a whole, or at least of a mighty complex of people, and make the higher stage of its development appear in the moral relation between these people. The first glance at this history could make us believe that the fixing of moral laws between different people as a law of nations realized itself only in Christianity and that Christianity alone accomplished it.[20] But careful attention to the circumstances within the Judaism of that age teaches us that that was not so. — Just as we recognized Christianity as an essential moment in the development of Judaism, though not as the complete expression of that development,[21] so too, one of the manifestations of this progress appears predominantly in Christianity, namely, the moral relationship between different states and nations in the idea of the law of nations and the balance of power.[22] But the unitive bond of religion between individuals who stand outside the national and political unity is much more strongly visible in the affairs of Judaism and the Jews of the Middle Ages. A Jew expelled from Spain who came to France, Germany, or Poland not only found a home in the religious association he joined by virtue of the citizenship of his faith, but he also found in every fellow Jew a brother, a fellow-man full of empathy and sympathy who, as a Jew, felt obliged to help him bear and lighten the burden of his misfortune. To this day, the Jew who arrives from distant lands sees his faith as credit on the sympathy and benevolence of his fellow-believers that no one may refuse.

In that way religion elevated itself in Judaism above the barrier of nation and state, namely, by forging a moral bond between its members that could do without external forms and limitations for its maintenance. But true progress does not merely want to know the limitations of the prior formation dissolved; it wants them adopted within the new form of existence. But the Judaism of the Middle Ages stood outside, rather than above, all political and national associations.

Perfectly aligned with the direction of its prior development, Judaism broke through the barrier of its confinement in theocracy and thus widened the territory of its external existence. But it lacked the force of action to make this soil its own and erect on it a new building, to enclose itself within new, though wider, limits. For where there is no limit there is no shape, and only in a particular formation can a development appear. Judaism remained unaware of its own progress; hence that constant desire for the return to those circumstances that it had long since outgrown; hence that forced conservation of external arrangements from bygone days; hence that indifference to the present; and hence at last that contradiction between life and religion that necessarily resulted from the contradiction between the internal and external development of Judaism.

The first step that Judaism must take to arrive at a true development of its past is to freely and consciously relinquish this past. It must give up on the return of the past so as to participate in its own present. It must no longer grieve the past as lost but relinquish it as overcome by its own development. It must not just declare the return to Jerusalem and the rebuilding of the Temple wishful dreams whose fulfillment it cannot hope to achieve, but it must openly acknowledge the contradiction in which they stand to Judaism's present destiny.[23] One should not object that, in our times, this is a matter of course. Ask the men of honest piety whether they have relinquished this hope rather than awaiting its fulfillment year after year anew; ask the orthodox who claim the level of contemporary education whether they are ready to renounce in public the eventual return of the past. But let us also recognize the important consequences that are necessarily associated with this concession. For with it, those who profess Judaism must cease to call themselves the Chosen People of the Lord, not just because they have entirely ceased to be a people but because the knowledge of God that was given them before all other nations is no longer their exclusive possession, or should not remain it if they themselves as well as Judaism are to fulfill their present destiny.[24] They need to recognize the highest duty conferred by the present destiny of Judaism in the voluntary act of relinquishing that preferred status they achieved without merit of their own. The Jew must recognize his fellow human beings as equal not just in the love of God but also in his own love and impose on himself the duty to contribute actively to their individual and collective wellbeing. If Judaism gives up the return of the situation in which its essence used to appear then it must also become aware of the fact that, at present, it lacks the soil on which religion and those who profess it can reach a coherent moral efficiency and must seek to gain this missing soil.

Two ways offer themselves here, and they will indicate the direction in which [Judaism] will need to accomplish its new development. For one, it must prepare the ground for a new formation in its own area and from its own resources to bring its autonomous and inner progress to external realization. But then it also must make that area the soil for its activity that is the ground for the moral creations of our time that came into being without any Jewish contribution and that until now only Christianity engaged with without having produced it on its own. Judaism, therefore, must create its own church within which its own life can take shape and enter into the lives of states and nations that are the carriers of the present development. It must exit the fragmentation of its present existence and shape itself into a coherent, living and organic whole. But while it gains its religious independence in this formation it must not only permit, but also command, its adherents to connect with the life of the present on its national and political soil and use its own powers to help prepare the way for it.[25]

We want to look at these two fundamental demands on Judaism issued by the present in greater detail. The rarely used expression "Jewish Church," which has as yet to gain a certain and generally accepted meaning, is still denied idiomatic legitimacy amongst us. We could have said "synagogue." But, after everything we have discussed, there cannot be any doubt how we understand this term.[26]

The Jewish Church is supposed to be the body whose soul is Judaism and whose members are its adherents. For now, we want to set aside the question whether such an association of all the adherents of Judaism is possible. Later on, we will need to determine how to limit the scope of a Jewish Church. But no matter how narrow or wide the circumference that will surround the whole thus united, the Church must always remain the expression of its entire religious life. Its shape must express the conviction of the whole so that the institutes and institutions it produces will satisfy its needs. That development that the religion is capable and in need of can and may complete itself only in the Church. In it the progress must become the property and action of Judaism itself, that until now only manifested in the consciousness and lives of its particular adherents and therefore never attained historic justification because it was merely the action of individuals, no matter how great their number.

We resolutely reject the founding of a church within Judaism that would demand of us to acknowledge its absolute divine power and whose proclamations can be binding on one's individual conscience. The Jewish Church may never demand of its members the confession of a particular creed, or it would completely misunderstand its own, and Judaism's, task. We will never suffer the introduction of a hierarchical element into Judaism, for Judaism knows no difference between those privileged to know and those for whom it is proper merely to believe, and there will never be a religious distinction between laity and priests.—The Church is to be the expression of the conviction of the whole and an organ of the will of the whole. It should serve as an authority that the individual can rely on to shape his religious life, but not a force of coercion for his conviction and freedom. It must possess the right to make general arrangements in the interest of the whole it represents and to demand the participation of all in the founding and maintenance of the institutes created for this purpose, but not to interfere on its own initiative with the lives of individuals. We recognize its unlimited authority, independent of all law and custom, to determine the form of public worship and all other religious rites; the authority to declare existing laws null and void and to proclaim new ones; but not the right to declare any one of its decisions for an authentic and hence unchangeable interpretation of the will of God.

How, we ask, is this union of the entire Jewry in a single Church to be born? How can it form that organ by which the conviction and will of the whole may appear? The first glance at the circumstances of Jews across different countries and parts of the world teaches us that such a reunification of all those who profess the Jewish faith is beyond all possibility.—But can we allow the irreversible loss of a complete unity among all Jewish believers to deprive us of the courage to seek it within the limits where it still seems possible? What is at stake is a matter of life or death for Judaism. We don't want to decide it without also hearing out our opponents. I clearly hear their admonition: "You are touching the formations of the past because you don't wish to take them for the work of God. You only grant the past a right because its laws were recognized at its time. Well, then, convene the same court that issued that judgment if you want to overturn it. All Israel spoke at Sinai, 'The commandments that you are bringing us, we will obey.'[27] All Israel made the Talmud its code of law. Hence as long as all Israel does not come and dissolve it, Mosaic and Talmudic law remain inviolable." I recognize how forcefully this strike threatens to shake our entire edifice, because it is carried out with the hammer that we ourselves had forged to take down the superannuated building. But let us see if the foundations we established are strong enough to withstand it.

Is it really us, I ask, who want to overturn the judgment of all Israel, or was it not rather the mightier hand of history that tore it—and the court itself—asunder for all times? For it said, "No longer shall there be unity among you and you shall live among all the nations of the earth so as to proclaim your truth one day in every language."[28] In order to carry out the new task of Judaism, its adherents had to take root in the soil of different nations and states and enter its particularity with every aspect of life so as to be able to make its religion a part of it. The formation of the new age did not manifest itself only extraneously, so that the adherents of Judaism, dispersed among the nations, gradually absorbed their morals and characteristics and thereby also developed different religious needs among them. It was Judaism itself that wished to enter into the different nationalities of the present to which it led its adherents. The formation of national churches within Judaism is a necessity, not just because the establishment of a universal church cannot be accomplished, and also not just because the actual difference of religious need likewise demand a different external form of religious life, but because Judaism itself needs a plurality of manifestations in order to let all of its rich forces come to life. Just as the vital force of a plant enfolds itself richer in the leaves than the stem, richer in the flowers than the leaves, and finally richer in the fruit than in the flower, so Judaism wants to become a German, a French, an English church, that is, it wants to manifest its own unique essence among all of these nations in forms that allow it to become an element in the lives of those nations. [. . .]

The building of a Jewish church is but one way by which Judaism can shape the future in the direction pointed by its own history: A path on which to create in its own territory a soil on which religion takes a moral shape. But Judaism should also make that territory the soil for the activity of its adherents that provides the ground for the moral creations of its time that have come into being without the contribution of Judaism. This is to enable the free and independent entry of its adherents to the social and political life of the present.

There is a threefold measure of influence that religion exerts on the more extensive participation of its adherents in the political and social creations of their time. It can permit them this participation; it can demand it of them; and at last it can also achieve it for them where its entitlement is hampered by external hindrances. We will need to make our claim on Judaism in all three regards.

Religion must permit its adherents this intimate participation by removing the obstacles it placed in its way. The Judaism of the past, however, limits this participation because it does not see the communal formations beyond its territory as moral phenomena. Though Mosaic Judaism is far removed from limiting the duty of love of the other to [love of] the fellow-believer alone, and indeed explicitly demands one to love the stranger as the native, [Judaism] nevertheless does not recognize the non-Jewish peoples as totalities and the state formed by them as moral.[29] The strict seclusion of the Jews from being in touch with them is the result and the expression of this denial of recognition. Talmudic Judaism likewise teaches love of members of other religions and likewise demands obedience to the government and the laws of the non-Jewish state, but it increases the rules that aimed at the separation of the Jews from the community of the members of other religions instead of diminishing or canceling them and thereby remains in protest against the moral legitimacy of the formations of general life created by Christianity or that have been created without Jewish input.[30] Judaism must openly and expressly renounce this contradiction, this indifference [toward non-Jewish religion], in which it has until now known and had to find itself in regards to the phenomena of history, because [it considered the members of other religions] not on the same footing with it. [Judaism must now] recognize them as moral, as historically justified, in order thereby to free its own adherents from the most important obstacle which hitherto has stood in the way of their entry into the life of the present.

We want to proclaim this as far as our voices reach: That we want to participate in the moral efforts of our time and that our religion demands this participation. We want to proclaim it and attest to it by action: That there is no law for us that could prevent us from living and acting in the most intimate communion with our Christian brothers, no doctrine that might make us think of the work of those who profess a different faith as lesser than our own, no rule that demands of us to seclude or separate ourselves from the members of other religions. But if such rules still exist, if the charge of our Christian fellow-citizens that avoidance of community is grounded perhaps not in the demands of our conviction or efforts but in those of our codes of law, then we want and may refuse to recognize those rules, and not just the individual but the Jewish Church itself must renounce them.

Judaism should not just permit its adherents this activity but demand it as a religious duty. By associating itself with the state the Church does not subordinate itself but its external appearance under it, and the obedience that it demands of its members is justified in the duty of obedience to the state and therefore presupposes it as necessary for the existence of the Church. The development of religious life within the whole therefore has the weal of the state as its precondition. In this way the very existence of the Church encourages participation on behalf of the public weal and especially for that of the state, and it will not require a particular religious law for this purpose. But the Church and its organs will need to draw attention to, and urge, the fulfillment of this duty, and community leaders and youth educators both must make it their task to disseminate and affirm more and more the love of fatherland and civic sentiment among the Jews.

Finally, religion will not just permit and command its members to engage in this activity in the sphere of public weal, but it must attain for them the right to engage in it.

The emancipation of the Jews is a task that Judaism as religion must realize. First, it must seek its own emancipation, its recognition by the state, in order to gain, as Church, a ground on which it can appropriate for itself a defined territory for its care for the public weal. From this standpoint of recognition of a Jewish Church within the state it will be able to attain the same for its adherents. For the state that grants the Jewish Church full citizenship in its territory cannot deny the same of its adherents without contradicting itself, just as the state cannot emancipate the Jew as a citizen without also recognizing the Church to which he belongs. Religion is unable to procure this right for its adherents by means of a particular action that emanates from it, but it will procure it by means of the dignity of its appearance and most of all by the determinate effort to permit the Jews to engage on behalf of the weal of the state and the whole and to demand it as their religious duty.

Thus, we believe to have found the way [forward] for the history of Judaism, a history we followed from its most distant past down to our present, on which it desires to enter into its future and hence onto the new stage in its development. It will consciously relinquish the ground of its moral appearance that it found in theocracy. It will separate religious and national existence and prepare the ground for the further development of the former in the Church, while in exchange for relinquishing the latter it will demand of its adherents the free participation in the general task of the time and thus elevate itself to one of the moving forces that are called upon to complete this task.

SAMUEL HIRSCH (1815–89)

Samuel Hirsch (b. 1815, Thalfang; d. 1889, Chicago), a German-American Reform rabbi, theologian, and philosopher, belonged to the first generation of university-trained German rabbis, earning his doctorate in 1842. He spent the first half of his career in Europe, as rabbi in Dessau and then in Luxembourg, before immigrating to Philadelphia in 1866, where he remained until his retirement in 1888.

Like his colleagues Abraham Geiger (see chapter 2) and David Einhorn, the final author in this chapter, Hirsch was a vocal and powerful advocate for reform, yet he also publicly maintained the importance of such ritual practices as circumcision and Hebrew prayer, seeing them as strong social and theological indicators of continuing Jewish religious difference. While in Dessau, Hirsch was nonetheless formative in the German rabbinical assemblies' declarations in the 1840s, including rejecting the authority of the Talmud as arbiter of Jewish law and ritual practice, and radically transforming the idea of the Messiah from that of a figure descended from the House of David to that of a universal vision enacted on Earth by all humanity. In his community in Philadelphia, he instituted the transfer of the observance of Shabbat to Sundays (a practice that fell away after his death), the better to instantiate his desire for Judaism and Christianity to effectuate an ethical revival as one great monotheistic family.

Throughout his career Hirsch wrote numerous articles on the cultural and philosophical history of the Jewish people. His major work, *Die Religionsphilosophie der Juden* (The religious philosophy of the Jews), sought to understand Judaism through the lens of Hegelian dialectic (meaning he saw Judaism as a religious development in constant antithesis and resynthesis with history and culture), yet as equal to Christianity in its expression of the pure essence of religion (an achievement Hegel thought only Protestant Christianity had reached).[31] It arguably contains thus the first serious discussion of Christian theology by a modern Jewish thinker.

In this selection, from part 5 (chapters 69 and 70), Hirsch vigorously argues against the theological doctrine that sin is inherent in Creation and that the time of the Messiah will only be possible in a world markedly different from our own.[32] Christianity, Hirsch says, went astray from the message of Jesus, which is the same as the traditional Jewish doctrine, holding that God's kingdom will be on Earth and that righteousness is possible right here and right now. "Since God created this world as sacred and pure," Hirsch writes, "sin should and need not be on this earth." The rift, he argues, resulted from Paul's interpretation of Jesus, particularly Paul's incorporation of Zoroastrian cosmology, with its dualist account of two divine forces: order and chaos, rightness and sinfulness. Judaism, Hirsch concludes, has always rejected such Manichaean ideas, and therefore retained the purer link with Jesus's own theology: that through repentance, prayer, and good deeds, all people can achieve a life without sin.

The Religious Philosophy of the Jews (1842)

Translated by Gershon Greenberg

The Jewish perspective is not different from that cherished by Jesus, which is as simple as it is clear: *A time will come when all evil on earth will have disappeared.* Since God created this world as sacred and pure, sin should and need not be on this earth. If it is indeed on earth, its presence is uniquely and solely the fault of human beings. No one should, and no one needs, to sin. If nevertheless one sins? On the one hand, as in paganism, God allows awareness of sin. Sin destroys itself through its own dialectic. On the other, as in Judaism, God educates towards holiness. At some point, by means of, and through the Jews, all human beings will come to the heartfelt conviction of the nullity and contingency, i.e., of the innecessity of evil, and to the conviction of the glory, truth, and unconstrained necessity of the good. God will forgive the sins of the past, and from then on, all human beings will lead that life which God wanted from the beginning—a life from which they should not have deviated, and for which humans were created. As Jesus speaks of the return of the son of man accompanied by the heavenly host,[33] he indeed thinks only of *this earth* as the place of his kingdom. For, according to the worldview of the time, even if always something wondrous, it was nevertheless not unusual for mortal but pious people to visibly associate with angels.[34]

Over against this, at that time there was yet another messianic doctrine in full swing, namely the Persian.[35] There, Ormuzd and Ahriman stood opposed to one another with equal power.[36] The earth was not created for the human being to live a holy and pure life. Given Ahriman's power, this was impossible. The earth was created solely for the human being to fight it out with Ahriman, in vain, over Ahriman's rule. For in time, Ahriman must come unnoticed to rule. The earth and everything on it was created for Ahriman's increasing pollution—while creation continued to advance. When the era of Ahriman would be over, this earth, polluted by Ahriman, would burn up. A new, pure earth would be created by Ormuzd. The *ferwers* of the creations, with the *yazatas* and the *Ameshaspand*, would lead an eternal, blessed, nonturbid life of light.[37]

Paul's doctrine of inherited sin is basically pagan.[38] It is distinct from Persian dualism only insofar as Paul seeks to repel its nasty practical consequences.[39] When it came to the doctrine of the messianic era, he of course had to throw himself totally into the arms of Parseeism.[40] Messianic hopes could not be fulfilled upon *this earth*, rather upon a new, heavenly, pure earth. All human beings were polluted through the *one*—the testimony to which is that all must die. Accordingly, every creature—for each must die—is necessarily defiled by the sins of *the one*. Every creature therefore awaits redemption, or the new heavenly condition.[41] This is expressed thusly:

> I consider that the sufferings of this present time are not worth comparing with the glory about to be revealed to us. For the creation waits with eager longing for the revealing of the children of God; for the creation was subjected to futility (original sin), not of its own will but by the will of the one (for the sake of man) who subjected it, in hope *that the creation itself will be set free from its bondage to decay* (entirely Persian) and will obtain the freedom of the glory of the children of God. *We know that the whole creation has been groaning in labor pains until now*; and not only the creation, but we ourselves, who have the first fruits of the Spirit, groan inwardly while we wait for adoption, the redemption of our bodies.[42]

One sees that the pagan teaching, that *the body is the prison of the soul*, is closely related to the Pauline doctrine. Paul knew that he was saved from inherited sin through Jesus. Nevertheless, for Paul, the body indeed still dies, it is indeed still ephemeral. *Consequently, it is still bad.*

The Bible, however, states that *the body is good*. It was created by God. Even if death, according to biblical doctrine, is the consequence of sin, this is indeed to be taken differently than Paul takes it. As soon as sin is there, the struggle with it begins—a serious struggle *over life and death. One must want to lose one's life*, Jesus says, *in order to acquire it again* (Matt. 10:39),[43] as do the rabbis.[44] Thereby, for Jesus, death becomes something holy; dying is something good. The body does not need redemption if the spirit is one day redeemed.

Paul follows with solace.[45] Neither internally nor externally does the present time impart any gratifying prospect:

> For in hope (at that time) we were saved. Now hope that is seen is not hope. For who hopes for what is seen? (So what we have now is not satisfactory.) But if we hope for what we do not see, we wait for it with patience. Likewise the Spirit helps us in our weakness; for we do not know how to pray as we ought, but that very Spirit intercedes with sighs too deep for words. And God, who searches the heart, knows what is the mind of the Spirit, because the Spirit intercedes for the saints according to the will of God.[46]

According to the student of Paul, for the Gospel writer Luke, this expression of Paul materialized into history. Its meaning is simply this: If amid the present sufferings we call upon God for relief, we nevertheless do not want to lose courage if our prayer remains unheard. Because the sufferings do not become assuaged, they certainly remain indispensable for the glorification of God. Luke has the apostles ask Jesus: "LORD, teach us to pray" [Luke 11:1].—"We know that all things work together for good for those who love God, who are called according to his purpose."[47] (Like John, Paul also knew that the conundrum, whereby so few show themselves to be receptive to the new means of salvation, is resolved only through the doctrine of *predetermined predestination*.)

[At the same time, the pride of the believers that they are better than the nonbelievers was to be rejected.] It forms a transition to what follows:

> *For those whom he foreknew he also predestined* to be conformed to the image of his Son, in order that he might be the firstborn within a large family. And those whom he predestined he also called; and those whom he called he also justified; and those whom he justified he also glorified. What then are we to say about these things? If God is for us, who is against us? He who did not withhold his own Son, but gave him up for all of us, will he not with him also give us everything else? Who will bring any charge against God's elect? It is God who justifies. Who is to condemn? It is Christ Jesus, who died, yes, who was raised, who is at the right hand of God, who indeed

> intercedes for us. Who will separate us from the love of Christ? Will hardship, or distress, or persecution, or famine, or nakedness, or peril, or sword? As it is written, "It is for Your sake that we are slain all day long, that we are regarded as sheep to be slaughtered."[48] No, in all these things we are more than conquerors through him who loved us. *For I am convinced that neither death, nor life, nor angels, nor rulers, nor things present, nor things to come, nor powers, nor height, nor depth, nor anything else in all creation, will be able to separate us from the love of God in Christ Jesus our Lord.*[49]

Paul closes with the firm conviction that the present could not make him waver about the future. If in the present the disciples of Jesus were so misunderstood and persecuted by the people, they nevertheless had the truth. For the world misunderstood the disciples only because the new salvation was still not at all certain. Even if Christians lapsed again into sin, they still would be saved. Because, according to the power of inherited sin, the new salvation could not be realized at all in this world. In this world, the new salvation could only impart hope for a better future world, free of inherited sin. Its inheritors are uniquely and solely those who become baptized in the name of Christ and receive his spirit. Paul closes his colossal edifice with this conviction. We also want to close with Paul.

Now Christianity stands there quite ready and as despisers of the Jews and Judaism. Until today, Christianity is not free of Paul, and has not come out from Paul. The entire history of Christianity, until this very day, both internally and externally, is but the inner completion and outer presentation of this proud Pauline temple. All dogmas and all dogmatic controversies are but the consequences of Pauline doctrine. The entirety rests upon the false foundation, and upon the false representation, which Paul shaped for himself from the law of the Jews. It was therefore easy for [German theologian and historian David Friedrich] Strauss [1808–74] to show in his *Christian Doctrine* that that entirety has gone out of fashion in scientific study—even if regrettably not yet in life.[50] But if one day the time would come, if one day the Church would *become Christian instead of Pauline*; if it chose to support itself not upon *the errors of Paul* but *upon the truth which was real and realized in Jesus Christ*, the Church would stand firm forever. No one would risk *staining its luster or disputing its sanctity*.

Note: Paul was a brother of the Jews in the flesh. He himself was so alarmed at the *inhumanity* he so plainly taught about the Jews that he sought to mitigate the ruinous consequences. It is touching how, in the subsequent chapters, he entreats for grace and compassion for the Jews. *He would surrender even the holiest, his share in Christ*, if by so doing he could acquire salvation for the Jews. He uses the doctrine of divine predestination in order to explain the unbelief of the Jews—"So it depends not on human will or exertion, but on God who shows mercy."[51] He believed he could repel the unavoidable astonishment connected to this, about this divine injustice with words: "But who indeed are you, a human being, to argue with God?"[52] He testifies that Jews had enthusiasm for God, and that they only erred by wanting to *earn* the grace of God, rather than have it *granted* to them (namely according to the opinion of Paul). Their will, however, was not bad (Rom. 10:2,4).[53] Finally, Paul solemnly avers that one day the Jews, one and all, will become believers (Rom. 11:1ff). Therefore, God now lets the Jews reject salvation, for salvation is to be preached to the pagans (Rom. 11:11). Paul does not want the secret that just as Israel shaped the *beginning of redemption* in Jesus and the Apostles it should also *conclude the redemption* (Rom. 11:25) be withheld from the pagans. Pagans should therefore beware of disdaining yet-unbelieving Israel, *or offending it*.

Meanwhile, Christians are not the brothers of the Jews in flesh. The Christians did not know why they should surrender the consequence of the doctrine of the law and grace, of inherited sin and redemption, in according to the pious wishes of Paul.

Apropos, we should be allowed to disclose here more of Paul's secret. Had the rich store of [Christianized] pagans really *entered* into the spirit of Jesus Christ, they would have really become, as a result of Christianity, what they wanted to be—brothers and inheritors of his kingdom. Had they lived as sinlessly and sacredly as their master; had the Christianity of the world not cost bloody tears; had love instead of hatred, humility instead of pride, intrinsic joint-property instead of self-interest erected their throne in the world—the Jew would have joyfully and with delight beheld the realization of their messianic hopes in Christianity. But because eighteen hundred years were still not enough to realize this in the *Christian countries,* it should not be taken amiss that Jews still always look hopefully into the future.

DAVID EINHORN (1809–79)

David Einhorn (b. 1809, Dispeck; d. 1879, New York) was a rabbi and leader of Reform Judaism in Germany and America, and a key ally of Abraham Geiger (see chapter 2). A rabbi in various communities across Germany from 1838 to 1855, he found himself continuously opposing more traditional views on religious and theological matters, advocating, for example, for the widespread introduction of the German language into prayer services and the elimination of liturgical references to the rebuilding of the Jerusalem Temple. But Einhorn also believed deeply in the unity of the Jewish community, and in the continuity of Judaism from ancient to modern times, and therefore opposed all reforms which he believed threatened to sever what he calls in this sermon "Israel's unchanging attachment to its mission." In 1855, Einhorn emigrated to the New World and became a leading figure in the American Reform movement, alongside esteemed colleagues Samuel Adler (1809–91) and Samuel Hirsch (in this chapter), and his sons-in-law Kaufmann Kohler (see chapter 7) and Emil Hirsch (1851–1923).

Einhorn delivered this sermon, entitled "Die Vorzüge der jüdischen Gotteslehre" (The benefits of the Jewish doctrine of God), on the holiday of Shavuot (Feast of Weeks), which celebrates the giving of the Torah on Mt. Sinai[54] For Einhorn, Shavuot becomes the perfect tableau against which to unfold his theology, for it is the one holiday which commemorates the origins of the Law itself, which celebrates Torah in its purest form, devoid of its Rabbinic encasement. In his sermon, Einhorn lays out the central characteristics of Judaism that he believes have allowed it to thrive across centuries, geographies, and national catastrophes. Three of these characteristics—correspondence with nature, trustworthiness, and flexibility—he argues, have marked Judaism as separate from other religions (most pointedly the monotheisms, Christianity and Islam), by never allowing it to go against reason (never preferencing faith without knowledge) while also fortifying it with a purity of spirit (what he calls "the winged flash of light that shines through it"). At the end, Einhorn calls on his generation of Jews to be like those who returned from Babylonia after the Captivity, reaffirming Judaism's dedication to serving God and reinvigorating its rituals for a new age.

The Benefits of the Jewish Doctrine of God (1852)

Translated by Michael A. Meyer

Perhaps no day is more suited to fill the heart of every Israelite with noble pride than the present one, the day that recalls the giving of the Law on Sinai, the only Law that bears the name "divine" and that shines upward from the ruins of grayest antiquity with a brightness that, instead of fading, is rather engaged in steady growth and will require a long time yet to evolve into full grandeur. To belong to a tribe that is called by God to be the recipient and guardian of such a treasure, a tribe that for the sake of its exalted vocation courageously proclaimed its willingness for sacrifice, regarding which the history of humanity in its entire compass knows of nothing comparable to equate with it; to belong to a tribe which, as a prince of God, never tires of being at once the priest and the sacrifice of the world, that on its immeasurably thorny path endured everything gruesome that tyranny could conceive, and, clearly protected by a Higher Power, with an ability to survive that is already legendary, could stride ahead unscathed past numberless abysses, across prickly ledges—whoever may boast of belonging to such a tribe, that individual can in truth, despite all of the bitterness of fate, declare his lot to be a delight and, more than anyone, has the right triumphantly to claim his patent of nobility.[55] Yes, my friends, if today we imagine that priestly band of hundred thousands which in those ancient times, when humanity was still in its cradle, stood about the flaming Horeb to mediate the marriage between heaven and earth and to dedicate itself to a struggle that their descendants now heroically carry on;[56] if we consider how all the destructive powers assaulted tiny Israel in vain, how it took its course unharmed through water and fire, past frenzied peoples, past graves of numberless generations, past collapsing worlds; how, like a sunny dove among the nations, despite all of the blows of fate, despite all of the burden of the years, and under all world-shattering upheavals, it nonetheless persevered in its unshakeable loyalty to its God and his teaching, an immovable rock in the billows of the sea—then our souls must rejoice at the thought that we are members of this heroic band and belong to that wondrous thorn bush which, at the sacrifice of its precious blossoms, burns on and on and is not consumed.[57] But then, as once did Moses, we cannot avoid investigating this miraculous phenomenon—raising the question: Whereon rests Israel's unchanging attachment to its mission?

There must be unusual—indeed incomparable—advantages that enable a teaching to withstand such fiery ordeals and to captivate its adherents in so unprecedented a manner! What then are these advantages? Our text illustrates them masterfully.[58] Its description of God's teaching calls to mind, above all, three of its characteristics that, in themselves, already suffice to secure their imperishability. They are: *correspondence with nature, trustworthiness,* and *flexibility*. What lends our sacred teaching an irresistible attraction is, to begin with, its conformity with nature, and, as with any purely human claim, its agreement with the demands of reason and of the heart. God's teaching—and in this regard it deserves praise like no other—is perfect, restoring the soul; God's mandates are just, rejoicing the heart; God's commandments are pure, enlightening the eyes! It is one of the most remarkable characteristics of the Israelite religion that, instead of splitting the human being into opposites and, as the price to be paid for reconciliation with God, dividing him in two, it rather, like a refreshing stream, flows over all parts of his being, and it is precisely where he is inwardly torn apart that it perceives the root or the fruit of sin. *Tam*.[59] Characteristically enough, being whole and being pious therefore have value for it as one and the same concept, and no teaching knows how it is that in order to satisfy the most daring and proud power of thought, as well as the most humble and childlike devotion of the spirit, it fully resolves all human contradictions in a higher unity.

Let us first examine the ardor of Judaism's relation to human reason! Cognition is the first of its foundation pillars! It is far removed from calling to the human being: "Close your eyes in order to be able to enter my Temple; be blind and you will be saved and look upon the glory of the Almighty; cast your spirit, ensnared by the devil, into chains so that wings of faith and salvation will then descend upon that chained individual in order to carry him upward into the luminous realm of freedom."[60] On the contrary, it is for the human spirit, which in accordance with its innermost nature is a pure and noble son of God, that the Father of all has engraved His holy law in indelible fiery writing.[61] God has called upon that spirit to unleash its powers ever more, to perfect its talents, and by means of such independence to gain likeness to God. Judaism does not seek blind submission to its truths and obligations, but rather their attainment as a crown of all budding knowledge and inquiry. The biblical sources in their entire compass have no designation whatever for any belief in revelation devoid of knowledge, one which, as a foreign beam, is forcibly stuffed into the inner human being either to stifle natural impulse in embryo or, where that doesn't succeed, result in a rootless life. The individual only hangs loosely to the tree of spirit like a tottering, nebulous creation that draws its sustenance only from hazy habit. In holy scripture the expression *emunah* nowhere means *belief* as opposed to *knowledge*, but rather loyalty, trust, reliability.[62] And wherever these qualities give rise to the adoption of the highest truths, this occurs in no other manner than on the basis of cognition and inquiry. "Cast your glance upward"—that is what Judaism teaches—"to the numberless hosts of stars and you will perceive in these astonishing works the Unfathomable who calls all by name and has sketched out everyone's unalterable course; He, the one and only, who has created all, guides and directs all. He is the source of all life and, were you able, O man, to fly from one end of the world to the other and, at every single point, your glance penetrate to the highest heights and the deepest depths—you would still find yourself everywhere within His realm, and you would hear every breath, every motion, every beam of light, and every drop in this immeasurable sea praise Him." Your reason may well quake at this thought—but only from joy and delight at seeing itself, on account of Sinai's teaching, carried upward to those steep heights where the wildest flight of pagan wisdom did not dare to ascend, heights where that wisdom's dark surmises of former times were led like lightning through the night of the spirit transforming it into shining light, into joy and delight at being freed from that blind god of nature, who, with iron arms encircles his own gigantic body, ever dashing himself to pieces in order, once more, to arise anew from his grave! Judaism further teaches: "Cast down your eye into your inner, unfathomable depths, and a thousand voices will bring you word of the divine breath that reigns within you. O man, God has created you in His image, your soul is a reflection of His majesty, and among all the myriads of creatures, He has called you alone to freedom and immortality. All things, to be sure, emerged pure and beneficial from His hand, but upon you alone the royal seal of self-consciousness, of free will, and of the power of sanctification were inscribed. The cosmos, which everywhere surrounds you, cannot bewilder you. After a brief slumber, your soul gathers itself up mightily, sets itself opposite Him, and speaks: 'I am!' A wondrous beam of light, brighter than the light of the sun, suddenly descends from an uncharted height upon your benighted spirit, a beam that in the midst of the rushing current of countless worlds and beings, feels itself, thinks and senses, and adorns a handful of dust with the ruler's crown. And should He disappear when this dust returns to earth? Nevermore! You have come to yourself in order to come to God and eternally to remain bound to Him." Whatever has once recognized and found itself is of divine origin and cannot be lost in the cosmic stream. The confined bundle may perish, but not the winged flash of light that shines through it.

Judaism further teaches: "There is but a single humanity, as there is but one God, a humanity sprung from the same holy source, endowed with one and the same basic excellence, and, though divided according to different regions, lands, and broadly beneficial activities, is oriented to one and the same high goal, a huge and mighty stream which, to be sure, in its extended course is divided into various channels in order to gain room for the development of its fructifying seeds, will, once it is richly loaded with treasures in all of its parts, again unite into an indissoluble bond." All manner of Israelite teachings do not merely fail to contradict the laws of reason, but are closely attuned to the results of advancing knowledge. And what is true for the faith teachings of our religion is true as well for its various obligations, to which Moses points specifically as witnesses to the wisdom and endurance of the Israelite people before the eyes of all nations. Human cognitive ability itself, at its highest summit, regards the Decalogue revealed at Sinai as the root of all ethics, as the fundamental pillar of the world's moral order.[63] It relates to everything that the wisest among the pagan peoples in their most daring flights of thought taught regarding the relationship of the human being to his God and to his fellow creatures. It is like the proud tree to the tiny seed or like the full brightness of midday to the first rays of dusk. All of the remaining laws, which make up only further implementations of these statutes, partially contain symbolic, and therefore changeable, signs that regularly awaken Israel anew to its lofty priestly vocation or, in ancient times, separated it from the pagan peoples in order to be able one day to bind it intimately to God and to itself.

So here too not a trace of that religiosity, lacking in thought and reason, which the later rigid legality imputed to Judaism, [is] clothing the elevated school of Mosaism in the darkness of night and disfiguring it with numberless flourishes. And let me tell you about the wonderful gifts that the Sinaitic teaching imparts to the heart: about the sweet relaxation under life's burden and stress, about the abundant consolation in times of suffering, about the heavenly blissful joy at every pure delight, about the hope and the surging enthusiasm that come to all who cling to it in loyalty and love. It calls God—your Father, and you—His child! Are you able to measure the blissful treasure that these unique sounds embrace—that which reveals to your heart its deepest secrets, which thrills you with thousand-fold jubilation, which pours the richest balsam upon all of your wounds, restores your sunken courage in deepest distress, and at death's door lends new wings to your fatigued soul? Is not all this contained in one thought: "Is He not your Father?" Is it not in this unique name that the greatest of all prophets [Moses], as if to place the capstone on his gigantic temple [the Torah], enunciates but once, and namely in his swan song, which the teaching of Moses first shouted into the frightful rocky caves of paganism so that it might never be allowed to fade away? Furthermore, with its Sabbath, this teaching opens up for you a source of numberless blessings; with maternal care it intends, after days of restless effort and labor to allow the refreshing shade of peace to descend upon you, leading your soul, which so easily loses itself, back into the hut of peace, to itself and to its God. In the midst of the surging, sweeping Sambation, churning up the slime of what is common, the Sabbath holds up before your eye a clear reflection of your earthly existence as well as a vision of the Most High.[64] Can a more precious refreshment be devised for a languishing heart than this oasis in the desert, this divine messenger and redeemer that bears word of eternal life and with its magic staff draws ever new circles of light around the inner person, around families and communities, to protect them against hostile forces?

And now too the great pleasure of its festivals—what a sweet meadow, what a fullness and depth of the noblest feelings! Like angels of blissful beauty, the festivals appear for you on your pilgrimage, extending the luster of heaven even to what is terrestrial and ephemeral in order soon to lead you into the innermost sanctum of life, into the joy of opening wide golden gates so that you may adorn and beautify everything in your house, and unite the varying tones of loving hearts into the sweetest harmony. Then in the temple of the Lord the angels spread their wings over reverent souls and carry the sounds of enthusiastic, jubilant choirs upward to the Father of love so that He may direct your glance both on your tribe's glorious origins, progress, and vocation, as well as upon your own past and future! And once one considers how, with this profound sacred earnestness, this complete immersion in the innermost life of the spirit and the heart, and this indefatigable allusion to the elevated goal of our existence, our religion at the same time reveals the most sincere care for our temporal welfare, how it does not want to suppress carnal pleasure, but rather to ennoble it, how in the place of that unnatural contempt for earthly life and its demands, it allows affectionate consideration and attention to all that is purely human and regards the corporal and visible in no way as the source of sin, but rather the reverse, as the reflection of the un-seeable, as the temple of the sacred and divine. At the same time, it eternally protests against that which sees in the human being, so to speak, God's failed, shoddy piece of work, its original qualities poisoned by sin. Rather, it sees human nature in all of its relationships and with all of its mixed elements as a remarkable royal creation of divine love. Who, then, would not exultantly join in with the Psalmist [19:8]: "The teaching of the LORD is perfect, renewing life"; who also wonder at the irresistible power with which, for millennia, such a teaching exercised sway over its adherents? Ours is a religion that stands in inner harmony with the whole person, that satisfies reason and the steepest height of inquiry no less than the childlike simplicity of the heart, that instead of presenting itself as the jailer of the spirit and body, raises them to the most lofty sentiment of their majesty and shields them as a habitation of the holy with its protective wings. With ravaging conflagrations it destroys the proliferating weeds that paganism transplants into the human being. At the same time, it pours itself out upon every noble human being like mild and thousand-fold fructifying light of spring. Such a religion is rooted in the eternal laws of human nature and is, like that nature itself, secured against all upheavals and tremors; like human reason and the human heart, it can be suppressed and mishandled, but never obliterated.

Though millions of times the earth completes its annual cycle, Judaism must—like our lineage—ever and again green up in youthful vigor and blossom anew.[65] Judaism sets its main focus neither upon an arid belief in God nor upon an empty cosmopolitanism, nor yet upon its ephemeral national shell, but rather on the unification that it grants to the person with himself and thereby also with God and his people. A single God, a single human being, and a single humanity—that [the word "single"] is the key word, the call that can never die away, because the fibers of the human spirit are the strings upon which it sounds, and these strings may allow themselves to be stretched but never to be torn!

An additional principal advantage of Judaism, one that assures its continuance, is its *flexibility*, its capacity to be at home in all lands and parts of the world, to adapt to the various customs and levels of education, and willingly to adopt everything that serves its enrichment. In this respect, as well, it lends itself to praise: *Torat YHVH temimah meshivat nafesh* ["the teaching of the LORD is perfect, renewing life," Ps. 19:8].

God's teaching is perfect, not one-sided or limited to certain areas, but rather a divine planting that flourishes everywhere. Among all the untruths with which Judaism has been slandered by its superficial detractors, history has refuted none more decisively than that which brands it with rigidity.[66] It certainly never gave up its God for another, not even then when the entire world still sank down before self-created idols; it never despaired of the dignity of the human race, of the future reign of light and truth, even when lies and depravity flooded the entire earth. It lowered its banner neither before the fire-spouting idols of Canaan nor before the enticing creations of Chaldean and Greek wisdom, nor before the dominion of the Romans. To be sure, it proved itself to be consistently inaccessible in relation to its innermost sanctum, but this firmness, with which it strides through all sovereign lands, has nothing in common with that pride which looks down contemptuously upon the spiritual life of the peoples, nothing in common with that hardness and tenacity that allows neither emergent nor declining worlds to have any influence upon it. Rather, it bears the deepest marks of the concepts and customs of those nations that, during its millennia-long career, came into close contact with it. At all times it possessed an open ear for the murmuring of the divine spirit evident in the cultural advance of the peoples. It had an open heart for everything that served its fructification and ennoblement, and above all, an open eye for the situation and requirements of its being.

I do not wish now to speak of that changeability of Judaism's forms which already comes clearly into view in the Books of Moses, not of that notable transformation which, even according to Talmudic evidence, the religious thought and feeling of its adherents experienced during the Babylonian captivity, not of the countless changes that its exterior underwent at the time of the Second Temple; but rather only of that flexibility and capacity for development to which the entire course of its destiny, ever since the destruction of the Temple, ever since the dispersion of Israel to all parts of the earth, attests, and which alone put it in a situation where, fructifying and binding in an as yet still narrow riverbed, it would traverse the entire world. Judaism did not die of the shattering blow that drove its adherents from their ancestral soil to all four corners of the earth and with a single blow tore away the proud adornment of its husk. For two thousand years it has been dwelling on what had been foreign soil—dwelling without Temple, without priesthood, without sacrifices, without purity laws, without the seventh-year prohibitions and the Jubilee, without a highest legal authority, without flagellation and capital punishment for the wicked. Indeed, during the dispersion it attained hundreds of victories, each of which can be set next to those of the Maccabees; the splintered Israel was raised to a high point of morality and sacrificial courage that exceeded its earlier situation while still in its homeland. But would it have been capable of achieving all of this without long ago having been mortally wounded in its innermost fundamentals, forced to sink away withered and parched, were it not for that undamaged rigor which sooner or later, again and again, pushes out strange intrusions as if they are incapable of being steeped in its own powerful juices? Within it dwells a flexibility that permits the willing acceptance of noble and enriching influences with regard to exterior form when they are directed toward the urgent requirements of spiritual, social, and political life. Only with such flexibility could the Sinaitic teaching emerge from the ashes of the national sanctuary, which buried their body, chained as it was to the soil, and allowed it to arise anew, refined and viable, in order that it might be able to begin its travels through the world. Only in this way was it able to contribute most intensively to the great progressive epochs of humanity and allow itself to be thoroughly shaken by the electrical shocks they produced without altering its basic tone. Only in this way could it occur that, bent under numberless turns and convolutions, it remained unbroken, and that such jolts, which often seemed to push it into the depths of an abyss, simply led to a greater deepening of its innermost essence.

In truth! Judaism does not attribute its continued existence to that indolence which tries to avoid moving from its place in the face of the urgent demands of the present, which ever and again points to what has been and what has come about, seeking by its outcries to silence history whenever history would allow the flutter of its wings to be heard, and not granting legal status to history's achievements until they have lost their breath of life. In fateful times that indolence serves neither for complaint nor lamentation, at most for insult, calumny, and denunciation. Not seldom it leads to a despicable hypocrisy that appears to the people like a roaring lion locked in the cage of convention. But behind its back, the lion having quickly slipped out through the little back door in order to pay tribute to that zeitgeist which they have damned, the roaring of the lion is transformed into the cooing of a dove. If these people had their way, Judaism and Jewishness would long ago have bled to death on account of its lacerations and injuries. But what is it that today still makes them both great and strong, what secures for our holy religion, not only an advanced age, but an imperishable youthful strength? It is that power of action which, always at the right time, assists its slumbering seeds; which possesses immeasurable germinating power and which, ready for sacrifice, shuns no scattering, no persecution in order *to protect* the endangered sanctum, to protect the energy with which Samuel gave his agreement to the alteration of the Mosaic constitution in order to establish the Israelite monarchy;[67] the power with which Zerubbabel, Ezra, and Nehemiah set themselves at the front of the Jewish colonies returning to Palestine and there, under unspeakable difficulties, sought once more to strengthen the divine teaching in widely alienated hearts; the power with which, following the destruction of the Temple, Rabbi Yohanan ben Zakkai undertook a thorough transformation of Israelite ritual;[68] and the power with which so many great teachers in Israel, applying of all of their talents, worked for the religious ennoblement of our tribe and assisted the ever living spirit of Moses' teaching to attain a glorious victory over the dead letters.

This lofty task has also fallen to us, my friends, and so let us then today, on the birthday of that wonder-working teaching, which we have come together to celebrate, praise our God anew, never tire or cool in our sacred strivings however great the hindrances may be that will stand in our path. Let us resolve never to lower the luminous banner that we have grasped nor ever to exchange it again for that useless battle armor which delusion and hypocrisy pass off as Judaism. Let us forever hold fast to the spirit of God, which in this house loftily unfurls its pinions, and carry its ennobling and purifying message into the family and into life. Thus, may we do our part to prepare that time when, according to the proclamation of the prophet, the LORD will enter into a new covenant with those of the house of Israel, place his teaching within them, and write it in their hearts.[69] We shall not be privileged to see that beautiful time, but it is already dawning from the womb of a not altogether distant future, and our descendants will be able to sun themselves in its full radiance. "Yes, God's sacred teaching, you will attain your victory!

You will one day draw near in full majesty and see before your glance the tottering realm of darkness and lies come crashing down! Not in vain have you withstood numberless gigantic battles, not in vain cast eyes upon the cradle and the grave of numberless peoples and stood firm amidst the tumultuous uproar of the millennia while spreading your net over all parts of the world! One day the love of you will blaze up into a flame in millions of hearts and spirits wherein the dust and decay that has turned you into a rock will go up in smoke, melting your chains and blending all the peoples of the earth into God's immense host. From this flame God will once again speak to our lineage, not in order to separate one people from another but rather to bind together those that are separated. You, the holy teaching, will be enabled to emerge in full royal regalia as a liberated Messiah who, born on a bare rock, will, with its scepter, extend from one end of the world to the other!" Amen.

4

God

God is one of the most difficult topics in all of religion, Judaism being no exception. God, it can be claimed, is at once deeply approachable—the guardian of pregnancies, the healer of the sick, the comforter of mourners, the redeemer of Zion—and at the same time unfathomably distant, the Being "who laid the earth's foundations . . . fixes its dimensions . . . closed the sea behind doors . . . assigned the dawn its place" (Job 38:4,5,9,12). The Hebrew Bible barely engages with the "idea" of God, choosing rather to describe God's actions and emotions, God's being*ness* rather than God's *being*.

For the most part, the classical rabbis followed suit. There is no tractate on "God" in the Mishnah or Talmud. Instead, there are stories, parables, emotions, dictates, conversations. There is the elucidation of law, and through God's laws the suggestion that we can perhaps come to glimpse what God, God's self, is like, and what God, God's self, cares most deeply about. As the English jurist William Blackstone (1723–80) is often purported to have said, "Law is the embodiment of the moral sentiment of the people," a belief that applies equally well to the Rabbinic conception if only we substitute "Divine" for its closing word.

Thus it fell to later Jewish thinkers, informed, as often as not, by Christian and Islamic theologians, to set out to describe what God *is*, and therefore what God is *not*, rather than just what God does and feels and desires. The greatest practitioners of what we now call medieval Jewish philosophy—the first Jewish attempt to systematically elucidate the core theological tenets of Judaism, especially concerning what we can and cannot know about God—were Saadia Gaon (ca. 892–942), Bahya

Ibn Pakuda (ca. 1050–1120), Judah Halevi (ca. 1075–1141), and Moses Maimonides (1135–1204). All four wrote in Arabic or Judeo-Arabic, and each in his own way left an indelible mark on all later Jewish thinking about God. They could not have been more different. Saadia's *The Book of Beliefs and Opinions* (933), the first known systematic treatise of Rabbinic theology, describes our understanding of God's character as stemming from our knowledge of God as, first and foremost, Creator, and seeks mainly to undergird Judaism's monotheistic contentions, primarily against Christian Trinitarianism. Ibn Pakuda, in *The Book of the Direction to the Duties of the Heart* (ca. 1080), argues that knowledge of God's creations leads to knowledge of God, that investigations into the workings of the world lead to an understanding of the essential characteristics of the Divine. Halevi, the greatest poet of Jewish Andalusia, drunk on the beauty and mystery of life, penned his dialogue *The Kuzari* (ca. 1139) as an expression and defense of an empathic, affirmative understanding of God, wherein all the emotions we attribute to God, and all the feelings engendered by God, are themselves part of God and add to our knowledge of God. And Maimonides, perhaps Judaism's greatest postbiblical genius, in his *Guide of the Perplexed*, most clearly elucidates the path of apophatic, that is, negative theology: the rejection of all anthropocentric terms as too limited to be appropriately applied to the Divine.

Modern Jewish theologians of the nineteenth century were the heirs of these medieval systematic treatises. This chapter offers one example of each of the two major modern responses. On the one hand, the nineteenth century witnessed the development of a theology of a so-called ethical monotheism, the idea (already implicit in Saadia and Ibn Pakuda) that God—by dint of being Singular, being Creator, and being (definitionally) purely Just—created Judaism to usher into the world a vision of moral perfection, over and against the ethically equivocal beliefs of the pagans. Ethical monotheism therefore holds that Judaism is a means by which the greatest truth is revealed—that as the pioneer religion of monotheism, Judaism becomes the handmaiden of a universal morality, the font from which a continuous message of righteousness and justice flows (also through, secondarily, its daughter religions, Christianity and Islam). Then again, other modern Jewish theologians, seeking to move away from the corporeal, even sensuous language of the classical rabbis and toward a more metaphysical spirituality, turned to Maimonidean philosophy, especially as exemplified in his *Guide*,[1] animated by its fundamental premise that human language is, at base, incapable of expressing even a single completely correct statement about God's ultimate Being.

JOSEPH LEWIN SAALSCHÜTZ (1801–63)

Joseph Lewin Saalschütz (b. 1801, Königsberg; d. 1863, Königsberg) was a rabbi, scholar, and early Jewish archaeologist. Writing numerous works on the development of Hebrew and Israelite religion based on the evidence uncovered about neighboring Near Eastern civilizations, in 1855–56 he published the groundbreaking work *Archäologie der Hebräer* (Archaeology of the Hebrews), which covered topics from ancient dress and home economics to governance and cultic practices. Briefly practicing as a rabbi and private instructor in Berlin and Vienna in the late 1820s and early 1830s, he returned to Königsberg in 1835, spending the remainder of his career there as a rabbi, as well as, from 1847 onward, a tutor in Israelite archaeology at the university. A prolific scholar, Saalschütz also wrote on ancient and modern theology, applying his knowledge of the Classical and Near Eastern sources to explore the development of Jewish religion.

In the following selection, excerpted from an 1844 article entitled "Der Monotheismus in sittlicher Beziehung" (Ethical monotheism), Saalschütz argues for the intrinsic, divine relationship between God's unique oneness and moral and ethical perfection.[2] "This unification of all forces, feelings, and life activities in beholding the holy God," he writes, "will at the same time offer [adherents of monotheism] the unifying standard of their moral self-perfection." In other words, the practice of monotheism itself is part of the maintenance of an ethical society, for otherwise, the dictates of errant doctrines or malevolent deities can lead people toward terrible actions—such as, he distinctly articulates, that of child sacrifice.

For Saalschütz, monotheism and its biblical dictates (be holy; love your neighbor) are reflections of the perfect nature of divinity itself. When God commands Israel to be like God, there is almost no need to dictate a further morality, for the whole field of ethics is already revealed: God, who created and loves all humans, demands us to be like God, which is to say, loving all our fellows. Only monotheism, Saalschütz writes, can inculcate such an all-encompassing, universalist morality.

Ethical Monotheism (1844)

Translated by Noa Sophie Kohler

The idea of godlikeness can have its absolute moral value only when combined with the belief in One, and therefore true and perfect God—the striving for a likeness to gods who were at times worse than men themselves could not lead the latter very far—and only within monotheism could this idea truly develop in all directions and gain its full validity for all relationships in life. If God is *unified,* as is intrinsic in the essence of divinity, and if, furthermore, the *likeness to God* is in fact not a mere theory but the actual manifestation of our inmost, spiritual nature, then we must also understand the endeavor to gain inner *unity*, to be the highest goal of our self-perfection and self-duty. Given that the highest task of our intellectual powers and the last stage of our drive for knowledge is the striving for the knowledge of God as the eternal most worth knowing; furthermore, given that a result of this knowledge will be, to an equal extent, joy in beholding the divine perfection, i.e., the love for God in its necessary association with gratitude, trust, and reverence—a love that will not just behave passively but will *actively* emerge where it can—then this side of the unification of our being is already denoted in the sentence: "Love God with all your heart, with all your life and all (temporal and spiritual) might" [Deut. 6:5], which thus signifies both a duty to God and a duty to oneself. But this unification of all forces, feelings, and life activities in beholding the *holy* God will at the same time offer them the unifying standard of their moral self-perfection with the biblical commandment: "You shall be holy, for I, the LORD your God, am holy!" [Lev. 19:2]. And this sanctification of our being in the reflection of the divine holiness will in two ways bring about the moral unity of the interior, the peace of mind, which is the foundation of our true happiness in life: *on the one hand*, that no claim can be asserted in the name of any higher power and deity; *on the other*, in our own, possibly temporal interest which contradicts the unshakable, godlike feeling of the good and right in itself, and so seeks to bring the conflict into the innermost [chambers] of our heart.

It is obvious that in polytheism, the *first*, as well as the *second*, condition of this self-unification was often endangered, and that only monotheism can completely fulfill it. Through oracles and priests, the gods made their will and their claims known to the people: delusion and superstition appeared as legislators! What moral perfection could legislation have that emanated from deities who themselves were thought of as imperfect?[3] How many things then appeared as *divine* demands that contradicted the better, *human* feeling! So, what authority should the mortal obey? And if he followed the *one*, overwhelmed by delusion and its helpers and priests, how could he be reconciled with the other? How disgusted must someone with pure and noble feelings be when faced with this fornication that was sanctified to the gods?—We shudder when we read in [Roman historian] Diodorus ([*Bibliotheca Historica*] XX. 14), how once in Carthage the children of the noblest houses were offered as a sacrifice to Saturn in order to avert this god's disfavor from the land. But how did those parents feel when they caused the horrible death by fire to their children? They were not permitted to evade the claims of this god, nor did they want to. But it would mean calling into doubt the divinity and authenticity of our inner moral law if we wanted to believe that it [the moral law] was completely destroyed in all of them and that it was entirely *taken up* by their terrible piety. And if this were not so, how could peace ever come to the heart that sinned so bloodily against itself?[4] How should it orient itself in the darkness of these doubts and contradictions? Only monotheism gave peace, light, and warmth in the gloomy madness of this desolation ("Thus there was the cloud with the darkness, and it illuminated the night" [Exod. 14:20]). For monotheism established as one of its most important principles that *God* demands nothing that contradicts the pure feelings of one's own heart, and on the other hand that *man* can find his true happiness only by convincing himself to walk with God: "And now, O Israel, what does the LORD, your God demand of you? Only this: to revere the LORD your God, to walk in His paths, to love Him, and to serve the LORD your God with all your heart and soul, keeping the LORD's commandments and laws, which I enjoin upon you today, *for your good!*" [Deut. 10:12–13, Saalschütz's emphasis].—"Surely, this Instruction which I enjoin upon you this day is not too baffling for you, nor is it beyond reach (solely external). It is not in the heavens, that you should say, 'Who among us can go up to the heavens and get it for us and impart it to us, that we may observe it?' Neither is it beyond the sea, that you should say, 'Who among us can cross to the other side of the sea and get it for us and impart it to us, that we may observe it?' No, the thing is very close to you, in your mouth and in your heart, to observe it" [Deut. 30:11–14]. It comes from God, whose image is now *His* revealed law (in human words that are on your lips), that you feel in your inner self as a deep premonition of your godlike nature (before which already Cain could not lift up his sinful gaze), and your heart warrants its truthfulness and *authenticity* that corresponds to the innermost human will. "With what shall I approach the LORD [to appear in a courteous way]? Shall I bow *down* before God on *high*? Shall I give my first-born for my transgression (cf. 2 Kings 3:27), the fruit of my body for my sins? He has told you, O man, what is good, and what the LORD requires of you; only to do justice, and to love goodness, and to walk modestly with your God" [Mic. 6:6–8].

Be holy! Be like the One God! This is man's bond of peace, not only with his creator but also with himself. Paganism was evidently often lacking a supreme principle of self-obligations. Stoicism, which put self-control at the forefront, thus became one-sided and extravagant. One could not say about it: "[It] is not too baffling for you, nor is it beyond reach" [Deut. 30:11]. And even though Stoicism had many followers, this was not for its naturalness but rather for its peculiarity, though it also gained followers for its moral striving in opposition to the general, prevalent lasciviousness and immorality, and from the desire to establish self-legislation, which the prevailing folk religion could not offer. Epicureanism had no spiritual, purely moral foundation, even if its starting point was: Be moderate in order to enjoy even more! It was just a refinement of the prevailing licentiousness and hedonism, and in its essence, it was suited to increase those. [The founder of Spartan militarism and legalism] Lycurgus and [the Athenian philosopher] Plato wanted the individual personalities with all their energy and all inclinations to be completely absorbed in the interest of the common good, in the love of the fatherland. This love will always occupy a high status in the realm of moral commandments; says Hillel: "If I am only for myself, what am I?" [PA 1:14]. But it can hardly be said that there are self-obligations for man—a being created for temporality and *eternity*—which would not include the love of the fatherland. Yet the highest moral command of monotheism not only encompasses the whole range of self-duties; it also teaches us to recognize their hierarchy and to reconcile the conflicts of earthly and spiritual duties in a higher unity.

And, in turn, also our duties and our relationship with our fellow human beings find their true rationale in the unity of God, and their supreme law in the godlikeness that we demand. Outside the realm of the highest knowledge, the idea of the love of man could never have developed in all its fullness and universality.

The One God is also the father of *all* humans ("Have we not all one Father? Did not one God create us?" [Mal. 2:10])—His love embraces them all. We are hereby told that we are to love them as our brothers, as godlike beings created equal to us, and that, ultimately, this love must likewise embrace all, in a godlike manner and [transcending] narrowmindedness. For the strength of this love for our fellow human beings, as equally feeling and thinking beings, the safest and highest standard is given, namely the feeling towards ourselves: "Love your fellow as yourself!" [Lev. 19:18]. The personal experience that we gain on our own bodies—to what extent something is pleasant or hurtful—shall guide our behavior towards our fellow to the fullest and noblest degree. As Hillel noted, this is the Basic Law. Everything else that can be said about the duties towards humans is nothing but the commentary, the explanatory clarification of the main idea.[5] Once the sentence is established—love your fellow as you love *yourself*, as you are *allowed* to love yourself, being godlike and destined for holiness, love him as a *child of God*—it is already indicated how we should behave towards our fellow when he is poor, sick, or otherwise suffering, when he is about to commit a sin against God, or commits offences against ourselves, as our enemy. It is indicated if we shall also love him, if he is not of the same descent as we are; if we are allowed to murder him, hate him, beat him, endanger his property or his health, deal with him with lies and deceit or any kind of injustice, or if we shall rather devote the most loving care to the preservation and integrity of his life, his property, his health, and his honor, to promote his spiritual and his external true self in every respect. Not a word needs to be said about any of this, and any moral being will be able to deduce it from that first sentence, with a little thought. So, to appreciate the monotheistic doctrine of revelation there is no need to anxiously research whether every single specific commandment of love for one's fellow is indeed written out, since they are all already included and given in that one first sentence. In fact, the divine law is here astonishingly complete ("The teaching of the LORD is perfect" [Ps. 19:8]). None of the points indicated were ignored or left to individual discretion; the duty of love—in all its special relationships and applications—is repeatedly declared, commanded, and warmly recommended with the most touching expressions of ultimate divine goodness.

DAVID KAUFMANN (1852–99)

David Kaufmann (b. 1852, Kojetein; d. 1899, Karlsbad) was an influential scholar of medieval Jewish philosophy and a famous collector of Judaica. Earning his doctorate in 1875 from the University of Leipzig, in 1877 he was ordained a rabbi at the Jewish Theological Seminary in Breslau, though he never occupied a pulpit. That same year he joined the faculty of the newly established Rabbinical Seminary in Budapest (Országos Rabbiképző Intézet) and remained in Hungary for the rest of his short life, teaching history, philosophy of religion, and homiletics. In Budapest, in his role as librarian of the Rabbinical Seminary, as well as a private personal collector and member of Mekitze Nirdamim (lit., "Rousers of those who slumber," a society dedicated to the preservation and publication of Hebrew texts), he discovered several invaluable manuscripts, among them the oldest complete text of the Mishnah (dating from the tenth century, and helping to explain the philological history of the traditional text), as well as dozens of medieval illuminated incunabula, including of Maimonides' *Mishneh Torah*, the Passover Haggadah, and the High Holiday *makhzor*. Indeed, alongside his magisterial work on philosophy, Kaufmann is often credited as the father of the field of the study of Jewish art, and the first modern scholar to persuasively disprove the common assumption that historical Judaism was aniconic (against images). (Subsequent manuscript research and archaeology in the Land of Israel has only confirmed Kaufmann's views.)

One of the most important representatives of *Wissenschaft des Judentums* in the late nineteenth century, he was especially embittered by the lack of interest in the results of *Wissenschaft* within the non-Jewish scholarly world and took it upon himself to explain and defend Judaism for many decades. In his writings on medieval Jewish philosophy and the history of Jewish art, for example, he was at pains to demonstrate the interconnection between Jewish, Christian, and Islamic thinking and artistry. In his writings on Jewish history, he focused on religious and political figures whose lives spanned the Jewish and non-Jewish worlds, including Israel Conegliano (seventeenth century, Padua) and Samson Wertheimer (1658–1724, Hungary). After his death, his students collected and published many of his sermons articulating his theology of Judaism, which he had delivered in German at the synagogue of the Budapest seminary.[6]

The text translated here is a short chapter, the "Epilogue" from his monumental work *Geschichte der Attributenlehre in der Jüdischen Philosophie* (History of the doctrine of attributes in Jewish religious philosophy, 1877), a comprehensive, five hundred–page study of the history of the teachings on the divine attributes in medieval Jewish philosophy.[7] Summarizing his own view of Maimonides' famous and controversial "negative theology," the claim that we cannot have any knowledge whatsoever of the divine essence (cf. *Guide of the Perplexed* 1:51–60), and proceeding exactly in the same way that the *Guide* proposes for gaining knowledge of God, Kaufmann proceeds to struggle with the radical nature of Maimonides' theory. Raising and rejecting a number of objections to the notion that "negative theology" can to produce knowledge, he eventually ends with a confirmation of Maimonides' thought that is in fact exclusively built on the negation of his opponents' arguments. The emotional language at the end makes it a document of a certain nineteenth-century religious conviction rather than an academic treatise.

That Maimonides' philosophy as developed in the *Guide* forms the center of Kaufmann's own views of a Jewish concept of God is an example of how the academic rediscovery of the *Guide* informed the personal religious orientation of many *Wissenschaft* scholars.

On Maimonides' Negative Theology (1877)

Translated by Shira Billet

What we can know of God is solely the fact of His absolutely necessary existence; this is the starting point and end point of Maimonides' theology. The immediate consequence of this cognition forms the basis of his entire doctrine of the Attributes, the conviction of the impossibility of any kind of compositeness in God, because such compositeness is now no longer possible in itself but only on the precondition [of the existence] of a composer.[8] Every proposition concerning the being of God is thus absolutely impossible; to attribute a quality to God is to bring bearing and being borne, and thus duality, into His being. Only those attributes may be identified by which the being of God remains inviolably complete, as in the attributes of action. However, it must always be kept in view that they do not correspond to something like different aspects within His being.

The [attributes] of relation also deserve some consideration. This allowance of positive attributes nevertheless ought to serve only as explanation of those [attributes] appearing in scripture, [and this allowance,] however, in no way implies a concession to unfettered uses of the same; rather, it is most strongly prohibited to use it even in prayer or to transgress the measure allowed through scripture and institution. They [the attributes of relation] could not have been done without, as supports of the God-concept for the weak human understanding, and thus constitute a necessary evil from which to liberate ourselves with the passage of time in general and with a more complete knowledge of God. If, however, on top of this, a series of attributes, which claim their origins in either actions or relations of God, emerge with the pretense of predicating something positive of God, what may thus be considered [each attribute's] true content is only the fact that its opposite is thereby denied of God. As humans, we cannot do otherwise than to fend off from God certain qualities that we consider to be imperfections, and to do this in such a way that we ascribe to Him their opposites. Only the negative content [of the God-idea] is hereby to be considered as true, whereas the positive form is vacant appearance; in truth, God is equally as elevated over the perfections seemingly attributed to Him as over the imperfections fended off from Him. Whereas even the permissible positive attributes could not be absolved of any appearance of a threat to the divine unity, with the negative [attributes] the appearance of a multiplicity within God is avoided; they are thus in truth the solely permitted [attributes]. One must thereby confine oneself to these; these alone may one augment: Only what God is not, can one cognize. [One's] striving must be directed to [the negative attributes], rather than, through an accumulation of perfections, to falsely believe one has approximated a cognition of God [in positive attributes]. [The negative attributes allow one] to perceive the fallacy of one's purported experiences of the divine being, [and] to step by step free oneself of the deceptions to which one is easily prone to abandon oneself in this context. Every advancement in the cognition of God has only this meaning—that we see our conviction that we can know nothing of God's being proven true again and again.

We must admit that this kind of inquiry makes it seem that the goal is to disperse any ideas about God in the seeker's mind, rather than consolidate them. Does this not rob human beings of their God, when every possibility of cognizing Him is taken from them, every hope of being able to come nearer to Him is destroyed? Instead of abundance and vitality which the believer would be allowed to coax himself to encounter in the God-concept, only the bleak and vacant now stares at him; the most secure and precious possession seems to turn into a cold, imperceptible, and repulsive silhouette. To be unable to know what God is is to forfeit God Himself [altogether]; the assertion of His inscrutability amounts to the sublation of His being. To abandon one determination of the divine being after another means for the believer nothing other than to sacrifice, piecemeal, his representation of God. How should continual not-knowing be our singular knowing? How can the ever-renewed declaration of our incapacity to cognize God amount to our true cognition of Him?

Had Maimonides any sense of the hopelessness of his teaching? Did he not notice that along the way of denying God's predications he came close to denying God Himself? We will now have to reject this conception of the incompatibility of his teaching with religion as superficial and merely seemingly valid, if we find the author free of any fear of his ruinousness for the thinking believer and, to the contrary, if we see him, with ceremonious words, presenting his opinion as truly felicitous. We know with certainty that God exists. This consciousness of His necessary existence must be most specially fortified and tended in us as our unique knowledge of God. Far from suffering a shock through the sublation of the attributes, this consciousness will, through the removal of the attributes, [tend and fortify] our own foremost and firmest conviction, thus clearing away all that would likely sublate or damage the absolute necessity of the divine existence by introducing multiplicity into His being. There is thus an increase in the knowledge of God. The possibility of a continuous fortification of His being in our thought remains open now as before; we will be ever more steeped in the existence [*Dasein*] of God the more we free ourselves from representations that endanger His necessity. The denial of qualities thus does not deny God but rather genuinely first restores Him to us truly and entirely. The unknowability of God does not condemn all human beings to the same humble level of ignorance; to the contrary, the diversity of human cognition of God first finds therein its true grounding: that the measure of that which is kept away from the concept of God is not equal for all [human minds]. It is a fallacy to believe that the levels of God-cognition are sublated if it is once certain that we can know nothing about God. It surely seems to us that continual negation would not be able to generate knowledge; however, experience counters this apparent proposition. Even on a negative path we can arrive at concepts, as vividly evidenced through examples from life, that enable us to come to a representation of a thing through nothing but negation. Thus, the negation of the attributes indeed has the advantages, without the disadvantages, of the positive path to God-cognition; any progress that we make in it [i.e., God-cognition] fortifies our conviction of the existence [*Dasein*] of the Necessarily-Existent.

Maimonides demonstrates this well by way of an example of how cognition of a thing can be reached on a negative path, and how it can even get at nuances therein. Is the issue not, however, hereby overlooked, that with respect to material things the cognition of an uncertain thing will be obtained by way of continual negations because the number of possible genera and species to which the object can belong is something to be known and therefore to be exhausted, whereas in relation to God, the continuousness of negations comprises no increase in approximation to the concept, for this [concept], from the outset, would have been considered as outside of all categorizations known to us? In fact, Maimonides can only have resorted to this example from the finite realm by way of comparison and approximation. As we could generate a concept of an object—with respect to finite things—through nothing but negations, [a concept] to which one approaches in measures, as one understands more in negating from it, so also with respect to God, in reference to whom each avoidance [of a misunderstanding, achieved through negation] must equally be considered a gain in understanding, can a continual approximation to His concept be mediated through negations.

The scope of the concept of God is certainly capable of no proliferation, for us—and surely equally for Moses as for the last confessors [of Judaism]—but if and when each false representation threatens the whole with respect to this concept that allows absolutely no compositeness and thus absolutely no partial truth, it can thus be claimed that whoever grasps fewer negations of God is further away from the cognition of God.[9] With every step on the track of negation we bring ourselves closer to a level of the cognition of the incomparability and transcendence of God. Not a new property in His concept, but a lessening of doubt in our knowledge; not an increase in experience, but a lessening of fallacy and ignorance designates, in this context, an increase in knowledge. If, on this path, we do not even gain a representation of God, it is nevertheless a sufficient gain, if we are released from the delusions of knowing God when we [actually] are far from His cognition [i.e., cognizing Him]. To indulge in no errors is, for the human being, the highest [attainment] that he can achieve; he knows the most about God when he learns to cognize the incorrectness of his purported knowledge of Him. How correct this idea is can be seen through a glimpse at the subsequent history of the teaching of the attributes, in which we measure the height and the significance of a thinker [through the measure of] how he exposed the deficient and the anthropomorphic in seemingly established attributes.

On this path, however, are the positive attributes not once again, as it were, admitted through a back door? The flipside of negation is positing. Of what avail is it to deny those attributes, if the representation of the opposite is thereby immediately awakened in the mind, and a positive quality is attributed to God? We want to negate impotence of God and to think that He is the not nonpowerful. The flipside of this negation entails the most decisive affirmation, and while we intended to fend off a predication from God, we [instead] ascribed to Him a different [predication], that of omnipotence. If, however, we want to raise God above even this predication, then we have truly denied God, since we thereby assert that neither of the two opposites can be predicated of God; He thus could be neither unpowerful nor powerful, neither un-knowing nor knowing. In truth, Maimonides' teaching is not affected by this objection. He absolutely concedes that in every negation, something is posited in God; for that reason, he also hastens immediately to sublate this position by saying that he represents it as merely homonymous with the concept commonly known to us by the same name. It certainly suggests itself, to derive from the judgment "God is not un-knowing" the conclusion "therefore he is all-knowing"; yet we cannot for even a moment consider this attribute [i.e., God as all-knowing] as a serious statement about God's being, for we, steeped in the impossibility of experiencing something about God's essence, must retain the attribute as merely homonymous with that which we understand under this concept. One cannot therefore claim that the teaching of the negative attributes divests God of all determinations, imperfections as well as perfections; to the contrary, it fully allows that perfections are present in God, only that we cannot know them, and thus are incapable of stating anything about them. If we are forced to think of God as free from all the defects that we already term human [defects] as such, then we are thus in no way allowed to ascribe to Him the merits corresponding to them, for a cognition of His being is absolutely impossible for us. The being that is, for us, the most certain of all beings is not indeterminate; only we are not permitted to gain a representation of His unparalleled being.[10]

If it is first established that we can know nothing about God, then it is clear that we thus far approximate more closely to this our unique knowing, that we know nothing, as we cast away from ourselves the fallacies, the heresies, the acquired misunderstandings and prejudices, in which we wrongly believe ourselves to possess something of [genuine] God-knowledge, toward clearer insight into their untruth and perversity. According to Maimonides' view, an accrual of negations is a positive augmentation of our knowing, and the positive attributes according to the proponents of the teaching of the cognizability of God render to Him, in a reversal, the negative attributes. That one [the proponent of God's knowability] thinks, the more of God he knows, the more he is in a position to express about Him; but this one [Maimonides] is convinced that the less he wrongly believes himself allowed to attribute to Him, the more he will have approximated to our uniquely possible cognition of Him. The work is the same on both sides. Whereas the confessor of the positive attributes believes that his God-concept is only solidified and fulfilled when he brings forth ever newer determinations of His perfection, the one who is steeped in the uncognizability of God believes His grandeur is only verified and strengthened when he progresses to ever higher levels at which he rejects dishonorable representations of God, which he had earlier believed to have honored Him.

To some extent, there is an ecstasy in this dreariness, [in the task of] purifying and shining light through the last hideouts and haunts of our putative knowledge of God with the torch of undaunted thought. The more we seem to move away from God, the more we feel ourselves proximate to Him; what to others seems to be a continual sacrificing of the most precious convictions, we consider to be a progressive gain, a sweet enrichment in pure representations of the most certain [being] of all existents. And what makes this dark approach so appealing is precisely that we cannot think of God in all those ways in which we could conceive His transcendence. This "I know not" is not vacuous;

it finds constant nourishment and fulfillment in the unmeasured succession of representations above which we must raise God. However, it also spares the believer the pain of seeing God's putative qualities kick about in contradiction with one another, as must inevitably be the case when originally finite concepts are utilized to impart a cognition of the infinite. For the one who abides by the uncognizability of God and His qualities, the sight of evil in the world does not refute God's omni-benevolence; [for such a person] there is no persistent intractable knot that [for others] grows out of the challenge of how to relate divine omniscience and human freedom of the will. For he does not think that by artificially adding the prefix "all" [omni] to our limited conception of goodness and knowledge, thus elevating those attributes to the level of inconceivability, as in all-goodness [omni-benevolence] and all-knowing [omniscience], that the limit and finitude of our conceptions of these concepts is thus removed. He keeps divine knowing free, from the start, from determinations, which the one who falsely considers them to be positively present in God must sooner or later decide to sublate.

2

Twilight of Modernity

The Early Twentieth Century

5

The Search for Essence

When in 1905 Rabbi Leo Baeck (1873–1956) titled his first, highly programmatic book *Das Wesen des Judentums* (The essence of Judaism), this was a direct response to German historian Adolf von Harnack's Das *Wesen des Christentums* (The essence of Christianity, 1900) as well as the summary of an entire project in modern Jewish theology that had begun with Moses Mendelssohn in the eighteenth century. For Baeck and his peers, the search for essence was supposed to be an antidote to what they perceived as the religious factionalism and social fragmentation of Judaism and the Jewish people in the modern era. Whereas in the nineteenth century modern Jewish theologians had argued that Judaism's lack of identifiable dogmatic beliefs and its nonhierarchical structure had been the very means of its survival as a more or less coherent religious community across all the years of exile, for Jewish theologians in the twentieth century the scene they witnessed appeared much different indeed. No longer could Judaism—once a single people with common prayers, common halakhah, and a common historical narrative about itself—be juxtaposed to Christianity, rife with factions, doctrinal denunciations, and a parade of historical schisms. At the turn of the twentieth century, against all historical precedent, Judaism seemed to be starting down the same road. Something needed to be done.

Into the breach stepped Leo Baeck and Solomon Schechter (1847–1915), two of the greatest Jewish scholars and social organizers of the modern period, and Hermann Cohen (1842–1918), one of modern Judaism's most profound philosophical minds. All three, along with their peers (including Heymann Steinthal and Max Wiener, likewise excerpted in this chapter), believed deeply in the continued unification of Judaism and the Jewish people—that something beyond ritual practice and legal obligation united all Jews and set them apart, not just from pagans but from the other major monotheisms as well. In short, there existed an essence to Judaism that lay outside the sum of commandments (mitzvot) and ritual obligations.

This theology of "Jewish essence" was greatly influenced by the philosophical school of neo-Kantianism and its method of "regulative idealization"—that is, the conscious selection of precisely those aspects of historical Jewish thought that supported a view of Judaism as rational and ethical monotheism, thus allowing these Jewish concepts to be not so much historically true as universally valid. In like vein, irrational aspects of Judaism, even those recognized as part of the history of Jewish thought, were dismissed as philosophically negligible. The essentialist project was the winnowing of the rational from the irrational. In other words, "essentialist" theologians held the view that logical or rational religious beliefs transcended their historical moment, while irrational or superstitious ones were the products of specific times and places. In identifying Judaism's rational elements, modern theologians sought to create a body of transhistorical and universal Jewish truths that were at the same time distinctly and particularly Jewish.

In this manner, modern Jewish theology gave new and rational meaning to almost all the major concepts of the Jewish religion. Creation, for example, was a continuous process of, in fact, preserving the world; Messianism was the nonpersonal, eternal hope for a better future for all of humanity, with the people of Israel being God's suffering servant (Isaiah) and accepting the scourge of antisemitism as a means to atone for all other nations' sins. Above all, such an abstract interpretation of "pure" Jewish monotheism offered a theological foundation for the whole direction in modern Jewish thought: The belief in One transcendent God came to mean One ethics, One humanity, and One common and better future.

HERMANN COHEN (1842–1918)

Hermann Cohen (b. 1842, Coswig; d. 1918, Berlin) was a German Jewish philosopher and the founder of the Marburg School of neo-Kantianism. Before moving to Marburg, Cohen attended the Jewish Theological Seminary in Breslau as well as universities across eastern Germany (Breslau, Berlin). He began teaching at the University of Marburg in 1873 and became a professor there in 1875.

Cohen devoted his life to expounding a view of Kantian philosophy that neither lapsed into metaphysics nor relied on empirical science for external legitimation. A leading thinker as well as public intellectual, his most famous work of Jewish philosophy, the posthumously published *Religion der Vernunft aus den Quellen des Judentums* (Religion of reason out of the sources of Judaism, 1919), argued that monotheism was the source of ethical law and universal values.

The selection here, "Das Judentums als Weltanschauung" (Judaism as a worldview), was first delivered as a speech at the Political People's Association in Vienna and later published in the widely read *Dr. Bloch's Oesterreichische Wochenschrift* (Dr. Bloch's Austrian weekly) in March and April 1898.[1] Cohen focused on three aspects of Judaism: its insistence on a single, transcendental God; its idea of charity linked with being humane; and its creation of a Sabbath as a day of rest for both master and slave. To him, these three aspects of Jewish moral law were "truly original ideas in the history of literature and culture," and they alone justified Judaism's continued existence as a distinct moral-religious entity in the modern era. All three were gifts of the prophets, who foresaw a Messianic Age in which kindness among people and economic equality would reign as a result of a unified human belief in one transcendental God.

Yet for Cohen, Judaism did not end with the prophets. Instead, it was continually reevaluating and fine-tuning the moral standards it set for itself and others. In this regard, his frequent references to the

Talmud throughout the lecture should not be overlooked. Unlike some of his friends in the Reform movement, Cohen interpreted the talmudic corpus not as an extended period of Rabbinical sophistry, heedless to the clarion call of the pure Mosaic law, but as a sophisticated attempt to refine (and often redefine) the Jewish moral character in a time of Diaspora. (Cohen's disparagement of Zionism partway through the lecture underscores this point.) Only by following the lead of the Talmud, and later of men like Maimonides and Ibn Ezra, could the Jewish worldview—with its strong moral vision rooted in the law of the one God—survive the pressures of modernity, Emancipation, and renewed racial antisemitism. Cohen's deep worries (and, it seems, dismay) at the last of these is an undercurrent throughout the essay.

Judaism as a Worldview (1898)

Translated by Samuel J. Kessler

Highly honored assembly!

Religion and politics—one might think they are opposites, and not only if one considers religion as the private form of piety and politics as the struggle for the existence of peoples. No—even when one regards religion as the education of the human race toward humanism and politics as the historical development toward morality—and perhaps even then—the contrast between these two directions—the power of the mind and the will—develops and intensifies. As you see it everywhere—in Classical Antiquity as in Biblical Judea, in the Middle Ages as in the Modern Age—ecclesiastical religion (presupposed and recognized by all ideal zeal) often reveals defects and damages in its fundamental justification of morality among men. It is still all the more explicable that the people—in addition to the dependence which they retain on the priests—at the same time strive in their own way not only for their own power and earthly welfare but also for peace and moral betterment.[2] It is perhaps the supreme triumph of religion that religion itself participates in this kind of politics.[3] And in no religion is this participation so definite and so clear and so poignant as it is in the religion of Israel, for the *politics of Israelite religion is prophecy.*

The prophets were the advocates of the people. Not only for the widows and orphans, the poor and the slaves, against the rich, the princes, and the kings, but no less against the priests and their world-historical missions, against social selfishness and superstition which underlies the pagan cult of sacrifice. In this—their [prophetic] politics—they became the founders of our religion. *Judaism does not want to be the Doctrine of Creation.* It has no dogmas about the astronomical world. It is very significant that in the Hebrew language the word for "world" also means "eternity," so surely was the concept of the world thought to be contained in the word *olam.* Everywhere in our literature "world" is taken in this moral meaning as "eternal world," which describes the *Problem of Religion* and becomes the verbal formulation:[4] *"The world is built on love"* [Ps. 89:3].[5]

But our task arises out of the sense of the word prevalent in Judaism: "Judaism as a worldview" has still a more specific meaning and utility. Religion as a worldview means the idealization of religion, the idealization of the idea of the moral world. If historical knowledge of religion itself were promoted from the point of view of the worldview, how much more so would be the true purpose of religion: *The peace and the connection among us peoples despite the diversity of religions!*

To view and understand religion as a worldview is in itself a reminder to expand and elucidate the confessional horizon of *self-criticism to one's own religion, as well as sympathy for the foreign* [religion], which to the truly religious must not remain foreign. If there is a sign that, in our time, in which religion is so much spoken about, the sense of religion is very uncommon and truncated, *then it is probably from this lack of goodwill with those of other faiths* and their sources of religion that makes our times so dark and worrisome.

The function of considering Judaism as a worldview is therefore the following: It frees one from the interests of *denominational polemics.* Here is the ground on which *every* religion can prove *what it does for the idea of the moral world; scholastic*[6] *keenness is by no means the same as brusqueness of affect.*[7] Worldview demands and fosters a world-historical sense and a world-historical heart.

Now, if we may, honored ones, try to deal with this task here, we now know the context of the task (which is [the same as] the purpose of a *political association*, a political people's association) and all that remains is the concern that [in our remaining time together] not all the many-branched relationships which link the religion of Judaism with political questions can come to light.[8]

The concept of a World Religion is by no means dependent on the number of its respective confessors but rather of the content of the evolving life of *their ideas*. The concept of a World Religion is conditioned by the concept of worldview, and that in the eternal progress of world history as a worldview our religion is a living force. Such a philosophy of history must be based on the belief in the *eternity of ideas*! It is required that our preservation as a religion *best serve the world* and the progress of humanity. Yet this historical understanding is very reserved and very sparse among our friends. It is little known among us—and it hardly seems believable to us—but it is literally a fact that there are those who do not acknowledge the survival of *our* religion as a religion, but only as the survival of a race,[9] which one might call our tribe.[10] But the saddest thing is that, among ourselves, the knowledge and the enthusiasm for the *worldview our religion* founded has, in the confusion of the age, become weak and insecure, and even in many cases lost altogether. Even outside of the circles which pursue politics, the sense of religion has greatly diminished in these times. For Jews this must be felt even more strongly, precisely because the Emancipation came about, or at least was proclaimed, and began to become a merciful reality in moderate doses.[11]

The consequences were inevitable. Judaism has lost its considerable power in the new spiritual and scientific services that opened to it, and the rarity of men with a broader spiritual perspective has, of course, made rare the courage that leads the soul to understand the *historical meaning* of our faith. Here may I call out the name of a man whose commanding leadership we greatly miss in these times: [Reform rabbi and scholar] *Abraham Geiger* [see chapter 2] had the faith and the courage to preach *Judaism as a World Religion, a Judaism of the future with world-historical meaning.*

By a general literary fact this decline can be seen in the self-confidence of our faith. For more than fifty years no *dogmatic theology of our religion* has been written.[12]

The Religious Spirit by [Salomon] Formstecher [see chapter 3] appeared in [Frankfurt] in 1841. In 1842, Samuel Hirsch [see chapter 3] published *Religious Philosophy of the Jews for Theologians of all Confessions* in Dessau, [Moses] Mendelssohn's old city.[13]

One might be consoled with the unscientific pretension that *Judaism has no dogmas*. Its articles of faith were thereby reduced to antiquarian value and repressed. One should know that, so long as it forms a system, every science has a dogma—every science, let alone a religion. After all, it is only inadequate education if, behind [the word] "dogma," one hears only "belief that contradicts reason." But by thus neglecting the dogmas of Judaism, by drying up the source of life—which in the Middle Ages had kept Judaism modern and made it the *teacher of Christian theologians*—and by ever loosening the connection between religious Judaism and worldly wisdom, we became so naïve as to think that a sober, meager *morality* could substitute for a *doctrine of faith*.[14] And so, we presented a collection of moral sayings and moral prescriptions that, perhaps, could defend against a vicious popular assembly, but which could not compel the reason for a Living Religion [to persist], [for such a reason] must always be the expression of a worldview. Our main aim in the remaining time must therefore be directed above all to clarifying and explaining the worldview and *living belief system of Judaism*.

First, the foundational idea is that of the transcendental God. For in transcendence lies the reason and the guarantee of God.

The transcendental world is the world-concept of Judaism, the *olam* given by God to men in their hearts. *God is the source of this transcendental world*; God is transcendental.[15] Because He is transcendental, therefore He is unique, He can be unique. For everything sensory is subject to division.[16] Everything sensory, and especially everything human, is excluded from Him. Only as a spirit should He be thought of. And only through the intellect will the relationship between Man and God be maintained.[17] In this restriction to intellect lives the image, the parable, of God as Father.

It is as Father that He is the source of the moral world and of the members of the moral world. *All human beings without exception* are His children. He is "the God of the spirit of all flesh" [Num. 27:16]. It is therefore a simple logical *consequence of the unity of God*—as the foundation of the moral world—that *the commandment of love of neighbor was to become the center of our faith*. "As He is merciful, so shall you be merciful!" [b. *Shabbat* 133b; Maimonides, Mish. Tor., *Halakhot De'ot* 1:6]. It is an always-important consideration that charity must be conceived as unlimited, unlimited by anything. No claim of faith can be acknowledged or even conceived of as conditional on this demand. God is the Father of all people, even if one does not recognize Him as such. It is not by faith in Him—let alone by the belief of another condition connected with this faith—that one achieves the filiation of God. Instead, it is a logical consequence that cannot be changed by one's behavior. *Thus, the commandment of love of neighbor here becomes true because it follows from the concept of God*. If, on the other hand, [the commandment of love of neighbor] were to be derived from the concept of Man, then it becomes ambiguous, because humans are ambiguous, because in humans it refers to an ambiguous concept—the ladder to the feeling of love being known as changeable and precipitous. Faust himself says that, alone, the love of God, "when it stirs, all impulses and all impetuous deeds are appeased."[18]

The concept *of love* in charity is by no means a sure leitmotif. One can examine dogmatic systems according to the value they place on love. But also, the religiosity of bygone ages can be tested by the extent to which they put an emphasis on love. It is not a matter of establishing the demand of charity, but of preparing in the context (and above all in the doctrine) of faith the conditions that make charity possible.

A more accurate guide than love is *respect*.[19] Love involuntarily makes distinctions, at least to a degree; *respect requires equality. The equality of men follows from the oneness of God*. If men were not equal, there would not be one God, but rather different men would have different gods, as they had and still have. The uniqueness of God has revealed the concept of equality of men. Love is based upon the equality of men, as the *teaching of Moses* understands them: *"Love him"; more precisely, "be his friend, for he is your equal"* [Lev. 19:18].[20]

This logical connection between charity and the Israelite idea of God can be recognized in two consequences resulting from the Talmudic development of this commandment. The first is of a purely religious nature. It is the religious manifestation, the reason as well as the effects of love—it is *salvation, the share of eternal life*.[21] In our religious books introduced in our religious schools, the Talmud's sentence is imprinted upon children: "The righteous[22] *among the nations of the world* have a share in the world to come" [b. *Sanhedrin* 105a].[23] This is the true expression of neighborly love, and this expression should be the goal of all neighborly love.

Salvation is the religious expression of moral equality. Equality is lacking—and with it respect—without recognition of salvation among all forms of faith; [there will be equality only] as long as [salvation] has piety—that is morality—as its effect and witness. But love is a wavering helm without respect. The naturalness and truthfulness of charity in the foundational conception of God as Father is attested to by the replacement of the "limits of the *faithful*"[24] with the concept of "Chasid"—the *interconfessional pious*[25]—and consequently in the *replacement of the concept of "salvation" with the concept of the "covenant of faith."*

The second consequence of the Israelite commandment of charity is of a political nature. It contains a concept which, in this political-legal context, represents a peculiarity of the Jewish spirit. It is the concept of Noahide, the sons of Noah. While in classical antiquity the constitution of the state and the law rested on the social basis of the cult of sacrifice and the sacrificial community, a concept developed in Talmudic Judaism that not only the Israelites should be called to participate in the administration of state and law, but also the Noahide, *whose equivalent membership in the state had to be recognized.* [See b. *Sanhedrin* 56a; Maimonides, Mish. Tor., *Halakhot Malakhim u'Milkhamot* 9:1; Nachmanides on Genesis 34:13.] This political abnormality—which is contrary to all other political views [among non-Jews]—is deeply rooted in the Israelite view and was even enforced in the sacrificial world. The stranger who came from a distant land is not only allowed to pray in the Solomonic Temple (may God hearken to him) but he may also offer sacrifices. The Noahide is representative of the doctrine that the connection of man to a moral state *does not presuppose confessional uniformity, but instead, acknowledgment and acceptance of natural morality is a sufficient condition* [for such connection].

In the seventeenth century, the Englishman [jurist, member of Parliament, and scholar of the history of law] John [Selden, 1584–1654] built his great work *Natural and National Law According to the Teachings of the Hebrews* on the fundamental concept of the Noahide and divided his chapters according to their seven rules.

[Dutch jurist and scholar] Hugo Grotius [1583–1645] also mentions this important concept. Since then it seems to have disappeared in the literature on Natural Rights. The "Chasid," the representative of morality among the various religions, has never anywhere been known, for even had he turned up, he would have remained an incomprehensible stranger. Not much is different in terms of an appreciation for these [precursor natural law theories, these] other foothills [leading up to] the Israelite idea of God, especially in the estimation of their [that is, these non-Jewish theories'] value in the present time. [. . .]

All peoples of antiquity, upon becoming dissatisfied with the conditions of their present age, transposed the dream of a better existence onto the past, onto the dark past, which at best they thought of as the cradle of their people. Therefore, antiquity has no "history" in the sense of "world history." The interest of the Greek historian extends only to the connection between the now and the past of national destinies, only to this connection between the now and the bygone age of one's own national history. The model of the Greek politician lies exclusively in the past, never in the future. *The hope for an ideal and its historical realization is not present in the consciousness of the Greeks* who, instead of hope, make opportunism a personified deity. These relations to the historical ideals distinguish our religion from the classical-antique. The prophet first—and he alone—linked his people with the other peoples in the name of their God, whose house of prayer should become a house for all peoples [Isa. 56:7]. The prophetic concept of history, therefore, is the concept of the future, of the Once of the end-of-days when the worship of the One God will unite Israel and the nations and will expand Jerusalem into the world.[26]

This "Once" of the messianic age created the concept of world history and [also] the idea of humanity.[27] In that "Once" the difference between Israel and the Nations disappears. Thus, the idea of humanity becomes the task of history, and through this task, history becomes world history. The Messiah who liberates Israel transforms together the Nations with Israel, making one Humanity that conforms to the one God. The idea of the Messiah is the idea of Humanity, the idea of World History.

In Christianity, this meaning of the Messianic Age had to be withdrawn from the beginning, for Jesus became the Messiah as Christ, the Once became the Now, and so there was nothing left in the historical sense for the Once (as, for instance, the vestige of the millennial kingdom). From the Once of world history comes the Once of individual Being, from the Once of future time comes the Once of the future life. The interest of eternal life, of eternal bliss, becomes the vital interest of religion. Well! We truly have our belief in immortality; we distinguish the future time from the future world or future life. This belief in the *future of humanity* is the belief of the eternal Jew who has discovered the idea of humanity. If, in a word, we want to answer the question of what alone could have caused the continued existence of the Jews, we may call on the idea of the Messianic Age. Those who believe in a future have a future. It is a strange symptom of the victory of the truth in our grievous age that a facet of the Messianic idea—namely, the universalism of the prophets—has come to recognition and has been acclaimed [only] through the critique of Protestant theology.[28] It [Protestant theology] is a real merit of theological-critical scholarship; a special merit of theological academic science in our age of hatred of the Jews;[29] a triumph of the free science founded after some preparatory work by [Jewish Andalusian philosopher, poet, and biblical exegete Abraham] Ibn Ezra [twelfth century] through [Dutch Jewish philosopher Baruch/Benedict] Spinoza [1632–77]. The stupid prejudice—that the prophets had only thoughts of their own people—has been thoroughly removed. Therefore, in the recognition of our universalism, the concession has finally been made that [the Prophets] conceived of the idea of humanity, and that they knew not the deification of Man but only the knowledge of God and the love of man. *Our Judaism is based on the world idea of the Messiah, and the messianic idea of world history is rooted in our moving and our continued existence among the nations.*

As a direct misjudgment of the messianic idea, I must bring up the modern movement of Zionism. "My heart for Moab," says the Prophet [Jer. 48:36]. How should we not grieve for our fellow believers in the East and ourselves in the West?[30] Anxiety has risen again. But we do not want to be pushed off the route of our world-historical track by anything that threatens of martyrdom. Our calling as Israelites is not exhausted in our political hardship. We do not relinquish our messianic vocation as the people of world history just to be swallowed up by dunes as a colonial state.[31] *We believe in the vocation to be scattered among the Nations until the "Once"—promised from the universalism of our prophets—will come true.*

As a third concept, I call up the idea of the Sabbath. It forms the supplement to the idea of humanity. In the struggle for status within the same people, in the conflicts between one person and another in the face of the social difference between rich and poor, the prophets discovered the concept of Man in the concept of Neighbor. Thus, in the context of social legislation there arose the commandment of charity. The *social-political idea of the Sabbath* is the comprehensive expression of charity in legislation and ethical expression. Charity means: There should be no differences between people [fundamental enough to] *question the concept of Man*. "Everybody else is like you"; but social contrasts—with their differences—are beneficial and essential for the blessings of culture. Work is the medium and the battlefield of culture; therefore, our religion brings the concept of charity to life.[32]

The reason for the establishment of the Sabbath is indicated in the Fifth Book [of the Pentateuch] through a political point: "So that your servant and your maid rest like you, the Eternal has commanded you to set up the Sabbath day" [Deut. 5:14]. While in the commandment of charity only the "other" is generally referred to and, if necessary, the stranger is introduced for a clearer instruction, the real impulse of social progress here appears to be the *worker*, the *slave*. The slave, who is resting one day in every week because of religious and state ways, is a contradiction in terms, which alone can arise and be made clear by the view—which stands opposed to all other ancient civilization—that the slave is a human being, *a person, and not a thing*. The revolutionary doctrine is proclaimed under the aggressive concept of equality. He should attain the rights of rest just as you yourself hold them. Resting from his work should make him equal to you; the *Sabbath rest makes the worker human*.

Clearly this third idea of Judaism has had its influence on modern culture. In recent times, it has even extracted political capital for the reputation and benefit of other religions. And—if we did not suffer directly from this—one might even be amused by such a crass example of historical irony, that this latter idea [the Sabbath], this cultural invention of Judaism, has in recent times been called "practical Christianity" (hilarity[!]), and the Sabbath and all the social legislation of the Pentateuch have been declared the creation of Christianity. Indeed, it is such a violation of literary property that can probably be atoned for by the fact that the intellectual creators of socialism are the Jews.

Incidentally, the Romans believed that the Jews who lived among them fasted on Saturday, so far is the Sabbath from being understood, even as it is now practiced and celebrated by all Christian parties.[33] [Indeed,] since it came into being our Sabbath celebration has maintained its coherence, for such is the connection between the social question and the foundations of religion. But this connection consists in the *relationship of the faith community to Torah.*

To be sure, the Torah is only a doctrine of religion. But in its voluminous constitution it has become a national project, one whose study makes full use of a person's intellectual powers.[34] Thus, the Torah is not only a science of religion, but a science [itself]. And this science of the Torah was the common property of the Jewish community, the *main source of the Science of Judaism [Wissenschaft des Judentums],* which contains a great deal of jurisprudence but on the other hand more than merely a little bit of poetry. Never, even in the darkest of times, has anyone made a fuss *about poor Jews learning a little catechism* [i.e., some Mishnah and Gemara]. Illiteracy, that is, the inability to pray or to "learn"—as the expression has it—has existed among us [Jews] only exceptionally, [and always] for individual motives. For just as the rich knew and sought no higher fame than that of being "sons of Torah," Judaism has always appreciated the powers that derived from poverty for the sake of scholarship. "Care for the children of the poor, for from them the Torah will issue forth" [b. *Nedarim* 81a]. So the elemental force of the lower classes was prized. Many were puzzled by how the Jews—once they had barely begun to speak and read the newer European languages—understood how to write in them as well. It was thought that they [the Jews] came from trade, but no one knew *how they combined—in so wonderful a union—the cultivation of science* [that is, religious knowledge] *with employment at the very lowest levels of retail.* Thus, it was also surprising [for the non-Jews to learn] that there is no proletariat among us, and [only] popular hatred drew the self-serving conclusion that all Jews are rich. What differentiates the proletariat from the poor? The difference comes from participation in culture. The poor Jew was not disenfranchised from scholarship, *so he never became a proletarian.* There can be no equality of the people without an equal share in culture.

The three ideas discussed so far—summarized in the Torah—may be regarded as particularly characteristic of Judaism, for they are the products of our very own Jewish spirit. There are very few truly original ideas in the history of literature and culture. I do not know the names of any others that were so wholly, so inwardly, produced from the spirit of a national literature, and so clearly without analogy in the other cultures. The immediacy between God and Men, as it is represented only by the *transcendental God*, was and is only present in Judaism, for the mediator between God and Man is human reason, says Maimonides [cf. Maimonides, *Guide of the Perplexed* 3:52, and Ibn Eza on Proverbs 22:21].[35] The idea of the future as the *golden age*, in which the swords of the peoples are forged into ploughshares [Isa. 2:4.]—this idea of the unity of the human race on the Sabbath of the Messianic Age—has, in the long history of human culture, only ever been discovered by the prophets. Furthermore, the *weekly day of rest* is not just an idea but also an economic system which is solely and exclusively the product of the Jewish religion. On these ideas is our religion based, and also its value as a worldview.

Honored ones! I would like to suggest to you the idea that our attitude towards our situation ought to be primarily that of the *enthusiastic upholding of our religion*, and therefore in the lively and active zeal for our theology. This [task] must be rooted in our personal honor, our *joie de vivre*, and our civil, idealist aspirations. In fact, we are judged by others according to how we ourselves relate to Judaism. The Jews are easily mistaken about this in superficial intercourse with Christians. Morally, it [honoring Judaism] is not only *the most natural and most worthy* [endeavor]; it is also the wisest thing to do.

We know, and willingly and gratefully acknowledge, that we have learned not only from the general, historical influence of the Christian worldview but also that Christian theology has supported our own insights and has deepened our moral principles. But we also know that not only the Christian worldview, but also Christian theology, owes a confession [of some influence] to our literature, our religious philosophy, and our dogmatics—or, not just owes, *it is in debt*. Our task is not combating other doctrines of faith. Instead, it is in the inner strengthening and equipping of our own [faith] through all the treasures of modern scholarship.

However, I cannot conclude with these words—especially in a Political People's Association—even though I maintain this policy to be the best and most resounding. One sees real liberation in direct political action.

Thus, let me touch, finally, on the connection that exists between the *tribal peculiarity of Jews and the idea of the modern state.*

In the German Empire—where the modern state as a state of national unity was longed for and finally founded by all German tribes striving for freedom and justice—in the German Empire, even today it can still be observed that those tribes, whose national commonality is the basis and prerequisite of the national state, still remain something of an obstacle for the [full] manifestation of the ship of state.[36] So precarious is the relationship between the individual tribes and the People in the *national* state, the jealousy and the strangeness of the various tribes must be appeased and repressed at times, and especially at critical moments, so that the state can carry out large and important cultural tasks.[37] And as happens still in parts of the German Empire, so similarly it happened in former times in England and France, and still does so in Italy today. And how much more challenging are the conditions in a unitary state, one built not only by tribes of the same nation but also by *different nations altogether*—I cannot even begin to deal with this in your state.[38] But all the more instructive is the relationship between Nation and State.[39] From the heavy struggles which are imposed on you, it is evident that the modern state—as the prophet says—must be created and maintained not by force and not by military might but by the spirit [cf. Zech. 4:6]. The spirit of the idea of the modern state is elevated above the *natural instincts of the races*. The modern state may have its roots in the natural foundation of national commonality, [but] its growth and health are gathered from the sap of culture, from the general ideas of history and law, freedom and science, which are not bound to any Nation. The *ideal goods* of all peoples form these eternal foundations of the state, form the idea of the modern state; the prosperity and welfare of the state rest only on these. The Jews, among all the modern peoples, are the living example that belonging to a modern state is not entirely conditional on the racial element.

The Jews' participation in the destinies of the peoples in whose midst they live is everywhere unpretentious, enthusiastic, and unselfish. Our enemies cannot deny this. We live and breathe the most sacred, choicest, and most beautiful national literature, and everywhere we take the most zealous part in the expansion of the rule of law. It cannot be the right thing when one calls us "foreigners." [Such name calling] can only rest on the fact *that the idea of the modern state has not yet achieved complete victory among all those who are on the journey to become modern people. In the struggle for these ideas our plight is justified; in the fate of this struggle lies the outcome of our cause.*

The messianic idea provides not only comfort but also guidance. It unites *cosmopolitanism and patriotism*, liberating them from the narrow standpoint of tribe and race, and educates them to the task of the modern idea of the state, which brings the difference between the tribes and peoples themselves to reconciliation in the moral task of establishing and expanding the rule of law and a national culture. With our messianic religiosity and our whole enthusiasm, we dedicate ourselves to the peoples in whose culture we have grown. The concept of the modern state rests not in the uniformity of faith nor of tribe but in the *education and development of nationality toward freedom and justice.*[40]

We have been described as a decomposing element among modern peoples, maybe in ways not quite well-intentioned. Certainly! We decompose the strange superstitions of the *exclusive salvation of the race* and serve as a reminder about the *urfactor* [original element]—which is more than mere putty—concerning the most important element in the structures of the state.[41] From this theoretical point of view—for the accuracy of which today the facts speak louder than ever—we draw our confidence and our courage to persevere from the *inevitable acknowledgment of our honor and the securing and consolidating of our religious continuity*. As long as messianic Judaism is the worldview it will assert its share in the foundation and purification of the moral world. And a time will come—perhaps it is no longer distant—in which one's share in, and thankfulness for, the manifestation of this *historical understanding will be generally recognized*. We confidently expect such a better age. We have proved that we have the power of patience and struggle. Our breath has outlived all the Scythian storms of past world history;[42] the present can sadden us but not weigh us down. We have a messianic belief in the future of the world. *Eternity is ours*

HEYMANN STEINTHAL (1823–99)

Heymann (Hermann) Steinthal (b. 1823, Gröbzig; d. 1899, Berlin) was a noted philosopher, philologist, and religious historian specializing in the study of folk mythology and national psychology. A gifted linguist, he spent his collegiate days at the University of Berlin, where he was deeply influenced by the works of Wilhelm von Humboldt (1767–1835), whose ideas pioneered the modern study of linguistics and the philosophy of language. In 1860, Steinthal cofounded (with his brother-in-law Moritz Lazarus, 1824–1903) the *Zeitschrift für Völkerpsychologie und Sprachwissenschaft* (Journal for national psychology and linguistics), which aimed to employ the modern methods of science and the lens of nation and race to understand human actions, development, and modes of communication. A professor of philology at the University of Berlin from 1863, Steinthal mentored some of the century's most noted philosophers, including Wilhelm Dilthey (1833–1911), Hermann Cohen (1842–1918, the previous excerpt), and Georg Simmel (1858–1918).

Throughout his life, Steinthal maintained an interest in Jewish theology and history, and in the modernization of the Jewish religion and culture. In 1870, alongside Abraham Geiger (1810–74, see chapter 2), he helped found and then taught at the Hochschule für die Wissenschaft des Judentums in Berlin, the premier institute of higher Jewish learning in the German capital, which integrated traditional Jewish learning with modern critical methodologies and scientific interpretation.

The following selection comes from a short essay first published in 1899 in the *Jahrbuch für jüdische Geschichte und Literatur* (Yearbook for Jewish history and literature).[43] Exploring the theological ramifications of the Creation story as recounted in Genesis 1–2, Steinthal here argues that the idea of a single God, Creator of Heaven and Earth, whose acts of Creation are fundamentally good, is a realization unique to the Jewish mind. Whereas other theological and philosophical traditions, from the Greeks to the Zoroastrians, had imagined a heavenly sphere entirely at the mercy and will of blind forces and amoral whims or locked in a cosmic struggle of good and evil, Judaism perceived Creation as the action of a supreme God, an invisible spirit who made His own self-reflective choices and gave to material reality the imprimatur of divine goodness. Finally, Steinthal notes, Genesis 1–2 gives us one more deep theological truth—the unique capacity of humans, created "in the image of God," for ethical decisiveness—thus humanity's ability to fashion a moral world that reflects the intrinsic goodness of God's Creation.

The Idea of the Creation of the World (1899)

Translated by Mary M. Solberg

Every people, once it has established its cultural beginnings, has very likely asked itself how the universe within which they live, and even how they themselves, came to be. But Israel-Judah is the only people that has answered this question: God, the one God, created the world.[44] We do not fully comprehend what this means, even those of us who learn it as children. Even the most advanced peoples — of India, Greece, and Rome — presumably did not know this! They were unfamiliar with the notion of the one God; nor did they think that one or another of their many gods had created the world! They simply did not have the concept of creation that they could have ascribed to any agent, and they knew of no being whose actions and existence might have revealed this concept: they were simply not intuitive enough to find a creative being at the source of it all. Naturally, can someone unfamiliar with the God who made Heaven and Earth have any notion of what Creation is? And so, he knows nothing otherwise about the world, either. True?

Now, we know that the Greeks were the fathers of philosophy. For them the world was a physical entity, eternally becoming, the gods and the world together and as one.[45] And this becoming consisted in both begetting and giving birth by material gods. Do not ask whether the gods begot the world or the world begot the gods; it is only a begetting, only a being born [e.g., Plato, *Timaeus*; Aristotle, *Physics*, bk. 3, chap. 4].

The concepts of God and world, true God and real world, are clearly interrelated. Only what can create a world is God, and only what God has created is a world.

What holds these two concepts so tightly together is the concept of spirit.[46] God, declares Israel-Judah, is spirit not flesh, and does not have a perceptible form.

All philosophy of religion emerges from this assertion. This is why the concept of creation turns up in the very first verse of our religious book: "In the beginning God created heaven and the earth" [Gen. 1:1], and in fact, as it turns out, in six days or acts. The text then relates the creation of light (before anything else) and thence the separation of day and night; next the world above and the world below, land and sea; then the creation of the plant kingdom beneath and the sun, moon, and stars above; the animals of the deep and the birds of the air; the land animals; and at last, the human being. With that, the text says, "The heaven and the earth were finished, and all their array" [Gen. 2:1] (which move upon and within them), and again, "God ceased from all the work of creation that He had done" [Gen. 2:3]. The world: God's or miraculous work.

The Hebrew language has three words that mean "to make," each one with different nuances. *Bara* denotes creating in its truest sense, that is, creating something completely new; *yotzer*, giving form to something; and *oseh*, completing something. All three are used in the first two chapters of the Bible. In addition, the remarkable expression *hivdil* appears, signifying that what has been created receives the divine imprimatur. So it is that light and darkness, what is above and what is below, land and sea, are separated from each other. Each of the "hosts" of sea- and land-creatures carries its reproductive seeds within it. This is how everything in the universe receives its limits—*ḥok* [law], *gevul* [limit/border/boundary]—so that nothing oversteps the boundaries set for it. Simultaneous with the creation, then, the preservation of the world is also secured. This is the Jewish perspective on the world.

A wise rabbi once pointed out that the Torah could have opened with the first laws given to the people of Israel [see Rashi to Gen. 1:1]. Of course it could have, if the Torah were intended only as a dried-up law book, as the portion of *mishpatim* [Exod. 21–24] presents, preceded by the Ten Commandments. When the people heard, "I am your God who brought you out of the house of bondage" [Exod. 20:2, modified following Steinthal], they might well have asked: Who is God? But now they knew: He is the one who created the world—Him alone, and of Him there is no physical depiction.

Two other important points are connected with this idea of creation. One is theoretical—humans' likeness to God [Gen. 1:26–27]; the other more practical—the establishment of the Sabbath [Gen. 2:2–3]. After six days of work, God rested on the seventh, and in doing so, sanctified that day. The human being, striving to be like God, sanctifies the Sabbath, setting work aside on this day. And in this rest lies the blessing that one experiences on the Sabbath. Man is only blessed by cultivating the earth, and then elevated out of slavery (*eved*) to all that is earthly and material by devotion to what is holy and divine; he becomes conscious of his freedom.

It was asked if Israel's religion has dogmas. If it has teachings, if it is not without content, then surely it must have dogmas, and the notion of Creation is such a dogma. But Israel's religion does not require that dogma be written down. If this were not so, then the original author of the first Mishnah of the fifth chapter of [*Pirkei*] *Avot* could be called a heretic. [See PA 5:1.][47] Instead, he demonstrates that the Bible itself does not depend on the letter.[48] Not even the three above-mentioned words for "create" are sufficient to him. In addition to its outer form, this whole text has also a refined meaning. In addition to the six days, the teacher of the Mishnah reminds us, there are "ten words" by means of which the world is created—ten words-of-becoming. According to this view, the expressions "to create, to fashion, to make" are still too tied to material filth. They are not suitable for God. The human works with, struggles with, material stuff; God creates without effort. The human makes use of, tries to master, physical materials and the forces of nature; God set them in place, gave them an immutable law and with it, limits that were not to be breached (*ḥok, gevul*), that is, laws. To speak is also an activity, not only the most immaterial but also the most purely spiritual. Just as we humans use words to transform our inner thoughts into an object that can be perceived, so too God transforms the divine thought-of-the-world into reality. And God did this not only during primeval times, but He continues to do it, as it says in our prayers: "who in his goodness continues to renew the work of creation every day" [from the first blessing preceding the morning *Shema*].

A deeper meaning is often reflected in childlike play. Those who do not take this to heart when considering the sayings of our sages will not understand them. The *tanna* [Mishnaic-era sage] who refers to the ten words-of-becoming raises this question:[49] Wouldn't it have been much easier for God had he spoken only once: "Let the world come into being?" For the psalmist says, "God speaks, and it was" [Ps. 33:9 (modified following Steinthal)]. But here is the answer the sage provides: In listing the parts of the world one by one, created through His word, God wanted to show how beloved, how valuable this world is to Him, how much He despises those who through their immorality bring disorder to the world, and in contrast, how dear to Him are the righteous who through their righteousness perfect it.

Here too the idea of humans made in the image of God shines forth—

humans to whom God assigns the ongoing cultivation of the world. The Bible signals this not only through the expression *l'avda u'leshamra* ("to till it and tend it" [Gen. 2:15]), but also suggests it in relating how God leads the animals to the humans so that they can name each one [Gen. 2:19–20], while God Himself names only the light, the heavens, the earth, and the sea. Thus, while the Bible does here show the likeness of humans to God, it actually wants to emphasize something else, namely, the divine institution of marriage and of human society generally. It says clearly that humans shall rule over both animals and inanimate nature, and stresses many a time that likeness to God is the characteristic of humans.

But the Bible bases this human status in the world upon the particular way in which Man's creation occurs. Man does not simply come to be, a product of the earth. Rather, God forms him, dust from the ground, and blows the divine breath into his nose [Gen. 2:7]. In this way, Man is called to rule and to continue creation [see Gen. 1:28].

Polytheism recognizes many gods, among them good ones and bad. But those that are good are not good because they want to be, or bad by choice; they are what they are by their very nature, because this is what fate wills, and thus they love and they hate this one or that one as their fancy takes them. The One, wholly good God, in contrast, has created the world because, in His utter goodness and holiness, He wills the good and only that. Thus it is that everything in the world which God brought into being with His word is good. Besides Him, there is no creator of an evil world, there is no Ahriman, as there is in the Persian religion [Zoroastrianism], which produces nasty winters and deserts and terrible vermin.[50]

And since everything created is good, so it is also that what is created is good not just in and for itself. Rather, everything is in harmony with everything else, the whole is very good, and even what looks bad to us proves in reality to be good. Only for Man was it not said after his creation: "and He saw that it was good."[51] In freedom, he still had to prove himself good.

So, this is the biblical idea of the creation of the world. Anyone who wants to can laugh over the childlike story of the six days and the blown breath. We, however, do not need a reinterpretation.

How did Israel-Judah come up with the idea of God's creation of the world? They lived in the world, were surrounded by the world on all sides; how did the thought of the Creator emerge? Did this people come to know the existence of God and His power of creation by means of the existence of the world? I do not think so! It was not until Israel recognized God that it added: And he is also the Creator, Sustainer, and Ruler of the world. But who was God for the people in the first place?

I would venture to say that Israel-Judah first recognized God as one who led them out of Egypt, the house of bondage, through the wilderness to the land promised to their forefathers, and gave it to them as a possession. This is how the prophet Hosea depicts God. Very likely this is how God appears in the earlier prophets.[52] This verse is of course a classic one: "Lift high your eyes and see: Who created these? He who sends out their host by count (like a field commander, not like a shepherd calling his sheep), who calls them each by name: because of His great might and vast power, not one fails to appear" (Isa. 40:26).[53] In contrast, an ancient Roman poet sings, "Look up at the brilliant heights that everyone calls Jupiter." Isaiah refers to the host of the stars without naming them; [he merely calls them] "these." God is neither the shepherd nor the great astronomer; He is Himself, and precisely because He is their Creator. Isaiah is not trying to prove God's existence; just like his predecessors, he assumes God and admonishes those who are weak in faith to trust Him, for as Creator of the universe he is able to do everything.

So: how was this most sublime idea discovered? I believe that it was only through a deep sense of ethical responsibility, in particular through the very vivid feeling of thankfulness toward the One who drew the people out of Egypt and gave them the land. Not only that they, the people of Israel, were slaves there—no, Egypt, a land of huge buildings, was in fact a land of tombs, its temples dedicated to the service of animals. It was truly and fundamentally a house of bondage. The Canaanite peoples, on the other hand, were deeply embedded in unnatural immorality [see Deut. 9:4–5]. A prophetic consciousness arose in the face of both of these, and this introduced the people to a living God, who rules over sea and land, because He created them; commands holiness, because He is holy; is Spirit, for only the Spirit creates in utter goodness.

LEO BAECK (1873–1956)

Leo Baeck (b. 1873, Lissa; d. 1956, London) was a leading Reform rabbi and scholar, and an internationally recognized advocate for European Jewry during the Second World War. Born into a rabbinical family, Baeck was educated in Breslau and Berlin, where he studied with the renowned philosopher and psychologist Wilhelm Dilthey (1833–1911) and taught at the liberal Hochschule für die Wissenschaft des Judentums. After leaving university, Baeck served as rabbi in Oppeln and Düsseldorf before eventually returning to Berlin, where, in 1933, he became president of the Reichsvertretung der Deutschen Juden (Imperial representation of German Jewry), an organization advocating on behalf of all German Jewry against National Socialist policies. Deported to the Theresienstadt concentration camp in 1943, he survived the war and emigrated to England, where he eventually became president of the World Union for Progressive Judaism and an international leader in interfaith dialogue.

This selection is from Baeck's *Das Wesen des Judentums* (The essence of Judaism), a work that made him famous in Germany almost overnight.[54] Composed as a book-length theological reply to *Das Wesen des Christentums* (The essence of Christianity, 1900) by the influential German theologian Adolf Harnack (1851–1930), Baeck strongly defended Judaism against all notions of Christian supersessionism. In the pages excerpted here, Baeck argues that ethics lie at the center of Judaism—that is, at its founding, Judaism was distinguished from all other religions by its ethical nature and its focus on moral law. An ethical religion, Baeck writes, does not evolve out of earlier spiritual forms. Morality cannot take center stage through a process of spiritual development. Instead, an ethical religion is something radically new in the world, a "revelation," a self-conscious displacement of all the religious ideals that came before it so as to make the focus on the moral law the center of an entirely new edifice of religious practice. Israel, Baeck says, was the first people to have made this revelatory break with past religion, and all ethical religions that exist today are the heirs and beneficiaries of Judaism's unique insight. Yet even while others have benefited and built on Judaism's creation of ethical monotheism, it remains Israel's special role—its "election"—to have brought ethical religion into the world and hence to seek to realize it most fully.

Revelation and World Religion (1905)

Translated by Victor Grubenwieser and Leonard Pearl

The ethical character, the fundamental importance of moral action, existed in the religion of Israel from its very beginning. However one may fix the date of its birth, and whatever view one may take concerning its progress, one thing remains certain: from the very beginning of the real, the prophetic, religion of Israel, its cardinal factor was the moral law. Judaism is not merely ethical, but *ethics constitutes its principle, its essence.* Monotheism came into being as a result of the realization of the absolute character of the moral law; the moral consciousness teaches about God. Where this principle takes its rise, the religion of Israel begins; its life has thereafter shaped this fundamental idea.

Its decided ethical character thus distinguishes the religion of Israel. [. . .] And this character is *completely new,* not merely the modified continuation of an older one. Ethical monotheism was not the outcome of an already existing development, but a conscious abandonment of it. For there never has been any development of a *nature religion* (that is to say, a religion in which the forces of nature are worshipped, and in which the gods are conceived as embodiments of nature) into an *ethical religion* in which God is something other than natural, in which He is the Holy One, the originator of morality, who is worshipped in the right deed alone. This is one of the most indubitable results of the history of religions. It is quite possible for nature religions to acquire ethical elements and to enter into relationship with morality. They can connect themselves with it by moralizing their gods, transforming them into guardians of the civic community. But a nature religion has never developed into a purely ethical religion of which morality is the real content. This transition is always effected by a break, a revolution. It is the work of intervening personalities, of founders of religion, and thus it means a discovery, and constitutes a fact which carries its reason within itself.

The ethical monotheism of Israel is not the product of a natural development, but is a *religion* that has been *founded*. The "One God" of Israel is not the *last word* in an *old* way of thinking which has reached this particular stage, but rather the *first word* of a *new* way of thinking: a new logic, the moral logic. In so far as this form of religion is a creation, an entirely new and fruitful principle, we are entitled to call it historically—disregarding first of all every supernatural interpretation—a *revelation*, marking a new sunrise in the history of the world.

We may say this all the more emphatically because it has remained an absolutely *unique* phenomenon. In the history of mankind there is nothing like it, nothing like the origin of monotheism as it was born in Israel out of the moral consciousness and out of the moral imperative. Whether, therefore, and in what form it might have come into existence on different soil and in different circumstances is an idle question. Historically it is a fact that it was given to mankind through Israel and through Israel alone. It is not necessary to create and to construct it, for it stands as a real phenomenon, as a revelation before our eyes.

In the fact that the religion of Israel is characterized as a revelation a *valuation* is implied. If the essential factor of religion lies in man's attitude towards the world—and this ancient view of the Prophets is today once more acknowledged—then there are but *two distinct forms* of religion: the religion of Israel and that of Buddha. The former bids us give a moral affirmation of this relation with the world by will and deed, and it declares the world to be the field of life's tasks; the latter takes as its aim the denial of this relation; man is to devote himself to himself in self-meditation and without volition. The one is the expression of the command to work and to create, the other of the need for rest. The one leads to the desire to work for the acknowledgment of God, to establish the kingdom of God in which all men may be included, whilst the other leads to the desire to sink into the One, into nothingness, there to find deliverance and salvation for the ego. The one calls for ascent, development, the long march towards the future, whilst the other preaches return, cessation, futureless existence in silence. The one seeks to reconcile the world with God; the other tries only to redeem from the world. The one demands creation, new men and a new world, the other "extinction," departure from humanity, departure from the world. The one is the religion of altruism, since it declares *that* man who has found his way to God in seeking his brethren, who serves God by showing justice and love towards men, to be striving towards perfection. The other is the religion of egoism, since it attributes perfection to the man who retreats from mankind in order to remain within himself, and to discover only the true approach to himself.

Between these two forms of religion the choice must be made; the one or the other must be religious revelation. The history of all religions besides these two consists in a greater tendency towards the one or the other; in the mixture which the great strata of life becomes, the one or the other shows more prominently. One can, at the very outset, discard religion altogether, and confine oneself to objective observation and intellectual exploration of the cosmos, according to the teaching of some of the Greeks. But he who would not live without religion, who seeks in religion a definitively religious relation with a real world, will be compelled to regard the religion of Israel as a revelation. This means as well that it [the religion of Israel] is the *classical* manifestation of religion, and that despite all the developments of its path, from the outset it was not simply a beginning, but an ideal. For every true idea is a whole, it represents a goal, which each period views in some fresh light.

Only in Israel did an ethical monotheism exist, and wherever else it is found later on has been derived directly or indirectly from Israel. The existence of this form of religion was conditioned by the existence of the people of Israel, and so Israel became one of the nations that have a mission to fulfill. That is what is called the *election* of Israel. Hence this word [election] primarily expresses only a historical fact; it defines an essential specific peculiarity which has here come to the fore. It indicates the fact that this people was assigned a peculiar position in the world, [and] that it achieved something which distinguished it from all the other nations.

But this statement simultaneously expresses a verdict. It declares that the *difference is justified*, that the *peculiarity is valuable*, and that the existing cleft rests on a clear and permanent possession. The difference is acknowledged as something which lends meaning to the life of this people, and in which it finds itself, as a mutual relationship between God and itself, as that *covenant* for which the LORD lifted it out of the darkness of its inarticulate past, and in which alone it discovered its straight path and the promise of its future, as that covenant which continues from generation to generation as that existence grants and demands. Thereby life sends down its roots into the depths where the human is born by the Divine, and above itself it discerns its height where the Divine endows the human with its confidence; thus the right to be different finds its basis and its certainty. A need of the soul finds herein its answer.

Everyone who is in possession of a truth experiences in it a peculiar possession which has been bestowed upon him, that which separates him from other men. He who is called is always the chosen one, one who has heard that word of God which indicates to him his peculiar way. Revelation and election are conceptions which imply one another. He who assigns to a religion a classical significance acknowledges also the special position of its champions, which they, and only they, possess.

SOLOMON SCHECHTER (1847–1915)

Solomon Schechter (b. 1847, Focșani; d. 1915, New York) was a rabbi and scholar who served as chancellor of the Jewish Theological Seminary in New York, founder of the United Synagogue of America (later, United Synagogue of Conservative Judaism), and a major contributor to the study of Second Temple Judaism as a result of his work on documents discovered in the Cairo Genizah (a trove containing thousands of discarded pages from Egypt's medieval Jewish community).

Schechter was raised in Moldova in a family of Chabad Hasidim, where he attended yeshivot and received a traditional Jewish education. From there he studied in Vienna with the great scholars of Midrash Adolf Jellinek (1821–93) and Meir Friedmann (1831–1908), and in Berlin at the Hochschule für die Wissenschaft des Judentums. In 1882, he emigrated to England, becoming, in 1892, Reader in Talmudic [*sic*] at the University of Cambridge. In the winter of 1896–97, through funding provided by Charles Taylor (1840–1908), Master of St. John's College, Cambridge, and the beneficence of the chief rabbi of Cairo, Raphael Aharon ben Shimon (1848–1928), Schechter secured the bulk of materials in the Cairo Genizah for Cambridge University and proceeded to organize and identify as many of the items as he could, in the process discovering one of the oldest Second Temple–era manuscripts ever found: the Hebrew original of the Book of Ben Sira (at the time known only by its later Greek copy). In 1902 he became the second chancellor of New York's Jewish Theological Seminary, where he remained until his death in 1915.

The following selection comes from Schechter's *Some Aspects of Rabbinic Theology*, a 1909 treatise which attempts to cull from the vast body of classical Rabbinic sources a discernable Jewish orientation toward foundational theological questions, such as the unique status of Israel;[55] notions of holiness, goodness, and sin; and the basic framework for a system of forgiveness and repentance. However, as discussed here, in the book's introductory remarks, Schechter was wary of any process of theological codification of Rabbinic viewpoints—that is, of any attempt to discern a definitive creed or dogma amidst the panoply of voices preserved in Rabbinic Judaism's original texts. The Rabbis, he wrote, "show a carelessness and sluggishness in the application of theological principles." This might be "distressing" to a certain type of reader, who has been taught to expect a systematicity of doctrine, and yet, he argues, Rabbinical diversity is not to its detriment. Instead, when we go in search of a "theology" of the Rabbis, we discover something that "resembles rather a complicated arrangement of theological checks and balances." Knowing, as we do, that such an arrangement has successfully undergirded the Jewish religion for thousands of years, we are forced merely to marvel at its ingenuity and insight, and to cease to expect a logical progression of beliefs and doctrines. And that itself, he concludes, might well be enough.

Some Aspects of Rabbinic Theology (1909)

A great English writer has remarked that "the true health of a man is to have a soul without being aware of it; to be disposed of by impulses which he does not criticize."[56] In a similar way the old Rabbis seem to have thought that the true health of a religion is to have a theology without being aware of it; and thus they hardly even made—nor could they make—any attempt towards working their theology into a formal system, or giving us a full exposition of it. With God as a reality, Revelation as a fact, the Torah as a rule of life, and the hope of Redemption as a most vivid expectation, they felt no need for formulating their dogmas into a creed, which, as was once remarked by a great theologian, is repeated not because we believe, but that we may believe. What they had of theology, they enunciated spasmodically or "by impulses." Sometimes it found its expression in prayer "when their heart cried unto God"; at others in sermons or exhortations, when they wanted to emphasize an endangered principle, or to protest against an intruding heresy. The sick bed of a friend, or public distress, also offered an opportunity for some theological remark on the question of suffering or penance. But impulses are uncertain, incoherent, and even contradictory, and thus not always trustworthy. The preacher, for instance, would dwell more on the mercy of God, or on the special claims of Israel, when his people were oppressed, persecuted, and in want of consolation; whilst in times of ease and comfort he would accentuate the wrath of God awaiting the sinner, and His severity at the day of judgement. He would magnify faith when men's actions were lacking inward motive, but he would urge the claim of works when the Law had been declared to be the strength of sin. When the Law was in danger he would appeal to Lev. 27:43, "Those are the commandments which the LORD commanded Moses," and infer that these laws, and no others, were to be observed forever, and that no subsequent prophet might add to them [see Tor. Koh. 115d (ed. Weiss, Vienna 1862)]. At another time he would have no objection to introduce new festivals, e.g., the Lighting of the Chanukah Candles, and even declare them to be distinct commands of God [b. *Shabbath* 23d; j. *Sukkah* 53d (ed. Krotoschin, 1866)] so long as they were, as it seemed to him, within the spirit of the Law. He would not scruple to give the ideal man [Abraham] his due, to speak of him as forming the throne of God [see Gen. Rab. 47:6], or to invest him with pre-mundane existence; but he would watch jealously that he did not become, as it were, a second god, or arrogate to himself a divine worship.[57] I shall have frequent occasion to point out such apparent or actual contradictions.

The Rabbis, moreover, show a carelessness and sluggishness in the application of theological principles which must be most astonishing to certain minds which seem to mistake merciless logic for God-given truths. For example, it is said: "He who believes in the faithful shepherd is as if he believes in the word of him whose will has called the world into existence." [. . .] "Great was the merit of the faith which Israel put in God; for it was by the merit of this faith that the Holy Spirit came over them, and they said *Shirah* to God, as it is said, 'And they believed in the LORD and his servant Moses. Then sang Moses and the children of Israel this song unto the LORD" [MdRI 33a (ed. Friedmann, Vienna,

1870)].[58] [. . .] Again, "Our father, Abraham, came into the possession of this world and the world hereafter only by the merit of his faith" [MdRi 33a]. Of [Palestinian Rabbinic sage] R. Jose [ben Halafta, second century CE] it is recorded that he said: "If thou art desirous to know the reward awaiting the righteous, thou mayest infer it from Adam the First, for whose single transgression he and his posterity were punished with death; all the more then shall the good action of a man confer bliss upon him, and justify him and his posterity to the end of all generations" [Tor. Koh. 27a]. Another Rabbi tells us that by the close contact of the serpent with Eve, he left in her a taint which infected all her seed, but from which the Israelites were freed when they stood before Mount Sinai, for there they came into immediate contact with the divine presence [b. *Yevamot* 103b]. To the professional theologian, it is certainly distressing to find that such sayings, which would have made the fortune of any ancient Alexandrian theosophist or modern Hegelian of the right wing, were never properly utilized by the Rabbis, and "theologically fructified," nor ever allowed to be carried to what appears to the scholastic mind as their legitimate consequences.[59] The faithful shepherd and the bliss-conferring righteous were never admitted into the Rabbinic pantheon; the concession made to the patriarch was never extended to his posterity, faith only modifying and vivifying works, but not superseding them; and even the direct contact with the Deity, which the fact of being present at the Revelation of Sinai offered to every Israelite, were conceived of only as the beginning of a new life, with new duties and obligations.

This indifference to logic and insensibility to theological consistency seems to be a vice from which not even the later successors of the Rabbis—the commentators of the Talmud—emancipated themselves entirely.[60] I give one example: We read, in the name of R. Akiba, "Everything is foreseen; freedom of choice is given. And the world is judged by grace, and yet *all is according to the amount of work*" [PA 3:15]. This is the usual reading. But some of the best Mss. have the words, "And *not* according to the amount of work."[61] The difference between the two readings being so enormous, we should naturally expect from the commentators some long dissertation about the doctrines of justification by grace or works. But nothing of the sort happens. They fail to realize the import of the difference, and pass it over with a few slight remarks of verbal explanation. Perhaps they were conscious that neither reading ought to be accepted as decisive, each of them being in need of some qualification implied in the other.

It will, therefore, suggest itself that any attempt at an orderly and complete system of Rabbinic theology is an impossible task; for not only are our materials scanty and insufficient for such a purpose, but, when handling those fragments which have come down to us, we must always be careful not to labor them too much, or to "fill them with meaning" which their author could never have intended them to bear, against which all his other teachings and his whole life form one long, emphatic protest; or to spin from the harmless repetition by a Rabbi of a gnostic saying or some Alexandrinic theorem the importance of which he never understood, a regular system of Rabbinic theology. All that these fragments can offer us are some aspects of the theology of the Rabbis, which may again be modified by other aspects, giving us another side of the same subject. What we can obtain resembles rather a complicated arrangement of theological checks and balances than anything which the modern divine [theologian] would deign to call a consistent "scheme of salvation." Still, I am inclined to think that a religion which has been in "working order" for so many centuries—which contains so little of what we call theology, and the little theology of which possesses so few fixities (whilst even these partake more of the nature of experienced realities than of logically demonstrated dogmas)—that this religion forms so unique and interesting a phenomenon as to deserve a more thorough treatment than it has hitherto received. It is not to be dismissed with a few general phrases, only tending to prove its inferiority. [. . .]

The question as to how far the theology of the Rabbis could be brought into harmony with the theology of our age is a matter of apologetics, and does not exactly fall within the province of these essays. With a little of the skill so often displayed by the writers of the life and times of ancient heroes, particularly New Testament heroes, it would certainly not be an impossible task to draw such an ideal and noble picture of any of the great Rabbis, such as [the great Babylonian-Palestinian Rabbinic sage] Hillel [ca. 100 BCE–ca. 10 CE], [Palestinian Rabbinic sage] R. Jochanan ben Zakkai [first century CE], or [Palestinian Rabbinic sage] R. Akiba [ca. 50–ca. 132 CE], as would make us recognize a nineteenth-century altruist in them. Nor would it require much ingenuity to parade, for instance, [Palestinian Rabbinic sage] R. Abuhah [Abahu, third–fourth century CE] as an accomplished geologist, inasmuch as he maintained that before the creation of *our* world God was ever constructing and destroying worlds [see Gen. Rab. 9:2]; or again, to introduce as a perfect Hegelian that anonymous Rabbi who boldly declared that it was Israel's consciousness of God which was "the making of God"; or finally, to arrogate for [Palestinian Rabbinic sage] R. Benaha [Benaiah, third century CE] the merit of having been the forerunner of [Provençal philosopher and theologian R. Abba Mari, called] Astruc [thirteenth century], because he declared that the Pentateuch was delivered not as a complete work, but in a series of successive scrolls. Indeed, the Rabbinic literature has already been described as a "wonderful mine of religious ideas from which it would be just as easy to draw up a manual for the most orthodox as to extract a vade-mecum for the most skeptical."[62] But I have not the least desire to array the ancient Rabbis in the paraphernalia of modern fashion, and to put before the reader a mere theological masquerade, or to present the Talmud as a rationalistic production which only by some miracle escaped the vigilant eye of the authorities, who failed to recognize it as a heretical work and exclude it from the Synagogue. The "liberty of interpretation," in which so many theologians indulge, and which they even exalt as "Christian freedom," seems to me only another word for the privilege to blunder, and to deceive oneself and others.

To show, however, that Rabbinic theology is, with the least modicum of interpretation or re-interpretation, equal to the highest aspirations of the religious man of various modes of thought, occasional illustrations have been given from the works of philosophers and mystics, thus proving the latent possibilities of its application by various schools in different ages. As to "modernity," it entirely depends whether there is still room in its program for such conceptions as God, Revelation, Election, Sin, Retribution, Holiness, and similar theological ideas; or is it at present merely juggling with words to drop them at the first opportunity? If this latter be the case, it will certainly find no ally in Rabbinic theology, or, for that matter, in any other theology.

MAX WIENER (1882–1950)

Max Wiener (b. 1882, Oppeln; d. 1950, New York) was a Reform rabbi and theologian. Born into a family of acculturated but still religious German Jews whose synagogue in Oppeln was led by Leo Baeck (see preceding extract), Wiener would go on to have a lifelong association with Baeck.

Wiener attended university in both Breslau and Berlin while simultaneously pursuing rabbinical ordination. Afterwards he took up rabbinical posts in Düsseldorf (where he was assistant to Baeck), in Stettin, and finally in Berlin, to which he returned in 1926 and where he remained until his emigration to the United States in 1939. In America, Wiener again took up the rabbinate, first in West Virginia, then on the Upper West Side in New York.

Though he spent a lifetime in the pulpit, Wiener was first and foremost a scholar. His works explored a variety of topics, from biblical scholarship to medieval philosophy to Zionism to theology, where his writings (including the one translated here) stressed the centrality of revelation and the unique status of the Jewish people as recipients of God's divine word.

In many ways Wiener's thought defies any sort of categorization within the traditional theological camps of his era, making him an interesting and surprising theologian to this day. This selection, a 1937 article entitled "Vom Sein und Sinn Gottes" (On the being and meaning of God), lays out his theological position, which sits at the intersection of a God who is beyond that which can be known (and therefore must be described, apophatically, in terms of what God is not) and a God whose being and essence is the model for religious and ethical action.[63] "Certainly," Wiener writes, "the unknowability of God does not mean that His real, positive essence lies beyond any meaning that human beings might find valid." The search for such meaning, Wiener argues, lies in the relation between religion and ethics—that is, in our knowledge that when we act ethically, and strive for the pure Good, we are resembling or symbolizing Divinity. Human goodness is not, of course, God's goodness. Nevertheless, Wiener writes, insofar as we strive for the good, "God is our God only because our sense of [ethical] value must assume that in God's perfection there inheres something both superior to us and yet related [to us]."

On the Being and Meaning of God (1937)

Translated by Robert S. Schine

The ultimate wellspring of religious certainty lies in the belief in a being that is superior to the natural world of our experience, that is fundamentally distinct from it and yet, in its effects, extends into it, again and again. To be sure, what we have in mind here is only the Biblical-Jewish type [of belief] and its offshoots. We will set aside specifically mystical attitudes, pantheistic forms of belief, and all those varieties of "religious worldviews" and philosophical constructions that pose as surrogates for religion. When we reflect upon our religious consciousness, we find that this insuperable dualism between God and world is already present. When we say that God created the world, it does not mean that He is absorbed into His creation, any more than the creation, which God has awakened to life, becomes divine. Every act of explanation, expression, or understanding, and every formulation derives from a treasure-trove of categories that are mainly useful only for orienting oneself in the world. When God intervenes in the reality that is familiar to the human being, when He speaks to one of His creatures, a miracle emerges, veiled in mystery, beyond disclosure. Any attempt to clarify the divine, to explain and describe it in the same manner that an object existing in the world would present itself to our cognizing mind—any such attempt means to draw it into the orbit of our natural world, no matter whether the divine is conceived of as cosmic origin, as the Prime Mover, or in some other way. Any rationalizing attempt to integrate the divine into a system of knowledge amounts to the annihilation of its true meaning. The God that would be rendered comprehensible by merging with the structure of the cosmos—and even if only to function as its origin—that God will thus itself become a part of the world, ceasing to be the God that is intended by religion.

In this spirit, we will avail ourselves of the religious meaning of the method of negative attributes.[64] This doctrine states that we have no access to knowledge of the "essence." Whatever logical and metaphysical motives have joined together to open this methodological path, in any case, it manifests an authentic religious disposition. [The doctrine of negative attributes] is the conceptual formulation of that consciousness of the believer; [it is a form of] consciousness that removes God beyond the grasp of any theoretical cognition, [that moves God into] the being that is incomparable in the strictest sense. For if all cognition is confined, rendered finite, and determined by concepts, then the basic quality of the religious quest—the quest that must remove the divine, as the absolutely unique, to a place beyond the familiar realm of the mundane—will remain unfulfilled. Certainly, the unknowability of God does not mean that His real, positive essence lies beyond any meaning that human beings might find valid; for a God conceived of as absolutely other can say no more to us and no more address us than a philosophical God belonging to the world can touch our religious disposition. What is meant by His unknowability is that no identifiable being, that is, no being known by our mind, can match the yearning for the infinite sublime, which, by its very nature, is unceasing.

For the doctrine of negative attributes will remain utterly incomprehensible and, from a theological point of view, meaningless, if one does not consider that a *conception of value* is inextricably embedded in its theory of being. This situation is the legacy of its Neoplatonic origin.[65] And because, in the construction of [Hellenistic philosopher] Plotinus' [204/5–70 CE] system, being and value are merged, it was able to incorporate this scheme into Jewish consciousness as a characteristically religious way of thinking.[66] Otherwise, the theological quest would have to take its last step just as it takes its first. But in fact, the certainty of revelation and, likewise, the intellectual translation of its content into concepts, never contain just the element of an enigmatic, obscure divine being that is beyond all cognition. The certainty of revelation also contains, along with this element of being, the idea that qualifies the essence of divine being: the idea of the perfect realization of value. Both the prophet, to whom divinity is an impenetrable, mysterious power, and the ruminating theologian, who shrinks from comprehending the essence of divinity, know one thing: the divine being is absolute perfection, the fulfillment of ultimate [moral] value. And this is, in fact, the fundamental claim about the divine, as it follows from the testimony of religious consciousness itself: the divine is *perfect being*, plain and simple. The infinitude attributed to God signifies His superiority, in dignity and value, over the human and mundane. That is the seal of His holiness. His infinitude gives Him the power that restrains the uncanny, perilous quality of strangeness and impenetrability. It generates the divine, worthy of veneration. Because of its infinitude, that which is infinitely remote and inconceivable becomes the object of an irresistible, loving yearning. Only within this sphere, in the region of moral value, is it possible to interpret the divine. Only then is it possible to make God, who is, in being and essence, beyond the limits of comprehension, of "whose essence there is no knowledge," into a God for human beings. For the human striving for perfection must be attuned to the essence of perfection, just as the genuine perfection of the true God must put itself on the level of human quest. Within the sphere of the divine being and essence there is no bridge leading from the human being to God; since such a bridge would rest upon a foundation consisting of the categories that set the conditions of our thinking, it would efface the difference between the Incomparable One and the world, making Him a thing of the world and an object of the reality that, in principle, is familiar to us, or at least accessible; that is, it would strip its character of its divinity. In the sphere of value judgment, as unconditional perfection, He is the ultimate measure of all life and judgment: supreme truth, goodness, beauty, and power. From this perspective, we can also understand why the ontological proof, though a logical and epistemological fallacy, is compelling for religious consciousness.[67] It is compelling not as a demonstration of the existence of God, but as a personal reflection on the part of the religious individual. For to such an individual, with the self-realization of God the existence of God is necessarily posited and thus the perfection of the divine is as well.

If these ideas are pursued further, it would become clear that the [divine] functions of creator, sovereign over the world, supervisor of providence, legislator and judge—functions that even the proponents of the doctrine of negative attributes do not deny God—all plainly originate from this source. For although there can be no knowledge of God's essence, it still seems clear in which direction one should go to seek whatever meaning the human being may anticipate from divine being. To interpret God is to interpret God from a human vantage point. Though human and divine being may be incomparable, the same kind of alienation does not prevail between the ultimate perfection and human understanding or even human striving.

This conclusion is now to be put to use for the purpose of clarifying the relationship between religion and ethics. Our purpose is, in particular, to clarify what is especially characteristic of Judaism. It is clear that both the religious attitude and the object to which it relates occupy their own space which is distinct from the sphere of practical-ethical activity. However, it must also be admitted that of all the value-concepts of our experience, no other stands in such a close relationship to religion as that of the Good. How can this be explained? Evidently as follows: in our mundane life we experience the ethical as the highest position in the scale of values. A conscious existence guided by an intelligent will can be endowed with meaning only by means of those practical norms that our moral consciousness exhibits. And the individual acquires the dignity and significance that is specifically human only as the bearer and the object of such motives. This view, at least, expresses the basic direction of the spirit of the Bible and of humanity educated in that spirit. Whatever ranking and distribution of values might be conceivable, our understanding of humanity and of the meaning that is represented in humanity stands or falls with certainty on this point. We are certain of it, certain that it is the highest ideal we can experience in our world.

God is perfect being, containing the fulfilment of all values, free of contradiction, and in infinite measure. We do not know how all these perfections are united in Him—goodness, wisdom, power, beauty, and whatever other perfections there may be, both those we can conceive and those we cannot. They must all be in Him, inasmuch as He is God, inasmuch as He can signify God to us. But our ignorance with regard to the how of His *perfection* is not the same as our unfamiliarity with the how of His *being*. Here, in the realm of value, our view is granted points of orientation from which lines, if extended into the infinite, must flow into the Divine. For the Divine can be nothing other than perfect. Now, inasmuch as we assign the ethical, in ourselves, the highest status, subordinating to it everything else, we can interpret the core of *divine* perfection only from His perspective. Whatever divine being may be in itself, it must contain a kind of order such that the ethical—if one may put it this way—may not be surpassed by any other divine interest.

Religion is equivalent neither to ethics nor to a practical guide for living, no less than divine perfection is identical to ethical sublimity. God is our God only because our sense of [ethical] value must assume that in God's perfection there inheres something both superior to us and yet related. And yet for us, God, too, remains obscure and unknowable in His being and His actions. His ways are not our ways, His thoughts are not our thoughts [cf. Isa. 55:8]. For, as much as it may be necessary for the human being to press ahead to the essence of divine perfection, it is also certain that, in that endeavor, he only interprets—in his own terms and only from his own perspective—that which by its essence is unfathomable, fundamentally beyond cognition, and is nevertheless a kind of being. If the Divine did not take its place within the field of value and thus did not speak a language intelligible to us, then for us the Divine would be utterly silent. If the human being did not, of his own accord, set goals for his strivings and norms of judgment, and if he did not experience one such level unambiguously as the highest, then the revelation of his God could never mean anything to him. The symbols with which the Divine is grasped and articulated as commanding word are drawn from human consciousness of value. One can speak of God's ethical character only insofar as one means, in so doing, that the human being sees divine perfection characterized and represented by that which he accords the highest status in his own sphere. Insofar as that is the Good, then there exists a primal connection between religion and ethics. Then goodness is the basic symbol of the Divine.

The way in which the human being experiences God, the way in which he is filled by His revelation, is never represented, neither in Holy Scripture nor in the Jewish spirit altogether, in such a way that miraculous letters were, so to speak, engraved on his soul and he was given a magic key for reading them. Instead, the intended meaning has always been that a power of interpretation, a certain kind of receptivity, resides in the soul. Because of the surfeit of His being, God is too great to be susceptible to cognition. But when He seizes the prophet, forcing His word on him, compelling him to be His emissary to the people, then it is certain that the human being who serves as the vehicle of this divine mission has a clear idea of what God expects from the prophet and from those he is supposed to lead. The Biblical revelations to the prophets, especially as they play out in the episodes relating each prophet's call, usually point to an obscure, enigmatic God [e.g., Isa. 6; Ezek. 1; Jer. 1]. Even where He discloses Himself as the God of the patriarchs, He loses nothing of this uncanny character [e.g., Gen. 28:10–15; Gen. 46:1–4.; Exod. 3:1–6]. The dark clouds in which He conceals Himself

[Exod. 13:21–22], the impossibility of seeing His face [Exod. 33:19], His inapproachability, felt and feared even by the highest-ranking among His servants [see Exod. 24:9–14[68]], the danger zone surrounding Him, encompassing both the Temple and the sacred paraphernalia—these make a profound impression on those who dedicate themselves to Him.[69] We may refrain from inquiring into the origin of these facts from the perspective of the history of religion.[70] But it is certain that they always recur in all the stages of the religious life, in prophecy as well as in the most sophisticated form of theological reflection. The description of the doctrine of attributes, in Maimonides in particular, surrounds the divine essence, beyond all cognition, with pathos and solemnity.[71] And this pathos and solemnity seems like a continuation of the mood of that moment when the prophet was illuminated by the God that remained dark and obscure. And in the one case as in the other, God comes closer to human comprehension, in that human beings experience God as the One who commands, judges, and protects them by His providence.

God is infinite. For us that means that our mind does not penetrate His essence. God is perfect. That permits us to have a fragmentary notion of His sublimity, in that we assume that the highest value within the scope of our lived-experience—ethical value—is realized within the context of His perfect being. By virtue of this, trust in Him is possible; communion with Him is possible.

One might think that what has been articulated here by means of concepts has already found appropriate expression in the form depicted by the calls of the prophets. We wish to illustrate this point briefly with a few examples. God addressed Moses at the burning bush (Exod. 3:2ff.). To be sure, the text says that the angel appeared to him in the blazing fire, from the midst of the bush. In fact, however, Moses sees only "this marvelous sight," that is, how the bush is ablaze, but is not consumed.[72] He wants to see this unusual sight up close, to discern why it is that the bush does not burn up. But God refuses him permission to come closer [Exod. 3:3–5]. The "holy ground" apparently has the same significance for this religious spirit as Mount Sinai, which is to be fenced off (Exod.

19:23) and which the people are not permitted to approach, lest the Eternal break out and wreak destruction in their midst. When God reveals himself to Moses as the God of his fathers, even then He remains the God that the human being may not see [Exod. 3:6]. Indeed, the intent of verse 3:6b, in which Moses hides his face because he is afraid to look at God, is to say that this God, who is familiar to you as the God of your fathers, persists in mysterious invisibility. Only thereafter is Moses sent on his mission. The fact that God then gives His own name at Moses' urging (3:14) is overshadowed by God's lengthy, elaborate characterization of Himself as the God of the patriarchs, uttered for pragmatic purposes both before and after He gives His name. [God as God of the patriarchs appears in Exod. 3:6 and 3:16; and God's giving of God's name in Exod. 3:14.] For whatever *ehyeh* may mean, whatever "being" is intended by this name, with the giving of the name, the mystery is not only not dispelled; on the contrary, it is cloaked in the deepest mystery of all. And the speculation that later developed about the Tetragrammaton always maintained this mysterious character. His enigmatic quality was guarded scrupulously: to gaze upon Him, to have knowledge of His essence—this idea is always present—exceeds human capacity. And yet He wants to appear to be familiar to those whom He deems worthy of His revelation—when, that is, and to the extent that they surrender themselves to His power. But to do His will, that is much more than morals and fulfillment of the Law. It also encompasses the humble shudder in the presence of the Unnamable One.

Isaiah's vision of his call [Isa. 6] is distinct from Moses' in its essential components, but in its general thrust it confirms our view. He does say that he has seen the LORD seated on His high and lofty throne. But he does not dare mention a word describing the features of the image of the one whose royal robe filled the temple. It is probably no coincidence that the prophet has something to say only about the most peripheral element of the divine form: the skirts of His robe [Isa. 6:1]. He averted his own gaze instantly—we may assume as much—from the actual form, and bowed low, in order not to profane the Holy One. He is able to say a good bit about the divine surroundings, the seraphim [Isa. 6:2–4]. Each seraph has three pairs of wings. Of these, he uses one to hover in the heavenly palace. Of the other two what is of greatest interest is the pair with which the seraph covers his face. Apparently, that is intended to mean that even the heavenly hosts, who are always considered worthy of nearness to God, are not permitted to look upon Him. How much less, then, a mortal human, who is granted a fleeting glance into the divine throne-room only in a few elevated moments of his life? For although verse 5 states "Yet my own eyes have beheld the King Lord of Hosts," one may well take that to refer to the view of the prophet of the entire form. Moreover, it is characteristic that here too, as above, so little is said about the face of God. Our sense of sight grasps an object, its essence; and in the case of a person, the essence manifests itself directly in his face. Isaiah's description shrinks discreetly from any such notion. But he hears the voice of God speaking. Spiritual perception, by means of the ear, is permitted. Hearing is the organ for receiving revelation [cf. Exod. 20:15–17]. Yet the voice of God conveys nothing to him that might inform about God Himself, about His inner essence. The message that he receives through the vehicle of the voice points him, rather, back into the world of the mundane where he is to inform the people of their divine task [Isa. 6:8–13].

This structure emerges in Ezekiel's *ma'aseh Merkabah* ("account of the chariot" [Ezek. 1]) with almost greater clarity. "The heavens opened and I saw visions of God" (Ezek. 1:1). The hand of the LORD that comes upon him (1:3) is what gives him access to his vision. His potent creative imagination enables him to depict the marvelous animals of the divine chariot [Ezek. 1:4–14]. But his imagination is restrained; because the subject is the divine throne and divine figure seated on it (1:26–28), the prophet does not succumb to speaking in terms that he would construe to be anything but analogies. The surfeit of terms that imply distance, terms such as "like," "appearance," and "form," is evidently intended to prevent the reader or listener from thinking that these words are a description of divine reality.[73] The prophet is able to report only on "the appearance of the semblance of the Presence of the LORD. When I beheld it, I flung myself down on my face. And I heard the voice of someone speaking" [Ezek. 1:28].

In his critique of Maimonides' interpretation of the *Merkabah* (chariot) vision of Ezekiel, [Portuguese Jewish philosopher and biblical exegete] Isaac Abarbanel [1437–1508] contests Maimonides' claim in the *Moreh Nevuchim* (Guide of the Perplexed) that the vision is an expression of Aristotelian metaphysics.[74] Following the example of others, in his first counter-argument he states that it is impossible that the kind of excessive, mysterious esoteric inquiry that has surrounded the preoccupation with the *Merkabah* since time immemorial could extend to the consideration of such metaphysical questions.[75] For according to Abarbanel, speculation on the construction of the world and its elements is regarded among philosophers as nothing more than a mystery. He is right. To draw the prophets' vision of images out of their own natural obscurity and to thrust them into the bright light of conceptual knowledge—conceptually difficult to be sure, but accessible in principle—to construe their visions and language as allusions to speculative wisdom and as symbols of it would mean to destroy the actual meaning of prophetic revelation. The very purpose of Ezekiel's phantasmagoria is, so to speak, to wrap God, who remains incomprehensible, in a broad sash of obscurity. Thus, Ezekiel's vision is obstructed by those marvelous celestial beings who are situated high above the human being, yet infinitely far below the Divine itself.

Thus, in the end, Ezekiel too remains a prophet with a calling who tells humanity what is good [cf. Mic. 6:8]. Where the mortal seems to touch the divine directly, he becomes blind and speechless. But for him it is a fertile blindness and a fertile speechlessness; for they teach him to interpret God in His significance for the way of the human being, and in so doing to use His own supreme idea, the idea of the ethical. God may not be seen but is to be heard.

6

Judaism and the Origin of Ethics

There are obvious justifications for Orthodox belief. That the words of the Torah record historical truth, that the Revelation on Sinai happened as depicted, that the sages' interpretations constitute the authentic tradition given to Moses and passed, uninterrupted and uncorrupted, down the generations—these are the traditional understandings of Judaism, the normative theological-historical-legal narratives that a great many of Judaism's finest thinkers have explicated and defended for the better part of two millennia. One could almost call Orthodoxy—or to use a less political word, traditionalism—Judaism's most natural expression, Judaism in its relaxed pose.

Living Jewish Orthodoxy is difficult. It commands one's whole being, every hour, every day. But its internal justifications are as smooth and lovely as silk—pleasant to behold and even more so to be adorned by—and as strong as iron, with roots deep in the soil of history and memory. In Orthodoxy in its purest sense, defending Judaism is, almost by definition, unnecessary. Judaism is a unique revelation, with its own theological justifications and ethical foundations, unbeholden to the demands and unreceptive to the critiques of those outside its sphere. That such a self-reflective narrative might not have perfect historical accuracy is of no relevance. When Orthodoxy becomes synonymous with the individual, it provides a complete framework for living a good and meaningful life.

But Orthodoxy—traditionalism—is not for everyone. For some, Orthodoxy is incompatible with their natural dispositions. They simply want to be different, to see differently, to be unmoored from social expectations and freed from the weight (often a burden even for those who embrace it) of historical communal memory. For others, Orthodoxy is antithetical to their own intellectual proclivities, an insular, uninteresting cavern of repetitious ideas and overweening authorities, of too many laws and too few poets, of too much pedantry and too little invention. Yet, arguably, without Orthodoxy, no matter one's other chosen path, the clarity that defines the purpose and meaning of Judaism's continued existence, and the boundaries that separate its moral insights from those of the other nations, begin to grow murky. Without the strictures of a law whose every detail begins with Moses, what remains to justify Judaism's unique place among the religions of the world?

By the early twentieth century, a small but influential cohort of modern Jewish theologians formulated their answer to that question: Judaism offered the first, and still clearest, example of the purity of religious *ethical learning*. In other words, Judaism wasn't unique because its traditions were perfectly preserved from antiquity. (Not even medieval Jewish sages quite believed that, and a basic tenet of *Wissenschaft des Judentums* was that Jewish culture and practice developed over time.) And it wasn't unique because it focused most clearly on monotheism (see chapter 3) or because its form of religion was the least tarnished by pagan influence (see chapter 5). Rather, Judaism was unique because of a combination of two intertwining factors: ethics formed the nucleus of its essence, and its fundamental structure was one of flexibility and adaptation. Ethics in Judaism, it was argued, was a process of learning, of uncovering the good. Surely it did not involve a mechanical acceptance of divine fiat, an absolute adherence to a strict standard written down—and then untouched—from the hoary days of antiquity. To imagine that Judaism observed, or should observe, the same moral law as in antiquity would be as absurd as to hope for the reinstatement of the Code of Hammurabi.

As the four essays in this chapter lay out, Judaism's contributions didn't need to be justified; they needed to be recognized. For Moritz Güdemann, the people Israel had always seen the Torah as a "delight."

Torah is not a legal code, he says, for who delights over a legal code? Instead, it is a font of eternal learning, a book that is always beginning. To Benzion Kellermann, such delight is the expression of the Jew's daily recognition of God's absolute goodness. As we increase our understanding of God, so too we increase our love of that which is just and upright. Taking Kellermann a step further, Moritz Lazarus defines the ethical as what is most pleasing to God—indeed, God's most favored attribute. Therefore, the more we strive to fulfill the ethical, the more we engage in the moral uplift of the world, and the more we bring ourselves into line with divinity, the more we align with the ultimate purpose of human life itself: that of *imitatio dei,* to be like God. Finally, Benno Jacob completely rejects the idea that Orthodoxy in any form is agreeable with Judaism. Anything that hints of the dogmatic, any attempt to cling to old ideas in the face of new knowledge, is immoral, since it will, by definition, create categories of those who are and those who are not on the right path. To Jacob, such a division is completely anathema to the core insights of Judaism that God is good and that human insight into God expands the moral universe. Judaism, by dint of developing and changing over time, and also by remaining unified without recourse to dogma, is therefore a unique example in modernity on which to model moral development without the strictures of doctrinal homogeneity.

MORITZ GÜDEMANN (1835–1918)

Moritz Güdemann (b. 1835, Hildesheim; d. 1918, Baden bei Wien) was an Austrian rabbi and historian. Educated in his hometown at both Jewish and Catholic schools, in the mid-1850s he moved to Breslau, where he completed his doctorate at the city's university and, in 1862, his rabbinical training at the Jewish Theological Seminary. That same year he accepted a rabbinical position in Magdeburg, where he stayed until 1866, when Vienna's chief rabbi Adolf Jellinek (1821–93) invited him to become preacher at the city's Leopoldstadt Temple. Eventually, he succeeded Jellinek as chief rabbi upon the latter's retirement in 1892.

A prolific writer of grand historical works, Güdemann published extensively on Jewish history across the centuries as well as on Jewish-Christian and Jewish-Arab interactions. A respected preacher and community leader, he, like his colleague Jellinek, attempted to hold a moderate path through reform, emphasizing the moral and theological aspects of Judaism while also seeking a continued place for ritual in modern Jewish life.

This selection is from one of Güdemann's later writings, entitled *Das Judentum in seinen Grundzügen und nach seinen geschichtlichen Grundlagen* (Judaism presented in its basic features and according to its historical foundations).[1] An attempt to synthesize the theological and historical underpinnings of Judaism for a popular audience, the work is divided into six sections, covering themes from family and beliefs to the unique status of humans and the coming redemption. This excerpt, from part 5, focuses on the underlying theological foundations of Judaism, and most importantly on the unique status and nature of Torah, which, Güdemann writes, is at once a constitution for Judaism (a basic law) but also a way of life, a mindset, a habit, and a daily regime. Torah, he says, means not "law" but "instruction," not "rule" but "teaching," and throughout the Bible it is described as "delightful" or "bringing delight." To Güdemann, this delight in teaching is the foundation of the Torah's role in Judaism, for the enjoyment of studying Torah is the bedrock of Jewish culture and its greatest gift to human society.

Instruction and Life (1902)

Translated by Brian Britt and Steve Britt

"Study and teach, preserve and take action," the words of God—this formula circumscribes the duties for followers of Judaism. One can see that its message is not about belief. Although articles of faith were established for different time periods by different great teachers of Judaism, these never took on canonical or binding authority. This is naturally not to diminish the significance of faith as the religious disposition, which is a matter of the heart and permeates and determines the human being. On the contrary, already because of the high estimation of faith in the sense indicated here—a traditional saying goes "God lays claim to the heart"—people have resisted substituting formulas for the essence of God. But faith asserts its value only when and to the extent that it is associated with the pursuit of knowledge.

This is why the latter [pursuit of knowledge] is emphasized more than the former [faith] in the sacred scripture of the people of Israel. In the fifth book of the Torah it says—perhaps this passage best expresses the suggested relationship—"Know therefore this day and keep in mind that the LORD alone is God in heaven above and on earth below; there is no other" [Deut. 4:39]. And the prophet Hosea proclaims, "And let us know, let us aspire, to know the Eternal One" [Hos. 6:3]. Further citations are superfluous. But this knowledge can naturally only gain depth and breadth through study and instruction.

The greatest emphasis was already placed on this in ancient times. In God's first address to Joshua he says, "Let not this Book of the Teaching cease from your lips, but recite it day and night, so that you may observe faithfully all that is written in it. Only then will you prosper in your undertakings and only then will you be successful" [Josh. 1:8]. The first Psalm addresses that same salvation, that "rather, the teaching of the LORD is his delight, and he recited that teaching day and night" [Ps. 1:2]. In another case, Psalm 119, it says, "Your teaching is my delight," "Your teaching is my delight," "Were not Your teaching my delight, I would have perished in my affliction," "O how I love Your teaching! It is my study all day long," etc. [Ps. 119:70,77,92,97].

Could a person reading the word of Torah for the first time in these passages, not knowing its meaning, possibly think that it could be translated as "law"? With all due respect to collections of state law—has one ever heard that one derived "his desire" from them? We could always imagine that a judge or legal expert from time to time, on certain occasions, "thinks day and night" about it, but the most diehard jurist will not describe it as his "delight," nor rave about his "love" for it, nor make it a topic of meditation "all day." Nevertheless, if the Torah were designated as law, as indeed it was by the Hellenistic Jews, it was only to convey the authoritative character of the Torah in terms consistent with the perception of the gentile world. For thus is the Jewish religion consistently designated in official Aramaic documents of the books of Daniel and Ezra, thus from the non-Jewish perspective, as an "edict" of the king and thus as the "law" (*dat*) [e.g., Dan. 6:6 (*dat elahe*); Ezra 7:14 (*dat elahakh*), 7:25 (*dati elahakh*)]. Consequently, the Torah and Judaism, outside the realm of the latter, were understood, or rather misunderstood, as if even their inner essence could be realized in legal terms.

The concept of law or the juridical always smacks of rigidity, strictness, severity, which is felt to be repulsive to the human consciousness of freedom, be it a law of nature, a law attributed to God, or a human law. This quality of law was now also grafted onto the Torah, and just as an unfortunately chosen name often has consequences, such is the case with the Torah. Beyond Judaism, it became customary to speak of a "burden of the law." Thus what the psalmist once described as a "desire"[2] would now be understood as a "burden."[3]

History has probably never seen a stranger case of reversal of judgment on a matter into its exact opposite. But for its part this reversal concerns a misunderstanding that stems from an infelicitous term. Etymologically, "Torah" means nothing other and can mean nothing other than "instruction." According to the author of the Proverb: "My son, keep your father's commandment [*mitzvat*]; do not forsake your mother's teaching [*torat*]" [Prov. 6:20]. Perhaps here the concept of the Torah of the mother as a representation of leniency is deliberately contrasted with the stricter father. And elsewhere: "The instruction [*torat*] of a wise man is a fountain of life" [Prov. 13:14]. That in both verses Torah refers not to law but rather to teaching and instruction is obvious. The same poet says of the worthy wife that "the Torah of love" is on her tongue [Prov. 31:26]. To whom would it occur to substitute the word "law" here?

The Torah is thus understood as instruction, and this view makes it comprehensible that this immersion, like its exercise, is a desire, a delight that could not have been the case had it been perceived as a burden, as an expression of legal rigor and strictness. The contents of the Torah also correspond to this point of view, for although they incorporate laws, ritual laws, criminal, civil, police matters, etc., they nonetheless largely consist of ethical precepts and meaningful stories from the past. The appeal of these parts and the piety thus aroused spread through the provisions of law, indeed all throughout [Scripture], and so we see how Psalm 119, with apparent deliberateness, and deploying a profoundly rich phrasing, glorifies the word of God [e.g., "Happy are those whose way is blameless, who follow the teaching of the LORD. . . . I rejoice over the way of Your decrees as over all riches. I study your precepts; I regard Your ways; I take delight in Your laws" (Ps. 119:1,14–15)]. His pronouncements, commandments, testimonies, laws, regulations, instructions, etc. are all united under the collective concept of the Torah. [German theologian and biblical scholar Heinrich] Ewald [1803–75] speaks of this psalm, composed in the time of Ezra, as "odd because of this constant connection to the Pentateuch."[4] But it is even more odd that Ewald consistently renders uses of the term "Torah" with "law" in this psalm,[5] while in the first psalm, which he places in the time after David, he translates as mentioned above: the poet calls out for salvation the one for whom "rather, the teaching [*torat*] of the LORD is his delight, and he recites that teaching [*torato*] day and night" [Ps. 1:2].[6] If one isn't translating for the sake of a historical construction, then one cannot recognize why the "Torah of God" should be "law" in Psalm 119 and "instruction" in the first. An unbiased consideration yields the conclusion that the Torah is always understood as instruction, that it is learned and further taught, and that numerous passages explicitly and firmly warrant this.[7]

In the Hebrew Bible a complete array of assorted expressions from a number of eras refer to "study and instruction" as one of the most central cases of a religious disposition, and as the most essential means to maintaining and safeguarding religion. As already expressed above, an instruction to Joshua attributed to God, "Let not this Book of the

Teaching cease from your lips, but recite it day and night" [Josh. 1:8], is praised; likewise, so is the above-referenced passage from the first psalm, where "the teaching of the LORD is his delight, and he recites that teaching day and night"; and finally [this holds true for] numerous passages, only some of which are cited here, from Psalm 119, where the poet describes the Torah as his "delight," his steady "meditation." All these expressions may indeed be seen as evidence that at the time when they originated, the Torah was an object of the most fervent study and teaching—for only this meaning can explain the sense of "day and night."

The Torah itself also illustrates this point. In the second book it is sometimes ordained for the father to explain the establishment of the Passover to the son, with the comment "in order that the Teaching of the LORD may be in your mouth" [Exod. 13:9]. The same statement appears in a dialogue between Moses and [his father-in-law] Jethro, that "the laws of God and his instruction" should be proclaimed or expounded to the people, [a phrase] which although initially refers to the decision of legal questions, more generally comprises public instruction [Exod. 18:16]. In the third book, one of the tasks prescribed for the priests is "you must teach the Israelites all the laws [*chukim*] which the LORD has imparted to them through Moses" [Lev. 10:11]. The actual terms of art for "study" (*lamad*) and "teaching" (*limmed*), which have remained ever since, appear first in Deuteronomy, and here both activities are most emphatically impressed upon the people.[8] For example: "Hear, O Israel, the laws and rules that I proclaim to you this day! Study [*lamad*] them and observe them faithfully!" [Deut. 5:1]. Or: "See, I have imparted to you laws and rules, as the LORD my God has commanded me. . . . Observe them faithfully, for that will be proof of your wisdom and discernment to other peoples," etc. [Deut. 4:5–6]. It notes further there of the "word of God": "Teach it to your children," and at another point, not in the same terms but in the same sense: "And make them known to your children" [Deut. 4:9], etc. These indeed are unmistakable witnesses to widespread learning and teaching activities.

We encounter related expressions in the prophets, in the Psalms, and in other scriptures of the people of Israel. In chapter 8 of Isaiah, we read: "Bind up the message, seal the instruction [*torah*] with My disciples [*limmudai*]" [Isa. 8:16]. Jeremiah says in chapter 31: "No longer will they need to teach [*yelamdu*] one another and say to one other: 'Heed the LORD; for all of them, from the least of them to the greatest, shall heed Me" [Jer. 31:34], etc. Further in chapter 32 of the same book: "Though I have taught [*lammed*] them persistently, they do not give heed or accept rebuke" [Jer. 32:33]. The other Isaiah[9] says in chapter 50 that God provided him a tongue for students [*limmudim*] and an ear, to listen as students [*kelimmudim*] [Isa. 50:4–5], and he prophesies in chapter 54: "And all your children shall be disciples [*limmude*] of the LORD" [Isa. 54:13]. The psalmist proclaims in Psalm 34: "Come, my sons, listen to me; I will teach you [*alamedchem*] what it is to fear the LORD" [Ps. 34:12], and Psalm 94: "Happy is the man whom You discipline, O LORD, the man You instruct [*telamdenu*] in Your teaching" [Ps. 94:12], while Psalm 119 uses the same expression for teachers [*melamdim*] [Ps. 119: 99] as Chronicles uses for students [*talmid*] [1 Chron. 25:8]. These multiple expressions for study and teaching also give rise to the concept of Talmud-Torah, or simply Talmud. Its direct descent from study and instruction that have been in practice since ancient times, and the object of which was precisely the "Teaching" [*Lehre*, Torah], cannot be doubted in light of the above evidence.

BENZION KELLERMANN (1869–1923)

Benzion Kellermann (b. 1869, Gerolzhofen; d. 1923, Berlin) was a radical Reform rabbi, teacher, and philosopher. Born into an Orthodox family, he soon turned to philosophy, went to Marburg to study with Hermann Cohen (see chapter 5), and became affiliated with the Marburg school of neo-Kantianism. Later he moved to Berlin and finished his rabbinical studies at the Hochschule für die Wissenschaft des Judentums. From 1900 to 1901 he interrupted his education to gain practical experience as the rabbi of the East Prussian town of Konitz.

Published from 1914 to 1916, Kellermann's two-volume German translation of *The Wars of the Lord*, the major treatise by Provençal Jewish philosopher, mathematician, astronomer, and exegete Gersonides, caused a great controversy in the Jewish intellectual world. In his extended neo-Kantian commentary, Kellerman had employed the Kantian terminology of the "a priori," a concept then unknown to Gersonides. To the charge of anachronism, Kellermann retorted that such a concept was exactly what the medieval thinker had had in mind—thus arguing radically for the notion of timeless philosophical ideas.

From 1917 to his death, Kellermann served as rabbi of the liberal Berlin Jewish community, while also writing major works on Kant (*Der wissenschaftliche Idealismus und die Religion* [Scientific idealism and religion, 1908] and *Das Ideal im System der Kantischen Philosophie* [The ideal in the system of Kantian philosophy, 1920]) as well as Spinoza (*Die Ethik Spinozas, über Gott und Geist* [The Ethics of Spinoza on God and Spirit, 1922]). These books intentionally intervened in contemporary Jewish-Christian debates about the prerogative of Kant's interpretation, as well as in internal Jewish discussions about the theological meaning of pantheism. On both issues, Kellermann took rather provocative positions, but which would take us too far afield here.

Most later scholars would come to dismiss Kellermann as an epigone of his teacher Hermann Cohen, but he was in fact the more radical theologian of the two. Whereas Cohen still allowed for the so-called nonrational, purely ritual traditions of Judaism to be part of one's service of God, as a means of Jewish education, Kellermann rejected all Jewish customs that did not seem to have an immediate rational explanation, including the Jewish dietary laws, because to serve God, one must be exclusively focused on moral behavior.

Nevertheless, being in many regards a faithful follower of Cohen, Kellermann was the designated author of the introduction to the posthumous edition of Cohen's *Jüdische Schriften* (Jewish writings). Only Kellermann's own untimely death in 1924 cleared the way for the introduction to be written by existentialist thinker Franz Rosenzweig (1886–1929, see chapter 8), who eventually produced a text that, using a number of unreliable anecdotes, portrayed at least "the late Cohen" as a predecessor of Rosenzweig himself and thus derailed Cohen scholarship for decades.

In this selection, from his 1907 essay *Liberales Judentum* (Liberal Judaism), Kellermann seeks to understand, through Kantian philosophical language, how Judaism can be led to reform itself, or open itself to reform.[10] Employing the concept of "movement"—that is, ideas, laws, and institutions responsive to changing social dynamics—Kellermann argues that Judaism must embrace the parts of itself that are most characterized by "movement." Ancient laws, appropriate in their time and place but irrelevant in our own, must be shed, and Judaism itself must be "divested of its claim to an absolute, eternal validity." Instead, writes Kellermann, Judaism must reinforce its already-present notion of God as developmental and responsive, and replace the ritual law with the moral one, for "all cases of the moral law . . . qualify as moving elements." If Judaism thus reforms toward movement, it will open the way toward the instantiation of pure religion and pure ethics, the most perfect realizations of human thought.

Liberal Judaism (1907)

Translated by Garrett E. Paul

If we look at the conceptual elements of the Jewish religion, they divide into two great complexes. On the one hand stands the entire complex of duties of an ethical and ritual character; and, on the other hand, the concept of God with His attributes as the ground, originator, and purpose of these duties. These two complexes stand in a completely reciprocal relationship to one another: no fulfillment of duties without the knowledge of God as the author and arbiter of these duties; no knowledge of God without the will to fulfill His commands. This gives rise to the question: Can this reciprocal relationship between duties and God be considered a cultural necessity? Does this relationship reveal specific tasks that can count as eternal cultural requirements? Obviously, this can be the case when the two components of the relationship and the relationship itself possess the capacity for flexibility and development,[11] as the cultural legitimacy of every construction of thought certainly lies only in the capacity for its development. In fact, every complex of duties contains both the flexible and the fixed; and, therefore also the concept of God, as the ground and purpose of all laws, is both possessed of a capacity for development and simultaneously opposed to development. In any case, moral law is the flexible element in this complex of duties. The concepts of "good" and "evil" will surely always be valid as the foundation of ethics. But their content changes. It is eternally produced anew, and moral reason in its own self is only realized in this eternal creation of new values. Every period has its particular moral tasks, its specific social and economic duties.

And as the moral law constitutes the true element of flexibility in this complex of duties, so too the concept of God that makes the moral law real entails an attribute of flexibility that corresponds to the one possessed by moral law.

God is not the maker of these moral values, no more than God may relieve moral reason from its moral task. Man himself produces the moral law with his reason; neither God nor revelation can relieve him of this sacred task.

God Himself is nothing other than the force behind the idea, which steers towards the realization of the moral law and constitutes the guarantee of its future fulfillment.

Without this belief in the future realization of the moral world, without the belief in an eternal moral progress in world history, ethics remains a fragment, a torso with no relationship to reality.

As surely as the content of the moral law eternally changes over the course of time, just as surely does the idea of God in its tendency to realization partake of that eternal development.

The relationship of the law and God works in a completely different way if the eternally creative and eternally productive reason of all humanity does not substantiate the law, but, instead, the psyche of particular individual persons invents the law. If, in place of this moral law, valid for all of humanity, or alongside this law for humanity, demands arise, these are valid only for individual persons, for individual groups. Then particular individual communities arise to take the place of the human community, and divide and rupture humanity. Such demands remain eternally rigid and unalterable, precisely because they strive for the rigid inalterability of the community—its eternal isolation. Particularistic ritualist laws come to ground and secure the character *indelebilis* (indelibly) in the community,[12] and a particular community is supposed to triumph over the human community; the past of mythical and naïve sentimentality is to take mastery over the present and its joyfully vital critical thought.

If Judaism is, instead, to signify a culturally necessary postulate, to play its part in configuring the great global law of movement and development, it must remove the rigid, anti-developmental elements from its consciousness, [or] at the least they must be transformed into an openness to development. It must be divested of its claim to an absolute, eternal validity if God is not to be reduced to the status of a preserver and protector of a particularistic, i.e., misanthropic community.

Therefore, Judaism must transform the rigid part in the relationship between God and law into a completely flexible one. And this transformation can be accomplished only by the removal of the rigid ritual laws from the complex of duties.

Only moral law can possess the compulsory force of a general and necessary law. Only through the moral law can the dynamic character of the Jewish religion be preserved. Only under this presupposition can the Jewish religion be [in] the truly pure stage of preparation for pure religion, pure ethics; only under this presupposition can its eternal value for the realm of general culture be affirmed. What religion intuitively beholds, reason critically develops. For pure reason, pure religion, and pure ethics are nothing other than the ripe fruit of the tree of historical religion.

MORITZ LAZARUS (1824–1903)

Moritz Lazarus (b. 1824 Filehne; d. 1903, Meran), a philosopher, psychologist, and activist in the fight against antisemitism, was arguably among the most influential German-Jewish intellectuals in the second half of the nineteenth century. Trained in Bible and Talmud in his youth, Lazarus studied philosophy in Berlin, but after earning his doctorate he changed to psychology, and during the 1850s founded the new discipline of *Völkerpsychologie* (comparative psychology or anthropology of cultures). In 1860 he was called to the university of Bern in Switzerland, where he became the first Jewish full professor in the humanities and later the dean of the philosophical faculty. Returning to Berlin in 1866, he first taught philosophy at the Prussian Military Academy and then psychology at the University of Berlin; among his students were soon-to-be famous scholars like philosopher and sociologist Georg Simmel (1858–1918) and anthropologist Franz Boaz (1858–1942). Lazarus's second wife, Nahida Ruth Lazarus-Remy, who converted to Judaism, became a celebrated journalist and activist for women's rights.

A lifelong defender of the Jewish religion, Lazarus took an active part in the great 1880 debate about antisemitism in Germany.[13] Writing in November 1879, the German Protestant historian Heinrich von Treitschke (1834–96) had "demanded" that Jews become thoroughly German, as "we do not want thousands of years of Germanic civilization to be followed by an era of German-Jewish mixed culture."[14] Lazarus responded by offering different visions of "nation" and "peoplehood" than Treitschke had proposed. Rather than an account of a Germanness based on blood descent (which he claimed was "a product of a general coarsely sensualist-materialist worldview"), Lazarus depicted Germany as the one nation with the most potential to represent humanity in its purest sense, that strove to embody a kind of universal spirit.[15] The Jews, then, as a diasporic people who "have been led to a consciousness of [their] national task by cosmopolitanism and world literature," were the truest partners in this endeavor.[16] Only Jewish Germans and Christian Germans together could create a state based on the most noble and humane ideals.

Lazarus was a religious liberal. He officiated as president of the first Israelite Synods in 1869 in Leipzig and 1871 in Augsburg, which assembled representatives from Jewish communities worldwide. These gatherings had decisive influence on the founding of Berlin's liberal rabbinical seminary (Hochschule für die Wissenschaft des Judenthums) in 1872, where Lazarus became president of the board and a frequent lecturer.

The selections reprinted here are taken from his major work in Jewish theology, the two-volume *Die Ethik des Judenthums* (Ethics of Judaism), published in 1898 (vol. 1) and posthumously in 1911 (vol. 2).

Lazarus saw ethics in a Kantian sense, where the basic question of ethics is "what *ought* I to do?" The response to such a question, argued Kant (and Lazarus), required not only an accounting of the foundational moral duties and responsibilities that apply to us as individuals, but also a robust notion of the Highest Good and its impact on the moral life. In the pages excerpted here, Lazarus attempts to portray the law of Judaism as a Kantian *ought*, arguing that God has commanded the law not as His pleasure or despotic will, but because it is moral. For Lazarus, practical reason is just another expression for the divine lawgiver, with God defined as the ideal of morality. Moreover, Judaism is the ideal Kantian moral system: a religion with a clear idea of the Highest Good and a divinity whose fundamental character is to be absolutely just.

The Ethics of Judaism (1898)

Translated by Henrietta Szold

§77. In its origin Jewish ethics is theological. For the Jewish mind its theistic rationale looms up in the foreground of all speculation upon morality. The whole Jewish conception of life is as little thinkable without God as our physical world is without the sun.

Within Judaism the essence of morality has never been considered other than the emanation of the divine order, the expression of a divine law, the fulfillment of a divine command. For man's will and conduct there are standards, that is, moral laws to be obeyed, and God is the lawgiver. Judaism regards what is morally good and what is pleasing to God, moral law and divine regulation, as inseparable.

§78. In practice this reference of all moral laws to God as the source of their enactment has had a highly significant expression, differentiating the life of the Jews essentially from that of other peoples. Legislation among the Jews does not emanate from an earthly authority. Neither deliberation, nor resolution, nor the will of one man or of many was the originator of a law. King, prophet, and priest could not create laws nor annul those in force. Not even the Great Assembly or the Sanhedrin could do it.[17]

If changed circumstances demanded peculiar ordinances at all, they were decreed on the basis of old laws, as an extension or relaxation of the old ones, or as new regulations in harmony with and as an emanation from them.

§79. What is morally good and what is pleasing to God, moral law and divine regulation, we called inseparable concepts—inseparable, mark you, not identical.

A deeper investigation of the essence and basis of the moral law reveals that Judaism everywhere clearly advances the thought, that not because God has ordained it a law is it moral, but because it is moral, therefore has God ordained it. Not by divine command does the moral become law, but because its content is moral, and it would necessarily, even without an ordinance, become law, therefore it is enjoined by God.[18]

§80. In the oldest version of the laws, dating from a time when conscious, abstract consideration of the content and essence of the moral law, of its purport and basis, was out of question, the thought appears with unmistakable clearness: the moral law does not exist by virtue of a divine act of will or an authoritative fiat; it flows from the essence of God himself, from his absolute and infinite moral nature. Therefore the fundamental law, "you shall be holy," which sums up all morality in one comprehensive expression, does not continue with "for I so will it," nor with "for I so command"; it reads, "You shall be holy, for I am holy," and other moral laws close simply with the declaration, "I am God" [Lev. 19:2].[19]

§81. The same thought runs through the whole of Rabbinic literature. The Divine Being and therefore the knowledge of His moral attributes, combined with the endeavor to imitate them in man's finite way, constitute at once the rule and the reason of morality: "Because I am merciful, thou shalt be merciful; as I am gracious, thou shalt be gracious, etc."[20]

In a word, the fundamental doctrine of Judaism reads: Because the moral is divine, therefore you shall be moral, and because the divine is moral, you shall become like God.[21] It may be said that the highest form and ultimate purpose of human life is likeness to God, and the ethical ideals are conceived as attributes of God, in whose image man was created, and whose image it is man's task to strive to increasingly become.[22]

§82. The Bible does not expound, and the Rabbis do not inculcate, metaphysical notions or dogmatic teachings concerning the divine nature, for the purpose of deducing the legislative authority of God.[23] Man's moral duty of obedience is based neither upon God's omnipresence, nor his omnipotence, nor even his supreme wisdom.[24]

The ethical ideals themselves are presented as attributes of God, and for the sake of their realization man is called upon to strive to become like unto God. When the "glory of God" is made manifest to Moses, only moral attributes are enumerated (Exod. 34:6).[25] And in the well-known verse from Jeremiah, we have a clear statement of what man can and should know concerning God: "Let not the wise man glory in his wisdom; let not the strong man glory in his strength; let not the rich man glory in his riches. But only in this should one glory: In his earnest devotion to Me. For I the Lord act with kindness, justice, and equity in the world" [Jer. 9:22–23].

§83. This, then, is the relation between divine law and human ethics: God is the lawgiver, but he did not promulgate the law as his pleasure or as an arbitrary or despotic command; and man is not to obey it as such. It is law for man, because he recognizes in God the prototype of all morality, because God is the creative force back of the moral order and moral purpose of the world. Moral law, then, is based, not upon some dogmatic conception of God, but upon the idea of his morality, that is, upon the essential nature of morality. Not God the master, but God the ideal of all morality is the fountainhead of man's moral doctrine.

§84. As a philosopher, a teacher of ethics, does not consider himself the lawgiver; as his desires and inclinations exercise no influence, and are meant to exercise none; as the genius of morality, or the idea of the good, working, as it were, through his person, dictates the substance of his teaching; as the moral idea of necessity shapes itself thus and so and not otherwise within him; as the principle underlying morality, whose bidding the will has but to do, assumes form in his mind; so in Judaism the majesty of the law produced the law.

"This is your wisdom and your understanding," says Deuteronomy (4:6) with reference to the law. When [German philosopher Immanuel] Kant [1724–1804] calls the force that actually decrees, teaches, makes demands, by the term "practical reason," he but uses another expression for morality.[26] Call it law, principle, idea, what you will, it is always an objective norm, in no wise dependent upon the pleasure of man, but constraining him as he knows himself to be constrained by the laws of logic when he thinks, by the laws of mathematics when he computes.[27] The all-important consideration is the absolutely impersonal character of the moral idea. This thought was strikingly expressed in early times by [Palestinian Rabbinic sage] Rabbi Yohanan [third century CE]: "The words of the law are fully established by him who considers himself naught [as compared with them]" [b. *Sotah* 21b.]—that is by one in whom objective truth has become subjective and living, who has identified the idea with his person.

§85. This view of the relation of human ethics to divine law can also be deduced from the Rabbinical utterances upon its relation to the Sinaitic law before, at, and after its revelation.

Morality was not created by the Sinaitic code; it springs from its own and from man's peculiar nature. It could therefore be said, as it was, that "Abraham observed all moral laws" [m. *Kiddushin* 4:14]. His own reason was the source of his ethical instruction. The Talmud distinguishes accurately between laws of reason, that is, laws independent of legislation, and formal, ritual ordinances, laws by virtue of their institution as such. It says with reference to Leviticus 18:4: "My judgments, that is, precepts—if they had not been laid down in Holy Scriptures, law (*Din*), or practical reason, would have demanded that they be put into writing; ordinances, however, rest upon institution" [b. *Yoma* 67b]. The examples cited in connection with this passage permit no doubt as to the antithesis intended. "Judgments" are illustrated by the laws of chastity, laws against bloodshed, robbery, etc.; "ordinances," by the prohibitions against eating swine's flesh, mixing diverse fabrics, etc.

Moral laws, then, are not laws because they are written; they are written because they are laws.

§86. Therefore, free moral convictions, not founded upon the authority and the act of legislation, are ranked above obedience to this authority.[28] [Palestinian Rabbinic sage] R. Simon ben Lakish [called Reish Lakish, third century CE] taught: "The stranger who accepts the law of his own free will stands higher in the eyes of God than the hosts of the children of Israel that surrounded Mount Sinai. They saw the lightning, and heard the thunder, the shofar, and the divine voice, else, perhaps, they would not have assumed the yoke of the divine order. The stranger saw naught of all this, yet, of his own impulse, he seeks to live in harmony with God—and submits to the moral order of the universe. Who can stand higher"? [Mid. Tan. (B.), *Lekh Lekha* 6].[29]

§87. It is in consonance with this that in the Talmud and the Midrash the authority of the teacher is in various ways represented as a circumstance of small importance in comparison with the significance and compelling force of the content of the law. Take, for instance, the principle that the dictum of the humblest, if it contains truth, is to be esteemed equal to the words of the great and even of the Most High:

What one has heard from a man of low estate should be looked upon as equal to what one has heard from a sage, from the Sanhedrin, from Moses, ay, from the mouth of the Most High [Sifre to Deut. 11:13 (*Piska* 41)]. Of still greater importance is the thought recurring again and again in Talmudic literature, that every age is justified in disregarding, more, is in duty bound to disregard, the written law whenever reason and conviction demand its nullification [m. *Rosh Hashanah* 2:9]. "Come," said R. Jacob ben R. Chaninah to R. Judah [the Prince], "let us investigate the laws again and again that no rust may gather upon them" [Sifre to Deut. 32:1 (*Piska* 306); "laws" here translates *halakhot*].

§88. Deep ethical wisdom lies in the Rabbinical view, that though man's moral character, based on freedom of action, eventually appears only in his will and acts, his moral nature is revealed, however, before the exercise of choice and volition, in the knowledge and acknowledgment of the good before and external to the will. Volition, then, forms only a second distinct step in moral activity [see Deut. Rab. 4:3].[30] This thought finds early and striking expression in the Biblical words, which teach that man need not exert himself to obtain knowledge of the law (from heaven or from beyond the sea), for it is to be found very nigh to him, in his mouth and in his heart [Deut. 30:11–14]. In Kantian language, the moral law is autonomous, not heteronomous.[31]

§89. In Judaism, then, and more particularly in the Rabbinic cycle of ideas, every moral injunction is looked upon as being at the same time a religious requirement. Man's destiny is sought in his relation to God, its goal being likeness to God and the means of reaching it being obedience and willing devotion to him, the prototype and fountainhead of all morality. Yet the intimate connection with religion does not annul the independence of the ethical idea. The reference to God is made, not to justify, but to urge the claims of the moral.

The Rabbinic thought is expressed with astonishing clearness in the saying: "All commands left to the human heart"—that is, to ethical research and conviction—"are accompanied in the Scriptures by the words, 'Thou shalt fear God'" [b. *Bava Mezia* 58b with reference to Lev. 25:17].

BENNO JACOB (1862–1945)

Benno Jacob (b. 1862, Frankenstein [Ząbkowice Śląskie]; d. 1945, London) was a German rabbi and arguably the first Jewish Bible scholar fully committed to the critical method. He attended the University of Breslau and then the Jewish Theological Seminary, where he became a student of Heinrich Graetz (see chapter 2), who taught history and biblical exegesis. Shortly after the 1890 publication of his dissertation on the book of Esther, Jacob became rabbi in Göttingen, where he served until 1906, when he became rabbi of the much larger community in Dortmund. After his retirement in 1931 he lived in Hamburg, and he emigrated to London in 1939.

A member of numerous Jewish associations, Jacob actively campaigned against antisemitism, writing hundreds of articles and letters throughout his life, and giving lectures across Germany. (As a student, he even founded a Jewish dueling fraternity, so that Jews could be represented in that most distinctly German university tradition.) Additionally, throughout his life he focused on biblical research, with a strictly philological approach, showing in his commentaries and essays the way letters, words, and grammatical forms revealed new meanings in the text. While he denied the Mosaic authorship of the Torah, he likewise rejected the Documentary Hypothesis (the theory that the Pentateuch is an editorial composite of multiple, distinct narrative traditions), on the grounds that its foremost proponents most often employed it antisemitically—as a way of dismissing Jewish contributions to anything but the final redaction of the biblical text.

The present text was written in 1902, in the aftermath of the controversial "Babel und Bibel" (Babel and Bible) lecture that the German Assyriologist Friedrich Delitzsch (1850–1922) had delivered to a lay audience in the presence of the German emperor, and which was published soon thereafter.[32] Delitzsch's contention that significant passages from the book of Genesis, especially the Creation and the Flood stories, borrowed from ancient Babylonian tales sparked a heated debate among both Jewish and non-Jewish scholars (the so-called Babel-Bible Controversy). In this essay, published in the weekly *Allgemeine Zeitung des Judenthums* (General newspaper for Judaism) the same year as the controversy, Jacob employed Delitzsch's lecture to emphasize his own opposition to the traditional belief in the divinity of the unchanged biblical letter, and in consequence, to the very possibility of a Jewish Orthodoxy in the first place. Jacob was firm in his conviction that Jewish belief cannot be harmed, but only strengthened, by the results of truly scientific research. Both Judaism and science are like-minded, he wrote, "because all honest research is a search for truth and leads to God."

Judaism and the Results of Assyriology (1902)

Translated by Noa Sophie Kohler

The Bible is the word of God and God cannot err. Jesus refers to the Torah as a work by Moses; therefore the five books are written by Moses, regardless of whatever Bible criticism has to say about it, for Jesus could not be wrong. Is this also the Jewish point of view?

It must be admitted that there was and is a Jewish Orthodoxy that is no less crass and strict. The Talmud teaches: "These people have no share in the World-to-Come: The one who says there is no resurrection of the dead according to the Torah, the one who denies the divine origin of the Torah, and whoever says of *a single verse* that God did not speak it, but Moses on his own initiative, and likewise whoever disputes the divinity of any traditional interpretation" [based on m. *Sanhedrin* 10:1, discussed in b. *Sanhedrin* 90a, which has only the first two criteria]. This sentence is a dogma of official Judaism, and its greatest dogmatist, Moses Maimonides, even declares as a heretic one who denies just *one word* in the Torah, although he himself has denied the *literalism* of a large part of the Torah.[33] It is therefore indisputable that every Israelite who denies the divinity and authority of even the slightest utterance of the written or oral teachings—let alone the writing of the whole Pentateuch by Moses, who wrote it down literally according to God's dictate—is a *heretic* according to the Talmud and the rabbis, and has no part in the afterlife, but is forever damned.

It is necessary to present the dogmas of Orthodoxy once in full clarity, to contrast them with mitigating but misleading reinterpretations. How many who call themselves "Orthodox" can guess the monstrosities they thus commit themselves to?

But no one shall tremble because of those threats! Whomever has to call himself a heretic according to the above rulings can take solace from the fact that God authorized neither the Talmud nor Maimonides to distribute the ranks in heaven and hell, and that nothing is more certain than this: that God loves those who sincerely seek the truth, and perhaps it is precisely the sincere doubters who are most likely to have a share in the World-to-Come, and find there the clarity they long for.

Every teaching Judaism produced has to prove its justification before the highest authority, the Bible. Whatever contradicts the spirit of Holy Scripture is un-Jewish, that is, unbiblical, or un-Israelite, even if it is confirmed by the highest authorities. According to *the spirit of the Bible*, however, a Jewish Orthodoxy in the sense of a "right faith" is as absurd as a wooden iron. Judaism, in its innermost essence, which is determined by the Bible, is not a right faith, but a right *conduct*. Judaism as a religion is morality based on God. This is what the prophets, Israel's most authoritative teachers, tirelessly preach. But the concept of Orthodoxy, especially in scientific, literary, historical, or archaeological questions, is completely foreign to the Bible. Biblical antiquity is so unconcerned with the historicity of Genesis or the authorship of Moses that the prophets, for example, hardly mention the names of the patriarchs and of Moses, let alone zealously insist on the literalism of the reports about them. One should try to put the above-mentioned sentences from the Talmud and Maimonides into the mouth of any of the prophets to immediately see their impossibility and realize the vast difference. We often find explained in the Bible how to be a pious person, and who is pleasing to God, but never the demand for dogmatic convictions.

Indeed, even the belief in God is demanded not as a dogmatic but as a moral conviction. The biblical rejection of atheism does not accuse it of inadequate or misguided thought and therefore does not seek to refute it with rationales. It sees atheism as a perverse moral condition that arose out of evil inclination and selfishness. Atheism is *nevela,* which is *frivolity,* a corrupt conception and treatment of moral obligations, and thus the inability to judge correctly in moral matters.[34] *Nevela* is moral ignorance, [because] judgment is rooted in the will.[35] Although if philosophical atheism had no consequences for practical morality, it would deprive [such morality] of its foundation, the Bible would not find it outrageous. Such philosophical atheism would soon turn out to be just a dispute over words if the term "God"—whose existence is absurd to deny—was correctly understood.

Passages like the one from the Talmud stem from a completely different world of ideas. They are pagan and Christian. It is a not sufficiently recognized fact that the Talmud is permeated by Greco-Roman, Christian, and other views, and that there is not a single area in which the Talmud represents an unadulterated tradition of ancient biblical times. Instead, the Talmud is oftentimes almost foreign to the spirit of the Bible, and the so-called tradition according to its *Orthodox* definition is nothing but a dogmatic construct. Essentially, the Talmud reflects the confrontation and amalgamation of post-exilic Judaism—which itself is no longer pure—with the religion, philosophy, science, law, and conventions of the declining Greco-Roman antiquity. But Judaism was already influenced to a great extent also by Christianity and even more by its sects. I claim that one cannot understand a single page of Talmud and Midrash without being constantly oriented towards contemporary education and culture, and that scholarship will show that precisely what is considered to be "specifically Jewish," e.g., the law as an ordering principle of life, the legalism as a moral principle, the Midrash, the dialectical spirit, etc., is of foreign and almost always of *Greek* origin. Likewise, all dogmatism is of foreign, of *Christian* origin. In order to recognize this, however, Jewish research must first turn with a completely different intensity to the study of the era in which that process took place. [. . .]

Christianity was founded on *faith* from the start: on the conviction that Jesus was the son and messenger of God, and on the fact that he rose from the dead. But as soon as Christianity came into being it split into a multitude of sects which interpreted its original doctrines in various ways and seriously endangered its existence. Against this backdrop, official Christianity felt compelled to formulate a dogma and to determine what one had to believe in to be a true Christian, and to brand heresy as damnable. Hence, the history of Christianity is a history of ever new formulations of the right *faith* against ever newly emerging heresies; in other words, it is the history of dogmas. Lists of heretics, produced as early as the second century, show the systematization of the condemnation judgments that were already common in the New Testament [e.g., 2 Peter 2:1].[36]

It was a time of unchecked turmoil, of an unheard-of religious confusion and unrestrained religious subjectivism, against which a positive creed had to be narrowly defined. Judaism did not escape this effort or necessity, and the first Mishnah of the [tenth] chapter of the tractate of Sanhedrin—from which the above sentence is taken—is nothing more than *a list of heresies in imitation of Christianity*, aimed in particular against the philosophy of the day, which was the common enemy of Judaism and Christianity.

A teaching that was particularly alien and offensive to the Greeks, i.e., to the educated people of the time, was the physical resurrection of the dead, which probably came from the Persian religion [Zoroastrianism] into Judaism and from there into Christianity.[37] This doctrine found its way into Judaism very early on and when, following the Greek example, the new knowledge, laws, institutions, and conventions that gradually emerged independently of the Bible were legitimized by corroborating them with hints from the Torah—through all sorts of interpretive arts—it was also not difficult to find scriptural evidence for the resurrection of the dead. This evidence was so important that anyone who denied it was declared a *heretic*. It must have been disputed, and with very good reasons, because otherwise there would have been no need to *command* belief in it.

Christianity, of course, had to attach even greater importance to this doctrine, and went to great lengths to make it acceptable to the gentiles. The claim about the *inspiration* of the Bible, and of the divine origin of its letters, already has significant points of reference in the Bible itself, but now it is used in the sense that even the telling of the biblical story is literally a divine revelation.[38] This is related to another idea, that God's Torah was completely ready from the beginning of creation, and after a certain time it was given to Moses. Through the mediation of Jewish-Alexandrian philosophy, such statements most likely go back to Greek thought, especially to Plato's doctrine of ideas, according to which there is a pre-worldly archetype of the world. Also, Egyptian theologoumena are involved here, influenced by Stoic philosophy.[39] Christianity made the same statement, only replacing Torah with Logos and Christ.

The *punishment* of the heretics is also unbiblical, as are the ideas of heaven and hell in general. As is well known, deliberately the Bible never speaks of an afterlife, not to deny it—because belief in it is a consequence of true religion that can hardly be denied—but rather to protest against the wild conjectures of paganism. However, in the century of Jesus, which no longer had the strength of biblical protest, this delusion powerfully befell the scared humanity. Descriptions of heaven and hell, taken from Egyptian and Greek imaginations, are the favorite subjects of the religious writers, who want to comfort the pious sufferers and terrify the villain.

This little [elucidation] may suffice to explain the origin of the Talmudic phrase and point out the source of the view according to which doubt about the letter of Scripture is heresy and sin, punished by condemnation.

Making such a claim was perhaps a historical necessity, and at certain times it may have had a certain disciplinary justification, but if one tries to make it absolutely binding, it is necessary to strongly emphasize that Judaism in its innermost essence knows neither Orthodoxy nor heresy. According to Judaism's pristine teaching, God judges humans not according to their faith but according to their deeds. A person is blessed or cursed not by virtue of his belief or unbelief, but by the life he leads. Jewish Orthodoxy is nothing else than the Christianization of Judaism, and particularly the Orthodox belief that the copyists of the Bible were also [divinely] inspired and faithfully passed it on to us, down to the very letter, is old Protestant Orthodoxy.

Those who are aware of this historical context shall not believe that thereby they have already gained the right to call themselves "liberal." They know what is Jewish and what is not, but liberalism is not knowledge; it is an ethos.[40] Otherwise, one would necessarily have to be learned in order to be liberal, and no scholar would be illiberal. Anyone who claims the opposite of the Talmud and, for example, elevates the currently prevailing view of the Pentateuch to the rank of a dogma and declares those who think differently to be heretics, is likewise Orthodox, propagating the "right faith." *Every* Orthodoxy is un-Jewish. Equally impossible is an Orthodox *Wissenschaft des Judentums*, which has recently been established.[41] There may well be an Orthodox *learnedness*—but independent research, for which the result is already determined from the outset, is an inherent contradiction. If Judaism is morality based on God, then the Bible is the textbook of this morality. The Bible's intention from beginning to end is to teach us the true God and His will, knowledge of God and fear of God. But because the scientific approach to God and the knowledge of that which is right and good is the highest truth, and the fear of God is the noblest flower and fruit of all wisdom, and because it is nowhere taught so purely and clearly as in the history and the holy writings of the Israelites, *the Bible is the most scientific book there is.*[42] It is a testimony to the wisdom of the Bible that it communicates its teaching, that is, its religious truths and demands, mostly not in doctrines but in narrations, and illustrates and inculcates them through symbolic acts and demands. The truly scientific way to research the Bible, namely in accordance with its intentions and essence, is therefore to determine its religious content. We should consider the mode of representation, concerning either natural science or historical narratives, just as unessential as the Bible itself does. The truth—that God has set up the order of the world in a perfect manner; that every being is special, has dignity and purpose; that all humans share the same origin; that humans are a combination of the worldly and the heavenly; that men and women are beings of the same kind and are intended to complement each other—is presented in narrative form, and to consider the narration itself to be essential means to value the frame more highly than the picture.

Nevertheless, the fact remains that there cannot be a more appropriate framework, and that no human has yet been able to devise a more perfect way of presenting those teachings. Nor does it affect the essence of our religion whether the Pentateuch was written down by Moses or not, although Moses' authorship has not yet been refuted for truly compelling reasons. The book that contains teachings like the ten commandments or the dictum "You shall love your neighbor as yourself" [Lev. 19:18] will remain the foundational book of humanity for all times, whatever title is written on its cover. The Bible is a holy book because of its content, and it carries its authentication within itself.[43] Our religion would have only one thing to fear: the denial of God and of the moral law. But we can rest assured about that: no science will prove away these foundations of Judaism.

What we have talked about here is the eternal and unchangeable fundamental content of Judaism. Empirical or *historical* Judaism—that is, the particular expression of the basic truths in different times—is not a constant at all but must necessarily change in its forms and formulas depending on the respective non-Jewish factors it is confronted with.

It is just as wrong to attribute different values to its various historical formations as it is a sheer impossibility to oppose constant change.

It is an illusion of Jewish Orthodoxy to believe that it represents the real and authentic, unadulterated, and immutable Judaism. As already indicated above, one can prove that Orthodoxy is Greek and Christian through and through. However, the modern form of Judaism, the way it developed especially under the influence of German rationalism, is also not a *higher* form than the Talmudic one, but just *different* and, according to its followers, more appropriate for their own reasoning. In all those transformations, we are only obliged to insist with steadfastness and prudence on the independence and the continued validity of the unchangeable and foundational Israelite ideas. Moreover, Judaism, according to its original structure, expresses its content not in articles of faith like Christianity, but in expositions of morality, in symbols and acts that represent or promote morality. Since Judaism rests on the basis of irrefutable truths and is essentially free to adopt any truth, it does not have to fear the freest research, but can welcome it as an ally. Both are like-minded because all honest research is a search for truth and leads to God. Every scientific truth, when thought through to the end, becomes an ethical truth and moral demand. All science works for Judaism and for the victory of ideas of the Old Testament, which will one day conquer the whole world as surely as they [such ideas] have already conquered part of it. Judaism is not *a* religion—its basic truths are *the* religion.

7

What Is Distinctive about Jewish Theology?

In the first prewar decades of the twentieth century, after nearly a hundred years of recognizably modern Jewish theology, a handful of thinkers began grappling with a new sort of question: What makes Jewish theology distinct from other forms of religious philosophy? This question arose organically, as part of the same set of circumstances that were transforming much of the Jewish community itself. By the twentieth century, a second generation of Jews were being raised in a social and cultural world far removed from that of their grandparents, and were enjoying increasing acceptance from their Christian neighbors. And more than a million Jews had already immigrated to America, a country where they could experiment with Jewish practice in ways that differed (often quite radically) from what was possible in Europe.

In this context, the theologians represented in the following pages sought to accomplish two fundamental tasks. First, like all the thinkers excerpted in the previous six chapters, they attempted to further strengthen the tradition (established by such medieval philosophers as Bahya ibn Paquda and Moses Maimonides) of theological rationalism — that is, the fundamental belief that Judaism is premised on rational principles and, as such, that its core beliefs and obligations can be explained without recourse to unverifiable acts of faith.

Second, as Jews and Judaism gained increasing acceptance within Christian circles, the theologians now concentrated on differentiating Judaism and Jewish theology from Christianity and Christian theology. Previously, when Jewish ethics was all but indistinguishable from Christian or liberal ones, it had been important to justify Judaism's continued *existence*, but in the new environments of modern Europe and America (and eventually the State of Israel), the persistence of Judaism was no longer the paramount issue. Rather, a new pressing need arose: to identify and explain the fundamentals of Judaism's *distinctiveness* from other religions, specifically Christianity (and to a lesser extent, Islam). One of the centerpieces of this theological analysis became (with perhaps just a touch of historical irony, considering the backdrop of immense communal fragmentation) a focus on the essential meaning and character of Jewish peoplehood itself—a marked turn from the intellectual to the corporeal realm.

For Alexander Altmann, Kaufmann Kohler, and Julius Guttmann, the question could not have been clearer: What was it about the Jews' unique role in the world, in being a nation both particular and universal (among the gentiles but not of them), that made Jewish theology fundamentally unique? Christianity, all three asserted, elides the question of peoplehood altogether, focusing instead on redeeming every particular individual and on expounding doctrines of universal salvation. Peoplehood, in contrast, represents a unification but also a challenging of the individual and the universal, partaking in both but not quite of either. In Christianity, there is but one universal humanity under Christ, just as there is only the one individual road to salvation. Christianity has no place in its theological vision for groups, kinships, families, neighborhoods, villages, languages, cultures, geographies—for any of these other aspects of the human experience. Christianity is but a doctrinal overlay, a coat that fits many bodies but, in the end, expresses no particular sartorial style.

Judaism, they argued, is different. Founded in a family, it grew into a people, then scattered across the lands to become a nation. But it always held fast to its original identity, forged at Sinai, of a single community with a shared divine covenant. As Altmann wrote, "In Judaism, the people stand in the place of the church. . . . In Judaism the people, and not the church, are the unmediated bearers of historical revelation." Such interplay between the universal and the particular becomes a quintessential set piece for this final incarnation of modern Jewish theology.

KAUFMANN KOHLER (1843–1926)

Kaufmann Kohler (b. 1843, Fürth; d. 1926, New York) was a Reform rabbi, biblical critic, and theologian. Born in Bavaria and raised in a strictly traditional household, Kohler studied for the rabbinate under (among others) the Orthodox intellectual Samson Raphael Hirsch (see chapter 2) in Frankfurt, but his interests quickly expanded to developments in the *Wissenschaft des Judentums*, and he spent the 1860s studying biblical criticism and Near Eastern language and history at universities throughout German lands, including Munich, Berlin, and Leipzig. His dissertation (submitted at the University of Erlangen), entitled, in translation, "Jacob's Blessing: With Special Consideration for the Old Version and the Midrash; Critically-Historically Examined and Explained," focusing on Genesis 49, was a major statement about the supremacy of biblical criticism and redaction history over and against received religious notions of the Torah's divine provenance. In 1869 he emigrated to the United States, taking a pulpit first in Detroit, then in 1871 in Chicago, and subsequently in 1879 in New York City (where he succeeded David Einhorn; see chapter 3), and finally in 1903 he became president of the Hebrew Union College in Cincinnati. Throughout these years, Kohler wrote dozens of books and articles on Jewish history and culture, ancient and modern.

This selection is taken from the first four chapters of his magisterial overview of Jewish theology,[1] published in German in 1910 and eight years later in a revised English edition.[2] At the outset Kohler attempts to set the parameters of Jewish theology, and to consider the myriad difficulties of writing a comprehensive Jewish theology, considering the religion's aversion to clear dogmatic statement and creeds: "Judaism has no such formula of confession which renders a Jew a Jew. No ecclesiastical authority ever dictated or regulated the belief of the Jew," he writes. Yet, he argues, there remains a need, especially in the modern era, to systematically outline the nature of Jewish theology, including both its development and its conclusions, however tentative these might be. To do this, the opening two chapters compare Judaism to Christianity and Islam, its two "daughter religions," which nonetheless represent very different models for theological development. The third chapter then addresses the unique insights of Jewish theology, its particular contributions to the religious understanding of God, and the peculiar interplay of parochialism and universalism at work in its historical development. Finally, the fourth chapter is a genealogy of attempts to define specific credal statements in Judaism.

Jewish Theology (1918)

CHAPTER 1. THE MEANING OF THEOLOGY

Theology and Philosophy of Religion differ widely in their character. Theology deals exclusively with a specific religion; in expounding one doctrinal system it starts from a positive belief in a divine revelation and in the continued working of the divine spirit, affecting also the interpretation and further development of the sacred books.[3] Philosophy of Religion, on the other hand, while dealing with the same subject matter as Theology, treats religion from a general point of view as a matter of experience, and, as every philosophy must, without any foregone conclusion. Consequently, it submits the beliefs and doctrines of religion in general to an impartial investigation, recognizing neither a divine revelation nor the superior claims of any one religion above any other, its main object being to ascertain how far the universal laws of human reason agree or disagree with the assertions of faith.

It is therefore incorrect to speak of a Jewish religious philosophy. This has no better right to exist than has Jewish metaphysics or Jewish mathematics. The Jewish thinkers of the Spanish-Arabic period [approximately 800–1400 CE] who endeavored to harmonize revelation and reason, utilizing the Neo-Platonic philosophy or the Aristotelian with a Neo-Platonic coloring, betray by their very conceptions of revelation and prophecy the influence of Mohammedan theology; this was really a graft of metaphysics on theology and called itself the "divine science," a term corresponding exactly with the Greek "theology." The so-called Jewish religious philosophers adopted both the methods and terminology of the Mohammedan theologians, attempting to present the doctrines of the Jewish faith in the light of philosophy, as truth based on reason. Thus, they claimed to construct a Jewish theology upon the foundation of a philosophy of religion.

But neither they nor their Mohammedan predecessors succeeded in working out a complete system of theology. They left untouched essential elements of religion which do not come within the sphere of rational verities, and did not give proper appreciation to the rich treasures of faith deposited in the Biblical and Rabbinical literature. Nor does the comprehensive theological system of Maimonides, which for centuries largely shaped the intellectual life of the Jew, form an exception. Only the mystics, [with rabbi, judge, and philosopher] Bahya [Ibn Paquda, ca. 1050–1120] at their head, paid attention to the spiritual side of Judaism, dwelling at length on such themes as prayer and repentance, divine forgiveness, and holiness.

Closer acquaintance with the religious and philosophical systems of modern times has created a new demand for a Jewish theology by which the Jew can comprehend his own religious truths in the light of modern thought, and at the same time defend them against the aggressive attitude of the ruling religious sects. Thus far, however, the attempts made in this direction are but feeble and sporadic; if the structure is not to stand altogether in the air, the necessary material must be brought together from its many sources with painstaking labor. The special difficulty in the task lies in the radical difference which exists between our view of the past and that of the Biblical and medieval writers. All those things which have heretofore been taken as facts because related in the sacred books or other traditional sources, are viewed today with critical eyes, and are now regarded as more or less colored by human impression or conditioned by human judgment. In other words, we have learned to distinguish between *subjective* and *objective* truths, whereas theology by its very nature deals with truth as absolute. This makes it imperative for us to investigate historically the leading idea or fundamental principle underlying a doctrine, to note the different conceptions formed at various stages, and trace its process of growth. At times, indeed, we may find that the views of one age have rather taken a backward step and fallen below the original standard. The progress need not be uniform, but we must still trace its course.

We must recognize at the outset that Jewish theology cannot assume the character of *apologetics* if it is to accomplish its great task of formulating religious truth as it exists in our consciousness today. It can no more afford to ignore the established results of modern linguistic, ethnological, and historical research, of Biblical criticism and comparative religion, than it can the undisputed facts of natural science, however much any of these may conflict with the Biblical view of the cosmos. Apologetics has its legitimate place to prove and defend the truths of Jewish theology against other systems of belief and thought, but cannot properly defend either Biblical or Talmudic statements by methods incompatible with scientific investigation. Judaism is a religion of *historical* growth, which, far from claiming to be the final truth, is ever regenerated anew at each turning point of history. The fall of the leaves at autumn requires no apology, for each successive spring testifies anew to nature's power of resurrection.

The object of a systematic theology of Judaism, accordingly, is to single out the essential forces of the faith. It then will become evident how these fundamental doctrines possess a vitality, a strength of conviction, as well as an adaptability to varying conditions, which make them potent factors amidst all changes of time and circumstance. According to Rabbinical tradition, the broken tablets of the covenant were deposited in the ark beside the new [see b. *Berakhot* 8b, *Bava Batra* 14a–b]. In like manner the truths held sacred by the past, but found inadequate in their expression for a new generation, must be placed side by side with the deeper and more clarified truths of an advanced age, that they may appear together as the *one* divine truth reflected in different rays of light.

Jewish theology differs radically from Christian theology in the following three points:

A. The theology of Christianity deals with articles of faith formulated by the founders and heads of the Church as conditions of *salvation*, so that any alteration in favor of free thought threatens to undermine the very plan of salvation upon which the Church was founded. Judaism recognizes only such articles of faith as were adopted by the people voluntarily as expressions of their religious consciousness, both without external compulsion and without doing violence to the dictates of reason. Judaism does not know salvation by faith in the sense of Paul, the real founder of the Church, who declared the blind acceptance of belief to be in itself meritorious. It denies the existence of any irreconcilable opposition between faith and reason.

B. Christian theology rests upon a *formula of confession*, the so-called Symbolum of the Apostolic Church, which alone makes one a Christian.[4] Judaism has no such formula of confession which renders a Jew a Jew. No ecclesiastical authority ever dictated or regulated the belief of the Jew; his faith has been voiced in the solemn liturgical form of prayer, and has ever retained its freshness and vigor of thought in the consciousness of the people. This partly accounts for the antipathy toward any kind of dogma or creed among Jews.

C. The creed is a *conditio sine qua non* of the Christian Church. To disbelieve its dogmas is to cut oneself loose from membership. Judaism is quite different. The Jew is *born* into it and cannot extricate himself from it even by the renunciation of his faith, which would but render him an apostate Jew. This condition exists, because the racial community formed, and still forms, the basis of the religious community. It is birth, not confession, that imposes on the Jew the obligation to work and strive for the eternal verities of Israel, for the preservation and propagation of which he has been chosen by the God of history.

The truth of the matter is that the aim and end of Judaism is not so much the salvation of the soul in the hereafter as the salvation of humanity in history. Its theology, therefore, must recognize the history of human progress, with which it is so closely interwoven. It does not, therefore, claim to offer the final or absolute truth, as does Christian theology, whether orthodox or liberal. It simply points out the way leading to the highest obtainable truth. Final and perfect truth is held forth as the ideal of all human searching and striving, together with perfect justice, righteousness, and peace, to be attained as the very end of history.

A systematic theology of Judaism must, accordingly, content itself with presenting Jewish doctrine and belief in relation to the most advanced scientific and philosophical ideas of the age, so as to offer a comprehensive view of life and the world (*Lebens-und Weltanschauung*); but it by no means claims for them the character of finality. The unfolding of Judaism's truths will be completed only when all mankind has attained the heights of Zion's mount of vision, as beheld by the prophets of Israel. . . .

CHAPTER 2. WHAT IS JUDAISM?

Religion and race form an inseparable whole in Judaism. The Jewish people stand in the same relation to Judaism as the *body* to the *soul*. The national or racial body of Judaism consists of the remnant of the tribe of Judah which succeeded in establishing a new commonwealth in Judaea in place of the ancient Israelitish kingdom, and which survived the downfall of state and temple to continue its existence as a separate people during a dispersion over the globe for thousands of years, forming ever a cosmopolitan element among all the nations in whose lands it dwelt. Judaism, on the other hand, is the religious system itself, the vital element which united the Jewish people, preserving it and regenerating it ever anew. It is the spirit which endowed the handful of Jews with a power of resistance and a fervor of faith unparalleled in history, enabling them to persevere in the mighty contest with heathenism and Christianity. It made of them a nation of martyrs and thinkers, suffering and struggling for the cause of truth and justice, yet forming, consciously or unconsciously, a potent factor in all the great intellectual movements which are ultimately to win the entire gentile world for the purest and loftiest truths concerning God and man.

Judaism, accordingly, does not denote the Jewish nationality, with its political and cultural achievements and aspirations, as those who have lost faith in the religious mission of Israel would have it. On the other hand, it is not a nomistic or legalistic religion confined to the Jewish people, as is maintained by Christian writers, who, lacking a full appreciation of its lofty world-wide purpose and its cosmopolitan and humanitarian character, claim that it has surrendered its universal prophetic truths to Christianity. Nor should it be presented as a religion of pure *Theism*, aiming to unite all believers in one God into a Church Universal, of which certain visionaries dream. Judaism is nothing less than a message concerning the *One and holy God* and *one, undivided humanity* with a world-uniting *Messianic goal*, a message entrusted by divine revelation to the Jewish people. Thus, Israel is its prophetic harbinger and priestly guardian, its witness and defender throughout the ages, who is never to falter in the task of upholding and unfolding its truths until they have become the possession of the whole human race.

Owing to this twofold nature of a universal religious truth and at the same time a mission entrusted to a specially selected nation or race, Judaism offers in a sense the sharpest contrasts imaginable, which render it an enigma to the student of religion and history, and make him often incapable of impartial judgment. On the one hand, it shows the most tenacious adherence to forms originally intended to preserve the Jewish people in its priestly sanctity and separateness, and thereby also to keep its religious truths pure and free from encroachments. On the other hand, it manifests a mighty impulse to come into close touch with the various civilized nations, partly in order to disseminate among them its sublime truths, appealing alike to mind and heart, partly to clarify and deepen those truths by assimilating the wisdom and culture of these very nations. Thus, the spirit of separatism and of universalism work in opposite directions. Still, however hostile the two elements may appear, they emanate from the same source. For the Jewish people, unlike any other civilization of antiquity, entered history with the proud claim that it possessed a truth destined to become someday the property of mankind, and its three thousand years of history have verified this claim.

Israel's relation to the world thus became a double one. Its priestly world-mission gave rise to all those laws and customs which were to separate it from its idolatrous surroundings, and this occasioned the charge of hostility to the nations. The accusation of Jewish misanthropy occurred as early as the Balaam [see Num. 22] and Haman stories. As the separation continued through the centuries, a deep-seated Jew-hatred sprang up, first in Alexandria and Rome, then becoming a consuming fire throughout Christendom, unquenched through the ages and bursting forth anew, even from the midst of would-be liberals. In contrast to this, Israel's prophetic ideal of a humanity united in justice and peace gave to history a new meaning and a larger outlook, kindling in the souls of all truly great leaders and teachers, seers and sages of mankind, a love and longing for the broadening of humanity which opened new avenues of progress and liberty. Moreover, by its conception of man as the image of God and its teaching of righteousness as the true path of life, Israel's Law established a new standard of human worth and put the imprint of Jewish idealism upon the entire Aryan civilization.

Owing to these two opposing forces, the one centripetal, the other centrifugal, Judaism tended now inward, away from world-culture, now outward toward the learning and the thought of all nations; and this makes it doubly difficult to obtain a true estimate of its character. But, after all, these very currents and countercurrents at the different eras of history kept Judaism in continuous tension and fluctuation, preventing its stagnation by dogmatic formulas and its division by ecclesiastical dissensions. "Both words are the words of the living God" became the maxim of the contending schools [b. *Eruvin* 13b].

The powerful and unique institutions of the Synagogue, intended for common instruction and devotion, are altogether creations of the Exile, and replaced the former *priestly* Torah by the Torah *for the people*. More wonderful still, the priestly lore of ancient Babylon was transformed by sublime monotheistic truths and utilized in the formation of a sacred literature; it was placed before the history of the Hebrew patriarchs, to form, as it were, an introduction to the Bible of humanity.[5]

Judaism, then, far from being the late product of the Torah and tradition, as it is often considered, was actually the creator of the Law. Transformed and unfolded in Babylonia, it created its own sacred literature and shaped it ever anew, filling it always with its own spirit and with new thoughts. It is by no means the petrifaction of the Mosaic law and the prophetic teachings, as we are so often told, but a continuous process of unfolding and regeneration of its great religious truth. [. . .]

Modern critical and historical research has taught us to distinguish the products of different periods and stages of development in both the Biblical and Rabbinical sources, and therefore compels us to reject the idea of a uniform origin of the Law, and also of an uninterrupted chain of tradition reaching back to Moses on Sinai. Therefore, we must attach still more importance to the process of transformation which Judaism had to undergo through the centuries.

Judaism manifested its wondrous power of *assimilation* by renewing itself to meet the demands of the time, first under the influence of the ancient civilizations, Babylonia and Persia, then of Greece and Rome, finally of the Occidental powers, molding its religious truths and customs in ever new forms, but all in consonance with its own genius. [. . .]

Instead of representing Judaism—as the Christian theologians do under the guise of scientific methods—as a nomistic religion, caring only for the external observance of the Law, it is necessary to distinguish two opposite fundamental tendencies; the one expressing the spirit of legalistic nationalism, the other that of ethical or prophetic universalism. These two work by turn, directing the general trend in the one or the other direction according to circumstances. At one time the center and focus of Israel's religion is the Mosaic Law, with its sacrificial cult in charge of the priesthood of Jerusalem's Temple; at another time it is the Synagogue, with its congregational devotion and public instruction, its inspiring song of the Psalmist and its prophetic consolation and hope confined to no narrow territory, but opened wide for a listening world. Here it is the reign of the *Halakah* holding fast to the form of tradition, and there the free and fanciful *Haggadah* [aggadah], with its appeal to the sentiments and views of the people. Here it is the spirit of *ritualism*, bent on separating the Jews from the influence of foreign elements, and there again the spirit of *rationalism*, eager to take part in general culture and in the progress of the outside world.

The liberal views of Maimonides and [Jewish philosopher, mathematician, astronomer, biblical exegete, and halakhik authority] Gersonides [Levi ben Gerson, 1288–1355, called Ralbag] concerning miracle and revelation, God and immortality, were scarcely shared by the majority of Jews, who, no doubt, sided rather with the mystics, and found their mouthpiece in [rabbi, biblical exegete, and talmudic commentator] Abraham ben David of Posquières [ca. 1125–98, called Rabad], the fierce opponent of Maimonides. An impartial Jewish theology must therefore take cognizance of both sides; it must include the mysticism of Isaac Luria [1534–72, called HaAri or Arizal] and Sabbathai Horwitz[6] as well as the rationalism of [rabbi and philosopher Joseph] Albo [ca. 1380–1444] and [historian, exegete, and philosopher] Leo da Modena [1571–1648]. Wherever is voiced a new doctrine or a new view of life and life's duty, which yet bears the imprint of the Jewish consciousness, there the wellspring of divine inspiration is seen pouring forth its living waters.

Even the latest interpretation of the Law, offered by a disciple who is recognized for true conscientiousness in religion, was revealed to Moses on Sinai, according to a Rabbinical dictum. Thus is exquisitely expressed the idea of a continuous development of Israel's religious truth. As a safeguard against arbitrary individualism, there was the principle of loyalty and proper regard for tradition, which is aptly termed by Professor Lazarus a "historical continuity." The Midrashic statement is quite significant that other creeds founded on our Bible can only adhere to the letter, but the Jewish religion possesses the key to the deeper meaning hidden and presented in the *traditional* interpretation of the Scriptures [see *Pesikta Rabbati* 5; Mid. Tan. (B.), *Vayera* 6 and *Ki Tissa* 17; cf. b. *Menachot* 29b]. That is, for Judaism Holy Scripture in its literal sense is not the final word of God; the Bible is rather a living spring of divine revelation, to be kept ever fresh and flowing by the active force of the spirit. To sum up: Judaism, far from offering a system of beliefs and ceremonies fixed for all time, is as multifarious and manifold in its aspects as is life itself. It comprises all phases and characteristics of both a national and a world religion.

CHAPTER 3. THE ESSENCE OF THE RELIGION OF JUDAISM

There can be no disputing the fact that the central idea of Judaism and its life purpose is the doctrine of the One Only and Holy God, whose kingdom of truth, justice and peace is to be universally established at the end of time. This is the main teaching of Scripture and the hope voiced in the liturgy; while Israel's mission to defend, to unfold and to propagate this truth is a corollary of the doctrine itself and cannot be separated from it. Whether we regard it as Law or a system of doctrine, as religious truth or world-mission, this belief pledged the little tribe of Judah to a warfare of many thousands of years against the hordes of heathendom with all their idolatry and brutality, their deification of man and their degradation of deity to human rank. It betokened a battle for the pure idea of God and man, which is not to end until the principle of divine holiness has done away with every form of life that tends to degrade and to disunite mankind, and until Israel's Only One has become the unifying power and the highest ideal of all humanity. [. . .]

Judaism is in a true sense a religion of the people. It is free from all priestly tutelage and hierarchical interference. It has no ecclesiastical system of belief, guarded and supervised by men invested with superior powers. Its teachers and leaders have always been men from among the people, like the prophets of yore, with no sacerdotal privilege or title; in fact, in his own household each father is the God-appointed teacher of his children [Deut. 6:7; 11:19].

Neither is Judaism the creation of a single person, either prophet or a man with divine claims. It points back to the patriarchs as its first source of revelation. It speaks not of the God of Moses, of Amos and Isaiah, but of the God of Abraham, Isaac, and Jacob, thereby declaring the Jewish genius to be the creator of its own religious ideas. It is therefore incorrect to speak of a "Mosaic," "Hebrew," or "Israelitish," religion. The name *Judaism* alone expresses the preservation of the religious heritage of Israel by the tribe of Judah, with a loyalty which was first displayed by Judah himself in the patriarchal household, and which became its characteristic virtue in the history of the various tribes. [. . .]

As it was bound up with the life of the Jewish people, Judaism remained forever in close touch with the world. [. . .] It is a religion of *life*, which it wishes to sanctify by duty rather than by laying stress on the hereafter. It looks to the *deed* and the purity of the *motive*, not to the empty creed and the blind belief. Nor is it a religion of *redemption*, contemning this earthly life; for Judaism repudiates the assumption of a radical power of evil in man or in the world. Faith in the ultimate triumph of the good is essential to it. In fact, this perfect confidence in the final victory of truth and justice over all the powers of falsehood and wrong lent it both its wondrous intellectual force and its high idealism, and adorned its adherents with the martyr's crown of thorns, such as no other human brow has ever borne. [. . .]

Christianity and *Islam*, notwithstanding their alienation from Judaism and frequent hostility, are still daughter-religions. In so far as they have sown the seeds of Jewish truth over all the globe and have done their share in upbuilding the Kingdom of God on earth, they must be recognized as divinely appointed emissaries and agencies. Still Judaism sets forth its doctrine of God's unity and of life's holiness in a far superior form than does Christianity. It neither permits the deity to be degraded into the sphere of the sensual and human, nor does it base its morality upon a love bereft of the vital principle of justice. Against the rigid monotheism of Islam, which demands blind submission to the stern decrees of inexorable fate, Judaism on the other hand urges its belief in God's paternal love and mercy, which educates all the children of men, through trial and suffering, for their high destiny.

Judaism denies most emphatically the right of Christianity or any other religion to arrogate to itself the title of "the absolute religion" or to claim to be "the finest blossom and the ripest fruit of religious development." [. . .] The full unfolding of the religious and moral life of mankind is the work of countless generations yet to come, and many divine heralds of truth and righteousness have yet to contribute their share. In this work of untold ages, Judaism claims that it has achieved and is still achieving its full part as the prophetic world-religion. Its law of righteousness, which takes for its scope the whole of human life, in its political and social relations as well as its personal aspects, forms the foundation of its ethics for all time; while its hope for a future realization of the Kingdom of God has actually become the aim of human history. As a matter of fact, when the true object of religion is the hallowing of life rather than the salvation of the soul, there is little room left for sectarian exclusiveness, or for a heaven for believers and a hell for unbelievers. With this broad outlook upon life, Judaism lays claim, not to perfection, but to perfectibility; it has supreme capacity for growing toward the highest ideals of mankind, as beheld by the prophets in their Messianic visions.

CHAPTER 4. THE JEWISH ARTICLES OF FAITH

The thirteen articles of Maimonides, in setting forth a Jewish *Credo*, formed a vigorous opposition to the Christian and Mohammedan creeds; they therefore met almost universal acceptance among the Jewish people, and were given a place in the common prayerbook, in spite of their deficiencies, as shown by Crescas and his school. Nevertheless, we must admit that Crescas shows the deeper insight into the nature of religion when he observes that the main fallacy of the Maimonidean system lies in founding the Jewish faith on *speculative knowledge,* which is a matter of the intellect, rather than *love* which flows from the heart, and which alone leads to piety and goodness. True love, he says, requires the belief neither in retribution nor in immortality. Moreover, in striking contrast to the insistence of Maimonides or the immutability of the Mosaic Law, Crescas maintains the possibility of its continuous progress in accordance with the intellectual and spiritual needs of the time, or, what amounts to the same thing, the continuous perfectibility of the revealed Law itself. Thus the criticism of Crescas leads at once to a radically different theology than that of Maimonides, and one which appeals far more to our own religious thought. [. . .]

Another doctrine of Judaism, which was greatly underrated by medieval scholars, and which has been emphasized in modern times only in contrast to the Christian theory of original sin, is that man was created in the image of God. Judaism holds that the soul of man came forth pure from the hand of its Maker, endowed with freedom, unsullied by any inherent evil or inherited sin. Thus man is, through the exercise of his own free will, capable of attaining to an ever-higher degree his mental, moral, and spiritual powers in the course of history. This is the Biblical idea of God's spirit as immanent in man; all prophetic truth is based upon it; and though it was often obscured, this theory was voiced by many of the masters of Rabbinical lore, such as [Palestinian sage] R. Akiba [ca. 50–ca.132 CE] and others [see PA 3:1; Gen. Rab. 21:5].

Every attempt to formulate the doctrines or articles of faith of Judaism was made in order to guard the Jewish faith from the intrusion of foreign beliefs, never to impose disputed beliefs upon the Jewish community itself. Many, indeed, challenged the fundamental character of the thirteen articles of Maimonides. Albo reduced them to three, viz.: the belief in God, in revelation, and retribution; others, with more arbitrariness than judgement, singled out three, five, six, or even more as principal doctrines.

The present age of historical research imposes the same necessity of restatement or reformulation upon us. We must do as Maimonides did—as Jews have always done—point out anew the really fundamental doctrines and discard those which have lost their hold upon the modern Jew, or which conflict directly with his religious consciousness. If Judaism is to retain its prominent position among the powers of thought, and to be clearly understood by the modern world, it must again reshape its religious truths in harmony with the dominant ideas of the age.

Many attempts of this character have been made by modern rabbis and teachers, most of them founded upon Albo's three articles. Those who penetrated somewhat more deeply into the essence of Judaism added a fourth article, the belief in Israel's priestly mission, and at the same time, instead of the belief in retribution, included the doctrine of man's kinship with God, or, if one may coin the word, his *God-childship*. Few, however, have succeeded in working out the entire content of the Jewish faith from a modern viewpoint, which must include historical, critical, and psychological research, as well as the study of comparative religion.

JULIUS GUTTMANN (1880–1950)

Julius Guttmann (b. 1880, Hildesheim; d. 1950, Jerusalem) is probably best known for his *Die Philosophie des Judentums* (The philosophy of Judaism, 1933), one of the most important works concerning the development of Jewish thought in the modern period, covering the history of Judaism from the Bible to the twentieth century. But Guttmann was also a religious philosopher in his own right. The son of Breslau's chief rabbi Jacob Guttmann (1845–1919), himself a historian of Jewish philosophy, Julius was trained at both the Jewish Theological Seminary and the University of Breslau. He remained in Breslau for some years, acting as Privatdozent (private lecturer) before accepting the chair of religious philosophy at the Berlin Hochschule für die Wissenschaft des Judentums, where he taught from 1919 until 1934. Rejecting several calls to work in the United States, he eventually emigrated to Jerusalem, where he headed the department for Jewish philosophy at Hebrew University until his death.

His major work, as well as the countless essays he authored, are all built on the premise that Judaism has a few original theological ideas (first and foremost monotheism) that can be found in biblical and Rabbinical literature and thus characterize Judaism as the "monotheistic religion of revelation." Religious philosophy, however, is not an original product of Judaism and could emerge only out of the absorption of external influences; indeed, all great Jewish philosophers labored within the framework of the great philosophical systems (from that of Aristotle down to Kant and Hegel). While Guttmann held (in the sense of German theologian Friedrich Schleiermacher [1768–1834]) that religion itself is not rational but largely a matter of individual feeling (*Gemüt*), the philosophical analysis of the root ideas of Jewish belief eventually led to a rational Jewish theology. The primordial spiritual heritage of Bible and Talmud, read through the universalistic philosophical method (of systematic, analytical thought) created distinctive Jewish dogma that still passed the test of reason. To this end, in a well-known debate with the German-American Jewish political philosopher Leo Strauss (1899–1973), Guttmann defended the possibility of a middle path between unreflective orthodoxy and atheism, based on the dual assumption that philosophizing is a religious obligation and also that philosophical thinking is an expression of religiosity. For Guttmann, in fact, this duality cleared the way for a meaningful Jewish theology. Strauss demurred, insistent that the tension between divine revelation and human rationality remained unresolvable.

The following selections are taken from one of the fundamental texts of Jewish theological modernity, giving an analysis of the basic structures and developments of Jewish belief: Guttmann's 1927 contribution to an extensive theological debate raging in the pages of the *Monatsschrift für die Geschichte und Wissenschaft des Judenthums* (Monthly journal for the science and history of Judaism), the flagship journal of the Wis-

senschaft movement.[7] Starting in 1924, several leading Jewish thinkers of the period, among them Leo Baeck (see chapter 5), answered, for the first time in a strictly academic framework, the centuries-old question: Does Judaism possess dogmas? Such a question and its affirmative answers are imperative, Guttmann insisted, because a meaningful discussion of Jewish theology itself becomes possible only if there are original, independent "norms of Jewish belief." To Guttmann, Judaism indeed has dogmas, but these are dynamic beliefs of the community, often expressed in liturgy, and not the product of formulation or fixation by a superior authority: "It is taken for granted that there is indeed a religious truth which is valid for all members of the Jewish community, but this truth is nowhere explicated systematically." As a result, "There is no firm line of demarcation between bindingly fixed and variable elements" of Jewish theology. That said, Guttmann drew a distinction between the premodern history of Judaism, for which he believed his analysis held true, and his own time. In the present era, Guttmann argues, "the affirmation of the Jewish character of the principles of belief becomes a matter of personal insight." In other words, Guttmann seems to suggest, in the postauthoritarian, modern age, Jewish belief has become individualized, with personal religious conviction taking the place of communal belief. While this concept perhaps solves the problem of dogma for Judaism, it brings religious Jewry very close to the similar concept of personal confession as it manifests in Christianity.

Establishing Norms for Jewish Belief (1927)

Translated by Gertrude Hirschler

I. In his argument against the existence of dogma in Judaism, [Reform rabbi and scholar Leo] Baeck [1873–1956, see chapter 5] cites the fact that the religious doctrines of Judaism were never authoritatively defined. This fact also plays a decisive role in our inquiry because it demonstrates that no attempt has ever been made by an authority in

Judaism to set down systematically the quintessence of those religious doctrines which are binding on every Jew. The best proof of this is the passage in Mishnah Sanhedrin—frequently cited in discussions of the question whether Judaism has dogmas—stating that anyone who does not believe in resurrection and the divine origin of the Torah will have no portion in the world to come [m. *Sanhedrin* 10:1]. The Mishnah thus seems to confer universally binding force on these two tenets. However, it is not the intention of the Mishnah to designate these two tenets as the only ones binding on all Jews; it merely singles them out from among a multitude of basically similar tenets in order to counter the influence of certain heretical views. Moreover, the Mishnah in no way intends to ascribe a primary position to these two principles. In the case of the belief in the divine origin of the Torah, such a position cannot possibly be intended even in the sense in which, say, the proclamation of a dogma by the Catholic church bestows official sanction upon a religious truth they had already been accepted as valid. The Mishnah presupposes the validity of these two principles and states merely that anyone who denies them thereby excludes himself from the community of Israel. This is even more true in the case of certain religious truths whose validity is demonstrated by the fact that they have been incorporated into communal prayer. Here too the intention is not to set down a religious truth as a dogma, but to give expression to certain religious convictions that are shared by the entire community. Thus [. . .] we have nowhere an act creating dogma. In making this statement, we are not simply emphasizing a scholarly nuance but are clarifying a fact of fundamental importance. In Jewish tradition there is no authoritative fixation or finalization of beliefs; tradition takes certain beliefs of the community for granted as something given and merely gives expression to them as the need arises.

Consequently—and this is an extremely important consequence—Judaism nowhere presents an exhaustive statement of beliefs held by the entire community. It is taken for granted that there is indeed a religious truth which is valid for all members of the Jewish community, but this truth is nowhere explicated systematically. The boundary line between the unchangeably permanent and the variable elements is nowhere clearly drawn. In fact, it is impossible to trace such a boundary line in accordance with the Talmudic tradition. This difficulty has arisen in connection with every attempt to set forth the substance of Jewish faith in dogmatic form. We first encounter it in the discussions of our medieval religious philosophers about the basic teachings of Judaism. Maimonides is criticized by later scholars for the fact that, in the compilation of his Thirteen Articles of Faith,[8] his selection of these specific doctrines from the totality of Jewish religious teachings had not been based on clearly discernible principles.[9] Yet when these thinkers themselves attempt to formulate the basic tenets of Judaism, they rely mainly on subjective criteria. They are unable to find any guidelines in Talmudic tradition. Even if we were to assume that they view the difference between the basic doctrines and the other religious truths of Judaism as having merely methodological (but not dogmatic) significance, they still would have to come to grips with the Talmudic statements about beliefs binding on all Jews—if they were able to find such statements. The same problem also confronts more recent attempts to determine the binding beliefs of Judaism based on Talmudic tradition. One may possibly contend that there is such a thing as "dogma" in Judaism, but one would be hard put to specify what the "dogmas" of Judaism are. [. . .]

This lability in the quantity of the religious truths generally accepted as binding on all Jews is associated with a similar, though lesser, lability in content. Even those doctrines which are regarded as binding are, for the most part, not defined in such unequivocal terms as to assure their uniform comprehension. In this respect, the absence of a fixed text is of the utmost significance. Inasmuch as the doctrines of Judaism have never been formulated authoritatively, Judaism has a potential for an infinitely greater freedom of interpretation and development in the content of its belief than has the Christian church. This can be readily documented from as early a source as the Talmudic Aggadah, but it is, above all, medieval religious philosophy which demonstrates that authoritatively accepted doctrines can be thoroughly recast under the influence of a completely different system of metaphysics. [. . .]

However, contrary to widely held opinion, the foregoing must not be interpreted to mean that Judaism offers complete freedom of belief. It is not correct to assume that the traditional conceptions of belief were deliberately formulated this way in order to permit relative freedom for the development of religious thought. Nor, indeed, does Judaism have freedom of belief in the basic accepted meaning of the term. In principle, traditional Judaism considers certain religious beliefs as authoritative. This applies, above all, to the belief in the divine origin of the Torah. The acceptance of this belief is demanded of every Jew; its denial is considered a heretical rejection of Judaism itself. Given this claim for the factualness of the divine revelation, it is no longer permissible to ask on what authority this belief is based; this "formal religious principle" is the very principle by which the concept of religious authority is constituted. Wherever there is such a thing as an authoritative religion, the principle of authority is of necessity primal and final. That the belief in the divine origin of the Torah and, in a wider sense, in the divine origin of the entire Scripture has this binding force in traditional Judaism can be seen without difficulty (if indeed proof is needed) from the fact that this belief is the basic assumption for the validity of the religious law, whose binding force rests solely upon its divine origin. Without this theoretical underpinning, the Halakha possesses no practical authority. Of course, it would seem that this principle is contradicted by the statement that universally binding norms exist only in the Halakha, while there is complete freedom in the Aggadah. However, this seeming contradiction shows merely that even this statement cannot be accepted without qualifications. The concept of Aggadah, which is defined in purely negative terms and embraces the entire nonlegal part of the Law, obviously includes elements of utterly different religious significance. If Aggadah is so defined as to subsume the ultimate religious truths, which alone validate the Halakha, it becomes clear that the principle of aggadic freedom cannot be applied to them. This doubtless is also the view held by tradition as a matter of course. It is, however, characteristic that the religious truths which are considered binding on all Jews are nowhere explicitly separated out as a sphere of their own. This fact alone is sufficient to show that any act to fix religious tenets is completely foreign to our tradition.

For our present purposes it is sufficient to point out that the belief in the divine origin of the oral tradition has the same claim to acceptance by Jews as has the written law. It is in this belief that the authority of all laws not contained in Scripture itself is grounded. The Talmud expresses this idea clearly when it characterizes as contemptuous of the word of God everyone who denies that any one of the generally accepted interpretations of the Law is of divine origin [see b. *Sanhedrin* 99a]. The Talmud's lack of concern for precise definitions of its dogmatic presuppositions is, of course, strikingly evident here. The Talmud is emphatic in its insistence on belief in the divine origin of the oral tradition, but it is difficult to derive from the Talmud a definitive understanding of the boundaries of this revealed oral tradition: what is of divine and what of human origin. The various statements in the Talmud on this subject are often mutually contradictory, and in some cases represent an indistinguishable blending of serious assertion and aggadic playfulness. It is, therefore, not surprising that the commentators of the Talmud represent diametrically opposed views on important questions, such as whether the halakhic precepts, derived from the Torah with the help of the traditional rules of interpretation, were divinely revealed or created by the sages, or whether they are to be taken literally or merely as an allusion.

At any rate, it can readily be seen that this conception of belief in revelation establishes the authoritative character of religious truth as such. Along with belief in the divine origin of the written and oral laws, every Jew is expected to affirm the truth of their contents. Revelation and tradition alike contain religious truth as a given fact, and every individual is bound to this given belief held by the entire community. The only purpose of a person's search and inquiry is to ascertain the true meaning of that religious truth. No matter how much latitude may thus be left for the development of individual religious thought, religious truth is consistently presented as a given fact. [. . .]

This conceptual deduction of universally binding beliefs from the principle of divine revelation reflects an interrelationship which also exists in historical reality. Historically seen, a number of religious beliefs were inextricably linked with the Jewish belief in divine revelation—beliefs which shared its authoritative character and, like it, did not need to be formulated explicitly in dogmatic terms in order to command adherence from the community. Thus the conviction that Judaism's religious truth is given in the Torah for all time does not dissolve itself into a mere postulate; rather it is fulfilled by a series of religious ideas which, by virtue of their linkage with the belief in revelation, themselves constitute a firm element of faith. Concepts such as divine providence, reward and punishment, and miracles, to name only a few, remained unassailably valid and had to remain so as long as the divine origin of the Torah was accepted as the basis of Jewish belief. Not even the freest philosophical reinterpretation of Judaism has ever negated these principles as such. It merely reinterpreted them, a procedure which was, of course, regarded by its opponents as incompatible with the concept of revelation.

Similar authority was, however, vested also in other beliefs which were not so intimately bound up with the principle of revelation. The beliefs in the Messiah, immortality, and resurrection have not only remained unchallenged but were considered unchallengeable. The messianic hope was so clearly expressed by the prophets that to doubt it was utterly unthinkable. The concept of resurrection was secured against any challenge by the Mishnah, which equated the rejection of this belief with the denial of the divine origin of the Torah. But it was primarily their expression in congregational prayer that turned these religious convictions into elements of a generally obligatory religious tradition. While their incorporation into the liturgy was not motivated by the intention to establish them as dogmas, the effect nonetheless was to confer upon them a dogma-like distinction. The same holds true for all the other cases we have cited. The authority of tradition is imparted to the beliefs which were clearly expressed in the authoritative traditional sources.

In recapitulation, we can say that the foundations for Jewish beliefs are not established through norms set by some official authority. At the same time, the authoritative character of revelation and tradition serves as the binding force of the community's religious beliefs. If we search Talmudic literature for statements explicitly granting dogmatic status to certain tenets, we find, at best, a haphazard conglomeration of data. The character of Jewish belief can be determined only on the basis of belief in revelation and of the ideas permeating Jewish worship. The notion that these fundamentals of Jewish belief should be singled out is alien to religious life itself, its truth is bound by tradition, without attempting to analyze the components of that truth. As a result, as we have already pointed out, there is no firm line of demarcation between bindingly fixed and variable elements. Even the content of the former is open to various interpretations. It is the elasticity of this bond [between religious life and tradition] that has permitted a relative latitude in the development of Jewish religious thought and has frequently created the impression that Judaism offers complete freedom of belief.

II. The facts outlined in the preceding section are highly informative about the religious character of Judaism. The norms for religious belief in Judaism are determined entirely by the concept of revelation. In this and all other respects, authority is based on the fact that Judaism is a scriptural religion and that "Scripture"—divine revelation promulgated for all time in the sacred book—rules as the supreme authority in every area of life. This, to begin with, establishes the historical character of the concept of revelation. Revelation in Judaism is a historical event which is the source of religious truth. All subsequent religious life conceives itself as being bound up with that origin and accepts the religious truth as a given fact. [...] Revelation, be it through prophet or priest, is considered to have ended. Thus, it becomes itself a part of history, and the definition of revelation as historical fact is, with full consistency, projected back into the interpretation of the past. The prophecy of Moses founding the

Jewish religion is sharply distinguished from the teachings of the later prophets; it is the norm binding upon prophets and priests and, indeed, upon every follower of Judaism in all fundamental religious questions. The revelation communicated to Moses established the validity of the religious norm as obligatory for all time.[10]

This historical view of revelation provides the basis for the formation of a much firmer, or at least more stable, authority than does the notion of an ongoing process of divine revelation. An even stronger impetus in this direction is given when revelation is set down in writing. Customs, usages, or the traditional ideas of a religious community that are fluctuating and changeable are firmed up once they are given a literary form. The scriptural religions, which view a sacred document as the norm for every aspect of religious life, constitute, indeed, a special category in the development of religious authority by making it possible to capture a religious idea firmly and to allow it to exert a historical influence in a manner that would hardly be possible otherwise. Judaism has carried through this principle of scriptural authority with particular determination. Even its concept of tradition, despite the possibilities it offers for the reinterpretation of the scriptural text, has basically served to reinforce the authority of Scripture.

The extent to which this formal principle of scriptural authority also leads to the establishment of norms for the content of belief depends, of course, on the contents of the holy writings. Hence the development of Judaism is also determined by the contents of the Bible, which includes not only religious laws but also the revelation of a world of religious ideas complete in itself. Though these ideas appear in the Bible as products not of intellectual reflection but of purely religious institution, they are stated with unmistakable clarity, as opposed to the figurative imagery and fantasies of mythology. Rooted in the concept of a supernatural God-Creator, they are set forth by the Bible, even to the deluded pagans, with a claim to exclusiveness not known before in religious history, as *the* one religious truth. After the principle of scriptural authority is fully developed, this exclusive claim to truth is of necessity applied not only to the revealed divine law, but just as much also to revealed religious truth as the nucleus of Jewish doctrine. Revealed religious truth thus becomes the norm for the community's religious beliefs, which are regarded as expressions of the truth set down in Scripture. This does not, of course, preclude the continued development of the ideas contained in the Bible any more than it arrests the evolution of religious law. But once this principle of tradition has gained ascendancy and such later concepts as the beliefs in resurrection and in retribution after death are classified as part of the original tradition and vested with its authority, and once the principal features of that tradition have been formulated, the belief of the community emerges as something final and definitive which every member of the community is expected to affirm.

Norm-setting in Jewish belief comes to a halt at this stage; the substance of Jewish belief has never been set down in the form of dogmas. An explanation frequently given for this state of affairs is that Judaism has lacked an authority which would be in a position to evolve dogmas and to determine their content. [. . .] However, the character of Judaism as a communal religion need not have precluded the development of dogmas, as can be seen from the development of Jewish religious law. There too the conceptual starting point is the individual; nevertheless, norms have evolved in religious law down to the minutest detail. [. . .] However, when it comes to interpretation of the divine law, the individual is not autonomous but bound to the authentic interpretation. This principle, which the Talmud can derive almost from the literal sense of the text of the Torah, makes it possible to develop an authority on the basis of the communal religion, a uniform way of regulating the religious life of the members of the community [*Sifre* to Deut. 17:10–11; b. *Sanhedrin* 87a]. This principle is the initial foundation for the authority of the Sanhedrin. However, the Sanhedrin's authority differs sharply from that of an ecclesiastical body in that it can demand acceptance of its rulings not because of the power it possesses in its own right but because it is the sole body legitimized by the Torah to interpret the Law. At the same time, the application of this principle makes it possible to regulate religious practice even after the disintegration of every Jewish central authority and organizational unity by placing the authority into the hands of scholars qualified by their expertise. This type of authority, emerging from the soil of communal religion, is by its very nature applicable both to questions of religious law and to problems of dogma; thus it also would permit an authentic interpretation of the Torah with regard to dogma. But the Talmud does not do this, and later teachers of the Law are unable to make up for this omission because their own authority is founded solely on the Talmud. Thus Judaism at that point indeed lacks an authority that could formulate dogmas. During the Talmudic era, however, the external conditions that would permit dogma formation are definitely present.

That this development does not occur is attributable not to the structure of the Jewish religious community but to the content of Jewish religiosity. [. . .] Talmudic Judaism knows none of the specific factors which could motivate the formulation of a formal creed. The method of norm-setting described earlier is entirely sufficient for the preservation of the communal unity of belief because disputes on dogma which would necessitate a definite ruling hardly ever arise. The defense against opposing religious trends from without or against dissident trends within (such as Sadduceeism, Christianity, or antinomian Gnosticism) call for other methods than authoritative statements of Jewish dogma. At the most, the immediate task at hand is to shore up the community's belief in specific disputed religious doctrines. But these trends never cause religious conflicts within Talmudic Judaism itself. The differences in aggadic speculation on basic religious questions do not touch on the tenets which are thought to constitute the collective faith of the community and therefore they do not require an authoritative ruling.

But this brings us to yet another, more profound, consideration. Judaism does not require dogmatic status for the content of its faith because it does not attribute to its tenets the salvational significance which motivated the development of dogma in Christianity. Judaism also considers the belief in God, in His Law, and in His promises as basic elements of piety and thus as prerequisites for salvation, but the concept of salvation through faith, be it in the sense of the Christian doctrine of vindication or in the sense of a gnostic concept of faith, is alien to Judaism. Accordingly, Judaism has no reason to formulate the content of correct belief conceptually and to set it down authoritatively. The acceptance of belief in the contents of the Torah and of the oral tradition, which Judaism demands of its adherents, does not presuppose a conceptual explication of these contents. Characteristically, this state of affairs changes during the Middle Ages when, under the impact of Aristotelianism, the correct knowledge of God is made a precondition for communication with Him and for eternal life. The objective of Maimonides and of some of his successors in fixing the dogmas of Judaism is to set down that correct perception which leads to salvation. The intellectualization of the concept of belief leads to the fixing of the content of belief. While Talmudic Judaism also reflects frequently on the content of belief, these reflections never probe belief as such. Judaism remains a naïve religion in its Talmudic phase and thus lacks any impulse to produce a conceptual explication of its contents.

III. Notwithstanding the changes which traditional Judaism has experienced since the Talmudic era, we have been able to treat it as a unified whole. The form of norm-setting which we have described is so closely intertwined with the Jewish belief in the revealed law and in the oral tradition that, along with that belief, it has survived all changes and continues to exist in present-day Judaism wherever belief in the divine origin of the written and oral laws in accordance with the traditional concept of revelation still constitutes the basis of religious life. Today we actually no longer have the options for the interpretation and reinterpretation of the biblical text which medieval rationalism could use in complete confidence. Stricter philological adherence to the biblical text has at the same time resulted in a more stringent adherence to religious concepts. Thus it is far more difficult today to reconcile, for instance, the theory of evolution in the natural sciences (or even only the current theories concerning the age of the earth) with the biblical account of creation than it was for a medieval thinker to bridge similar contradictions in his time. But this study is not the place for a detailed investigation of the problem or of possible ways of resolving it.

However, we must still show briefly that this situation changes radically once the belief in the verbal inspiration of the Torah and in the Sinaitic origin of the oral tradition is discarded. As this form of belief in divine revelation is surrendered, the Bible, and especially the oral tradition, cease to be norms of belief in the sense that every passage in them is authoritative and binding. By its very nature, the freer concept of inspiration, which replaces the idea of verbal inspiration, no longer requires adherence to the literal text of the Bible. Moreover, the world of Jewish belief can be examined in the light of historical development, making it evident that these beliefs have gone through a process of thoroughgoing evolution in the Bible itself and that important religious principles of Judaism are of postbiblical origin. In this respect, the consequences of abandoning the ancient supernaturalist concept of revelation in Judaism are basically the same as in the Christian churches.[11] This fact is not always clearly recognized because, in Judaism, these consequences affect the area of religious law much more strongly than they do the creedal content. In contrast to Christianity, the struggle between religious movements in Judaism occurs primarily in the area of religious law, not in the sphere of dogma. The basic ideas of biblical monotheism—the belief in man's moral freedom, in his predestination for an eternal life, and in the coming of the kingdom of God—are shared by all branches of Judaism. A reading of the crucial passages in a modern presentation of the beliefs of Judaism will hardly reveal the religious group to which the author belongs.

Nevertheless, the break with the authoritative concept of religion has by no means been without consequences in respect to dogma. Parallel to the development in the Christian churches, Judaism's attitude toward the biblical accounts of creation and of miracles has changed. Without going into detail, I want to mention merely two factors which have played a significant role in the struggles about reforms in the Jewish prayer book:

the abandonment of belief in resurrection and the changes in belief in the messianic future. The belief in physical resurrection has not been able to stand its ground anywhere without the support of the dogmatic authority of tradition; indeed, it has vanished almost entirely from the consciousness of many Jewish circles. Already during the Middle Ages Maimonides clearly attached little significance to it. However, he considered it as an equivalent of dogma; it remained in force as a component of the traditional doctrine of Judaism. The belief in a messianic era per se is common to all trends in Judaism, but its content has undergone an essential change. Its most obvious manifestation is that the belief in a personal Messiah had been given up, leaving only the belief in a messianic era.[12] But the transformation of the messianic idea goes much farther. The idea that God's messianic kingdom will be established by a single miraculous act from Heaven and will replace the present world order has vanished together with the belief in a personal Messiah. The messianic kingdom of God is regarded as the ultimate goal toward which the moral and religious development of mankind is striving. This recasting of the messianic idea into the ideal of moral-religious progress—for which there certainly is no lack of foundation in Jewish tradition—has profound implications. Above everything else, it has given Judaism a completely new orientation to the present-day world: today's world will not be replaced by an entirely new messianic world in which Israel's destiny will be realized, nor is it merely the arena in which Israel must suffer and prove itself worthy of future redemption. The present-day world itself is to evolve into a messianic world, and it is in this world, the here and now, that Israel has a religious task to perform. In this way, a religious basis for the integration of Judaism into the world of modern culture and for its active participation in worldly concerns is established. [. . .][13]

The abandonment of the original principle of authority makes it necessary for Jewish theology to find new means of identifying its beliefs as Jewish and of differentiating clearly between what is Jewish and what is not. This problem has not become very significant within Judaism itself, because there has, indeed, been no change in the fundamental principles of Jewish belief, and the unity of belief (to the extent that is still determined by religious factors) has remained intact.[14] However, this does not alter the theoretical significance of the problem. Its solution lies in the definition of the concept of the "essence" of Judaism, which more recent Jewish religious philosophy has rightly adopted as the basis for its work.[15] The Jewish character of our belief is guaranteed by its harmony with the spirit and essence of Jewish doctrine. However, these concepts present enormous theoretical difficulties. As similar discussions in Christian theology show, a clear definition of the concept "essence" is an extremely complicated task which we cannot even begin to undertake in the present study.

To conclude these reflections, only the following still remains to be said: The concept of "essence" cannot help in establishing new authoritative norms for the content of Jewish belief. The criteria by which it can be defined are internal and, as such, necessarily "subjective." If this is true for the purely historical definition of the essence of Judaism, it is all the more true for the application of that definition to norm-setting. This subjectivity obviously rules out an authoritarian fixing of belief. Even in instances in which its separation from the old principle of authority has left the substance of belief unaltered, its validity undergoes a fundamental change. Not only the acceptance of the truth of its contents, but also the affirmation of the Jewish character of the principles of belief become a matter of personal insight and religious conviction. This is increasingly apparent as one comes to realize that the essence of Judaism does not consist of a series of individual tenets, but of a unified fundamental religious conviction which is the very basis of these tenets and which alone gives them their religious meaning. To extract this religious conviction from its conceptual and ideational expression is the crucial task involved in defining the essence of Judaism—a definition which alone makes it possible to comprehend the multiplicity of individual tenets as the expression of *one* religious spirit, and to discuss the unchanging religious content in the changing conceptual forms in which it manifests itself.

The definition of "essence" is therefore also the basis for any decision whether a given doctrine is inextricably linked with the essence of Judaism. This formulation of the task at hand underscores even more strongly the subjective nature of any definition of the essence of Judaism—a subjectivity, however, which need not create fear of arbitrariness and individual whim. In place of a theoretical substantiation of this fact, may it suffice to point to the actual result of studies made to date, studies which have essentially followed the procedure outlined here and which, through this process, have arrived at a remarkable consensus in their conception of Judaism.[16] But even more significant than this accord in the scholarly definition of Jewish belief is the unity which has survived in Jewish belief itself. The inner bond with the basic religious beliefs of Judaism which has taken the place of external norms for these beliefs has proven strong enough to preserve the uniform religious basis of Judaism.

ALEXANDER ALTMANN (1906–87)

Alexander Altmann (b. 1906, Kassa; d. 1987, Boston) was a German American rabbi and scholar, and professor at Brandeis University. The son of the chief Orthodox rabbi of Trier, Altmann received a traditional Jewish education, completed his doctoral thesis on the work of the phenomenological anthropologist Max Scheler in 1931, and that same year received rabbinical ordination at the Rabbinical Seminary for Orthodox Judaism (called the Hildesheimer Seminary), where he remained and taught until his emigration to England in 1938. He served as a communal rabbi in Manchester until 1959, when he accepted a professorial position at Brandeis University, where he would remain for the rest of his career.

An authority on the life and times of Moses Mendelssohn, Altmann wrote on an exceptionally wide range of issues, including Bible, medieval Jewish philosophy and mysticism, and modern Jewish thought. His theological essays reflect an attempt to bring the full force of traditional Jewish learning into conversation with the momentous events of the twentieth century.

In the following selection, published in German in 1933 and later included in a 1991 collection of Altmann's essays entitled *The Meaning of Jewish Existence*, Altmann seeks to determine the scope and purpose of Jewish theology, which, he writes, plays a fundamentally different role in and for Judaism than it does in Christianity.[17] For Christianity, he says, theology is essentially about defining the relation between God and the Church, since the latter is responsible for mediating between a fallen humanity and a forgiving God. Not so in Judaism, which does not possess a mediating ecclesiastical institution; instead, "the people," the nation of Israel, is the direct recipient of revelation. Because of this, he says, "the work of revelation is essentially uncompleted and is demanded anew historically each day. Out of this grows the historical dynamic of the labor of Jewish theology." Jewish theology, then, is the continual attempt to understand this "unfolding" revelation, which manifests in Judaism through halakhah, the civil and ritual law. In Altmann's conception, there is no separation between the purpose and meaning of law in Judaism and Jewish theology, for "at the center of Jewish theology stands the work of halakhah." Law and theology are manifestations of the same religious urge—to understand and act upon God's daily revelation to the Jewish people.

What Is Jewish Theology? (1933)

Translated by Edith Ehrlich and Leonard H. Ehrlich

I [. . .] Two phenomena, revelation and peoplehood, may, in fact, be considered the two sufficient and not further reducible elements through which one can determine *a priori* the meaning-structure of a Jewish theology that is to be fleshed out concretely. In their mutual relation they form the structural schema "Jewish theology." The task that is a necessary consequent of this insight consists in analyzing these two weighty ideas down to their last ramifications, and in establishing a mutual relationship in which all the aspects are structurally ordered.

An enterprise of such proportions cannot be the subject of the present essay. Here I would like to attempt to explicate only a few essential points of view that are decisive for laying the foundation of a theological understanding of the existence of Judaism.

Is there a "Jewish theology" at all? The opinion has been expressed frequently that in Judaism the "law" has taken the place of theology. This theoretical observation, which goes back to [Jewish philosopher Moses] Mendelssohn [1729–86], coincides with the undoubted unpopularity in Orthodox circles of the term "Jewish theology." We admit that this state of affairs is based on certain important phenomena that make "Jewish theology" appear as something fundamentally different from the nature of "Christian theology." We agree wholeheartedly with [rabbi and liberal theologian] Ignaz Maybaum's [1897–1976] most recent statement that for Judaism the function of theology is of only secondary importance.[18] With this ranking, however, one implicitly posits the presence or possible presence of a "Jewish theology." For the present we must treat this possibility merely as a problem. First we must examine whether the complex, for which one claims the name "Jewish theology," indeed deserves this appellation. The reason for this doubt is supplied by the consideration that the word and concept of theology have remained alien to Jewish consciousness in its immanent region of meaning. We shall not analyze, in this connection, the historical phenomenon of the medieval Jewish philosophy of religion. It is sufficient to indicate that its type of structure should not be considered normative at all, that it demands at least a fundamental examination of the question whether its mix of Platonic-Aristotelian metaphysics and Jewish "theology" does not represent a distortion of both the theological structure and that of the philosophy of religion.

What is essential for answering the question of whether it is permissible at all to speak about a "Jewish theology" seems to be the fact that all

Christian theology receives its characteristic function through reference to the sacral authority of the church. This relationship characterizes not only Catholicism, within which the correlational component "church" represents a wholly stable authority, but even Protestantism right up to the revolutionary group of dialectical theologians struggling for the revelational concept of the "word of God." [. . .] Theology is either, as in Catholicism, the explication of what has been proclaimed by the ecclesiastical authority, or, as in dialectical theology, "the place where the church renders an account of its actions." In each instance it is therefore a mutual service between church and theology that is essential to the structure of the task of theology.

These formal determinations, however, do not suffice to make visible to us the concrete depth of meaning and the full import of this correlation. One must also bring to mind what the metaphysical presuppositions are that have produced this formal schema. One must point out that the structure "theology-church" is not an organic meaning-relation, grounded in realities, not an elementary fact, but a theologoumenon [lit. "that which is said about God"], the by-product of a certain theological construction.[19] Whereas the being-complex "Judaism" signifies already in its "mute existence" (Maybaum) a given, an existence grounded in meaning, the salvific institution "church" is not a reality as such but a theological construct, an organizational formation, and not the kind of organic growth that is represented by Judaism in its peoplehood. "Church" is possible only by virtue of certain theological presuppositions. Judaism is here and creates certain theological consequences through its theophany.

Here we touch upon the most essential point of difference between Jewish and Christian theology. This difference becomes all the more pronounced if we call to mind the specific theologoumenon that lies at the foundation of the construct "church." It is the doctrine of original sin, which necessitates inserting a charismatic salvific institution between God and man. The church, as successor to its founder, takes over the function of bestowing grace. With this, however, it enters a situation of permanent crisis. The church necessarily becomes a paradox. It wants to be divine and human in one. More so, it claims to be both sinning humanity and repository of the otherworldly. [. . .]

This theological structure of the concept of the church naturally exhibits the mark of the same paradoxical situation in the theology that is dependent upon it. It brings about the dialectical moment of theological speech concerning God. Since theology is the theology of the divine-human church in permanent crisis, it also partakes, as *theologia post lapsum* [theology after the Fall] of the crisis of all paradoxes.

We now take up our question anew: Is there a "Jewish theology"? Our interim answer must be: There cannot be, within Judaism, a theology that is the explication of what is proclaimed by ecclesiastical authority or that acts as guardian over the statements of a dialectically moved church. In other words: If one understands by theological work essentially reflection on the contents of revelation transmitted through the mediation of an authoritative holy institution, then a Jewish theology in this sense is impossible. This is so because Judaism does not know ecclesiastical authority, even in the weakest sense of the term. In Judaism, the people stand in the place of the church. The people and not the synagogue or community. Let us examine this fact more closely.

II. In Judaism the people, and not the church, are the unmediated bearers of historical revelation. It is the people who received the teachings of God, the Torah, and it is the people who have to actualize it in their daily life through all time. The expression of this immediate relation is the symbol of the *b'rith* [covenant], which, according to the events at Sinai, unites God and people in a spiritual *cum* moral *cum* metaphysical covenantal relation (and not a purely biological-ritualistic one, as some claim). Absolute theocracy is the political constitution corresponding to this *b'rith* relationship.[20]

The realization of this covenant through the daily actualization of the Torah demands an ever new questioning, born of each situation, of an eternal revelation that certainly does not regulate unequivocally every occurrence. Hence the work of revelation is essentially uncompleted and is demanded anew historically each day. Out of this grows the historical dynamic of the labor of Jewish theology. The living people are called to theological action. In this way, one can also comprehend the principle of the unfolding of halakhah from the nature of the *b'rith*-constituted revelation. The word "evolution" would be open to misunderstanding, and it is better to say "unfolding." Each and every word of the Torah has—as is repeatedly emphasized in the Talmud—numerous possible aspects, which, in the historical process of existence with its exigencies, are dealt with cooperatively through the generations. This dynamic work of thorough investigation and application, performed directly on the unique and static revelation, in short, the halakhic labor on the Torah, should be called the theological labor of Judaism.

This does not mean that we declare the task of hermeneutic "understanding" of the meaning complexes that are "theological" in the narrower sense (such as creation, revelation, messianism, doctrine of attributes, reward and punishment, etc.) to be essentially not theological and eliminated from theology. That they belong to theology can already be seen in that the *b'rith*-process brings to revelation purely legal demands as well as historical-metaphysical and specifically theological matters. However, the core of the relation to the covenant is represented precisely through the theocratic-legal element. In this way we gain a fundamental point of view: at the center of Jewish theology stands the work of halakhah. Theoretical efforts regarding the concept of "Jewish theology" must inevitably arrive at this insight, through understanding the fundamental phenomenon of the *b'rith* which, as *b'rith*, has, and can only have, the character of a demand.

This demonstrates that every Jewish theological system that does not do justice structurally to the central position of halakhah is wrong. Wrong, thus, are all theological systems into which the factor of halakhah is built only secondarily and artificially, those, conversely, that do not grant primacy to halakhah. Medieval philosophy has, in fact, detached the metaphysical from the authentically theological. Maimonides is a theologian as the author of the *Yad ha-Ḥazaka* (The Code of Jewish

Law or *Mishneh Torah*), but as the author of the *More Nebukhim* (*Guide of the Perplexed*) he is a philosopher of religion. [Rabbi and biblical commentator] Malbim [Meir Leibush ben Yehiel Michel Wisser, 1809–79] and [Orthodox rabbi Samson Raphael] Hirsch [1808–88, see chapter 2], for example, preserve the theological unity of the halakhic and the metaphysical-theological aspects of Judaism.

Thus it is evident that the relation to revelation alone is not sufficient to legitimize a Jewish theology as such. Maimonides' *Guide*, too, stands entirely in relation to revelation. The section concerning the "reasons of the commandments" with its rationalistic constructions, which ultimately devalue halakhah, is entirely related to revelation; and yet is a chapter not of Jewish theology but of the psychology of religion. *Only a theology standing in relation to revelation and, at the same time, having halakhah at its center is entitled to be called Jewish theology.*

As I have stated above, neither church nor synagogue nor communal institution, but the people, are called to do this theological work. There is no real theological rank (the function of the priests [*Kohanim*] is not theological but related to divine service); rather, everyone is legitimized to do halakhic labor, his knowledge and pious attitude being presupposed. This is the basic situation. We shall not here go into its complication through the theological concept of *semicha* (ordination). But it, too—I want to point out in brief—cannot touch the basic state of affairs.

However, the institution of the Sanhedrin seems to raise a serious objection to our thesis. Is it not a kind of ecclesiastical authority within Judaism? A kind of divine-human teaching authority with pneumatically grounded ultimate authority analogous to the church? No. Seen metaphysically, the Sanhedrin is a purely human institution. To be sure, the Torah demands it. This is the basis of its authority, and opposition to its decision signifies revolution against the divine command itself [cf. Deut. 17:8ff]. But this does not mean that the Sanhedrin can base its decisions in each case on an actual pneumatic experience, on being addressed ever anew by the "word of God." Characteristic here is the talmudic tale of the quarrel between R. Eliezer and the Sanhedrin [b. *Bava Metzia* 59b–60a]. Here the Sanhedrin denies even to a *bat qol* [a divine voice], i.e., an actual utterance emerging from transcendence, the right to influence in any way the logical decision that is now left to the human authority of the Sanhedrin. [. . .]

Thus it is quite clear: The Sanhedrin is not a sacral authority like the church, which, as the "body" of its founder (who himself is the "head" of this "body"), contains his *pneuma* and thus makes decisions based on its sacral authority. It is rather, according to its claim, merely "halakhic authority," or better halakhic *agency*, receiving its sanction only through the single fact of being appointed by the Torah, but not through an actual pneumatic relation to the word of God. The theological consideration that the ruling of the Sanhedrin is a right one even metaphysically does not constitute a counterargument to our thesis. For this consideration is based on the doctrine of an *analogia entis* [analogy of being] between God and man, a doctrine that is decisive for the basic attitude of Jewish theology. That man was created in God's image and—contrary to every theory of original sin—did not lose in principle the character of "purity" validates the human labor on revelation even for the realm of transcendence. In *one* form, however, the Sanhedrin perpetuated itself: its decrees remained binding. However, what is essential for this state of affairs [. . .] is the insight that all the legal decisions of the Sanhedrin are considered to be non-abrogable only if they have already gained acceptance among the people. On the other hand, each custom is considered to be nonrescindable—"even Elijah could not abrogate it"—if it has already become the property of the people. Hence, the foundation of all halakhic work based on the given revelation has recourse to the halakhic attitude of the whole people. In the same way it is evident, if we look carefully, that all the later codifiers and decisors, e.g., [rabbi, legal decisor, and mystic] Rabbi Joseph Karo [1488–1575] or [leading authority of Orthodox Jewry and vociferous opponent of German Reform] the Ḥatam Sofer [Moses ben Samuel Schreiber, 1762–1839], received their authority not by virtue of a sacral authorization but precisely because it was bestowed by the consciousness of the people. Hence it follows that the elementary theological state of affairs has prevailed empirically; the people, as the immediate correlational link to God, are the subject of theology.

Jewish theology, in its living fulfillment, is thus the total accomplishment of the Jewish people as regards the unfolding of revelation, primarily as regards halakhah, secondarily with respect to metaphysics and theology. [. . .] Accordingly, Jewish theology is fundamentally not a systematic-literary labor but an actualistic-decisional function. It is, thus, essentially an "open system." The form and conception of its standard work, the Talmud, correspond to this situation. Nonetheless, the systematic point of view has validity if placed at the service of a progressive, eternally fluid process.

Thus it seems to us that the most urgent requirement of Jewish theology today is to examine anew the principles of halakhic decision-making and to guide decisions in accordance with achieved results. The result of this theological investigation of principles will tell us whether the examination will indeed be fruitful enough to be able to take into account the halakhic requirements of the present (as, for example, the newly arising halakhic problems concerning the sanctification of the Sabbath in the agricultural enterprises in Palestine). Such an investigation is necessary under all circumstances. The *metaphysical* problems of special theology are surely urgent. However, for the existence of Judaism as a national entity primarily determined by halakhic thought it is the halakhic decisions, the ones regulating practical life, that are undoubtedly more urgent. Here we need precisely the clarification of the questions of principle. [. . .]

It has been shown that the Jewish people are the bearers of the halakhic labor on divine revelation and thus the ultimate authority of halakhah. The halakhic authority of the single individual and his decisions is able to be meaningful only on the basis of halakhically thinking and authority-founding peoplehood. The halakhic atmosphere of this peoplehood produces the authority, and it receives, in return, the decision of authority, to which it bows as belonging to its essence. Today wide areas of the Jewish people (especially in western Judaism) lack a halakhic atmosphere. Hence we need not be surprised that there is a dearth of authorities brave enough to make decisions. If the rabbinic authority does not feel itself backed by a halakhic atmosphere among the people, it must necessarily lower itself to become a kind of isolated church agency. On the other hand, lacking, of course, the organized ecclesiastical *potestas* [power], it sees itself deprived of all possibilities for making authoritative decisions. Thus it becomes the most urgent task of the present, in order to establish the necessary interaction between the people and their leaders, to educate the great mass of the people to think halakhically again, to restore to it its historical function of shaping halakhah. Only then would the meaning of Jewish-theological labor be realized again in its most noble region, the halakhic, and the people of Israel would regain the dignity as partner in the covenant, the *b'rith*.

III. Liberalism has the tendency to dissolve the halakhic element of Judaism—which, being tied to the people, is necessarily particularistic—into the universal, commonly human dimension. Recently the liberal camp, too, has recognized the indissoluble particularist character of halakhah. However, as [. . .] there has now opened up for the liberal consciousness an unbridgeable abyss between the particularist element of Jewish theology, the halakhah, and the universal ideas that are contained in Judaism, those elicited by special theology (by which we understand the philosophical teachings about God, His nature, and rule). I do not believe that there is such an abyss. In order to understand this, it will be necessary to focus our attention on a fundamentally particularistic character that is also suited for a special theo-logy.[21]

The primacy of the halakhic aspect in Jewish theology is realized not only in the status-relationship of halakhah and authentic theology but also in the special character of theo-logical labor itself. The theo-logical element in Jewish theology is dominated methodically and objectively by the halakhic aspect so that the theology as a whole (halakhah and theo-logy in the specific sense of the word) has a halakhic coloration and a halakhic nature. We indicated this dependence in two directions, the methodological and the objective.

The first tells us: the methods of halakhic scholarship (exegesis based on the traditional rules of interpretation) are applied also to the theological (in *aggadah*). As the multiformity of life always brings forth new legal problems, a book of laws can be treated exegetically in such a manner that independently of the originally intended meaning of the words new possibilities of meaning can be discovered by way of hermeneutics. When dealing with questions regarding theological matters, however, the use of exegetical rules should be prohibited, based on the view that no ideas may be held about God's being and reign other than those that are established and expressly revealed. Actually, however, the halakhic method, as we have seen, has also determined the *aggadic* one. The legitimation for this is found in the fact that theo-logical knowledge of God was also influenced by halakhah and transposed itself dynamically from static knowledge, from being a dead possession, into being the live possession of everyday; and from here it has transformed itself into a posture of struggling exegetically for the word and its meaning. Theo-logy has become dramatized and thus halakhized in Judaism. The theo-logical *having* of conceptions became inner *action*. Precisely because there was no composed church that could preserve or contribute self-assured knowledge of salvation, and therefore no possibility for formulating authoritarian dogmas, the special theology could assume the open unfolding character of halakhah, whose use of the *middot* [principles of scriptural explication] can be considered its symbol and mark.

Second, we spoke about the objective dependence of theo-logy on halakhah. We may describe the particularism of halakhah as the objective characteristic of its nature. The halakhic summons, being Jewishly theological (and not noachistically universal),[22] is addressed to a specific people, to Israel. A very special law seeks its very special bearer and shaper. Both members of the correlation "law and people" bear a particularistic meaning. The people are chosen, they represent a noninterchangeable sector of mankind. The meaning of its existence cannot be equated with that of "man as such." By virtue of its task and inherent destiny, Israel cannot be reduced to the concept of mankind pure and simple. There is an irreducible remainder, a not entirely comprehensible mysterious fact connected to its destiny. To be sure, this can be related to the meaning it bears for the salvation of humanity, yet it always remains, in itself, an ungraspable problem. As Israel is an enigma among peoples, so the codex of halakhah is the solitary, peculiarly puzzling block among the codices of people. The demands of halakhah cannot be dissipated into the universals of ethics or of "rational religion." Halakhah cannot be translated into a book of laws that is ethically, religiously, philosophically, psychologically, or mythologically comprehensible or universally "understandable." It cannot be transposed into a universal normative language. Philo's attempts at allegorizing, as well as Hirsch's symbolism, are subject to this dictum, although in different degrees. Nor was medieval philosophy of religion able to include halakhah in the system of universal philosophy.

But what about the specifically theo-logical doctrinal content of Judaism, which obviously manifests a universalistic character? What is its relation to the particularism of halakhah? Wiener considered the most urgent task connected with the foundation of a Jewish theology to be to grasp clearly and to take seriously the dualism: "universal philosophy of religion—halakhah tied to a people." This dualism is represented objectively as well as personally in the figures of Maimonides and others (who thought particularistically as halakhists and universalistically as philosophers of religion).

We do not find a tension here that is characteristic for the structure of Jewish theology. The shape of Jewish theology is completely homogenous in itself. It does not permit any polarity of universalism and particularism within Jewish theology itself, insofar as it is not confused with the philosophy of religion, the reason being that authentic Jewish theo-logy, like halakhah, bears wholly particularistic features. To be sure, all thought, in contrast to action, has the tendency toward the universal, and theological thinking is not exempted from this. But it is the formulation of a thought that first objectifies it and exposes it to criticism, i.e., to universal criteria. Thus, Catholicism, for example, exposes the contents of its teachings to criticism and to the universal (metaphysical and scientific) approach through the process of exact formulation and dogmatization. However, this situation does not occur in Judaism. Its nature as a popular covenantal religion is revealed in its unfamiliarity with dogma and its silence about its knowledge, which is revealed solely through the deed informed by this knowledge. It does not court believers and thus necessarily enlighten them; it does not sell its possessions by making them public. It does not dogmatize. God's revelation, says the Midrash, resounded through the world in seventy languages [b. *Shabbat* 88b; also Exod. Rab. 5:9; cf. t. *Sotah* 8:6 (some editions 8:5)]; but Israel itself is silent, and even where Midrash speaks, it merely paints pictures of its experiences without turning them into negotiable coin through dogmatic-unequivocal formulations. Of the Sabbath it is said, even from God's vantage point, that it is given "in the stillness of," in the intimacy of "between me and the children of Israel" [see Exod. 31:16–17].

Thus, Israel's knowledge of God, its experience of God's closeness and distance, never enters the crass, blinding light of the public. It is a chaste knowledge that ennobles Jewish theo-logy. It is a thinking that is indeed oriented toward the universal, as is all thinking, but that time and again fails to a certain extent to advance into formulation, into that which is generally understandable, into the universal; for: "if the soul speaks, then, alas, the soul no longer speaks."[23] If one comprehends this tendency of the Jewish theological attitude, which manifests itself at every step in talmudic and midrashic literature as well as in the facticity of all great theological forms of Judaism, then one cannot uphold whatsoever the talk of an inner rupture of Jewish theology caused by the polarity of universalism and particularism. Rather, one should refer to the formal structure of Jewish theology as essentially particularistic.

This holds true even if only because a genuine theological thought—insofar as it is that and not diffused through a philosophical point of view into its generally valid "quintessence"—cannot signify a universally comprehensible meaning. Theological ideas—and this pertains to all religions—are never concepts that can be schematized and thus universalized in some way without forfeiting the true essence of their being. But let us remain with Judaism. Its specific theology too cannot be translated into the universalistic. It cannot be interpreted into the rational nor can it be regarded within a universalistic aspect through irrational auxiliary concepts such as that of the "holy" ([proposed by German theologian, philosopher, and historian] Rudolf Otto [1869–1937]) in such a manner that the Jewish character is retained.[24] And this is so precisely because the formal quality of "the holy," like every other universal category, silences the specific value-tones of valuation within the ever-differentiated meanings of the "holy." There is no simple "holy," but the always specifically structured qualified meanings which, in each religion, constitute its specific phenomenon of holiness. It is the task of theology to preserve and refine this specific nuance. It is not universalization but differentiation that is the function specific to its nature; through it alone is it able to live and testify to its theological experience. While the meaning of religious-philosophical labor will always be to apply external universalistic criteria to theology, and thus to maintain the dispute between religion and science, theology must always be conscious of its particularistic character. A theology that abandons its characteristic coloration, its untranslatability, surrenders itself.

This illustrates how wrong the intention of Jewish liberalism was in extolling the perspective of universalism as a principle of Jewish theology. By endeavoring to transfer the specifics of Judaism to the universally human, it allowed authentic Jewish theology to slip through its fingers. The Jewish atmosphere, which alone can make Jewish contents palpable, dissolved into nothingness. How can one find a way out of this nothingness into a Judaism that again does justice to the inner unity of halakhah and theology?

IV. [. . .] However, it is precisely the emphasis on what is Jewishly particular in the spiritual situation of the Jews that is essential for the problem raised here of reawakening the Jewish individual to the specific coloration of Jewish theological existence. [. . .] This special feature of the ontic character of Jewish existence is present even if in his outer existence the Jew is not made to feel this specialness in some way. It is always latent. It is part of the ontic character of the Jew and is already there in what we call his outer destiny. The special nature of his existential self-comprehension is proved by the fact that the Jew in his historic situation reacts in a very definite, typical way which remains the same; that, for him, suffering and enduring, hope and work are always transposed into an interpretation of theological meaning. Most likely the existential moments, adduced by Heidegger, of "heritage" (*Erbe*) and "destiny" (*Schicksal*) could prove to be decisive for an understanding of Jewish existence. Even these structures, however, are not quite adequate for the singular phenomenon of Jewish existence. Rather, in the Jewish case these concepts display a very conscious turning toward the transcendent moment of divine revelation. It is characteristic of the Jewish people that they are conscious of their heritage, as well as of their destiny, believing that they are always being addressed anew by God in the course of history. Israel stands anew time and again before the ineradicable givenness of its spiritual heritage which it must somehow master and satisfactorily incorporate. It is the actuality of the "Hear O Israel."

It is the function of Jewish destiny in its tragic singularity to see to it that this claim of actuality be heard. The path leads from Jewish destiny to heeding ever anew what has been revealed. For this destiny, which cannot be normalized and which always corroborates anew what has been prophesied, is itself revealed to the Jewish individual, the bearer of Jewish destiny, the always new call of God, who with a mighty grasp discloses to him the entrance into an actualized Jewish being. [. . .] [An] incomprehensible destiny [. . .] rests, fateful and indissoluble, on the

Jew and testifies to *his* specific existence, one that cannot be associated with any other. From this destiny there is only an either/or: the way into the darkness of impotent despair, i.e., retreat into immanence; or the way into the light, the thrust into the Jewishly experienced theological sphere. However, this way does not proceed from the individual; it proceeds only from the discovery of his peoplehood. The individual who feels himself merely to be an individual, must lose. From the vantage point of peoplehood the meaning is disclosed and the circle is closed, a circle the direction of whose current is determined precisely by the two poles of "revelation" and "Jewish people." [. . .]

Here it is worth mentioning that today a concept that was accorded too emphatic an importance during inauthentic phases of the theological process begins to recede into the background, namely, the concept of "congregation." Its place is being taken by a primary regard for the overarching concept of peoplehood. Originally, the congregation did not have any theological meaning of its own in Judaism. The individual *tzibbur* [community] is not a configuration theologically composed in itself that can be thought in isolation from God. It has an actual function. It can be the vessel of God's presence. But it is—unlike in Christianity—only a fluctuating partial configuration, absorbed in a higher entity. The concept of "congregation" as an institution, as something that completes and endures, is Christian. The church is not thinkable without the "congregation" as its organ. Judaism is essentially a community of a people. The people as the people, and not as a congregational group, are already theologically qualified. The congregations are representations of the whole of the people. [German Jewish philosopher] Hermann Cohen [1842–1918, see chapter 5] and [Reform rabbi] Leo Baeck [1873–1956, see chapter 5] are wrong in saying that in Judaism the congregation takes the place of the church. Rather, in place of the Christian structure "church-congregation," there is the Jewish one of the people. It's a manifestation of *galut* [exile] that in the consciousness of Judaism the problem of establishing congregations has been so overvalued and the idea of the community of the people overshadowed. [. . .]The Jew of today, if he is to be renewed and revived theologically, demands this synthesis of revelation and peoplehood which, we believe, will also solve satisfactorily the other problems of synthesis. The time is ripe to tackle this formative task. The *theoretical* analysis of the nature of "Jewish theology" leads us to the projection of the *practical* theological task.

3

The Existentialist Turn

The Weimar Years and Beyond

8

Theological Existentialism

The end of World War I proved to be a watershed moment in Jewish theology. Though the atrocities of the Second World War were still completely inconceivable, the Great War of 1914–18 nonetheless surpassed in horror anything that Europeans had theretofore witnessed: industrial mass slaughter, tens of thousands of disabled war veterans flooding European cities, violent political unrest following the armistice (especially in Germany), the toppling of multiple empires and the birth of entirely new nation-states, and a broadening recognition of the sheer intellectual and ethical absurdity of every justification leading up to the war. All these things together led to widespread disillusionment concerning the power of human moral reasoning and the argument that idealism could build a better society. Many intellectuals even questioned the utility of abstract, theoretical, and scientific thought at all.

The focus of Jewish thinking before the war—both the intensive search for a theological essence of Judaism and the study of newly discovered ancient and medieval Jewish texts to demonstrate their contributions to human civilization and culture—were now almost entirely replaced by different issues, with the change rooted in serious suspicions of rationalism and rationality itself. All unquestioned authority of the natural sciences was abandoned; *Wissenschaft* had to make room for intuition, instinct, and urge. New questions arose about life and death; about the dynamics of being; about creativity and the deepest layers of the human soul—about all that exists beyond and outside of pure reason. Human experiences, shaped by historical conditions, replaced timeless conceptional thought. Inherited tradition and culture was now seen as forming the human being, instead of the human as molding culture in a rational act of free agency.

In the specific realm of Jewish theology, the universalistic approach of the nineteenth century—putting ideal humanity before the (Jewish) individual, and universal ethical virtues before ethnic affiliations—was largely discontinued (if not discredited) after 1918. Arising in the shadow of the war was a retreat into Judaism, now understood as a place of ancestral belonging and not as a confessional choice. The idealistic humanism of free agency was assumed to have failed, given the atrocities of the war. What remained was the existential aspect of the I, its identity as a Jew "running in its blood"—but keenly felt at the same time was the subjection to forces from the outside, first and foremost the fear of death.

There is perhaps no better example of this drastic shift in Jewish thought than the very first lines of Franz Rosenzweig's highly influential treatise *The Star of Redemption* (1921), a work that symbolizes the general turn to existentialism in Jewish theology: "From death, it is from the fear of death that all cognition of the All begins."[1] Only four years earlier Hermann Cohen (see chapter 5) had proclaimed death to be a problem for physicians or for mystics but not for the Jewish theologian.

Jewish existentialists now rejected the essentialist thinking (of that which is above and beyond experience) about Judaism dominant thus far. As seen in prior chapters, nineteenth-century Jewish theologians wrote extensively on the concept of the "essence of Judaism." Viewing a search for essence as rooted in a failed rationalist paradigm, Jewish existentialists, as well as some scholars of mysticism, such as Gershom Scholem (1897–1982), introduced a search for Jewish authenticity as the main aim of their theology. (Famously, Buber and Rosenzweig would claim discovery of Jewish authenticity in Eastern European Hassidism.) In sharp contradistinction to nineteenth-century theology, the empirical search for the Jewish *Volksgeist* (national spirit) became the core of the Jewish challenge in post–World War I modernity.

The most influential representatives of this radical shift in Jewish thought after 1918 were Franz Rosenzweig and Martin Buber. Despite their differences (especially on Zionism), both became the paradigmatic Jewish proponents of the new existentialism and rapidly found widespread acceptance, especially among younger Jews who had experienced the war themselves, often as soldiers.

Like Rosenzweig, Buber discovered a form of Jewish authenticity in the Hasidic tradition, but unlike Rosenzweig, Buber combined his personal *Lebensphilosophie* (philosophy of life) with active Zionism. Of Buber's philosophical thought, only a few works can be characterized as theological in a narrow sense; Buber's relation to Judaism is better explained as a dialogical religious anthropology than an attempt to understand God as such.

But in the realm of theology, Buber's rejection of all transcendence and his conscious use of the metaphor of "blood" to describe the core of Jewish identity would prove extremely influential well into the latter decades of the twentieth century. The Jew senses in the immortality of the Jewish people "a community of blood," Buber proclaimed even before the First World War, in the first of his famous speeches given before Jewish students in Prague. "Our innermost thinking and our will are colored by it."[2] This idea made a powerful impression on a whole generation of young intellectuals searching for a foundation of their Jewish identity beyond the traditional obligations of religious law. Philosopher Samuel Hugo Bergman (1883–1975), who was present when Buber gave this speech in 1909, wrote in 1944: "All who were there will never forget these words for the rest of their life."[3]

Rosenzweig followed suit. In his *Der Stern der Erlösung* (*The Star of Redemption*) from 1921 (parts of which are presented in this chapter in a new translation) he also speaks of the Jewish people as a community bound by blood, "for only the blood gives to hope for the future a guarantee in the present. . . . The community of the same blood alone feels even today the guarantee of its eternity running warmly through its veins."[4]

In this way, Buber and Rosenzweig replaced the revolutionary theological ideas that had been the nineteenth century's justification for future Jewish existence among the peoples of the world with an intuitive consciousness of common ancestry—of belonging to an almost mystical chain of generations—as the true identity marker of the Jew. Theirs marked a truly provocative departure from the idealistic, theology-centered view preferred by most nineteenth-century Jewish thinkers, which invested in Judaism's universality, its common grounding in one indivisible God.

The other great project Buber and Rosenzweig shared was to propose a new beginning in Jewish thought after the Great War, in response to what they saw as the failure of the idealistic, universal, almost naïve optimism of their parents' generation. The nineteenth century had watered down Judaism to humanist ethics, they claimed, disregarding the much wider and multifaceted literary past of the Jewish religion. To reappropriate this literature, one had to start with reading the Hebrew Bible. All the more, to let the Hebrew Bible be the testimony of the "advance of the Holy" into history and nature once again, Buber professed, we have to read the Bible, "as if we had never read it before."[5] To achieve this refreshing effect, Buber and Rosenzweig felt the urgent need for a completely novel translation of the entire Bible into German.

In this enormous project, Buber and Rosenzweig were arguably the first translators to prefer strict loyalty to the (Hebrew) source language instead of to the target language, rendering the German text sometimes almost incomprehensible for conventional readers. But with regard to theology, the Buber-Rosenzweig translation proved at least as disruptive as their particularistic Jewish existentialism. It aimed toward full "unintermediatedness," to re-create the orality of the spoken word of revelation and hence displace the allegedly corrupted concept of Scripture. In the name of a new beginning, the translation dramatically cut off millennia of rabbinical exegesis and philosophical interpretation of the biblical text.

MARTIN BUBER (1878–1965)

Martin Buber (b. 1878, Vienna; d. 1965, Jerusalem) was one of the most influential Jewish philosophers of the twentieth century, introducing existentialism into Jewish thought and bringing an end to the dominance of ethical idealism. He was also an important exegete and translator of the Hebrew Bible into German, in collaboration with Franz Rosenzweig.

In many ways, however, it was Buber's "discovery" of Hasidism for Western Jewry that solidified his continuing fame. As a popularizer of Hasidism, he pictured it as an open-minded and "authentic" model of Jewish piety (a description that sometimes shaded into romanticization), thus emphasizing ethnic culture and downplaying the abstract theological analysis of Judaism, prevalent still during the nineteenth century. Likewise, and in stark contrast to his Jewish predecessors, Buber was theologically much more tolerant of Christianity, viewing both religions as ultimately only two different ways of expressing the same belief (*zwei Glaubensweisen*).

Buber grew up in Lviv (Lemberg) with his grandfather Salomon Buber (1827–1906), a pioneering scholar and editor of midrashic and medieval Jewish literature. In his youth Buber joined the Zionist movement but soon opposed its mainstream iterations, both because of his preference for cultural (as opposed to religious) Zionism and his ideal of a binational state in Palestine.

Buber lived for some years in Vienna and Berlin, and later in Hesse, Germany, where he taught at the University of Frankfurt until 1933. Five years later he left Germany for Jerusalem, becoming professor of the sociology of culture at Hebrew University. He remained in Israel until his death in 1965.

The main idea underpinning Buber's philosophical writings is that human life finds its meaningfulness in dialogical relationships. There are two ways for the "I" to address its existence: it can relate to an "It" or to a "Thou." The "It" represents the world as we experience it, as separate objects. With the "Thou," however, we enter a relationship where the other is not separated from us, and we thereby enable real encounter and dialogue. God, Buber argues, is the *Eternal Thou*, the culmination of all human relationality. Every time we address a "Thou," we also address God; in Buber's theology this enables direct dialogue with the Divine.

The text presented here is excerpted from the first of Buber's famous Prague speeches from 1909—speeches that would prove to be a watershed event for Jewish self-identification in the modern age.[6] Speaking as a kind of guru to a group of largely secular Jewish students struggling to find meaning in their Jewishness, Buber rejected both the religious and the nationalistic paths to Jewish identity and suggested replacing them with a "community of blood." In speaking of blood, Buber was not propounding a racial, biologically deterministic understanding of Jewish identity, but rather overhauling the then-prevalent, theologically grounded view of Jewish affiliation—which focused on shared belief in the one indivisible God of Judaism—by giving value to a Jew's ancestral connections as the true root of Jewish identity.

What Buber said in Prague became nothing less than a manifesto for a whole generation of young Jews, mostly Zionists, which rapidly spread from Prague throughout the Ashkenazi world—if only because many of the students present there in 1909 themselves soon became influential Jewish thinkers: Hugo Bergman, Franz Weltsch, Max Brod, and in a certain way also Franz Kafka. But also in a wider sense, Buber's explicitly nonreligious but at the same time ethnic-popular approach proved to be the salvific word for this generation, which found affirmation in a Jewishness that was both secular and at the same time rooted in national traditions.

In the spoken text Buber went as far as to say "Today we don't have a god"—a passage he later edited and (from 1923 on) completely deleted from all subsequent editions of the speech. In like manner, the drastic decline in his use of "blood" metaphors throughout his mature years indicates a later change of mind on his part. Nonetheless, the metaphor and its influence suggest the profound revision undergone by Jewish theology in its existentialist phrase.

Judaism and the Jews (1911)

Translated by Eva Jospe

On these three constant elements within his experience—native surroundings, language, and mores—the individual's sense of belonging to a community is built. This community reaches farther than the primal community of family, or the community of friends, born of choice. The individual feels that he belongs to those whose constant elements of experience are the same as his, and on this level he perceives them, in their totality, as his people. [. . .]

We are interested in taking a look at the one who proceeds from there. What leads him on is an innate desire [. . .] for perpetuity, for lasting substance, for immortal being. He discovers that there is [. . .] a constancy of existence which steadily sustains all experience. [. . .]

As man discovers his I, his desire for perpetuity guides his range of vision beyond the span of his own life. [. . .] Stirred by the awesomeness of eternity, this young person experiences within himself the existence of something enduring. He experiences it still more keenly [. . .] with all the artlessness and all the wonder that surrounds the matter-of-fact, when he discerns it at the hour when he discovers the succession of generations, when he envisions the line of fathers and of mothers that had led up to him. He perceives then what commingling of individuals, what confluence of blood, has produced him, what round of begettings and births has called him forth. He senses in this immortality of the generations the community of blood, which he feels to be the past life of his I, the perseverance of his I in the infinite past. To that is added the discovery, promoted by this awareness, that blood is a deep-rooted nurturing force within individual man; that the deepest layers of our being are determined by blood, that our innermost thinking and our will are colored by it. Now he finds that the world around him is the world of impressions and of influences, whereas blood is the realm of a substance capable of being impressed and influenced, a substance absorbing and assimilating all into its own form. And he therefore senses that he belongs no longer to the community of those whose constant elements of experience he shares, but to the deeper-reaching community of those whose substance he shares. [. . .] The people are now for him a community of men who were, are, and will be—a community of the dead, the living, and the yet unborn—who, together, constitute a unity [. . .] the ground of his I, this I which is fitted as a necessary link into the great chain.[7] [. . .] Whatever all the men in this great chain have created and will create he conceives to be the work of his own unique being; whatever they have experienced and will experience he conceives to be his own destiny.

FRANZ ROSENZWEIG (1886–1929)

Franz Rosenzweig (b. 1886, Kassel; d. 1929, Frankfurt) grew up in an assimilated Jewish family in Germany. After writing a dissertation on the development and reception of Hegel's political philosophy (*Hegel und der Staat* [Hegel and the state]), Rosenzweig flirted with conversion to Christianity before recommitting to Judaism. He studied with Hermann Cohen (1842–1918, see chapter 5) at the Lehranstalt für die Wissenschaft des Judentums (Higher institute for Jewish studies) in Berlin in 1914, and was a close interlocutor of Cohen's during the latter's final years. In the closing months of the First World War, while serving in an antiartillery unit on the Balkan front and then subsequently recovering from the respiratory flu sweeping Europe at the time, Rosenzweig began writing what was to become his magnum opus, *Der Stern der Erlösung* (*The Star of Redemption*). It was published in 1921, shortly after he moved to Frankfurt to assume the leadership of an innovative Jewish adult education program known as Freies Jüdisches Lehrhaus (Free Jewish school).

A year later, Rosenzweig was diagnosed with ALS. Despite the ensuing paralysis, he continued to write, translating a collection of Judah Halevi's poems (1924) and undertaking a monumental translation of the Bible with Martin Buber (see earlier in this chapter) in 1925. At the time of Rosenzweig's death in December 1929 the two had translated through the book of Isaiah.

In *The Star of Redemption*, Rosenzweig seeks to grasp the totality of all being—natural, personal, and divine—as linked to one another through a series of relations stretching from Creation through Revelation, and culminating in a future redemption. The Star (of David) here graphically represents the inherent connection between these three key theological concepts, and intertwines them with the other three corners of the Star, which stand for God, the universe, and the human being. Rosenzweig also unveils his original theory of language, called "speech-thinking," as the unifying relation between beings, and offers sweeping histories of art, politics, religion, and philosophy. Like Buber, he presents Judaism and Christianity as closely related theologically; as an example, both religions introduced eternity into time through their liturgical calendars and ritual institutions.

In spite of these elements, *The Star of Redemption* is not a work of systematic theology. Its sometimes almost mystical language and the assumed implicitness of its main concepts have made it possible for generations of readers (far beyond Judaism) to find numerous ways of access to its central ideas, and thus to turn it into one of the most influential works of modern Jewish thought still to this day.

The description of Revelation in part 2, book 2 of the work, which Rosenzweig famously called the *Herzbuch* (literally the "heart" of the Star), is, as readers will see, an evocative narration of God as a lover, declaring His love to man as the "beloved one." The experience of divine revelation depicted in it is understood as a central moment of awakening—to oneself, to the Divine, and ultimately, to one's place and mission in the world.[8]

The Star of Redemption (1921)

Translated by Benjamin Pollock

GRAMMAR OF EROS (THE LANGUAGE OF LOVE)

DIALOGUE FORM. We will continue to advance, not, as in Creation, from word-type to word-type, but rather from actual word to actual word, according to the wholly actual course through which language becomes spoken, in which we tarry here in the middle-part of this whole written work. Only reflecting can we—as indeed we must—know the actual word as representative of its word-type, as well. But we find it not as such a representative of a type, but rather immediately as word and answer.[9]

SELF-TALK. Within God, a You answers the I. It is the double-sound of I and You in God's self-talk, in the creation of the human being. But so little as the You is a genuine You, because it still remains within God, so little is the I already a genuine I. For there is still no You that has stepped over against Him. Only when the I recognizes the You as something outside itself, thus only when it passes over from self-talk to genuine dialogue, does it become that I which we just claimed as the primordial No become-audible. The I of self-talk is still no "I, however," but rather an unemphatic I. Because it is merely the I of self-talk, it is so too just a self-evident I, and thus in truth still no revealed I, but rather one still concealed in the secret of the third person, as we knew it already in the "Let us" of the story of creation [Gen. 1:26]. The real I, which is not self-evident, the emphatic and underlined I, can first become audible in the discovery of the You. But where is such an independent You, a You freely standing over against the concealed God, by which He could discover Himself as I? There is an objective world, there is a closed self. But where is a You? Yes, where is the You? So God asks too.

THE QUESTION. "Where are you?" [Gen. 3:9]. It is nothing but the question after the You. Not, say, after the essence of the You. This is not at all in sight at the moment. Rather, at first only after the Where. Where if anywhere is there a You? This question after the You is the only thing that is already known of it. But this question suffices for the

I to discover itself. It doesn't need to see the You. In that it asks after it, and testifies through the Where of this question that it believes in the existence of the You, even without its having come before its eyes, it addresses and expresses itself as I. The I discovers itself in the moment where it claims the existence of the You through the question after the Where of the You.

THE CALL. It discovers itself—but not, say, the You. The question after the You remains mere question. The human being conceals himself, he doesn't answer, he remains mute, he remains the self as we knew it. The answers which God ultimately elicits from him are no answers. No I, no "It is I," "I have done it," answers the divine question after the You. Rather, instead of the I, a He-She-It comes out of the answering mouth: the human being objectifies himself into "man": the woman, and indeed she wholly objectified as the woman "given" to man, has done it, and this latter tosses the guilt upon the ultimate It: it was the snake. For the self to open its mouth to the I, it wants to be conjured with a stronger spell than the mere question after the You. In place of the indefinite, merely indicative You—the You thus also answered by the human being with mere indication—the woman, the snake—steps the vocative, the call. And every escape to objectification is cut off for the human being, in that in place of his universal-concept, which can flee behind the woman and behind the snake, that which cannot flee is called, the quintessential particular, conceptless, transcending the realm of power of the two articles, definite and indefinite, which encompasses all things, even if only as objects of a universal and not particular providence: the personal name. The personal name, which is indeed no name of one's own person, not a name which the man has arbitrarily given himself, but rather the name which God Himself has created for him, and which only for this reason, only as creation of the creator, is his own. The man who, upon God's "Where are you?", had still been silent as defiant and stubborn self, now answers, called by his name, doubly, in the highest definitiveness such as cannot be misheard, wholly open, wholly outstretched, wholly ready, wholly—soul: "Here I am" [Gen 22:1].

LISTENING. Here is the I. The single human I. Still wholly receptive, still only open, still empty, without content, without essence, pure readiness, pure obedience, wholly ear. Into this obedient listening, it is the command that falls as first content.[10] The summons to listen, the call by the personal name and the seal of the speaking divine mouth—all this is only introduction, preluding each command, spoken out to its full extent only before the one command which is not the highest, but rather in truth the only command, the meaning and essence of all commands which may indeed come out of God's mouth. Which is this command of all commands?

THE COMMAND. The answer to this question is known by all. Millions of tongues testify to it late and early: "You shall love the Eternal your God with whole heart and with whole soul and out of all your power" [Deut. 5:6]. You shall love—what a paradox lies herein! For can love be commanded? Is love not fate and being-seized and, if indeed free, then yet only free gift? And now it is commanded? Yes certainly, love cannot be commanded. No third person can command it and compel it. No third person can do this, but the One can. The command of love can only come out of the mouth of the lover. Only the lover, but he actually, can speak and speaks: love me. In his mouth the command of love is no external command, but rather nothing but the voice of love itself. The love of the lover has no other word at all to express itself than the command. Everything else is already no longer immediate expression, but rather explanation—declaration of love.[11] The declaration of love is very poor; like any declaration it always comes after the fact and thus, because the love of the lover is present, really always too late. Were the beloved not to open her arms wide in the eternal faithfulness of her love in order to accept it, then the declaration would fall wholly into the void. But the imperative command, the immediate, springing-up from the moment, and already become audible in the moment of its thus springing-up—because becoming-audible and springing up are one in the imperative—the "love me" of the lover, this is the wholly consummate expression, wholly pure language of love. While the indicative has the whole circuitous grounding of objectivity at its back, and thus appears at its purest in the form of the past, the imperative command is wholly pure, unprepared-for present. And not just unprepared for, unpremeditated too. The imperative of command bears no foresight for the future; it can only conceive of the immediacy of obedience. Were it to think of the future or of an always, it would not be command, not order, but rather law. The law reckons with times, with future, with duration. The command knows only of the moment; it expects the result in the very moment of its becoming-audible, and if it possesses the spell of the genuine tone of an order, then it will also never delude itself in this expectation.

PRESENT. So the command is pure present. While now, however, were one to see any other command only from the outside and as it were in hindsight, it could also just as well be law, the one command of love is quintessentially incapable of being law. It can only be command. All other commands could also cast their content in the form of law. This one alone denies itself such re-casting. Its content tolerates only the one form of command, of the immediate presence and unity of consciousness, expression and the expectation of fulfillment. For this reason, as the only pure command, it is the highest of all commands, and where it stands as such at the top, there everything which otherwise and seen from the outside could just as well be law, likewise becomes command. Because God's first word to the soul, opening herself up to Him, is the "Love me," so everything that He otherwise may still reveal to her in the form of law becomes, without further ado, words which he commands her "today" [Deut. 6:6], becomes the carrying-out of the one and first command, to love Him. The whole revelation steps under the great today. "Today" God commands, and "today" it holds to listen to His voice. It is the today in which the love of the lover lives—this imperativistic today of command.

REVELATION. And as this imperative can only come out of the mouth of the lover, but out of this mouth no other imperative comes than this, so now the I of the speaker, the root-word of the whole dialogue of revelation, is also the seal which, imprinted upon each word, marks the individual command as command of love. The "I the Eternal" [Exod. 20:2], this I with which revelation begins—as the great No of the concealed God, negating His own concealedness—this I accompanies it through all individual commands.[12] In the Prophets, this "I the Eternal" creates for revelation its own instrument and its own style. The prophet is not mediator between God and human beings; he doesn't receive the revelation and pass it on. Rather, the voice of God sounds directly out of him, God as I speaks immediately out of him.[13] The genuine prophet does not, like the master of the great plagiarism with respect to revelation, let God speak and pass on the revelation which has happened to him in private to the astounded who surround him. He does not let God speak at all, but rather in that he opens his mouth, God already speaks. The prophet can scarcely bring out his "Thus speaks the Eternal," or the still shorter, still more hurried "speech of God," sparing even the verbal form, that God has already taken possession of his lips. God's I remains the root-word that runs through the revelation as an organ-point; it bristles at any translation into a He; it is I and must remain I. Only the I, no He, can speak the imperative of love; it must ever only resound: Love me.

RECEIVING. But the soul—the ready, opened, wholly mutely listening soul—what then can she reply to the command of love? Because there must be a reply. The obedience to the command cannot remain mute; it must likewise resound, likewise become word. For in the world of revelation everything becomes word, and what cannot become word, lies either before or after that world. Thus the soul, what does she answer to the charge of love?

SHAME. To the lover's charge of love it is the beloved's confession of love which answers. The lover doesn't confess his love—how should he? He has no time at all for it. Before he were to confess it, it would already be past, no longer present. Were he to try nevertheless, then the lie that lies in the confession of the present would punish itself. For everything once confessed is already known,[14] turned thereby into the past, and is no longer the present that was meant in the confession. For this reason the confessing of the lover turns into a lie straightaway. And it is only right, and a sign of how deeply this all is anchored in the unconscious, that faith too renounces mere confession, and the just opened soul of the beloved is thereby closed up again before it. Truly, the lover speaks only in the form of the charge of love, not in that of the confession of love. Otherwise, the beloved: for her confession does not become lie. Her love, once born, is something that stands, a constant; so she may stand for it, she may confess. Her love too is present. But unlike that of the lover, it is present only because it endures, because it is faithful. In confession, love is confessed as a present that has duration, wants to have duration. For the future all appears bright and alit for the confession; the beloved is conscious of herself only wanting to continue to be in the future what she is: beloved. But back in the past there is a time where she was not yet that, and this time of not being beloved, of lovelessness, appears to her to be draped in deep darkness. Yes, because love only becomes enduring for her as faithfulness, thus only with a view to the future, so that darkness fills the whole past right up to the moment of the confession. Only the confession jolts the soul into the bliss of being loved.[15] Up till then everything is lovelessness, and even the readiness in which this self called-by-name opened itself into soul, still lies in that shadow too. That's why it's not easy for the soul to confess. In the confession of love she uncovers herself. It is sweet to confess that one loves in return, and that in the future one wants nothing but to be loved. But it is hard to confess that one was without love in the past. And yet love would not be the shocking, seizing, jolting-about, if the shocked, seized, jolted-about soul were not conscious of herself having been up to this point unshocked and unseized. It was thus necessary that there first be a shock, so that the self could become beloved soul. And the soul is ashamed of her past self, and that she has not broken the spell in which she lay by her own power. That is the shame which sets itself before the beloved's mouth who wants to confess. He must confess his past and still present weakness, in that he would like to confess his already present and future bliss. And so the soul to whom God calls out his command of love is ashamed of herself, ashamed to confess her love to him. Because she can only confess her love in that she confesses her weakness along with it, and to the "You shall love" of God, answers: "I have sinned" [from the Rosh Hashana liturgy].

ATONEMENT. I have sinned, speaks the soul, and dismisses shame. In that she speaks thus, purely back into the past, she purifies the present from past weakness. I have sinned, means: I was a sinner. With this confession of having sinned, however, the soul frees the way for the confession: I am a sinner. But this second is already the full confession of love. It tosses the force of shame far away and submits itself wholly to love. That the human being was a sinner is dismissed in confession; for this confession he had had to overcome shame, but it remained near him so long as he confessed. Only now, where despite the fact that he has dismissed past weakness, he all the same still confesses to be a sinner, shame withdraws from him. Yes, that his confession is dared in the present, is the sign that it has overcome shame. So long as it still lingered in the past and did not yet have the courage to express itself fully and trustingly, it could still doubt the answer which would come to it. For indeed up to now only the call-by-name and love-demanding command came out of God's mouth to the soul, still no "declaration," still no "I love you." And as we know, there may still be none that comes, for the sake of love's being bound to the moment, in which the genuineness of the lover's love rests, and which would have run aground for him in confession, in the explanation that is always in the form of a sentence, actually aground, aground in "grounds."[16] Because the love of the lover is groundless, in contrast to the love of the beloved, which indeed has its ground in the former. So the soul, who would have liked to confess, still doubted whether her confession would find acceptance. Only in that she dares herself out of the confession of the past into the confessing of the present, doubt falls away from her. In that she confesses her sinfulness as still present sinfulness and not as "sins" past and done, she is certain of the answer, so certain that she no longer needs to hear the answer aloud. She hears it within herself. She does not need God to purify her from her sins, but rather in view of His love, she purifies herself. In the same moment where shame withdraws from her and she submits herself in free present confession, she is certain of divine love, as certain as if God Himself had spoken that "I forgive" [Num. 14:20] in her ear for which she longed before, when she confessed to Him the sins of the past. Now she no longer needs this formal absolution; she is free of her burden the moment she has dared to take it all on her shoulders. So too the beloved no longer needs the confession of the lover, longed for before she had confessed her love. In the moment where she herself dares to confess, she is as certain of his love as if he had whispered his confession in her ear. The confession of the still present sinfulness, for the sake of which alone the past sins are confessed at all, is just no longer confession of sin—that is there in the past like the confessed sin itself—it confesses not the past's emptiness of love, but rather the soul speaks: I love even now, even in this most present of moments, still not as much as I know myself loved. This confession however is already highest bliss for her; because it encompasses the certainty that God loves her. This certainty comes not out of God, but rather out of her own mouth.

CONFESSION. Thus in that the soul, at this highest point of her self-confession, freed of all shame, spreads out wholly before God, her confession already confesses more than herself, more than her own sinfulness. It doesn't merely become but rather already is immediate confession—of God. As the soul gives itself up to shame and dares to confess itself in its own present, and thus becomes certain of divine love, it can now testify to and confess this divine love that it has known. Out of the confession of sin springs forth the confession of faith: a connection that would be inconceivable, if we did not know that the confession of sin, both in its beginning as confession of the past, as in its completion as confession of present sinfulness, is nothing but the confession of love of the soul in its stepping forth out of the shackles of shame to a state of submission that is completely full-of-trust. The soul who confesses her being in love, testifies therewith most certainly to the being of the lover. All confession of faith has only the one content: he, whom I have known as lover in the experience of my being beloved—he is. The God of my love is truly God.

The confession of Islam, "God is God," is no confession of faith, but rather a confession of the lack of faith.[17] In its tautology, it confesses itself not to the God who has been revealed but rather to the hidden God.[18] [Renaissance humanist Nicolaus] Cusanus [1401–64] rightly says that the pagan, even the atheist, could confess thus too. In the genuine confession-of faith, this unification of two, be they names, or be they natures, always happens: it is always this testimony that one's own experience of love must be more than an experience of one's own; that he, whom the soul experienced in his love, is not the mere delusion and self-deceit of the beloved soul, but actually lives. Just as the beloved, in that she becomes conscious of her love in the blissful confession, can in no way do otherwise, she must believe that the beloved is truly a man, she cannot be satisfied therewith that he is merely the one who loves her, so the soul becomes certain in her belovedness that the God who loves her is truly God, is the true God.

And just as only in the beloved's faith in the lover does the latter first actually become human being—the soul may well awaken and begin to speak in loving, but she only achieves being, a visible being for herself, in becoming beloved—so too now God only achieves the tasteable and visible actuality, from His side, this side of His hiddenness, which He previously, beyond His hiddenness, had once possessed in a different manner in paganism, here, in the testimony of the faithful soul. In that the soul confesses before God's countenance and therewith confesses and testifies to God's being, God too, the revealed God, first achieves being: "if you confess me, so I am." What does God now answer to this "I am yours" of the beloved soul confessing him?

KNOWLEDGE. Now, after God has achieved being, within and on the ground of revelation, thus a being that he achieved only as revealed God, wholly independent from all being in secret: now he can also, for his part, let himself be known, without danger for the immediacy and pure presence of experience. Because the being that he now lets be known, is no being that is beyond experience any longer, no being in the hidden, but rather it has wholly grown up in this experience, it is wholly in the revealed.[19] He doesn't let himself be known before He has revealed himself; rather His having-become-revealed must precede so that He can let Himself be known. He cannot let Himself be known to the soul, before she has confessed Him. But now He must. Because it is through this that revelation first comes to conclusion. It must, in its groundless presentness, now come permanently to the ground, to a ground that lies beyond its presentness, thus in the past, but which it itself only makes visible out of the presentness of experience. That much invoked relating-back of revelation to creation is ultimately what we mean here. But, as just said, revelation is not explained out of creation; then creation would indeed be something independent over against it. Rather the past creation is proven from out of the vitally present revelation. Proven, namely pointed out. In the shining-light of the experienced miracle of revelation, a past preparing and foreseeing this miracle becomes visible; the creation which becomes visible in revelation is the creation of revelation. Only at this spot, where the character of revelation as experience and as present is irrevocably determined, only here may it receive a past, but here it also must now receive it. To the confessing "I am yours" of the soul, God does not answer just as simply His "You are mine." Rather He reaches back into the past and points himself out as the author and inaugurator of this whole conversation between Him and the soul: "I have called you by your name. You are mine" [Isa. 43:1].

THE GROUND. The "I am yours" of the beloved soul can be said groundlessly, indeed only groundlessly. The soul speaks it purely out of the living overflow of her blissful moment. But the answer, the "You are mine" of the lover, as a statement which does not have the I as subject, is more than merely word of his own heart. It sets a relation—even if only in the most narrow, innermost circle—into the world of things. So this word may only be spoken if it adapts itself to the form of the world. There must be a ground prepared for it, a past as grounding of its present. For this present no longer wants to be merely the inner immediate present, but rather claims itself as present in the world. The lover who speaks "You are mine" to the beloved, is conscious that he has engendered the beloved in his love, and has given birth with pain. He knows himself as the creator of the beloved. And with this consciousness he now encompasses her and wraps her with his love in the world—"You are mine."

But in that God does so, His revelation to the soul has now stepped into the world and become a piece of the world. Not as if something foreign steps into the world with it. Rather, revelation, although it remains at once wholly present, recalls back to its past and knows its past as a piece of the past world. But therewith it also gives its present the position of something actual in the world. For what is grounded in a past is also an actuality in its presentness, not merely inwardly but rather visibly. The historicity of the miracle of revelation is not its content—that is and remains its presentness—but its ground and its guarantee. Only in this its historicity, this "positivity," does the self-experienced faith, after it has already found out of itself the highest bliss determined for it, now experience the highest possible certainty for it, as well. This certainty doesn't precede that bliss, but it must follow it. Only in this certainty of a long-ago occurring call by name to faith, does the experienced faith find rest. Certainly, already before this nothing could separate it from God, but indeed only because in its immersion in the present it saw nothing outside of itself. Now it may calmly open its eyes and look around itself in the world of things. There is no thing that could separate it from God. For in the world of things he catches sight of the objective ground of his belief in the irrevocable factuality of a historical event. The soul can look around in the world with open eyes and without dreaming; she remains now ever in God's proximity. The "You are mine" that is said to her, draws a protective circle around her steps. She now knows that she only need stretch out her right hand in order to feel God's right hand coming towards her. She can now speak: my God, my God [Ps. 22:2]. She can now pray.

THE APPEAL. This is the last that is achieved in revelation, an overflowing of the highest and most-consummate trust of the soul: prayer.

We are not at all asking here whether there will be fulfillment for the prayer. The prayer itself is the fulfillment. The soul prays with the words of the Psalm: Let my prayer and your love not be taken away from me [Ps. 66:20]. She prays for the ability to pray, which was already given to her with the certainty of divine love. That she can pray is the greatest of what is gifted to her in revelation. It is only an ability to pray. In that it is the highest, it already steps out over the limits of this realm. Because with the gift of the ability to pray, a need-to-pray is imposed upon it. Her faith finds rest in the proximity to God of unconditioned trust, whose force God has granted to her with his "You are mine," grounded in the past. Her life, however, remains in unrest. For what she possesses as grounding of her faith in the world is only a piece of world, not the whole. Her experience fills her completely. But the historical actuality that grounds experience in creation, is not the whole of the world, but rather only a part. Thus her ability to pray becomes a need to pray. God's voice, which filled her within, fills her world only in the smallest part; enough in order to be able to be certain of her worldly actuality in faith; not enough in order to live this faith. The ground-miracle of revelation that happened once in the past longs for its complement in a further miracle, which has not yet happened. The God who has once called the soul by her name—which is set firm like everything past, but has yet to come to the knowledge of any third party—He must do it "again" once, but then "before the eyes of everything living" [see the Sabbath *Musaf* liturgy].

THE CRY. So the soul must pray for the coming of the kingdom. Once God descended and has grounded His kingdom. The soul prays for the future repetition of this miracle, for the completion of the once grounded edifice and for nothing further. The soul cries: O that you would tear open the heavens and descend.[20] The parlance of the primordial language of revelation expresses such a "O that you" quite deeply through the question form: "Who would give that you."[21] Revelation culminates in an unfulfilled wish, in the cry of an open question. That the soul has the courage to wish thus, to question thus, to cry thus, this consummation of the trust held in God is the work of revelation. But to fulfill the wish, to answer the question, to still the cry, this no longer lies in her power. The present belongs to her; into the future it can only cast the wish, the question, the cry. Because the future does not appear in the present other than in these three configurations, which are but one. And for this reason, prayer, this last, although highest for it, yet only half belongs to it, only as ability to pray and need to pray, not as—actual praying. The prayer for the coming of the kingdom is ever only a crying and sighing, only a quick prayer.[22] There is yet another praying. So the last, which belongs wholly to the realm of revelation, indeed to the fully quieted faith, remains the stillness of the soul in God's "You are mine," the peace, which she found in His eyes. Love's exchange of speech is there at an end. For the cry which the soul moans in the moment of the highest immediate fulfillment, steps out over the bounds of this exchange of speech. It no longer comes out of the blissful stillness of being-beloved, but rather climbs in new unrest out of a new depth of the soul as of yet unknown to us and sobs over the unseen yet felt proximity of the lover, far out into the twilight of infinity.

LOGIC OF REVELATION

GRAMMATICAL GLEANINGS. . . . In the hurrying back-and-forth of speech we could hardly designate with sufficient perspicuity the points where the speaking language of revelation took its leave from the establishing, re-counting, conditioning language of creation. Let this be made up for summarily, in as it were tabular brevity. To the temporal form of the past, in which creation was grounded as act and culminated as result, there here corresponds predominantly the present. Revelation is present, yes it is being-present itself. The past into which it also looks back, in the moment where it wishes to give its presentness the form of proposition, only becomes visible to it in that it shines into it with the light of the present. Only in this glance backwards does the past prove itself as ground and prediction of the present experience, housed in the I.[23] In itself and at first, however, experience does not possess the form of the proposition, as it is to the occurrence of creation.[24] Rather, its presentness is satisfied only through the form of the command that springs up immediately in one, the command spoken, heard, and carried out: the imperative belongs to revelation like the indicative does to creation; only it does not leave the circle of I and You. What pre-sounded in that all-encompassing, lone, monological "Let us" of God in the creation of the human being [Gen. 1:26], this passes into fulfillment in the I and You of the imperative of revelation. The He-She-It of the third-person has faded away. It was only the ground and the soil out of which the I and You grew forth. The verb no longer serves as expression for occurrence, but rather for experience. Thereby the noun turns from object into subject; its case is now the nominative instead of the accusative. As subject of experience, however, the noun ceases to be thing, and no longer displays the ground-character of the thing as a thing among things. It is, because subject, now an individual; it stands fundamentally in the singular. It is individual, better yet someone individual, as it again was pre-sounded in the creation of the human being, of the first individual, of the "image of God."

THE PERSONAL NAME. The I or the You, seen thus in its objectivity, is quintessentially individual, not individual through the mediation of some multiplicity. It is no "the" because it is "a," but rather an individual without genus. In place of the article, there steps here the immediate definiteness of the personal name. With the call of the personal name, the word of revelation entered into actual exchange of speech; in the personal name a breach has been set into the firm wall of thingliness. That which has a personal name can no longer be thing, no longer be everyone's business; it is incapable of dissolving without remainder into the genus, because there is no genus to which it belongs. It is its own genus. It also no longer has its place in the world, its moment in the occurrence, but rather it carries its here and now around with it. Where it is, is a middle-point, and where it opens its mouth, is a beginning.

In the multiply-interlaced world of things there was no middle-point and beginning at all. The I with its personal name, however, in that it, according to its creation as human being and "Adam" at once, is in itself middle-point and beginning, now brings these concepts middle-point and beginning into the world. For it demands a middle-point in the world for the middle-point of its experience, a beginning for the beginning of its experience. It longs for orientation, for a world in which things don't lie next to each other indifferently, or flow by one after the other in equanimity; but rather one which undergirds the inner order, the order which always accompanies it in its experience, with the firm ground of an outer order. The personal name demands names outside of itself, as well. Adam's first act is giving names to the beings of the world [Gen. 2:19]. Again this is only a presounding. For Adam names the beings, as they step towards him in Creation, as genuses, not as individual beings; and he names them himself, thus expressing only his demand for names. The demand remains as yet unfulfilled. For the names that he demands are not names which he himself would give, but rather names which are revealed to him like his own, names in which the personal name's character of being one's own would attain ground and soil. It is thus not yet necessary that the whole world be full of name; but there must at least be enough name in it in order to give ground for his personal name. One's own experience, tied to one's personal name, thus requires grounding in creation, that creation which we just previously designated as creation of revelation, as historical revelation. Such grounding must, because in the world, be spatio-temporal. Precisely therewith it can give the ground for the absolute certainty of experience to have its own space and its own time. The grounding must thus establish for experience both middle-point and beginning in the world, the middle-point in space, the beginning in time. These both, at the very least, must be named, even if the world otherwise still lies in the darkness of namelessness. It must give a Where, a still visible place in the world, from which revelation radiates out; and a When, a still resonating moment, in which it opened its mouth. The two must, no longer today, but at one time, have been a single one, one that is just as singular in itself as my experience is today, because it should set the ground for my experience. Even if revelation's spatial quality of having taken place in a given place, and its temporal quality of having been an occurrence, may live on, in their after-effects today, in separate carriers—the former in God's community, the latter in God's word—once it must have been grounded with a single stroke. Ground of revelation, middle-point and beginning in one—this is the revelation of the divine name. Out of the revealed name of God, the constituted community and the composed word live their life up to the present day, up to the present moment and up into one's own experience.[25] Because, truly, name is not sound and smoke, as unbelief ever again in proud-stubborn emptiness would like to take for true, but rather word and fire.[26] One is to name the name and to confess: I believe it.

Notes

Introduction

1. This has never been a question in Christian circles. Departments of Protestant and/or Catholic theology—sometimes called "divinity"—were ubiquitous at colleges and universities into the late twentieth century, and many of Europe's elite universities retain such departments to this day.
2. Schechter, *Some Aspects of Rabbinic Theology*, 12.
3. Maimonides' Thirteen Attributes [or Principles] of Faith can be found in his commentary to m. *Sanhedrin* 10:1 (translated in *Maimonides' Commentary on the Mishnah*, 151–57.)
4. See Shapiro, *Limits of Orthodox Theology*. Such treatment of Maimonides' Thirteen Attributes is symptomatic of Jewish theology. Even if, for example, there is agreement about the importance of messianism, the actual content of the messianic doctrine of Judaism is unstable and controversial.
5. The classic example is Gen. 8: 20–21.
6. Formstecher, *Die Religion des Geistes*, 5.
7. K. Kohler, *Jewish Theology*, 6.
8. Guttmann, "Establishing Norms for Jewish Belief," 56.
9. It is no coincidence that most Jewish ethicists writing at the beginning of the century belonged to the school of neo-Kantian philosophy, since Kant had provided them with an ethics that often seems to have been taken directly out of talmudic legal thought. For example, the talmudic regulation "greater [is one who] is commanded [to do a law] and performs it than one who is not commanded and performs it" (b. *Kiddushin* 31a, later codified by Maimonides), seems not only to contradict common sense but also widespread Christian attitudes to legal observance. Nevertheless, this coincides remarkably with Kant's ethical writings.
10. The first such work was arguably Margarete Susman's *Das Buch Hiob und das Schicksal des jüdischen Volkes* (The Book of Job and the fate of the Jewish people), published in 1946.

1. The Essentials of Judaism

1. Salomon, "Die dreizehn Grundlehren der Religion."
2. See also the continuation: Ps. 96:11–12.
3. *Religionsgenossenschaft* (religious fellowship). Salomon appears to understand Judaism first and foremost as a religious denomination; therefore, for him, the people united in common religious belief and practice are the *Israelites*.
4. *Maimonides' Commentary on the Mishnah*, 151–57. Maimonides' original was written in Arabic, while the well-known version discussed by Salomon here is a sixteenth-century popular Hebrew adaption for the Jewish prayer book (commonly referred to as "Yigdal," after its opening word), whose authorship is variously attributed to the scholar and poet Immanuel of Rome (1261–1328) or the poet Daniel ben Judah (fourteenth century).
5. "He exists—unbounded by time is His existence." [Salomon's note.]
   A quotation from the first line of "Yigdal."
6. "He is One—and there is no unity like His Oneness." [Salomon's note.]
7. "He has no semblance of a body nor is He corporeal." [Salomon's note.]
8. Interestingly, already at this early stage (the 1820s) in the development of modern German Jewish theology, Salomon makes a striking connection between imageless monotheism and ethical perfection (*sittliche Vollkommenheit*), one he treats as self-evident. Thus he becomes a harbinger of a doctrine that later in the century dominates much theological writing, that of "ethical monotheism."
9. "He preceded every being that was created." [Salomon's note.]
10. Another central element of Jewish theology for Salomon: that the deity is not only not identical with (as in pantheism) or part of nature (as in incarnation theories) but essentially *above* nature, the free ruler of it, forming and changing nature according to His will.
11. "Behold He is Master of the Universe, and every creature proclaims His greatness and majesty." [Salomon's note.]
12. A reference to the medieval concept of God's realm being divided between a book of nature and a book of revelation.
13. "The fullness of His prophecy He bestowed, on those whom He treasured [and in whom he gloried]." [Salomon's note.]
14. "Never arose again in Israel like Moses, a prophet [who beheld God's image]." [Salomon's note.]
15. *Der Ewige* (the Eternal), meaning YHWH (the tetragrammaton or ineffable name), first introduced into German Bible translations by Moses Mendelssohn in the 1770s.
16. "God gave to His people a Torah of truth, through the hand of His prophet, the faithful one of His house." [Salomon's note.]

17. Salomon's reading of the *divinity of Torah*, as in Maimonides' original.
18. *Lehre* (Teachings), which indeed translates "Torah" according to the word's literal sense. This became a subject of theological debate later in the nineteenth century, with several Jewish thinkers pointing out that Paul's translation of Torah as *nomos* (law) was wrong, not only in a philological way: as Salomon points out here, some of the Torah's laws might become obsolete in time, but never God's Torah (teachings) as such.
19. "God will not change or alter His Law, for anyone, ever." [Salomon's note.]
20. Probably Salomon's rendering of the *immutability of Torah* in Maimonides' list. But both the universality and the "four pillars" are Salomon's own additions.
21. "He sees and knows our secrets, He foresees the end of a thing at its beginning." [Salomon's note.]
22. "He rewards one with kindness according to his deeds, He sends evil to the wicked one according to his wickedness." [Salomon's note.]
23. "At the end of days He will send our Messiah, to redeem all who await His final deliverance." [Salomon's note.]
24. Here, Salomon's interpretation is ahead of its time: a reinterpretation of Jewish messianism along the (nonpersonal) lines of an earthly age of reason and universal brotherly love of a united humanity became the common doctrine of liberal Jewish theology around the 1840s and through the nineteenth century.
25. NJPS: "But I know that my Vindicator lives; in the end He will testify on earth" (Job 19:25).
26. "God will revive the dead in His abundant kindness." [Salomon's note.]
27. Creizenach, "Grundlehren des israelitischen Glaubens."
28. This rendering follows Creizenach's translation of the Hebrew.
29. See b. *Horayot*, esp. chap.1, for discussions concerning rabbinical rulings made in error.
30. On the contrary, the Talmud expressly asserts that exegesis alone is valid on all points of belief (see b. *Makkot* 23b). [Creizenach's note.]
31. R. Bahya is best known for the theological work *The Book of the Direction to the Duties of the Heart*, composed in Judeo-Arabic but translated and disseminated in Hebrew as *Chovot Halevavot*.
32. It would be very good if someone made the effort to publish a version of the book for the educated Israelite, leaving out all the too-scholastic ornaments. [Creizenach's note.]

    To that end, see Ibn Pakuda, *Book of the Direction to the Duties of the Heart*.
33. The subsequent list is not a translation of the Maimonidean original but of the version Creizenach offers in the present essay.

34. Maimonides' original does not mention the divine spirit. Rather, it explains (consistent with his later philosophical teachings) that the prophets were morally and intellectually perfect human beings whose human intellect would eventually join the "active intellect."
35. Maimonides' original does not mention divine revelation but only Moses' ultimately superior intellect that made his direct communication with God possible (i.e., the argument in Maimonides is bottom-up rather than top-down).
36. Maimonides' original explicitly mentions both the "Written Torah" and the "Oral Torah," a distinction Creizenach fails to make here, likely purposefully, perhaps to avoid introducing a contradiction or difference between the two, or to avoid being forced to say which one is not revealed, in his view.
37. In the original, Maimonides clearly identified good with the keeping of the biblical commandments and evil with their transgression.
38. This is stated in the Thirteenth Attribute (*Maimonides' Commentary on the Mishnah*, 157).
39. An oft-cited example is Maimonides' doctrine of the Messiah (Twelfth Article). The Talmud holds a variety of opinions here (see discussions in b. *Sanhedrin*, chap. 11), including that the Messiah has already come and the Messianic Period is over (see b. *Sanhedrin* 99a and Rashi's comments *ad loc.*).
40. For example, from Provençal rabbi, commentator, and mystic Abraham ben David of Posquières (ca. 1125–98, called Rabad), who doubted the validity of Maimonides' Third Article. He argued that believing in God's corporeality could be debated but not declared heresy, since, if declared heretical, great numbers of faithful Jews would suddenly be excluded from the community of Israel against their wills.
41. See b. *Sanhedrin* 99a.
42. For creation ex nihilo, Maimonides seemed to allow for a view ("of the philosophers") that assumed precreational matter, as long as time itself was held to be created (cf. *Guide, part* 2, chap. 13). Interestingly, the same view appears in Albo's *Sefer Ha-'ikkarim* (1:12).
43. Probably a reference to the midrashic compilation *Pirkei de Rabbi Eliezer* (3:3).
44. The three middle blessings of the Rosh Hashanah *Musaf* are: Kingship (*malchuyot*), Remembrances (*zichronot*), and Shofars (*shofarot*).
45. Dernburg, "Das Wesen des Judenthums."
46. *Glaubensgebäude* (structure of faith). In this essay, Dernburg's use of *Gebäude* (structure) gestures toward his ultimate desire for a comprehensive system in which to understand Jewish theology.
47. I.e., the distinction between Torah law (*d'oraita*, written law) and Rabbinic law (*d'rabanan*, oral law). Such criticism was leveled at traditional Judaism not

only by Christians but by nineteenth-century Jewish Reformers, who saw the Rabbinic (oral) law as a gratuitous, even scabrous, encrustation on the purer spirit of the Bible.

48. An adoption and subversion of Christian language, wherein the "firstborn son of the Father" becomes any person of deep religious faith.
49. Frankel, "Rede."
50. Referring to Jonah (Jonas) Frankel (d. 1846), a leading businessman and banker in his home city of Breslau (Wrocław).
51. See also Maimonides, Mish. Tor., *Sefer Shoftim*, Laws of Mourning 4:4.
52. *Gemüt* (soul) can also refer to a "state of mind" or "disposition."
53. *Wille* (will). The German term carries a meaning beyond mere volition, having a stronger connection to action than its English counterpart.
54. Frederick William IV (1795–1861; reigned 1840–61).
55. *Pflanzschule* (academy). Note here the botanical metaphor and the related language of cultivation. A more literal translation would be "nursery."
56. *Ebenbild Gottes* (God's image). *Urbild* (archetype), playing on the relationship (more visible in German) between "God's image" (*Ebenbild Gottes*) and "archetype."
57. Famous statement of French philosopher René Descartes (1596–1650), often rendered in Latin (*cogito, ergo sum*) or French (*je pense, donc je suis*).
58. See Beer, "Die neuere jüdische Literatur und ihre Bedeutung." [Frankel's note.]
59. *Gur Aryeh*, the Torah commentary of R. Judah Loew ben Bezalel, called *Maharal* (b. 1520, Poznan; d. 1609, Prague). Translation of Frankel's German rendering of the Hebrew.
60. See m. *Sanhedrin* 10:2, commentaries of Maimonides (s.v. *shelosha melakhim ve-arba'ah hedyotot ein la-hem chelek*); Ovadia Bartenura (s.v. *ein la-hem chelek le-olam habah*); and Tosafot Yom Tov (s.v. *bilam*). See also Maimonides, Mish. Tor., *Hilchotot Teshuvah* 3:5.
61. Translation of Frankel's German rendering of the Hebrew.
62. See t. *Shabbat* 6:7; m. *Pesachim* 4:9 and Maimonides there. [Frankel's note.]
63. See m. *Sanhedrin* 6:1; b. *Bava Kamma* 83; b. *Makkot* 7a.
64. See Shul. Aruk., *Choshen Mishpat* 369. [Frankel's note.]
65. See PA 3:2. [Frankel's note.]
66. Philippson, *Der Pentateuch*, 6–7.
67. For Philippson, this narrative is not meant to be a historical account but rather a general description of the state of humanity pre-Sinaitic Revelation. Philippson rejects the idea of man's fall, as well as the literal reality of the narrative of the Garden of Eden (a distinct contrast with almost all premodern biblical commentators, even including Mendelssohn).

68. *Geist* (spirit), meaning both "spirit" and "intellect." *Recht* (law) can mean both "law" and "justice." Interestingly, Philippson here clearly associates lawfulness (the sense of justice) with divine Revelation, and not with the natural abilities of human reason.
69. The election of Israel was a difficult subject for nineteenth-century Jewish theologians, owing to the need they felt to avoid any emphasis on divine privilege. Many liberal thinkers followed Philippson here in pointing out that the *historical task* of being elected was to teach and act as exemplar, and indeed not to be naturally elevated in status.
70. *Offenbarungsvolkes* (People of Revelation).
71. *Unmittelbar* (imminent), lit. "immediate" or "not mediated."
72. As another sign for the mixture of old and new in Philippson, he here seems to indicate that the laws of kashrut are indeed grounded in considerations of a healthy nutrition, while most of Jewish theology views them as revealed ritual (and thus impossible to explain through logic or nature.)
73. Luzzatto, *Lezioni di teologia dogmatica Israelitica*, 15–30.
74. Stewart, *Outlines of Moral Philosophy*, 171–241.
75. Maimonides, *Guide*, part 3, chap. 13. Luzzatto includes the Hebrew translation in his text.
76. The Epicurian doctrine that the physical universe is composed of atoms that "swerve" survived in Lucretius's famous philosophical poem *De rerum natura* (*On the Nature of Things*).
77. Likely a reference to Fontenelle's *Entretiens sur la pluralité des mondes* (*Conversations on the Plurality of Worlds*), his major—and popular—work on cosmology.
78. Virey, *Histoire des moeurs et de l'instinct des animaux*, 258–92.
79. The same thing is equally, and more marvelously, observed in the various instincts of the various animal species. I have decided, however, to omit their discussion in the text, because the instinct was contested by various philosophers, although today it seems to be admitted by the greatest philosophers and naturalists alike. [Luzzatto's note.]
80. See Cicero, *De natura deorum*, 2:38.
81. The following words, "I wounded and I will heal" [Deut. 32:39], demonstrate (as was already noticed in the b. *Sanhedrin* 91b) that we are dealing with the same individual who dies and then resurrects. The matter is explained more openly by the mother of the Prophet Samuel (1 Sam. 2:6). [Luzzatto's note.]

2. Torah as Law and Ritual

1. E.g., see m. *Pesachim* 4:1 and b. *Berakhot* 17b concerning labor on the eve of a festival.

2. The title has sometimes been read as *Iggerot tzafon* (Letters from the north). See, e.g., the Hebrew translation (Vilna, 1890). However, Hirsch clarified the title as *Iggerot tzafun* (Letters from a hidden one) in a letter to Z. H. May (September 8, 1835). See reference to Martin Cohen's "100 Jahre, 'Neunzehn Briefe,'" in Breuer's review of Rosenbloom, *Tradition in an Age of Reform*, 146.
3. S. R. Hirsch, *Iggerot tzafun*, 87–104.
4. Hirsch refers to the academies of Sura and Pumbedita, both in Babylonia.
5. *Geist* (spirit), encountered numerous times in this paragraph, is perhaps the keyword of the eighteenth letter. It is generally translated as "spirit" but, when rendered otherwise, the original is noted in brackets.
6. In this context, *Geist* (mind) refers to a specific person, i.e., Maimonides.
7. Hirsch explains this classification, which he develops in his larger work *Horeb* (1838), in the tenth letter: *mishpatim* are expressions of justice toward beings equal to the agent; *chukim* are expressions of justice toward subordinate beings such as the Earth, plants, and animals; *edot* are verbal or symbolic signifiers of truths that form the mission of the *Mensch-Jissroel*, or *homo Israelis*, the Jew in whom humanity is exemplified; *mitzvot* are commandments prescribing love to all beings.
8. E.g., Gen. Rab., *Lekh Lekha* 44:1; Tor. Koh., *Acharei Mot* 18:9; and similar passages. The expression that one should not expound the reason of the verse, which was not infrequently cited in response to me, means in any event nothing other than the very correct proposition that one ought to ascribe no consequences in practical decision-making to the conjectured ground of a *mitzvah* precisely because it is only conjectured. See also Ramban on the Torah, *Kedoshim* 19:19 [s.v. *et chukotai tishmoru*]. [Hirsch's note.]
9. b. *Sanhedrin* 24a: "What does the name 'Bavel' [Babylonia] mean? R. Yohanan said: It means soaked [*belulah*] in Scripture, soaked in Mishnah, soaked in Talmud." In Tosefot, ad. loc., Rabbenu Tam (1100–71) comments that it is because of this feature of the Babylonian Talmud that "we exempt ourselves" from the talmudic prescription to divide study time equally between these three areas of investigation. In *Soferim* 15:9, as if attempting to head off such an interpretation, it is said: "Happy is the man whose labour is in the study of Shas, but this does not mean that he should skip Scripture and Mishnah and come immediately to Shas; rather, on condition that he studies Scripture and Mishnah should he come to Shas."
10. *Geistesforschungen* (Intellectual research).
11. Reference to the Shulchan Arukh (1565) by Joseph Karo, which was a digest of his more expansive work, *Beit Yosef* (1550–59), a commentary on the *Arba'ah turim* (Four rows) of Jacob ben Asher.

12. Namely, *Orach chayyim* (Way of life), the first of the four divisions of the *Arba'ah turim* and hence of the Shulchan Arukh.
13. *Avodot*, in Hirsch's system, are verbal and symbolic actions that exalt and sanctify our inner life.
14. Mendelssohn led a group project that produced an edition of the Pentateuch, *Netivot shalom* (Berlin, 1780–83), that included a translation of the Bible into *Hochdeutsch* (High German), written in Hebrew letters, as well as a commentary. While Mendelssohn did indeed emphasize the aesthetic value of the Hebrew Bible, he also insisted on the need for an edition that cohered with Rabbinic interpretation, and he excluded a lengthy philological essay, much to the chagrin of its author, Solomon Dubno (1738–1813), who left the project in protest.
15. Do not misunderstand me. Here only the total impression of his impact on Judaism is under discussion. Yet it is also the case that his *Jerusalem* defends freedom of thought and belief, vindicating Judaism, and, in contrast to the *Guide* [of Maimonides], highlights the practical essentiality of Judaism, and also expresses a view of the *edot* which, had it only been followed through in detail by him or his followers, would perhaps have given an entirely different direction to the whole subsequent time. Yet neither one nor the other occurred. The *Wissenschaft des Judentums* was not guided any further by him. Meanwhile, his followers, who lacked their master's religious sentiment, were not satisfied with his highlighting of the eternally obligating force of the law as divine utterance and had no option with respect to the spiritual comprehension of the law but to throw themselves into the hands of Maimonidean adjustment. [Hirsch's note.]
16. Not explicitly named in *Nineteen Letters*, Hirsch elsewhere develops an alternative to the "and yet" approach that he ascribes to Mendelssohn under the slogan, taken from *Avot* 2:2, *Torah im derekh eretz*, lit., "Torah with the way of the land"—that is, Torah accompanied by and thus expressing its sovereignty by means of the culture of the land shared with non-Jewish neighbors and fellow citizens. Fully committed to Torah observance and study while participating just as fully in economic, civic, and political life, the ideal Jew—the *Mensch-Jissroel*—is to exemplify humanity at its highest level, fulfilling Israel's particular duties including its mission to the world, and thereby unifying particularity and universality.
17. Cf. 2 Cor. 3:6.
18. A word about methods of Torah research: Two revelations lie before you: nature and Torah. For both there is only one method of research. As in nature the phenomena stand before you as *facta*, and you strive only retrospectively to construct a law of each detail and the context of all; proof of the truth or

rather of the probability of your assumptions is, once again, dependent only on nature itself, on the basis of whose phenomena you adopted your assumptions provisionally, and the highest degree of certainty attainable by you remains the ability to say that everything comports itself as if your assumptions were true, i.e., all observable phenomena may be explained in accordance with your assumption. Hence only one recalcitrant phenomenon makes your assumption untenable, and you must therefore seek all and only possible experience of the phenomenon that is the topic of your research, so that it may be available to you, where possible, in its totality. So too, ultimately, insofar and to the extent that you have not yet been able to catch sight of the law and context of any present phenomenon as itself a *factum*, the phenomenon itself still remains a *factum*. Just so is research of the Torah. It is a *factum* for us like the heaven and earth; as *facta* its determinations lie before us; in the Torah as in nature, the ultimate ground is God; as in nature, so too in the Torah, no *factum* is to be denied, even if its ground and context are not evident; instead, just as in nature, so too in the Torah, God's wisdom is to be traced. The determinations of both nature and Torah, therefore, are first to be taken up as phenomena in their whole scope, and their interrelations should be determined in accordance with these phenomena along with the object rendered definite by them. Your assumptions should once again be tested against their details, and your highest certainty here too consists in being able to say that everything comports itself as if your assumption were true. But, as in nature, the appearance stands there as *factum*, although you have not yet cognized it according to its ground and context. Its existence is not conditioned by research, but the other way around. Thus the details of the Torah stand there before you as law, even if you have not yet researched their ground and context, and your fulfilment is not conditioned by your research; except that the laws of the category *edot*, fulfilling their purpose as cognition and life-feeling, remain essentially incomplete without such research. [Hirsch's note.]

Hirsch here uses the term "*facta*" as either truths or actions, e.g., experiments, whose validity or performance is accepted on the basis of observation and/or testimony. The term was taken from legal discourse, in which, e.g., someone may be guilty "before or after the *factum*," and in which *facta* may be accepted or stipulated by the court.

19. Cf. the words (published in 1799) of Protestant theologian and scholar Friedrich Schleiermacher: "For Judaism is long since a dead religion, and those who at present still bear its colors are actually sitting and mourning beside the undecaying mummy and weeping over its demise and its sad legacy," *On Religion*, 113–14.

20. Prayerbook, Morning Service [*Shacharit*], blessing before recital of the Shema. [Hirsch's note.]
21. A more literal translation of the Hebrew would be: "To the quarry from which you were dug out." However, Hirsch translates *makevet* as "hammer"—not as the hole made but as the hole-making tool. He thereby connects the verse to Isa. 44:12, where *makavot* is generally understood to mean "hammers" (NJPS: "hammering"). Cf. m. *Kelim* 29:7 (*makevet shel satatin*, "stone-trimmer's axe").
22. Isa. 51:1–2 (translation follows Hirsch's German); cf. NJPS *ad loc.*
23. Geiger, "Das Verhältniß des natürlichen Schriftsinnes," 53–81, 234–59.
24. Cf. PA 1:1.
25. Here and in the next sentence, *äußerliche* is translated as "superficial," although it likely means something closer to "external," as in "external to the letter of the biblical text."
26. m. *Berachot* 1:5; *Shekalim* 1:4; 6:6; *Yoma* 8:9; *Yevamot* 10:3; *Ketubot* 4:6; *Sotah* 5:1–5; *Chullin* 5:5 ff; *Pesachim* 10:4; *Megillah* 2:2. [Geiger's citations.]
27. See 1 Kings 17.
28. m. *Yoma* 1:6; *Hagigah* 2:1; *Sanhedrin* 11:2. [Geiger's citations.]
29. m. *Shabbat* 8:7 and 9:4; *Sanhedrin* 8:2. [Geiger's citations.]
30. m. *Sanhedrin* 11:3. [Geiger's citation.]
31. b. *Hagigah* 10a–11b. [Geiger's citation.]
32. Compare for example m. *Shabbat* 9:4 with the b. *Yoma* 76b and *Niddah* 32a. This also happens with the older beraita, which still upholds the view of the Mishnah (cf. m. *Berachot* 2:6 and b. *Megillah* 20b, b. *Pesachim* 7b and *Niddah* 8b). [Geiger's citations.]
33. Holdheim, *Das Ceremonialgesetz im Messiareich*.
34. "The place of the Jewish people," i.e., as God's chosen, righteous people, who worship only God and follow only God's laws.
35. Cf. b. *Menachot* 68b and b. *Berachot* 9b. This is also the halakha given in Shul. Aruk, *Orach Hayim* 224:9. See *Magen Abraham* ad. loc., that the Messiah is here meant to be a Jewish king. [Holdheim's note.]
36. For an extended discussion of the coming of the Messiah, see b. *Sanhedrin* 96b–99a. See also Maimonides, Mish. Tor., *Kings and Wars* 11:1.
37. See t. *Avodah Zarah* 9:4. See also Nachmanides to Gen. 34:14; b. *Sanhedrin* 56a and 59b; and Maimonides, Mish. Tor., *Kings and Wars* 9:1–2.
38. Cf. Maimonides, Mish. Tor., *Kings and Wars* 11:4. [Holdheim's note.]
39. There is a talmudic ruling: Israel does not accept converts in the time of glory, and the examples given are the reigns of David and Solomon.
40. Lit., "blood mixing" (*Blutsvermischung*).
41. Maimonides, Mish. Tor., *Kings and Wars* 11:4.

42. Idolatry: *Heidentum* (or paganism).
43. Stein, *Die Schrift des Lebens.*
44. Compare here Cicero's excellent words in his work "On the Laws" 1:11. [Stein's note.]

    Stein's exact citation is probably a typographical mistake, since 1:11 consists simply of introductory remarks, but 2:11 includes a discussion directly addressing Stein's point. See Cicero, *On the Republic and On the Laws*, 157.
45. Called *Sati* (after the goddess Sati, the first wife of Shiva, who self-immolated out of shame and was reincarnated as Parvati). Some Hindu communities in India practiced widow self-immolation through modern times. The British officially banned *Sati* in 1829.
46. Baal-Moloch: a combination of names attributed to the ruling deity of the ancient Levant. The Phoenicians were a coastal people, inhabiting primarily the Levant (today Lebanon and its environs), likely related to though culturally distinct from the Canaanites. Baal (meaning "Lord") was a general title, and Moloch is perhaps a long-held mispronunciation of *melekh* (meaning "king"); thus, the name of the Canaanite-Levantine god, Lord-King, is similar to the LORD God (*YHWH Elohim*) of the Hebrew Bible.
47. For decisive rejections of this practice in the Hebrew Bible, see Lev. 18:21, 20:3; Deut. 12:31, 18:10; Jer. 7:31, 19:5; and Ps. 106:37–38. However, for instances of children sacrificed (or of attempted sacrifice) as burnt offerings to the God of Israel, see Abraham and Isaac (Gen. 22) and Jephthah and his daughter (Judg. 11:29–40).
48. Mylitta (called Ninlil or Mulliltu/Mullissu [Akkadian]; named Mylitta [Greek] by Herodotus), goddess of creation and childbirth, wife of Enlil (Mesopotamian pantheon) or Ashur (Assyrian pantheon).
49. "Rava said: one is obligated to become intoxicated on Purim until one can no longer distinguish between: cursed is Haman and blessed is Mordechai" (b. *Megillah* 7b)—And this overblown expression of a single man runs as a religious rule through all codes of law! See Maimonides, Mish. Tor. *Megillah* 2:15; Shul. Aruk., *Orach Chayim* 695:2. [Stein's note.]
50. Dionysus (Greek) or Bacchus (Latin), god of orchards, harvests, wine, and fertility, famous for the Roman festival of Bacchanalia, records of which describe lavish parties, drunkenness, and immodest sexuality.
51. All male children in ancient Sparta were trained under a highly disciplined regime called *agoge*. This practice of punishing boys not for stealing but for being caught is described in Plutarch's *Lives* ("Lycurgus," paragraph 17), part of his writings on Spartan lives and practices.

52. Referring to the famous saying of the French socialist and philosopher Pierre-Joseph Proudhon—"Property is theft!"—proclaimed in his 1840 treatise, *What Is Property?*
53. Gen. 20:12. [Stein's citation.]
54. See Gen. 29.
55. For the law forbidding Abraham's marriage to Sarah, see Lev. 18:9; for Jacob's marriage to Leah and Rachel, see Lev. 18:18.
56. b. *Shabbat* 88b. [Stein's citation.]
57. In Rabbinic thought, there were seventy original nations, stemming from the seventy named descendants of Noah (see R. Bahya to Gen. 10:1). Originally, all the world spoke Hebrew (see Midrash Tanhuma, *Noah* 19:1; Rashi to Gen. 11:1), but after the Tower of Babel incident (Gen. 11:1–9), each nation acquired its own language. Though the diversity of languages is originally depicted as a punishment (Gen. 11:6–7), Stein's point is that the Rabbis imagined an overcoming of that punishment at Sinai, not with the reunification of all language, but through simultaneous translation. (See b. *Shabbat* 88b ["each and every utterance that emerged from the mouth of the Almighty divided into seventy languages"].) The Rabbis went further, however, mandating that the Great Sanhedrin, the high court in the Second Temple period, had to have at least two judges who spoke all seventy languages and additional judges who understood all seventy. (See t. *Sanhedrin* 8:1; quoted and explicated in j. *Shekalim*, chap. 5, halakhah 1.)
58. [Graetz], *Briefwechsel einer englischen Dame*.
59. *Stamm* (tribe). This was common when seeking to designate Judaism as something different from a mere faith community (*Religionsgemeinde*) and broader than a national people (*Volk*).
60. Likely a reference to the Tiszaeszlár Affair of 1882, a blood libel in Austria-Hungary that led to a rise in antisemitic events. After the disappearance of a young girl in the Hungarian town of Tiszaeszlár, the local Jews were accused of her ritual murder. Her body was later found in a nearby river, where she had likely drowned. Though all the accused were eventually acquitted after a lengthy trial, the affair caused much consternation among Central European Jewry. (Graetz dedicated the revenue from the sale of this book to the victims of the affair.)
61. *Volksstamm* (national tribe).
62. Before being permanently placed in Solomon's Temple, the Ark often accompanied the Israelite army to war: see Josh. 6; Judg. 20; 1 Sam. 4.
63. The biblical account (e.g., Josh. 3, 10, 21, 24) records that the invading Israelites killed or subjugated all the inhabitants of the land; yet the appearance of these

nations later in the biblical narrative (e.g., Judg. 1) suggests some hyperbole in the initial statements concerning their destruction. Adonis: The god known by this name (from the Canaanite word *adon*, meaning "Lord"), or, often, by the name Dumuzid (Sumerian) or Tammuz (Syriac), was worshiped in Mesopotamia and the Levant. He was said to die each year and be reborn in spring, which inspired a cult of mourning. Later adopted into the Greek pantheon, Adonis retained his Near Eastern origins. (Ovid, book 10, places him as a son of Cyprus.) Ezek. 8 describes women sitting at the north gate of the Jerusalem Temple "bewailing Tammuz." Astarte: Wife of Adonis, called Innana (Sumerian) or Ishtar (Akkadian). Likely the progenitor of the Phoenician god Astoreth, and perhaps of the Greek goddess Aphrodite.

64. Born in the Kingdom of Israel, Athalia (reigned ca. 841–35 BCE), wed to King Jehoram (r. ca. 849–42 BCE) of Judah, became queen regnant after the untimely death of their son, Ahaziah (r. ca. 842–41). She was later overthrown and executed by those loyal to her grandson, Jehoash (see 2 Kings 8–11 and 2 Chron. 22–23). Jezebel: Wife of King Ahab of Israel (r. ca. 871–52 BCE). Jezebel was deeply despised by the biblical authors (see 1 Kings 16–19), who accused her of introducing foreign worship into Israel, especially that of Baal and Ashera. Baal: (meaning "Lord") A general title of the reigning deity of the Levant. The name of Jezebel's father, Etbaal, captures within it the family worship of the regional deity (1 Kings 16:31). Astarte: It would follow local practice for the daughter of the king to also be a priestess in the cult of a powerful female deity like Astarte, a practice she would then bring with her into her new marriage. Graetz might also have meant to write "Ashera," the divine queen-consort associated with the reigning deity (Baal or El) of the Levantine and Canaanite peoples. "Astarte" and "Ashera" are sometimes interchanged in later biblical and postbiblical narratives. "Had to hide their sentiments": See 1 Kings 18.
65. Priest in the southern kingdom of Judah during the reigns of Ahab and Jezebel's children, credited with ending the worship of Baal in Jerusalem; see 2 Chron. 23–24.
66. "Pure Jehovahdom," i.e., worship only of YHWH. Example secessions and reactions: King Hezekiah (r. 729–687 BCE) ended Baal worship (2 Kings 18); his son, King Manasseh (r. 697–43 BCE), reinstated it; and his grandson, King Josiah (r. 640–609 BCE), again ended it.
67. The argument that the ritual law of Judaism is not given for its own sake but is in fact a means to eradicate idolatry is a standard element of rational Jewish theology from Maimonides through Moses Mendelssohn to Hermann Cohen.
68. See PA 1:1 and the commentaries of Maimonides and Ovadia Bartenura *ad loc.*
69. E.g., Lev. 18:30.

70. For the lengthiest talmudic discussion of the Messianic period, see b. *Sanhedrin* 96b–99a. Talmudic literature frequently discusses the annulment of ritual law in the Messianic era (e.g., b. *Niddah* 61b; Lev. Rab. 9:7.) Perhaps Graetz is referring to the famous line said to have been spoken by the Messiah himself in regards to when he will come (b. *Sanhedrin* 98a): "Today!"
71. Likely a reference to radical Reform theology such as that espoused by Samuel Holdheim in Graetz's time: if universal messianism is about uniting humanity in peace, in order to advance the Messianic Age, separatist ritual laws of Judaism must be abandoned already in the present.
72. See Lev. 17:10–11. See also there the commentaries of Maimonides and *Sefer HaChinukh*, which concur with Graetz on the negative moral consequences of consuming blood. "Flesh of wild animals": Presumably, unslaughtered meat of either pure or impure animals. Jewish law permits the consumption of many wild animals (e.g., birds, goats, buffalo), so long as the animal is captured, killed, and prepared appropriately.
73. Tacitus, *Histories* 5.5.2.
74. See Exod. 23, 34; Lev. 23; Deut. 16.
75. The Bible describes each of the pilgrimage festivals as connected with the yearly agricultural cycle. Biblically, two of the festivals (Passover and Sukkot) also commemorate historical events in the life of the Israelites, the Exodus from Egypt and the wandering in the wilderness, respectively. Rabbinic tradition later associated Pentecost with the reception of the Torah at Mt. Sinai (see b. *Pesachim* 68b).
76. The tenth day of the seventh month, on which Israel must practice "self-denial." (See Lev. 23.)
77. See b. *Yoma* 85b–86b.
78. High priest during the Second Temple period (early–mid-third c. BCE), considered one of the last men of Great Assembly.
79. Joel, *Zur Orientierung in der Cultusfrage*, 3–14.
80. The term "cult" held greater relevance in the nineteenth century, and especially in the first hundred years of modern anthropological research, than it does today. As Joel uses it, "cult" refers to the whole motivation and pathos of religious life, a central topic of discussion in the history of religion until the second half of the twentieth century. Today, scholars of biblical studies still employ this term, mainly to refer to the sacred practices associated with the Jerusalem Temple, but its broader meaning—i.e., the passions that underlie its origins and the origins of religion in general—is an object of little scholarly attention.
81. By "if it is a normal one," Joel means to separate normative (or what are often referred to as "positive") religions from religious movements (such as Baccha-

nalian or messianic revival) that erupt with passion but do not last beyond a limited timeframe. For Joel, a "normal cult" is an agglomeration of experiences and traditions that gains its lasting momentum and interior organization from its cross-generation inclusivity.

82. *Perhorresciren* (lit. "to object to a judge"), a term adopted from legal discourse.
83. Cf. Maimonides, *Hilkhot Tefillah* 3:16–17, and the comment on the time when the prayer for rain begins. [Joel's note.]
84. *Freisinnig* (liberal; lit. "free-minded")
85. "Synagogue" here and below means normative Rabbinic Judaism.
86. A reference to Strauss's *Das Leben Jesu, kritisch bearbeitet* (The life of Jesus, critically examined, 1835–36), which attempted to derive a historical personage for Jesus from within (what Strauss characterized as) the mythological framework of the Gospels.
87. Namely, the divinity of Jesus as the Son of God, which, less a "dogma," is the very foundation stone upon which the Christian religion is built.
88. The Karaite movement of Judaism rejects the Oral Law of the Rabbis for a literalist interpretation of written Scripture. Arising sometime in the tenth century, and modeled on groups existing in the late Second Temple period, it flourished as a minority denomination alongside the larger Jewish communities, mainly in the Islamic world and its environs (e.g., Russian Crimea).
89. A reference to Ritter, *Geschichte der jüdischen Reformation*.

3. Relevance of Judaism

1. Formstecher, *Die Religion des Geistes*, 4–16. Additional sections of the work are translated in Greenberg, ed., *Modern Jewish Thinkers*, 139–70.
2. I.e., if Jews do not actively engage in the study of Judaism, then only Christians will. Formstecher outlines what he sees as the unfortunate outcome of this in the remainder of the paragraph.
3. Regrettably, experience teaches that so many a Christian believes himself to be at this stage of pure education—but is still very far from it. [Formstecher's note].
4. Not to be confused with the king from the Scroll of Esther (although likely named after him), Ahasuerus (Ahasver) is the name given to the Jewish protagonist of the 1602 German work *Kurze Beschreibung und Erzählung von einem Juden mit namen Ahasverus* (Brief description and narration of a Jew named Ahasuerus), which retells the medieval legend of the Wandering Jew. Ahasuerus (and the nameless Wandering Jews of legend before him) is cursed to be without a homeland after having taunted Jesus on the Via Dolorosa prior to the crucifixion.

5. A descendant of Japhet, one of Noah's three sons (see Gen. 5:32). Before the nineteenth century, he was often understood as the forefather of the peoples of Europe and Asia Minor.
6. Cf. a similar argument in Einhorn (this chapter), "The Benefits of the Jewish Doctrine of God."
7. The development and justification of Israelite doctrines of belief is a matter of scientific research, and not churchly authority. Each may decide here in the highest court. Just the same, we will constantly hold the names Maimonides and Mendelssohn in high esteem. They might have erred hundred-fold—still we will always recognize the spirit of Judaism in their endeavors, which does not find witness for belief in supernatural appearances, and which merely finds the credit for truthfulness in rationality. [Formstecher's note.]
8. Eisenmenger is best known for his book *Entdecktes Judenthum* (Judaism unmasked, 1700), an early Christian attempt to, supposedly, "understand" (*Entdeckt*) the development of Judaism beyond its biblical origins. However, as Formstecher notes here, and as the book was clearly intended from the outset, Eisenmenger sought not to educate his readers about Judaism but to "unmask" the Jewish critique of Christianity, for he often shone the least flattering light on various aspects of Rabbinic thought. The volume was and continued to be a source for popular anti-Jewish prejudice.
9. Anton Theodor Hartmann (1774–1838), a Hebrew Bible scholar and Protestant theologian, published the pamphlet "Johann Andreas Eisenmenger und seine jüdischen Gegner" ("Johann Andreas Eisenmenger and His Jewish Opponents") discussing Jewish reactions to Eisenmenger from 1700 to his day. Hartmann was involved in several public theological and political debates with Jewish thinkers, including with Gotthold Salomon and Abraham Geiger.
10. Cf. 2 Tim. 2:19.
11. Stern, *Die Aufgabe des Judenthums*, 132–57.
12. For example, in ancient times, monarchy, Temple priesthood, and sacrifice; in classical Rabbinic times, halakhah and prayer. The implication is that as Judaism evolves again, so will its rituals.
13. I.e., its knowledge of one God, Creator and loving preserver of the world.
14. What is being disseminated is this knowledge of God that is unique to Judaism, not Judaism as a religion, which Stern, alongside traditional Rabbinic doctrine, holds is not an evangelizing religion.
15. E.g., see Gen. 12:7–8.
16. E.g., see Gen. 48:15, 50:24 and Exod. 3:6.
17. E.g., see Exod. 20:2–3.
18. E.g., see Deut. 34:9. See also the book of Judges, which depicts Israelite theoc-

racy at its purest, and the books of Samuel and Kings, where theocracy (rule by priest and prophet) functions alongside monarchy. For the uneasy alliance between prophet and king, see Samuel's speech upon the anointing of Saul as king over Israel (1 Sam. 10:18–19).

19. Stern presumably means after the end of Israelite monarchy but before the advent of Rabbinic culture, a period of some five hundred years.
20. That is, if one were looking for a religion that excelled at the universalization of biblical ethics, Christianity would appear much more suited to the task than Judaism, and therefore we might best understand Christianity as the undoubted intention of history rather than diasporic Judaism.
21. A profound concession, and worthy of note, stemming from two possible sources: 1. increasing Jewish emancipation across Europe, which, though still relatively modest in 1845, was widely discussed among the continent's intelligentsia; 2. the scholarly reevaluation of Jesus and early Christianity, portraying Jesus and his followers as intimately bound up in the controversies of Second Temple Judaism, rather than as an entirely new prophetic lineage.
22. Stern here credits Christianity with inventing moral statecraft. But in the following paragraph, he credits Judaism with transcending statehood and the need for land altogether, trusting as it did not in citizenship but in religious affiliation. He deems this interpersonal arrangement to be of the highest moral caliber.
23. This is not an anti-Zionist message (for modern political Zionism does not really develop until the final quarter of the nineteenth century) but rather a theological one, aimed at Jewish philosophy and liturgy. Jewish prayers abound in calls for the return to Zion and the rebuilding of Jerusalem, most clearly perhaps on three occasions in the *Amidah* (the Eighteen Benedictions, recited three times daily), in which it is said, "gather us again together from the four corners of the earth," "may You rebuild [Jerusalem] soon, in our days," and "return the [Temple] service to the sanctuary of Your House."
24. A profound and perhaps disquieting argument. Jews are God's Chosen People because, Stern describes, they have a unique knowledge of God and a particular association with a geographic homeland. But Judaism's historic mission, he says, is to share its knowledge of God and relinquish its claims to a homeland. Once done, the Judaism that results is no longer the same Judaism as before, and the Jews certainly not the Chosen People as understood by the biblical texts.
25. I.e., Jews must be encouraged to see their situation in Europe not as Diaspora but as the settled pleasantness of eventual inclusion and integration.
26. I.e., "synagogue" representing all that is interior-looking and parochial about Judaism, closed to all but the small community of the faithful, as opposed to a

Church, which is outward-looking and magnanimous, open to accepting and edifying all who are inclined to listen and hear.

27. A paraphrase of Exod. 19:8.
28. In essence, the diasporic nature of Judaism, as decreed upon it by history, has already undermined any claims to the unity of Mosaic and talmudic law.
29. See, for example, Lev. 19:34, Deut. 10:19, and b. *Bava Metzia* 59b.
30. The principle of "obedience to the government and the laws of the non-Jewish state" known as *dina d'malkhuta dina*, "the law of the country is the law," is attributed to the amoraic sage Samuel of Nahardea (165–254 CE, called Samuel). See b. *Bava Kamma* 113b and *Bava Batra* 55a. See also Maimonides, Mish. Tor., *Laws of Robbery and Lost Property* 5:14; the responsa of Simeon ben Zemah Duran (1361–1444, called Rashbatz), *Sefer haTashbatz*, part 3, 138; and Shul. Aruk., *Choshen Mishpat* 369: 2, 9.
31. Samuel Hirsch, *Die Religionsphilosophie der Juden*, 761–86.
32. Part 5 is titled "The Extensive Religiosity or Christianity"; chapter 69, "Paul"; and chapter 70, "Influence of Pauline Doctrine on the Other New Testament Writings."
33. See Luke 19:10 (cf. its insertion as Matt. 18:11); Mark 8:38–9:1; Matt. 16:27–28.
34. From Isaiah's point of view (65:17), it is probably superfluous to remark that this passage is to be taken only figuratively. [Hirsch's note.]
35. Zoroastrianism.
36. Ormuzd: More commonly referred to as Ahura Mazda (Wise Lord), creator and chief deity of Zoroastrianism. Ahriman: The destructive spirit in Zoroastrianism's dualist theology, standing in opposition to Ahura Mazda.
37. *Ferwer*: In Zoroastrian theology, the active spirit of an individual, some combination of an external force and the soul. *Yazata*: In Zoroastrian theology, the positive powers (sparks), of whom Ahura Mazda is the greatest and most venerable. *Ameshaspand* or *Amesha Spenta:* In Zoroastrian theology, the seven divine beings emanating from Ahura Mazda, existing before creation and aiding in the coming-into-being of the world.
38. In the section just before the pages excerpted here, Hirsch lays out his understanding of Paul's doctrine of inherited sin: "The main features of Paul's world view, which remain with the Church until today, are as follows: All human beings are biased towards sin. The law brings the wretchedness of this situation—that of an inherited split in the human breast—to consciousness. This provokes sin to the point of eruption. Only Christ remains excluded from inherited sin. By means of wondrous divine grace, we are capable of appropriating the life of Christ. In and through Christ we become capable of leading a new, free, holy,

and sacred life—instead of dying off because of inherited sinfulness." Samuel Hirsch, *Die Religionsphilosophie der Juden*, 760–61.

39. Many scholars understand Zoroastrian theology as reflecting a dualistic (Manichaean) theology, where all creation is balanced by the two opposing divine forces of order and chaos. Hirsch argues here that Paul, by setting sin as something outside the individual, and as a force toward which human beings are drawn, reflects the same cosmology as Zoroastrianism: Divine goodness and order are set in dualist opposition to sin and chaos.
40. Meaning "Persian," referring to Zoroastrianism.
41. We must therefore declare Salvador's *Life of Jesus* [*Jésus-Christ et sa doctrine histoire de la naissance, de l'église et de ses progrès pendant le premier siècle* (1838), published in German in 1841] as an unsuccessful work, for it imputes this view of Paul to Jesus. [Hirsch's note.]

    Joseph Salvador (1796–1873), French scholar of Sephardi origin, wrote extensively on the history of Judaism and Christianity.
42. Rom. 8:18–23. Italics and notes in parenthesis are Hirsch's own intertextual comments.
43. "Those who find their life will lose it, and those who lose their life for my sake will find it."
44. The passage to which Hirsch refers readers is from Gen. Rab. 8:11.
45. See Rom. 8:23.
46. Rom. 8:24–27.
47. Rom. 8:28.
48. Ps. 44:23 (in some versions, 44:22).
49. Rom. 8:29–39.
50. Strauss, *Die christliche Glaubenslehre*.
51. Rom. 9:16.
52. Rom. 9:20.
53. In [Rom.] 10: 4–9, Paul uses the words of Moses from Deut. 30:11–14 (where even Paul overlooks the Hebrew *mitzvah*, "command," in v. 11) to set Christ in opposition to Moses. This was a process which Hegel knew how to appropriate. [Hirsch's note.]
54. Einhorn, "Die Vorzüge der jüdischen Gotteslehre," 295–305.
55. Einhorn, like others, employs the word *Stamm*, here translated as "tribe." Often *Stamm* was employed when seeking to designate Judaism as something different from a faith community (*Religionsgemeinde*) and broader than a national people (*Volk*).
56. The Bible records the number of Israelites who left Egypt at six hundred thousand men plus women and children (Exod. 12:37).

57. Exod. 3.2.
58. Ps. 19:8–10.
59. *Tam*, meaning "simple" or "innocent" as well as "complete" or "perfect." In Ps. 19:8, the Torah is called *temima*, "pure" or "perfect."
60. The meaning of these and other uncited quotation marks in this sermon is uncertain. Einhorn appears to be free-verse writing his own biblical-style poetry, as they are not biblical or Rabbinic citations (so far as can be ascertained).
61. A subversion of normative Christian language, wherein "son of God" is the general human spirit.
62. *Emunah*, often translated as "faith," but also meaning "trust" or "devotion." Einhorn might be referring to Mendelssohn's discussion of *emunah* in *Jerusalem* (100).
63. See Exod. 20.
64. The mythical river across which the Ten Lost Tribes are said to have been exiled by Assyria during the conquest of the Northern Kingdom, ca. 720 BCE. It is reported to "surge" and "sweep" and "churn" for six days of the week, but be calm on the Sabbath, when it is forbidden for Jews to travel beyond a prescribed limit. Hence, many classical commentators equate the name Sambation with "Sabbath" or "sabbatical."
65. Einhorn's use of the term *Geschlecht*, often translated as "race," here more decidedly refers to "lineage," pointing toward covenant and religion rather than blood.
66. A traditional Christian argument against Judaism was that, whereas Christianity enriched the biblical spirit through the fructifying powers of faith, Judaism atrophied that selfsame spirit through a continual encrustation of ritual and law.
67. See 1 Sam. 8–9.
68. See b. *Gittin* 56.
69. Jer. 31:33.

4. God

1. See G. Y. Kohler, *Reading Maimonides' Philosophy*.
2. Saalschütz, "Der Monotheismus in sittlicher Beziehung," 159–64.
3. Cf. Hermann Cohen's central idea of the inherent connection between ethics and jurisprudence, as he developed it in his *Ethik des reinen Willens* (Ethics of pure will, 1904). The idea of the monotheistic God stands here as a symbol for the concept of truth, common to both fields.
4. That is, we must *know* that some moral abhorrence at their own customs remained in the hearts of the Carthaginians, and that they repented later in

life; otherwise we could not claim the absolute divinity of an inner moral law that rejects such murderous customs.

5. See b. *Shabbat* 31a.
6. Kaufmann, *Achtzehn Predigten.*
7. Kaufmann, *Geschichte der Attributenlehre*, 471–80.
8. "Attributes" here refers to what can and cannot be known about God—i.e., what can and cannot be *attributed* to God.
9. Modern Jewish theologians were often critical of Maimonides' attempt to depict the biblical Moses as superhuman, the never-challengeable master of all prophets. This depiction, they claim, was driven more by theology than reason—that is, by Maimonides' belief in the absolute divinity of Torah and therefore the superiority of the Pentateuch over the rest of the Bible. Nineteenth-century liberal Jewish theologians often preferred the social and messianic message of the prophetic books.
10. Cf. Hermann Cohen's *Ethics of Maimonides* for a more Kantian solution to the same problem. Cohen used Kant's notion of the "infinite judgement" (A = non-B) to claim that Maimonides thus came to an even more fruitful expression of the divine attributes.

5. Search for Essence

1. Cohen, "Das Judentum als Weltanschauung." "Judaism as a Worldview" was not included in Cohen's three-volume *Jüdische Schriften* (1924).
2. Throughout the speech, Cohen uses the German *Völker* to refer both to people in general and to the non-Jewish peoples in particular. When the translator has deemed Cohen's usage to be for the former, as here, he has translated the word as "people"; when the latter, which occurs mainly in the context of biblical imagery—when Cohen is referring to the Hebrew *goyim*—he has translated it as "nations."
3. I.e., peace and moral exaltation.
4. The phrase "Problem of Religion" (*Problem der Religion*) might also be translated as something like "Question/Challenge of Religion." Cohen is not arguing that religion is a "problem" in the sense of something that must be overcome, as did Marx or Freud, but rather that religion—and especially religion in the modern period—raises certain questions that require more sophisticated answers than those offered by pietism or traditional exegesis.
5. Cohen may have encountered this line in a number of common sources: b. *Sanhedrin* 58b; Tor. Koh., *Kedoshim* 11:11; TDER 29:1; and Maimonides' *Guide*, part 3, chapter 53. Also cf. PA 1:2.

6. Here, *wissenschaftlich* is translated as "scholastic," though elsewhere a version of the same word appears as "science," "scientific," or "scholarship."
7. In the phrase "scholastic keenness is by no means the same as brusqueness of affect," Cohen is seeking to combat the antisemitic stereotype that the Rabbinical focus on legal particularities resulted in a religion without kindness or feeling.
8. A reference to the group that invited Cohen to give this lecture, the Politischen Volkverein (Political people's association) of Vienna.
9. In late nineteenth-century discourse around race and religion, there were those who questioned whether Judaism was a religion or a race. The latter would have excluded the faith of the Jews from being called a World Religion.
10. *Stamm* (tribe). This was common usage when seeking to designate Judaism as something different from a mere faith community (*Religionsgemeinde*) and broader than a national people (*Volk*).
11. "Emancipation" is the term used for the gradual extension of civil rights to the Jewish communities of the European continent. The process began in 1790 in France and was completed (at least for a time) after the 1917 Russian Revolution.
12. Cohen uses the word *Dogmatik* (here translated as "dogmatic theology") to refer to systematic theology and credal statements about religion.
13. Cohen conflates the book's general title, which translates as *The System of the Religious View of the Jews and Its Relationship to Paganism, Christianity and to Absolute Philosophy, for Theologians of All Confessions such as Presented for Educated Non-Theologians and Provided with the Explanatory Evidence from the Holy Scriptures, Talmud, and Midrash,* with the specific title of volume 1 (*The Religious Philosophy of the Jews or the Principle of the Jewish Religious View and its Relationship to Paganism, Christianity, and to Absolute Philosophy and Provided with Explanatory Evidence from the Holy Scriptures, Talmud, and Midrash*) and misstates the place of publication (Leipzig). Hirsch had been living in Dessau until 1841 but was forced to leave his post because of his radical views on religious reform.
14. Cohen's teacher Manuel Joel (1826–90, see chapter 2) and Cohen's friend Jacob Guttmann (1845–1919) each published writings that demonstrated (far beyond the facts known at their time) how much Judaism (especially Maimonides) influenced the thought of Albert the Great (1200–1280, called Albertus Magnus) and Thomas Aquinas (1225–74). See G. Y. Kohler, "'Scholasticism Is a Daughter of Judaism,'" 319–40.
15. *Der Grund* (the source). A complex philosophical expression playing on the multiple definitions of *Grund,* which can mean "reason" (in the philosophical sense), "cause" or "foundation" (in the metaphysical sense), and/or "ground" (in the literal, earthly sense). In Cohen's philosophy, *der Grund* more accu-

rately translates as "the origin" or "the source"—i.e., the world is not "built" or "founded" on God's transcendence, but rather emerges from it.

16. *Sinnliche* (sensual, sensory), i.e., the opposite of transcendental.
17. *Geist,* translated here and in the following sentence as "intellect" (one could also use "reason") rather than its more literal "spirit," as in the previous sentence.
18. Cohen probably quoted this from memory, as it appears in several of his works and always in the same incorrect form. Cf. Goethe, *Faust* 1, "Studierzimmer": "Entschlafen sind nun wilde Triebe / Mit jedem ungestümen Tun."
19. *Achtung* (respect), in this context might also mean "deference" or "esteem."
20. In German, "Liebe deinen Nächsten, denn er ist wie du," with Cohen substituting "he is like you" (dir gleich) instead of "as [you love] yourself." This exegetical midrash, possibly dating to Moses Mendelssohn's *biur (biblical commentary),* was later adopted by Franz Rosenzweig (1886–1929, see chap. 8) and Martin Buber (1878–1965, see chap. 8) in their Bible translation and commentary. In Cohen, it also appears in *Religion der Vernunft,* 137f.
21. *Grund* (reason).
22. From the Hebrew *chasidei,* translated here as "righteous." Cohen subsequently equates this same term with the German *Frommen,* which is more commonly translated as "religious" or "pious."
23. The quote *chasidei umot haolam yesh lahem khelek l'olam habah* appears not only in the relevant Tosafot, but is also found in Maimonides, Mish. Tor., *Hilkhot Teshuva* 3:5, and Ovadia Bartenura's fifteenth-century commentary on m. *Sanhedrin* 10:2.
24. *Schranken der Glaubensfrommen,* a phrase connoting someone "locked inside the confines of a specific dogmatic theology."
25. *Frommen* (pious). When Cohen uses the term "Chasid," here and below, he does not mean the various forms of this proper noun that have been used to refer to Jewish communities, such as the medieval pietists of the Rhineland or modern Hassidim. Rather, he has adapted the Hebrew term *chasid* from the above-quoted Hebrew phrase *chasidei umot haolam,* righteous/pious among the nations of the world.
26. Here Cohen uses the term *des Einst* as a proper noun; it is translated throughout as "Once" or "the Once."
27. "Humanity" (*Humanität*) plays also on the word "humaneness."
28. Cohen uses the word *Kritik,* which in the academic sense means a detailed analysis or assessment. It carries none of the negative connotation it has acquired in contemporary vernacular English. In this instance, Cohen is bemoaning that Protestant theologians have recognized the moral virtues of the Hebrew prophets to a greater extent than have the Jews.

29. In the last decade of the nineteenth century, antisemitism was on an upswing across Europe. The Dreyfus Affair (1894–1906) was ongoing in France. And less than a year before Cohen's lecture, Karl Lueger (1844–1910), a notorious antisemite and populist, was elected mayor of Vienna.
30. Violence against the Jews of Eastern Europe, and especially in the Russian Empire, had been on the upswing since the early 1880s. See Zipperstein, *Pogrom*.
31. The word *versanden* (swallowed up by dunes) is usually translated as "fizzle out" or "peter out." But Cohen is clearly playing on the root of the verb, *sand* (sand), and, to him, the outlandish and dangerous notion of attempting to build a new Jewish country in the deserts of the Near East instead of fulfilling Judaism's messianic potential in the Diaspora.
32. The wordplay in this and the subsequent paragraph is the same in German and English: *Arbeit* (work) is the battlefield of culture; the *Arbeiter* (worker) is the focus of the Sabbath command.
33. Probably a reference to Tacitus, *Histories*, book 5.
34. *Staatlichen Wissenschaft* (national project; lit. "state science")
35. Cohen cites this same passage in an essay two years later, "Liebe und Gerechtigkeit in den Begriffen Gott und Mensch," 98.
36. *Stämmen* (tribes). The same word Cohen uses for the Jewish tribe.
37. *Stämmen und Völkern* (individual tribes and the People). Cohen is making a contrast between smaller bands of people and the national unity of the *Volk*. Later he will use the term *Nation* (nation).
38. Cohen's reference is to the Habsburg Empire, a polyglot assemblage of nations politically dominated by the Austrians and Hungarians but also composed of Slavs, Jews, Italians, Ruthenians (Ukrainians), Romani, and others.
39. *Nation und Staat* (nation and state). One understanding would be Cohen's progression toward increasingly inclusionary unity, from tribes (*Stämmen*) to peoples (*Völkern*) to nation (*Nation*) to state (*Staat*).
40. *Volksthum* (nationality), a sense of "feeling like a people," the ending ("*-thum*") being something along the lines of the "-ness" in "Americanness."
41. That is, the *urfactor* is more than merely the matrix out of which other things are formed; it is something moral and worthy in and of itself. Recall Cohen's discussion of God as the transcendence *out of which* the world comes into being.
42. The Scythians is a generic name for various nomadic tribes who inhabited the Eurasian steppe in the biblical and Classical periods. They became famous for their tactics as horse-mounted warriors who would suddenly appear on the horizon—thus the allusion to "Scythian storms."
43. Reprinted in a collection of Steinthal's writings on Jewish theology: Steinthal, *Über Juden und Judentum*, 126–30.

44. In using the phrase Israel-Judah, Steinthal is perhaps emphasizing two different sides of Jewish culture: on the one hand, the unique monotheistic idea (Israel); on the other, the tribal element at the heart of Jewish communal cohesion (Judah). Or his usage may be historical. Authors in the nineteenth century extensively discussed the alternate usages of the terms Israelites and Jews. Christian theologians sought to find a break with Jesus, and therefore to create a before and after (Israelites before, Jews after). Jewish thinkers generally resisted such a stark contrast, insisting instead on continuity in Jewish history, and to stress this, they used the same word—very often Israelites—when discussing the biblical, Second Temple, and Rabbinic periods.
45. In Classical Greek thought the world is eternal, without beginning or end (Aristotle) or in an endless cycle of birth, death, and rebirth (the Stoics). As such, the gods of the Greek pantheon exist within this eternal universe, rather than (as the Hebrew Bible suggests of God) as creators outside of it.
46. *Geist,* meaning in German both spirit and intellect, as in *Geisteswissenschaften* (humanities).
47. The author of this Mishnah is referring to the ten instances of the word *vayomer* ("and he said") used in relation to God in Genesis 1.
48. In suggesting that the world *could* have been made with only a single utterance but was done with ten so as to punish the wicked and reward the righteous, the author of PA 5:1 has interpreted the biblical text well beyond any plain-text reading. Steinthal suggests that imputing such motives to God is a heretical act if the Bible is straitjacketed by adherence to literal interpretation. But, Steinthal says, because Judaism does not preach the dogma of literalism, the author of the Mishnah is well within the bounds of normative Rabbinical theological interpretation.
49. Here Steinthal is referring to the anonymous author of PA 5:1.
50. Ahriman, the destructive spirit in Zoroastrianism's dualist theology, stands in opposition to Ahura Mazda (Wise Lord), the supreme creator god.
51. This is not exactly true. After Creation on the second day there is likewise no mention of God seeing that it was good.
52. It has not escaped my attention that even in Amos (4:13), a generation older than Hosea, God is praised as the one who forms the (mighty) mountains and is Creator of the (ever-moving) wind, the one who tells humans what they themselves are thinking, who makes light out of darkness, and who treads upon the heights of the earth, the Eternal One, God of Hosts is his name. [Steinthal's Note; translation adapts Amos 4:13 to follow Steinthal.]
53. Parentheticals are Steinthal's elucidation.

54. Leo Baeck's *The Essence of Judaism* was originally published in German as *Das Wesen des Judentum* (1905). The excerpt included here, from the version translated by Victor Grubenwieser and Leonard Pearl in 1936, has been edited for clarity.
55. Schechter, *Some Aspects of Rabbinic Theology*, 11–17.
56. Carlyle, *Characteristics*.
57. See *Gen. Rab.* 1:1 [1:4] about the pre-mundane existence of the *name* of the Messiah. Cf. *Gen. Rab.* 2:4, about the soul of the Messiah. In *Gen. Rab.* 8:4, mention is made of the souls of the righteous with whom God took counsel when he was going to create the world. See also PDRE 3, text and commentary. Cf. Also Joel, *Blicke in die Religionsgeschichte*, vol. 2, p. 181 and *Seder Eliahu Rabba und Seder Eliahu zuta (Tanna d'be Eliahu)*, ed. Friedmann (Vienna, 1900), 160. See also Ginzberg, "Die Haggada bei den Kirchenvätern," 541n1. [Schechter's note.]

    Perhaps Schechter is interpreting "ministering angels" (*malakhei hasharet*) as "souls of the righteous."
58. *Shira* refers to the Song of Moses (Exod. 15). For a translation and elucidation of the *Shirta* (Exod. 15) section of MdRI, see Goldin, *Song at the Sea*.
59. Followers of the German philosopher Georg Wilhelm Friedrich Hegel (1770–1831), whose ideas on the teleological flow of history and the supremacy of Protestant Christianity as the endpoint of religious development were broadly influential, and, as Schechter notes, utilized by right wing and conservative thinkers to advance an ideology of Protestant German intellectual, cultural, and moral hegemony.
60. Schechter means here the *tannaim*, the Mishnaic-era rabbis, the originators not only of the Mishnah and its laws but also of the deeply unsystematic hermeneutic of exegetical midrash.
61. See Taylor, *Sayings of the Jewish Fathers*, Appendix [Additional Notes, p.] 152. I add here Ms. Oxford Heb., c. 17. Parma, 802, 975. See *Machzor Vitri*, pp. 514, 515. Cf. Müller, ed., *Die Responsen des R. Meschullam*, p. 11, note 19. [Schechter's note.]
62. From Schechter's introduction to *Studies in Judaism*, xviii.
63. Wiener, "Vom Sein und Sinn Gottes."
64. "Method of negative attributes," also called apophatic or negative theology, was Maimonides' preferred method for obtaining knowledge of God, as developed in his *Guide*, part 1, chapters 51–60. Cf. David Kaufmann (here in chap. 4).
65. Neoplatonism, a modern term for the youngest school of ancient Platonism, emerging around the middle of third-century Rome, dominated the entire philosophical thought of the period, suppressing all other directions of ancient philosophy.

66. "Plotinus' system" refers to the three basic principles of his philosophical system: the One (the simple and absolute transcendent source of all being, sometimes referred to as "the Good"), the Intellect (the source of what is intelligible or conceivable), and the Soul (the principle of desire for that which is external to the self).
67. The *ontological proof* consists of arguments for God's existence based solely on reasoning, without recourse to experience, observation, or historical events. Famously, German philosopher Immanuel Kant (1724–1804) argued against the validity of ontological proofs on the grounds that existence itself stands in no logical connection to understanding.
68. Here, the priests and elders are invited to the foot of Mount Sinai, but Moses ascends alone.
69. The Tabernacle in the Wilderness, and subsequently the Temple in Jerusalem, were composed of spaces of increasing holiness. At the very center stood the throne room of God, which could only be entered by the High Priest one day each year (on Yom Kippur).
70. Wiener here gestures at the study of the relationship of biblical injunction and related cult practices in the ancient Near East, a field that has revealed many new insights into the meaning of biblical practice, separate from traditional Rabbinic interpretation, since the mid-nineteenth century.
71. The "doctrine of attributes" in general refers to the logical construction that the concept of divinity demands omnipotence, omniscience, and omnibenevolence. Here, however, Wiener refers to the specific form of this doctrine as found in Maimonides' *Guide*: There are five groups of possible attributes that we can think of. Maimonides denies that the first four groups can be applied to God because any addition, even that of a nonmaterial attribute, would harm the concept of God's oneness and uniqueness. Only the fifth group, the so-called attributes of action, can be said to be possessed by God, since these have no influence on His essence (*Guide*, part 1, chapter 54).
72. Exodus 3:2 is usually translated as two sentences: "An angel of the LORD appeared to him in a blazing fire out of a bush. He gazed, and there was a bush all aflame, yet the bush was not consumed." Wiener is suggesting that, while the text tells us that there is an angel of God who is separate from the flames, Moses only sees the flames, but does not realize it represents, or is the embodiment of, an angelic presence.
73. This is captured well in the English translation by Robert Alter, who, for example, in Ezek. 1:22–28, uses the word "like" (to mirror the Hebrew prefix k-) eleven times.

74. Cf. *Guide*, part 3, chapters 1–7, where Maimonides discusses the *Merkabah*. But Wiener is actually referring to the introduction to the *Guide*, where Maimonides indeed equates the *Merkabah* with metaphysics. For the Abarbanel critique to which Wiener refers, see Maimonides, *Moreh Nevuchim*, 71.
75. See Kreisel, "From Esotericism to Science." The "others" whose example Abarbanel followed are translator and philosopher Samuel Ibn Tibbon (1165–1232) and rationalist philosopher and leading halakhic authority among Spanish Jewry Hasdai Crescas (1340–1410/11), both medieval commentators on Maimonides' *Guide*.

6. Judaism and the Origin of Ethics

1. Güdemann, *Das Judentum in seinen Grundzügen*, 67–72.
2. *Lust* (desire).
3. *Last* (burden).
4. Ewald, *Die Dichter*, 475; Ewald, *Commentary*, 268.
5. E.g., verse 1, *die im geseze Jahve's gehn* [*sic*] ("who go in the law [*torat*] of Jahvé"): Ewald, *Die Dichter*, 476; Ewald, *Commentary*, div. 1, vol. 2, 269. Verse 34, *Fertig mich mach' zu wahren dein gesez* [*sic*] ("Fit me to keep Thy law [*toratekha*])": *Die Dichter*, 478; *Commentary*, 271. This is not actually universally true; e.g., verse 18, *des wunders viel aus deiner lehre* ("much wonder from Thy doctrine [*toratekha*]"): *Die Dichter*, 477; *Commentary*, 270; verse 29, *mit deiner lehre begnad'ge mich* [*sic*] ("with Thy teaching [*toratekha*] be gracious to me"): *Die Dichter*, 478; *Commentary*, 271. Indeed, looking across all of Psalm 119, it appears that Ewald adapted his translation of Torah based upon his understanding of the particular verse and its context.
6. Ewald translates the verse as [*sic*] *sondern lust an Jahve's lehre safs, über sein lehre nachsinnt tag und nacht* [*sic*]: ("but has pleasure in Jahve's doctrine, on His doctrine meditates day and night"): *Die Dichter*, 219; *Commentary*, 318.
7. A polemical passage that is not borne out even in Jewish Bible translations; e.g., NJPS renders the famous passage as "There shall be one law [*torah*] for the citizen and for the stranger who dwells among you" (Exod. 12:49). See also: "The same rule [*torah*] applies to both" (Lev. 7:7); "Such are the rituals [*torah*] of the burnt offering" (Lev. 7:37); "Such is the ritual for every eruptive affection" (Lev. 14:54); "and the priest shall carry out this ritual [*torah*] with her" (Num. 5:30); "the same ritual [*torah*] and the same rule shall apply to you and to the stranger" (Num. 15:16).
8. By "terms of art" Güdemann means something artificial or nonnatural—terms made up for human use.

9. A reference to the prophet whom scholars call Second Isaiah or Deutero-Isaiah. Second Isaiah is the author of Isaiah 40–66, who, though born in Babylon, lived to see the restoration of Israel from exile and the return to Jerusalem. First Isaiah, the author of chapters 1–39, lived in Judea before the destruction of the First Temple and foretold—but never witnessed—its destruction.
10. Kellermann, *Liberales Judentum*, 4–7.
11. *Beweglich* (flexibility).
12. *Indelebilis* is a term from the Christian teaching of the Sacraments meaning that a person who has received a sacrament is indelibly marked by it, like a coin.
13. Lazarus's essay has been translated in Stoetzler, *State, the Nation, and the Jews.*
14. Quoted in Stoetzler, *State, the Nation, and the Jews*, 1.
15. Lazarus, "What Does National Mean?," 330.
16. Lazarus, "What Does National Mean?," 342.
17. Proofs are superfluous; however, see b. *Megillah* 14a. [Lazarus's note.]

    Indeed, all these were important and powerful legal institutions in Jewish antiquity.
18. Cf. Plato's famous dilemma of *Euthyphro* ("Consider this: Is the pious being loved by the gods because it is pious, or is it pious because it is being loved by the gods?" [*Euthyphro*, 10a, p. 9]), which poses the same problem.
19. Almost all modern Jewish theologians (before and after Lazarus) invoke this verse for this purpose.
20. There is absolutely no doubt in my mind that what is meant is to express both "as I am" and also "because I am." Strictly, the meaning "as I am" is an impossibility; man can approach the divine pattern, but he can never be equal to it. The rationale underlying the moral, however, can and should be the same for man as for God. As God can have no reason for morality but the nature of the moral, so there shall be no other for man. [Lazarus's note.]

    Cf. b. *Shabbat* 133b. The reference is to Exod. 34:6.
21. *Gottähnlich* (shall become like God), i.e., not fully identical.
22. This idea might be traced to the *Guide*, part 1, chapter 54, where Maimonides seems to interpret the traditional Thirteen Attributes of God (from Exod. 34:6–7) as the only knowable attributes of the deity, the "attributes of action." Thus, Maimonides defines our knowledge of God as ethical knowledge. Interestingly however, Lazarus made a point of not referring to the "Aristotelian" *Guide* in his book, much to the frustration of Hermann Cohen in his review of Lazarus's *Ethik* (Cohen, "Das Problem der jüdischen Sittenlehre"). Eventually, Cohen himself expounded the option of an ethical reading of Maimonides on this

subject in his extensive 1908 essay *Charakteristik der Ethik Maimunis* (translated as *Ethics of Maimonides*).

23. On principle, metaphysics and mystical speculation were confined to the most intimate circles (b. *Chagigah* 11b [a reference to m. *Chagigah* 2:1 and its Gemara], and elsewhere). [Lazarus's note].
24. Proverbs, especially chapters 1 and 8, seems to be an attempt in this direction made in the time of Hezekiah. The Prophets do not continue the train of thought, and the only other passages that can possibly be made to bear upon it are the chapters in Job indicating the peripetia. [Lazarus's note].
25. It seems, however, that in Exodus 33–34 the Thirteen Attributes are not identical with the *glory*, but with the "ways of God," because seeing God's glory is denied to Moses there, while to be able to understand God's *ways* would also fit the ethical nature of the attributes mentioned, as modes of ethical behavior. This is at least how Maimonides and Hermann Cohen read the biblical passage.
26. *Critique of Practical Reason* (1788), the title of Kant's second major work, which deals with rational ethics. For Kant, practical reason (as opposed to "pure reason") would not ask "what am I able to know," but "what shall I do"—although the answer to this question is also given by practical reason without the support of experience. Practical reason is a priori the self-legislation of the will. For Kant, practical reason, although it cannot contradict pure reason, still has primacy over theoretical thought.
27. This is of course a more complex matter: Judaism considers its law to be God's will—that is, coming from an outside ("heteronomous") source—which, for Kant, should (and did) disqualify it as a part or product of practical human reason. Lazarus hints in several other places in this text at a solution: to define God as Himself bound by reason; indeed, to define God as the autonomous force compelling the human will.
28. This seems to move away from Kant, however. For Kant, moral conviction is never free but indeed law bound, the product of (self-)legislation (autonomy).
29. Lit. "and accepted the yoke of heaven, who is more loved?"—"The *moral* order" is Lazarus's interpretation of the midrash. This seems to contradict his earlier identification of God's Revelation with practical reason, but probably the emphasis is put here on the influence of the *outer signs* accompanying the event at Mt. Sinai and not the content of the revealed law. In b. *Kiddushin* 31a we find the opposite: "Higher stands him who follows the law because it is law, than him who follows it although he is not commanded."—This would be the more Kantian rule.
30. This is an interesting point, because the philosophy of ethics often discussed the primacy of reason or, alternatively, of the will in moral decisions.

31. Although the difference between the two concepts in Kant is not about human exertion but about rational self-legislation and the acceptance of influences of experience. To the contrary, morality is not inherent in human beings but must be learned.
32. Jacob, "Das Judenthum und die Ergebnisse der Assyriologie."
33. *Buchstäblichkeit* (literalism), referring to Maimonides' general tendency to interpret the Torah in a nonliteral, allegorical sense in cases where the literal meaning contradicts his philosophical convictions—most importantly in cases of clear anthropomorphisms. See Maimonides, "Thirteen Principles of Jewish Faith," no. 8, found in his commentary to m. *Sanhedrin* 10:1, translated as *Maimonides' Commentary on the Mishnah*, 151–57.
34. *Nevela*, in biblical Hebrew, a corpse—that which has died a natural death (Deut. 14:21). (It often means "villainy" in modern Hebrew.)
35. I.e., "moral ignorance" is the immoral opposite of judgment rooted in reason. In ethical theory, the source of the moral faculty in an old and complex question, with most philosophers taking a middle position between strict voluntarism and extreme rationalism.
36. *Ketzerkataloge* (list of heretics), referring to the "list of heresies" regularly produced by the Catholic church.
37. "Greek" is meant here in the broadest sense, i.e., Hellenistic philosophical as opposed to biblical morality.
38. The idea of divine inspiration of the Bible was a common doctrine of Christian theology for centuries, developed with the aim to preserve biblical doctrine as the *Word of God* but reject the idea that God dictated Scripture word-for-word. (Jacob explicitly rejected this Christian notion.)
39. Egyptian: Likely meaning Egyptian Gnostic ideas, a general term for any number of ancient philosophical systems originating in the early centuries CE, generally cultivating notions of an individualized spirituality (*gnosis*), and often espousing a certain dualism: differentiating the goodness and metaphysical ineffability of God from the flawed and fallen state of material existence. Theologoumena: Theological statements without direct revelatory or scriptural authority.
40. *Gesinnung* (ethos; also "attitude" or "cast of mind").
41. From its beginnings in the early nineteenth century, *Wissenschaft des Judentums* was strongly associated with the Reform movement. Later in the century, Jewish Orthodoxy attempted to join the project, including establishing a modern rabbinical seminary in Berlin. The reference here is probably to the founding of the Jüdisch-literarische Gesellschaft (Jewish literary society) in 1902 (the year of Jacob's writing), an Orthodox society for the advancement of the scientific study of Judaism. In Jacob's field of biblical scholarship, however, modern

Orthodox authors largely remain bound by traditional dogmatic assumptions. See, e.g., Berman, *Ani Maamin.*

42. *Die Wissenschaft von Gott* (scientific approach to God; lit. the science of God).
43. This issue dates to a dispute within Jewish philosophical circles of the Middle Ages: Does the divine authority of the Torah originate from the historical event of its delivery (i.e., the Revelation at Sinai) or from its content (i.e., the words and letters of the text itself)? Whereas for medieval poet and philosopher Judah Halevi (1075–1141), the historical act of bearing witness by hundreds of thousands of Israelites at Mount Sinai grounded the truth of Torah, for Maimonides, the Torah's validity must exclusively be measured against the law's content and its effectiveness to facilitate the constant and infinite approaching of divine holiness (cf. *Guide, part* 2, chapter 40). In this instance Jacob sides with Maimonides.

7. Theological Distinctiveness

1. K. Kohler, *Jewish Theology*, 1–28.
2. K. Kohler, *Grundriss einer systematischen Theologie des Judentums.*
3. "Positive" in this usage means "defined" or "identified," as in a religion with a clear set of historical events and communal norms (with no valuation implied).
4. The Latin *symbolum* is commonly translated as "creed," referring to a doctrinal statement of belief, as in *Symbolum Nicaenum* (Nicene Creed) and *Symbolum Apostolorum* (Apostles' Creed).
5. A reference to the idea within biblical scholarship that the priestly writers and redactors of Pentateuch adapted the Creation, Flood, and Tower of Babel stories from preexisting Near Eastern myths.
6. Referring either to Shabbethai Sheftel Horowitz (sixteenth–seventeenth c., called "the Elder"), mystic, author of *Nishmat Shabetai haLevi* (1612), and brother of the rabbi and mystic Isaiah Horowitz (ca. 1555–1630); or to Shabbethai Horowitz (ca. 1590–1660a, called "the Younger"), son of Isaiah Horowitz and editor of his father's famous work *Shnei Luchot HaBerit (Shelah).*
7. Guttmann, "Die Normierung des Glaubenshinhalts im Judentum" (English translation, "Establishing Norms for Jewish Belief").
8. *Maimonides' Commentary on the Mishnah*, 151–57.
9. The reference is to medieval Jewish philosophers Hasdai Crescas (ca. 1340–1410/11) and Joseph Albo (ca. 1380–1444). Critical discussion of Maimonides' list of the Thirteen Articles (Attributes) of Jewish Faith continues to this day. While some of his immediate successors reduced the list to seven (Crescas), or even to three (Albo), there is also a widespread opinion that Judaism does

not possess dogma at all, or, alternatively, that Jewish belief must focus on all of the 613 biblical commandments, not accepting any hierarchy.

10. The passage in the Talmud stating that no prophet is authorized to add anything new to the Torah (b. *Megillah* 2b) refers directly only to the halakhic sphere; however, it clearly shows that the later prophets basically were subordinate to the Mosaic revelation upon which the Jewish religion is based. [Guttmann's note].
11. That is, the loss of biblical authority for its own sake.
12. This change had already begun during the 1840s in Germany as a result of the reformation of Jewish liturgy. The need for a new approach to messianism in prayer forced the nascent Reform movement to rethink the messianic concept of Judaism. However, the movement was more than willing to retain messianism in principle, since it guaranteed a religious orientation toward the future and a turning away from ever repeating the past.
13. This reading of messianism answered a pressing need of Jewish belief in the modern era: Why adhere to (religious) Judaism other than for the sake of tradition and piety?
14. This 1927 assessment by Guttmann is arguably challenged today by the rise of Jewish religious nationalism in its various forms (e.g., kabbalistic neomysticism, the Israeli settler movement).
15. Compare here Leo Baeck's important work in Jewish theology, *The Essence of Judaism* (see chapter 5), a first edition of which was first published in 1905 as a reply to the Christian critique of Judaism and republished in 1922 as a fully developed philosophy of the Jewish religion.
16. It is difficult to understand what is meant by this consensus. While indeed the twentieth-century theological works by Hermann Cohen and Leo Baeck come to similar conclusions in their search for Judaism's essence, the time after 1918 also saw the rise of Jewish existentialism—especially in the thought of Martin Buber and Franz Rosenzweig—where essence-thinking was replaced by the search for Jewish "authenticity," something both thinkers found first and foremost in Eastern European Jewish culture. These thinkers root authenticity, however, in a return to a collective identity, different from Guttmann's thesis of individual, subjective belief.
17. Altmann, *Meaning of Jewish Existence*, 40–56.
18. A reference to Maybaum, "Das Konsistorium des Israel Jacobsohn."
19. A theological statement of individual opinion or assertion lacking doctrinal authority or the support of Revelation.
20. Martin Buber has brought out well the meaningful, religiously phenomenological unique form of this theocracy. Cf. Buber, *Königtum Gottes*, 60 [*Kingship of God*, 93]. [Altmann's note].

21. In the coming section, Altmann adds a dash inside "theo-logy" (and its derivations), seemingly to highlight the fact that he's describing a particular kind of study (*logy*) of God (*theo*).
22. The idea of a universal morality based on the seven Noahide laws. See b. *Sanhedrin* 56a–b; cf. t. *Avoda Zarah* 9:4.
23. Schiller, *Sämtliche Werke,* "Speech," in *Tabulae Votivae,* 313.
24. Reference to Otto's influential 1917 work *Das Heilige* (*Idea of the Holy*).

8. Theological Existentialism

1. Rosenzweig, *Star of Redemption,* 9.
2. Buber, *On Judaism,* 15.
3. Bergman, *Hagut,* 12.
4. Rosenzweig, *Star of Redemption,* 317.
5. Martin Buber, "Zu einer neuen Verdeutschung der Schrift," published as a supplement to the first volume of his and Rosenzweig's translation, *Die fünf Bücher der Weisung,* 3–44.
6. Buber, *On Judaism,* 11–21. This excerpt is presented in conformity with fair use protocol.
7. The original speech read in translation: "which is fitted as a necessary link into the great chain in its predestined place."
8. Rosenzweig, *Der Stern der Erlösung,* 194–209. (Taken from: Part II, Book II: "Revelation, or the Ever Renewed Birth of the Soul.")
9. *Wort und Ant-wort* (word and answer).
10. *Gehorsames Hören* (obedient listening).
11. *Erklärung-Liebeserklärung* (explanation-declaration of love).
12. "The Eternal" here is a translation of "the LORD," itself a translation of the tetragrammaton, the ineffable name. Cf. Rosenzweig's essay "Der Ewige" (The eternal) in Buber and Rosenzweig, *Die Schrift und ihre Verdeutschung,* discussing this translation of the four-letter divine name, which Moses Mendelssohn first introduced in the 1770s.
13. See Heinrich Graetz's explanation of prophecy in the first volume of his *History of the Jews* for the same idea.
14. *Alles einmal Bekannte ist schon ein Bekanntes* (for everything once confessed is already known).
15. *Die Seele in die Seligkeit* (the soul into the bliss)
16. *Zugrunde gehen würde, wirklich zugrunde, zugrunde in "Gründen"* (Actually aground, aground in 'grounds' [reasons]').
17. *La ilaha illa llah* (there is no God but God).

18. Contra Rosenzweig, it could also be meant in the sense of the Jewish liturgical declaration "The LORD is God" (*YHVH hu ha-Elohim*), found prominently in the Yom Kippur liturgy.
19. *Im Offenbaren* (in the revealed).
20. Likely a reference to Isa. 63:19 (64:1 in Christian Bibles)—an important verse for Christian theology.
21. Perhaps a reference to Job 14:13.
22. Cf. the prayer in Matt. 6:9–13.
23. *Voraussage* (prediction).
24. *Aussage, Voraussage* (proposition, prediction).
25. Here Rosenzweig uses the same word (*verfaßte*), meaning both "constituted" and "composed."
26. *Name is nicht [. . .] Schall und Rauch* (name is not sound and smoke)—a reference to Goethe's drama *Faust* (part 1, scene: Marthen's Garden). The same rejection of the meaninglessness of the divine name is found in Hermann Cohen's posthumous *Religion der Vernunft* (*Religion of reason out of the sources of Judaism*), from which Rosenzweig probably adopted it. *Namen sind Schall und Rauch* has since become a popular proverb in German.

Bibliography

Albo, Joseph. *Buch Ikkarim: Grund- und Glaubenslehren der Mosaischen Religion*. Translated by Wolf Schlesinger and Ludwig Schlesinger. Frankfurt: n.p., 1844.

———. *Sefer Ha-'ikkarim*. Vol. 1. Translated by Isaac Husik. Philadelphia: Jewish Publication Society, 1929.

Alter, Robert. *The Hebrew Bible: A Translation with Commentary*. New York: Norton, 2019.

Altmann, Alexander. *The Meaning of Jewish Existence: Theological Essays 1930–1939*. Edited by Alfred L. Ivry. Hanover MA: Brandeis University Press, 1991.

Baeck, Leo. *Das Wesen des Judentums*. Berlin: Rathausen & Lamm, 1905.

———. *The Essence of Judaism*. Translated by Irving Howe, based on Victor Grubenwieser and Leonard Pearl. New York: Schocken, 1948.

Beer, Bernhard. "Die neuere jüdische Literatur und ihre Bedeutung." *Monatsschrift für Geschichte und Wissenschaft des Judentums* 3, no. 7 (1854): 249–68.

Bergman, Samuel Hugo. *Hagut: Teshurah li-Shemu'el Hugo Bergman bi-melot lo shishim shanah*. Jerusalem: Be-hotsa'at ha-Ḥevrah ha-filosofit, 1944.

Berman, Joshua. *Ani Maamin: Biblical Criticism, Historical Truth, and the Thirteen Principles of Faith*. Jerusalem: Maggid, 2020.

Breuer, Mordechai. Review of *Tradition in an Age of Reform: The Religious Philosophy of Samson Raphael Hirsch*, by Noah H. Rosenbloom. *Tradition* 16, no. 4 (Summer 1977): 140–49.

Buber, Martin. *Drei Reden über das Judentum*. Frankfurt: Rütten & Loening, 1911.

———. *The Kingship of God*. Translated by Richard Scheimann. New York: Harper & Row, 1967.

———. *Königtum Gottes*. Berlin: Schocken, 1932.

———. *On Judaism*. Edited by Nahum N. Glatzer. Translated by Eva Jospe. New York: Schocken, 1995.

Buber, Martin, and Franz Rosenzweig. *Die fünf Bücher der Weisung*. Cologne: Hegner, 1954.

———. *Die Schrift und ihre Verdeutschung*. Berlin: Schocken, 1936.
Carlyle, Thomas. *Characteristics*. Edinburgh: Constable, 1831.
Cicero, Marcus Tullius. *De natura deorum: Academics*. Translated by Harris Rackam. Loeb Classical Library 268. Cambridge MA: Harvard University Press, 1951.
———. *On the Republic and On the Laws*. Translated by Davit Fott. Ithaca NY: Cornell University Press, 2014.
Cohen, Hermann. "Das Judentum als Weltanschauung." In Dieter Adelmann, *"Reinige dein Denken": Über den jüdischen Hintergrund der Philosophie von Hermann Cohen*, edited by Görge K. Hasselhoff, 322–23. Würzburg, Ger.: Königshausen & Neumann, 2010. Originally published in *Dr. Bloch's Oesterreichische Wochenschrift* 12–13 (1898): 221–24, 241–43.
———. "Das Problem der jüdischen Sittenlehre: Eine Kritik von Lazarus' Ethik des Judentums." *Monatschrift für Geschichte und Wissenschaft des Judentums* 43, parts 9–10 (1899), 385–400, 433–49. Reprinted in Cohen, *Jüdische Schriften*, vol. 3, 1–35.
———. *Ethics of Maimonides*. Translated by Almut Sh. Bruckstein. Madison: University of Wisconsin Press, 2003.
———. *Ethik des reinen Willens*. Berlin: Cassirer, 1904.
———. *Jüdische Schriften*. 3 vols. Edited by Bruno Strauss. Berlin: Schwetschke, 1924.
———. "Liebe und Gerechtigkeit in den Begriffen Gott und Mensch." *Jahrbuch für jüdische Geschichte und Literatur* 3 (1900): 75–132.
———. *Religion der Vernunft aus den Quellen des Judentums*. 2nd ed. Frankfurt: Kauffmann, 1929.
———. *Religion of Reason out of the Sources of Judaism*. Translated by Simon Kaplan. Atlanta GA: Scholars, 1995.
———. *Writings on Neo-Kantianism and Jewish Philosophy*. Edited by Samuel Moyn and Robert S. Schine. Waltham, MA: Brandeis University Press, 2021.
Cosgrove, Elliot J., ed. *Jewish Theology in Our Time: A New Generation Explores the Foundations and Future of Jewish Belief*. Woodstock VT: Jewish Lights, 2010.
Creizenach, Michael. "Grundlehren des israelitischen Glaubens." *Wissenschaftliche Zeitschrift für jüdische Theologie* 1, no. 1 (1835): 39–51.
Dernburg, Joseph. "Das Wesen des Judenthums nach seinen allgemeinsten Grundzügen." *Wissenschaftliche Zeitschrift für jüdische Theologie* 4, no. 1 (1839): 12–18.
Einhorn, David. "Die Vorzüge der jüdischen Gotteslehre (1852)." In *David Einhorn Memorial Volume*, edited by Kaufmann Kohler, 295–305. New York: Bloch, 1911.
Elbogen, Ismar. "Neuorientierung unserer Wissenschaft." *Monatsschrift für Geschichte und Wissenschaft des Judentums* 62, no. 2 (1918): 81–96.
Ewald, Heinrich. *Commentary on the Psalms*. Translated by Edwin Johnson. London: Williams and Northgate, 1880–81.

———. *Die Dichter des Alten Bundes: Die Psalmen und die Klaglieder.* Vol. 1, part 2. 3rd ed. Göttingen, Ger.: Vandenhoeck & Ruprecht, 1866.

Fontenelle, Bernard Le Bovier de. *Conversations on the Plurality of Worlds.* Translated by H. A. Hargreaves. Berkeley: University of California Press, 1990.

Formstecher, Salomon. *Die Religion des Geistes: Eine wissenschaftliche Darstellung des Judenthums nach seinem Charakter, Entwicklungsgange und Berufe in der Menschheit.* Frankfurt: Hermann, 1841.

Frankel, Zecharias. "Rede bei der am 28. Januar 1855 stattgehabten Gedächtnißfeier am jüdisch-theologischen Seminar zu Breslau." *Monatsschrift für Geschichte und Wissenschaft des Judentums* 4, no. 2 (1855): 45–55.

Friedmann, Meir, ed. *Seder Eliahu rabba und Seder Eliahu zuta (Tanna d'be Eliahu).* Vienna: Israel-theol. Lehranstalt, 1900.

Geiger, Abraham. "Das Verhältniß des natürlichen Schriftsinnes zur thalmudischen Schriftdeutung." *Wissenschaftliche Zeitschrift für jüdische Theologie* 5, nos. 1–2 (1844): 53–81, 234–59.

Gersonides (Levi Ben Gershom). *The Wars of the Lord.* 3 vols. Translated by Seymour Feldman. Philadelphia: Jewish Publication Society, 1999.

Ginzberg, Louis. "Die Haggada bei den Kirchenvätern und in der apokryphischen Litteratur." *Monatsschrift für Geschichte und Wissenschaft des Judentums* 42, no. 12 (1898): 537–50.

Goethe, Johann Wolfgang von. *Faust: Eine Tragödie.* Tübingen, Ger.: Cotta, 1808.

Goldin, Judah. *The Song at the Sea: Being a Commentary on a Commentary in Two Parts.* New Haven CT: Yale University Press, 1971.

[Graetz, Heinrich]. *Briefwechsel einer englischen Dame über Judenthum und Semitismus.* Stuttgart, Ger.: Levy & Müller, 1883.

Graetz, Heinrich. *History of the Jews.* Philadelphia: Jewish Publication Society, 1891–98.

Greenberg, Gershon. *Modern Jewish Thinkers: From Mendelssohn to Rosenzweig.* Brighton: Academic Studies, 2011.

Güdemann, Moritz. *Das Judentum in seinen Grundzügen und nach seinen geschichtlichen Grundlagen.* Vienna: Löwit, 1902.

Guttmann, Julius. "Die Normierung des Glaubenshinhalts im Judentum." In *Wissenschaft des Judentums im deutschen Sprachbereich,* vol. 2, edited by Kurt Wilhelm, 753–68. Tübingen: Mohr, 1967. Originally published in *Monatsschrift für Geschichte und Wissenschaft des Judentums* 71 (1927): 241–55.

———. "Establishing Norms for Jewish Belief." Translated by Gertrude Hirschler. In *Studies in Jewish Thought: An Anthology of German Jewish Scholarship,* edited by Alfred Jospe, 54–69. Detroit MI: Wayne State University Press, 1981.

Halevi, Judah. *The Kuzari (Kitab al Khazari): An Argument for the Faith of Israel*. Translated by Hartwig Hirschfeld. New York: Schocken, 1964.

Hirsch, Samson Raphael (Ben Usiel). *Iggerot tzafun—Neunzehn Briefe über Judenthum*. Altona, Ger.: Hammerich, 1836.

Hirsch, Samuel. *Die Religionsphilosophie der Juden oder das Prinzip der judischen Religionsanschauung und sein Verhältniß zum Heidenthum, Christenthum und zur absoluten Philosophie*. Vol. 1. Leipzig: Hunger, 1842.

Holdheim, Samuel. *Das Ceremonialgesetz im Messiareich: Als Vorläufer einer größern Schrift über die religiöse Reform des Judenthums*. Berlin: Kürschner, 1845.

Ibn Ezra, Abraham. *Ibn Ezra's Commentary on the Pentateuch: Exodus (Shemot)*. Translated by H. Norman Strickman and Arthur M. Silver. New York: Menorah, 1996.

Ibn Pakuda, Bahya ben Joseph. *The Book of the Direction to the Duties of the Heart*. Translated by Menahem Mansoor. Portland, OR: Littman Library of Jewish Civilization, 2004.

Jacob, Benno. "Das Judenthum und die Ergebnisse der Assyriologie." *Allgemeine Zeitung des Judenthums* 66 (1902): 187–89.

Joel, Manuel. *Blicke in die Religionsgeschichte zu Anfang des zweiten christlichen Jahrhunderts: Volume 2: Der Conflict des Heidenthums mit dem Christenthume in seinen Folgen für das Judenthum*. Breslau, Ger.: Schottlaender, 1883.

———. *Zur Orientierung in der Cultusfrage*. Breslau: Schletter, 1869.

Kant, Immanuel. *Critique of Practical Reason*. Rev. ed. Translated by Mary J. Gregor. Cambridge: Cambridge University Press, 2015.

Kaufmann, David. *Achtzehn Predigten*. Edited by Ludwig Blau and Max Weisz. Budapest: Jabneh, 1931.

———. *Geschichte der Attributenlehre in der jüdischen Philosophie des Mittelalters von Saadja bis Maimûni*. Gotha, Ger.: Perthes, 1877.

Kellermann, Benzion. *Liberales Judentum*. Berlin: Poppelaur, 1907.

Kepnes, Steven, "Introduction." In *The Cambridge Companion to Jewish Theology*, edited by Steven Kepnes, 1–19. Cambridge: Cambridge University Press, 2020.

Kohler, George Y. *Reading Maimonides' Philosophy in 19th Century Germany: The Guide to Religious Reform*. Dordrecht, Neth.: Springer, 2011.

———. "'Scholasticism Is a Daughter of Judaism': The Discovery of Jewish Influence on Medieval Christian Thought." *Journal of the History of Ideas* 78, vol. 3 (July 2017): 319–40.

Kohler, Kaufmann. *Grundriss einer systematischen Theologie des Judentums auf geschichtlicher Grundlage*. Leipzig: Gustav Fock, 1910.

———. *Jewish Theology: Systematically and Historically Considered*. New York: Macmillan, 1918.

Kreisel, Howard. "From Esotericism to Science: The Account of the Chariot in Maimonidean Philosophy till the End of the Thirteenth Century." In *The Cultures of Maimonideanism: New Approaches to the History of Jewish Thought*, edited by James T. Robinson, 21–56. Leiden, Neth.: Brill, 2009.

Lazarus, Moritz. *Die Ethik des Judenthums*. Frankfurt: Kauffmann, 1898.

———. *The Ethics of Judaism*. Translated by Henrietta Szold. Philadelphia: Jewish Publication Society, 1900.

———. "What Does National Mean? A Lecture (1880)." In *The State, the Nation, and the Jews: Liberalism and the Antisemitism Dispute in Bismarck's Germany*, edited by Marcel Stoetzler, 317–59. Lincoln: University of Nebraska Press, 2009.

Luzzatto, Samuel David. *Lezioni di teologia dogmatica Israelitica*. Trieste, It.: Colombo Coen, 1863.

Maimonides, Moses. *The Guide of the Perplexed*. 2 vols. Translated by Shlomo Pines. Chicago: University of Chicago Press, 1963.

———. *Maimonides' Commentary on the Mishnah: Tractate Sanhedrin*. Translated by Fred Rosner. New York: Sepher-Hermon, 1981.

———. *Mishneh Torah: Hilchot Kri'at Shema Hilchot Tefilah*. Translated by Eliyahu Touger. New York: Moznaim, 1997.

———. *Mishneh Torah: Hilchot Melachim U'Milchamoteihem — The Laws of Kings and Their Wars*. Translated by Eliyahu Touger. New York: Moznaim, 1987.

———. *Mishneh Torah: Hilchotot Teshuvah — The Laws of Repentance*. Translated by Eliyahu Touger. New York: Moznaim, 1990.

———. *Mishneh Torah: Sefer Shoftim*. Translated by Eliyahu Touger. New York: Moznaim, 1998.

———. *Moreh Nevuchim im Peirush Efodi, Shem Tov, A[sher b. Abraham] Crescas, Abarbanel*. Part 3. Vilna: 1904.

Maybaum, Ignaz. "Das Konsistorium des Israel Jacobsohn: Anmerkungen zu einer Schrift aus dem Jahre 1932." *Jüdische Rundschau* 20, no. 4 (1932): 153.

Mekilta de Rabbi Ishmael. 3 vols. Translated by Jacob. Z. Lauterbach. Philadelphia: Jewish Publication Society, 1949.

Mendelssohn, Moses. *Jerusalem: Or on Religious Power and Judaism*. Translated by Allan Arkush. Waltham MA: Brandeis University Press, 1984.

Meyer, Michael A. *Response to Modernity: A History of the Reform Movement in Judaism*. Detroit MI: Wayne State University Press, 1995.

Müller, Joel, ed. *Die Responsen des R. Meschullam, Sohn des R. Kalonymus*. Berlin: Rosenthal, 1893.

Nadler, Steven. *A Book Forged in Hell: Spinoza's Scandalous Treatise and the Birth of the Secular Age*. Princeton NJ: Princeton University Press, 2011.

Nordau, Max. *Entartung*. 2 vols. Berlin: Duncker, 1892–93.

Novak, David. "What Is Jewish Theology?" In *The Cambridge Companion to Jewish*

Theology, edited by Steven Kepnes, 20–38. Cambridge: Cambridge University Press, 2020.

Otto, Rudolph. *The Idea of the Holy*. Translated by J. W. Harvey. New York: Oxford University Press, 1923.

Philippson, Ludwig. *Der Pentateuch—Die Israelitische Bibel, enthaltend den heiligen Urtext und die deutsche Übertragung von Ludwig Philippson*. Leipzig: Baumgärtner, 1844.

Plato. *Euthyphro*. Translated by G. M. A. Grube. In *Plato: Complete Works*, edited by John M. Cooper, 1–16. Indianapolis: Hackett, 1997.

Plutarch. *Lives*. Vol. 1 Translated by Bernadotte Perrin. Loeb Classical Library 46. Cambridge MA: Harvard University Press, 1914.

Proudhon, Pierre-Joseph. *What Is Property?* Edited and translated by Donald R. Kelley and Bonnie G. Smith. Cambridge: Cambridge University Press, 2002.

Ritter, Immanuel Heinrich. *Geschichte der jüdischen Reformation*. 3 vols. Berlin: Peiser, 1858–65.

Rosenzweig, Franz. *Der Stern der Erlösung*. Frankfurt: Kauffmann, 1921.

———. *The Star of Redemption*. Translated by Barbara E. Galli. Madison: University of Wisconsin Press, 2005.

Saadia Gaon. *The Book of Beliefs and Opinions*. Translated by Samuel Rosenblatt. New Haven CT: Yale University Press, 1948.

Saalschütz, Joseph Lewin. "Der Monotheismus in sittlicher Beziehung." *Wissenschaftliche Zeitschrift für jüdische Theologie* 5, nos. 1–3 (1844): 44–53, 152–74, 391–95.

Salomon, Gotthold. "Die dreizehn Grundlehren der Religion." In *Festpredigten für alle Feyertage des Herrn*, 159–78. Hamburg: Nestler, 1829.

Salvador, Joseph. *Jésus-Christ et sa doctrine histoire de la naissance, de l'église et de ses progrès pendant le premier siècle*. Paris: Guyot et Scribe, 1838.

Schechter, Solomon. *Some Aspects of Rabbinic Theology*. New York: Macmillan, 1909.

———. *Studies in Judaism*. Philadelphia: Jewish Publication Society, 1896.

Schiller, Friedrich. *Sämtliche Werke*. Vol. 1. Edited by Gerhard Fricke and Herbert Georg Göpfert. Munich: Hanser, 1962.

Schleiermacher, Friedrich. *On Religion: Speeches to Its Cultured Despisers*. Translated and edited by Richard Crouter. Cambridge: Cambridge University Press, 1996.

Shapiro, Marc B. *The Limits of Orthodox Theology: Maimonides' Thirteen Principles Reappraised*. Oxford: Littman Library of Jewish Civilization, 2011.

Sifre: A Tannaitic Commentary to the Book of Deuteronomy. Translated by Reuven Hammer. New Haven CT: Yale University Press, 1986.

Silver, Daniel Jeremy. *Maimonidean Criticism and the Maimonidean Controversy, 1180–1240*. Leiden, Neth.: Brill, 2012.

Stein, Leopold. *Die Schrift des Lebens: Inbegriff des gesammten Judenthums in Lehre,*

Gottesverehrung und Sittengesetz (Dogma, Cultus und Ethik). Strasbourg, Ger.: Schneider, 1877.

Steinthal, Heymann. "Die Idee der Weltschöpfung." *Jahrbuch für jüdische Geschichte und Literatur* 2 (1899): 39–44.

———. *Über Juden und Judentum*. Edited by Gustav Karpeles. Berlin: Poppelauer, 1906.

Stern, Sigismund. *Die Aufgabe des Judenthums und des Juden in der Gegenwart: Acht Vorlesungen, gehalten in Berlin, vom 15. Jan. bis 12. März 1845*. Berlin: Berliner Lesecabinets, 1845.

Stewart, Dugald. *Outlines of Moral Philosophy*. Edinburgh: Cadell, 1829.

Stoetzler, Marcel. *The State, the Nation, and the Jews: Liberalism and the Antisemitism Dispute in Bismarck's Germany*. Lincoln: University of Nebraska Press, 2009.

Strauss, David Friedrich. *Das Leben Jesu, kritisch bearbeitet*. Tübingen, Ger.: Osiander, 1835–36.

———. *Die christliche Glaubenslehre in ihrer geschichtlichen Entwicklung und im Kampfe mit der modernen Wissenschaft*. 2 vols. Tübingen, Ger.: Osiander, 1840.

Susman, Margarete. *Das Buch Hiob und das Schicksal des jüdischen Volkes*. Zurich: Steinberg, 1946.

Tacitus, Publius Cornelius. *Histories: Books IV–V; Annals: Books I–III*. Translated by Clifford H. Moore and John Jackson. Loeb Classical Library 249. Cambridge MA: Harvard University Press, 1998.

Taylor, Charles. *Sayings of the Jewish Fathers Comprising Pirqe Aboth in Hebrew and English with Notes and Excursuses*. Cambridge: Cambridge University Press, 1897.

Virey, Julien-Joseph. *Histoire des moeurs et de l'instinct des animaux, avec les distributions méthodiques et naturelles de toutes leurs classes*. Vol. 1, *Animaux vertébrés*. Paris: Deterville, 1822.

Weisz, M. *Machsor Vitry*. Budapest: Neumayer Ede Könyvnyomdája, 1895.

Wiener, Max. "Vom Sein und Sinn Gottes." *Monatsschrift für Geschichte und Wissenschaft des Judentums* 81 (1937): 3–12.

Zipperstein, Steven J. *Pogrom: Kishinev and the Tilt of History*. New York: Liveright, 2018.

Contributors

SHIRA BILLET is assistant professor of Jewish thought and ethics at the Jewish Theological Seminary of America. She holds a PhD in religion from Princeton University and is completing a monograph on the German Jewish philosopher Hermann Cohen.

BRIAN BRITT is professor of religion and cultural theory at Virginia Polytechnic Institute and State University. His books include *Religion Around Walter Benjamin* (Penn State University Press, 2022); *Postsecular Benjamin: Agency and Tradition* (Northwestern University Press, 2016); and *Biblical Curses and the Displacement of Tradition* (Sheffield Phoenix, 2011).

STEVE BRITT works as a translator in Europe, where his clients have included the Vatican and several research institutions. He also has scholarly expertise in applied hermeneutics.

EDITH EHRLICH (d. 2015) received her doctorate from Yale University and was the translator of works by Karl Jaspers and Alexander Altmann, among others.

LEONARD H. EHRLICH (d. 2011) was a professor of philosophy and Judaic studies at the University of Massachusetts, Amherst, and the author of *Karl Jaspers: Philosophy as Faith* (University of Massachusetts Press, 1975).

EMANUEL FIANO is associate professor of Syriac studies at Fordham University. He is the author of *Three Powers in Heaven: The Emergence of Theology and the Parting of the Ways* (Yale University Press, 2023).

PAUL FRANKS is the Robert F. and Patricia Ross Weis Professor of Philosophy and Judaic Studies at Yale University. He is the translator and commentator, along with Michael L. Morgan, of *Franz Rosenzweig: Philosophical and Theological Writings* (Hackett, 2000), and the author of *All or Nothing: Systematicity, Transcendental Arguments, and Skepticism in German Idealism* (Harvard University Press, 2005). He is working on a new account of the vital role of Jewish thought, including kabbalah, within European philosophy.

GERSHON GREENBERG is visiting professor in the field of religious thought through the Holocaust at Hebrew University in Jerusalem and at Bar Ilan University. He is professor of philosophy and religion at American University in Washington DC, where he created and directed the Jewish studies program. He recently translated and introduced Eliezer Schweid's *Siddur Hatefillah: The Jewish Prayer Book: Philosophy, Poetry, and Mystery* (Academic Studies, 2022).

VICTOR GRUBENWIESER (d. 20th century) was the translator of Leo Baeck's *The Essence of Judaism*, among other works.

GERTRUDE HIRSCHLER (d. 1994) was a translator, editor, and lecturer. She was the assistant editor for the *Encyclopedia of Zionism and Israel* and the coauthor (with Lester S. Eckman) of *Menahem Begin: From Freedom Fighter to Statesman* (1979).

EVA JOSPE (d. 2011) was the translator of works by Moses Mendelssohn, Hermann Cohen, Franz Rosenzweig, and Martin Buber, and taught modern Jewish thought at Georgetown University and George Washington University.

SAMUEL J. KESSLER is Åke and Kristina Bonnier Endowed Chair in Jewish Studies and assistant professor of religion at Gustavus Adolphus College. He is the author of *The Formation of a Modern Rabbi: The Life and Times of the Viennese Scholar and Preacher Adolf Jellinek* (Brown Judaic Studies, 2022).

GEORGE Y. KOHLER is associate professor of Jewish philosophy and director of the Joseph Carlebach Institute at Bar Ilan University. He is the author of *Kabbalah Research in the Wissenschaft des Judentums (1820–1880): The Foundation of an Academic Discipline* (De Gruyter, 2019) and *Reading Maimonides' Philosophy in 19th Century Germany: The Guide to Religious Reform* (Springer, 2012).

NOA SOPHIE KOHLER holds a PhD in Jewish history from Ben-Gurion University of the Negev and is research fellow at the Jacques Loeb Centre for the History and Philosophy of the Life Sciences, Ben-Gurion University of the Negev.

MICHAEL A. MEYER is the Adolph S. Ochs Professor of Jewish History emeritus at Hebrew Union College–Jewish Institute of Religion in Cincinnati. His most recent book is *Rabbi Leo Baeck: Living a Religious Imperative in Troubled Times* (University of Pennsylvania Press, 2021).

GARRETT E. PAUL is professor of religion emeritus at Gustavus Adolphus College, where he served as department chair for fifteen years. His research is presently focused on German theology and politics in the period from 1914 to 1922, with particular emphasis on Ernst Troeltsch's philosophy of history.

LEONARD PEARL (d. 20th century) was the translator of Leo Baeck's *The Essence of Judaism*, among other works.

BENJAMIN POLLOCK is Sol Rosenbloom Associate Professor of Jewish Philosophy in the department of Jewish thought at Hebrew University in Jerusalem, where he also serves as director of the Franz Rosenzweig Minerva Research Center. He is the author of *Franz Rosenzweig and the Systematic Task of Philosophy* (Cambridge University Press, 2009) and *Franz Rosenzweig's Conversions: World Denial and World Redemption* (Indiana University Press, 2014).

DANA RUBINSTEIN is a doctoral student in the department of Jewish thought at Hebrew University in Jerusalem.

MAREN SCHEURER is a researcher and lecturer in the department for comparative literature at Goethe University–Frankfurt. She is the author of *Transferences: The Aesthetics and Poetics of the Therapeutic Relationship* (Bloomsbury, 2019).

ROBERT S. SCHINE is the Curt C. and Else Silberman Professor of Jewish Studies at Middlebury College. He is the author of *Jewish Thought Adrift: Max Wiener 1882–1950* (Brown Judaic Studies, 1992) and the coeditor, with Samuel Moyn, and main translator of *Hermann Cohen: Writings on Judaism and Neo-Kantian Philosophy* (Brandeis University Press, 2021).

MARY M. SOLBERG is associate professor of religion emerita at Gustavus Adolphus College. Her most recent book is *A Church Undone: Documents from the German Christian Faith Movement, 1932–1940* (Fortress, 2015). She is currently a stained-glass artist in Saint Peter, Minnesota.

HENRIETTA SZOLD (d. 1945) was a writer, translator, and Zionist leader, and founder of Hadassah, the Women's Zionist Organization of America.

THOMAS ABRAHAM TEARNEY holds a PhD in Germanic languages and literatures from the University of Pennsylvania. He conducts research with the university's history of art department and works as an indexer at the University of Southern California Shoah Foundation.

MICHAEL ZANK is professor of religion, Jewish studies, and medieval studies at Boston University. He is the author of *Jerusalem: A Brief History* (Wiley Blackwell, 2018); *Jüdische Religionsphilosophie als Apologie des Mosaismus* (Mohr Siebeck, 2016); and *The Idea of Atonement in the Philosophy of Hermann Cohen* (Brown Judaic Studies, 2000).

ALEXANDRA ZIRKLE is assistant professor of Jewish thought at the University of Buffalo, SUNY. She is a scholar of modern Jewish thought, biblical hermeneutics, and Jewish-Christian relations.

Index

In the JPS Anthologies of Jewish Thought Series

Modern Musar: Contested Virtues in Jewish Thought
Geoffrey D. Claussen

Modern Conservative Judaism: Thought and Practice
Elliot N. Dorff
Foreword by Julie Schonfeld

Modern Orthodox Judaism: A Documentary History
Zev Eleff
Foreword by Jacob J. Schacter

A Kabbalah and Jewish Mysticism Reader
Daniel M. Horwitz

Modern Jewish Theology: The First One Hundred Years, 1835–1935
Edited by Samuel J. Kessler and George Y. Kohler

The Growth of Reform Judaism: American and European Sources
W. Gunther Plaut
Foreword by Jacob K. Shankman
New introduction by Howard A. Berman
New epilogue by David Ellenson
With select documents, 1975–2008

The Rise of Reform Judaism: A Sourcebook of Its European Origins
W. Gunther Plaut
Foreword by Solomon B. Freehof
New introduction by Howard A. Berman

The Zionist Ideas: Visions for the Jewish Homeland— Then, Now, Tomorrow
Gil Troy

To order or obtain more information on these or other Jewish Publication Society titles, visit jps.org.

Printed in the USA
CPSIA information can be obtained
at www.ICGtesting.com
LVHW041546061023
760170LV00002B/2